MEDIA AND PSYCHOANALYSIS

A Critical Introduction

MEDIA AND PSYCHOANALYSIS
A Critical Introduction

Jacob Johanssen
Steffen Krüger

 KARNAC

First published in 2022 by Karnac Books, an imprint of Confer Ltd.

www.confer.uk.com

Registered office:
Brody House, Strype Street, Spitalfields, London E1 7LQ

British Library Cataloguing in Publication Data
A catalogue record for this book is available from the British Library.

ISBN: 978-1-913494-57-5 (paperback)
ISBN: 978-1-913494-58-2 (ebook)

Typeset by Bespoke Publishing Ltd.
Printed in the UK.

Contents

Acknowledgements

This book is the result of an intense work process and countless dialogues and discussions we had on, with, in and via digital media. We are glad it's done, but we are still glad we've done it.

Thank you, Jacob. Thank you, Steffen. *The authors.*

Introduction

In 1907, Sigmund Freud wrote to his family while he was on holiday in Italy. On the Piazza Colonna in Rome, a screen had been installed on the roof of one of the buildings onto which magic lantern slides and moving images were projected:

> They [the magic lantern slides] are actually advertisements, but to beguile the public these are interspersed with pictures of landscapes, Negroes [sic] of the Congo, glacier ascents, and so on. But since these wouldn't be enough, the boredom is interrupted by short cinematographic performances for the sake of which the old children (your father included) suffer quietly the advertisements and monotonous photographs. They are stingy with these tidbits, however, so I have had to look at the same thing over and over again. When I turn to go I detect a certain tension in the crowd, which makes me look again, and sure enough a new performance has begun, and so I stay on. Until 9 p.m. I usually remain spellbound; then I begin to feel too lonely in the crowd. (Freud, 1992, pp. 261–2)

Written well over a hundred years ago, the scene that Freud describes here may nevertheless sound familiar to us. Big screens in public places on mild summer nights have long since become a cultural mainstay and frequently attract hundreds, even thousands, of people to experience, say, a sporting event together.

As art and media historian Pasi Väliaho (2013) observes of Freud's report, under 'the pull of the technological spectacle, the external environment of the Piazza becomes secondary' (2013, p. 169). His eyes glued to the screen, Freud finds himself suffering through the advertisements, as so many television viewers in the decades that would follow, but he admits to being *spellbound* by the moving images offered in between the ads and the slideshows. Indeed, the spectacle of movement on the screen fascinates him so much as to render him immobile, if only for a short moment. More than that, each time he attempts to turn his back on the screen and leave, he can sense in the physical responses of other spectators that something new is catching their attention, which makes him turn around again only to become spellbound once more.

Although the magic lantern was one of the key inventions predating and anticipating cinema – with the first *properly moving* images having been made and shown by Louis Le Prince in 1888 – we can link the repetitive, tidbit nature of the screening at the Piazza Colonna to contemporary media technology. Indeed, the historical scene is reminiscent of the photo- and video-sharing app Snapchat, for example, where users can share up to 60-second-long videos with friends. Furthermore, the magic lantern slides can also be seen as early instances of animated gif images that have become commonplace on social media: punchily short film sequences that are a few seconds long and repeat endlessly. The silent films and slideshows of Freud's era were often accompanied by live music to add an additional stimulus. This comes remarkably close to another current social media platform, TikTok, which draws its highly affective strength from the often funny and joyful visual illustrations of short samples of well-known pop music songs.

Turning to more traditional media, Rome, the 'eternal city', has been featured in countless Hollywood films, from *La Dolce Vita* (Fellini, 1960) and *The Talented Mr. Ripley* (Minghella, 1999), to *Zoolander 2* (Stiller, 2016) and many others. It is also possible today to learn about Rome by watching videos of virtual walks on YouTube or to 'visit' the city through a virtual-reality headset like Oculus Rift where users can interact with a virtual artificial intelligence (AI) tour guide. Videogames from *Street Fighter Alpha* (1995) and the *Assassin's Creed* series (2007–16), to *Gran Turismo 6* (2013) have all featured levels set in the Italian capital. Hence, although technology and media change rapidly, we can always find traces of the old in the new. As we shall see in the coming chapters, the spatio-temporal dynamics of repetition and in/visibility that we have evoked in the above passages are characteristic of both media and psychoanalysis. In this Introduction, we outline basic ideas of psychoanalysis and define key technological terms such as 'media'. Lastly, we provide a summary of the book's main arguments.

What is psychoanalysis?

This book is a critical introduction to media and psychoanalysis or, more precisely, the study of diverse media through a psychoanalytic lens. The coming chapters feature the technologies, practices, uses and genres already broached above: film and television, the internet and social media, videogames and AI. We present and develop the field of psychoanalytic media studies and show how scholars have drawn on psychoanalysis in their thinking about them.

But, first of all, what is psychoanalysis anyway? Founded by the Austrian neurologist Sigmund Freud (1856–1939), psychoanalysis is, first and foremost, a theory of the human mind, or the human being in general (the 'subject', a term many psychoanalysts prefer) and its peculiar ways of functioning. Taking its cues not from the well-functioning and healthy, but from the ailing mind, it consists of a clinical practice of caring for what today is referred to as 'mental health issues': for example, an inexplicable and overwhelming sadness (called 'depression'), states of extreme, mysterious fearfulness ('anxiety'), obsessive–compulsive behaviours such as 'hoarding', and radical mood swings and emotional instabilities (classified today as 'bipolar' or 'borderline', depending on the strength and character of the phenomena), as well as many others.

We can say that, together with his mostly female patients – or 'analysands', as one calls them nowadays, so as to denote a more equal relationship in which both analyst and patient/analysand engage in mental work – Freud 'discovered' that people suffering from psychological turbulences could be significantly helped by talking about themselves and what is difficult in their lives during daily sessions. Although much has changed since then,[1] the basic principles have remained the same. The analysand lies down on a couch and freely associates – that is, talks about everything and anything that comes to their mind – while the analyst sits at an angle behind them, taking in the analysand's stream of (un)-consciousness with evenly hovering attention, trying not to focus their attention on any specific aspects of the analysand's discourse, but bringing out the import of the overall scene thus created.

Psychoanalysts (or psychoanalytic therapists, psychodynamic therapists or depth psychologists, as they are often called) are trained in psychoanalytic institutes, not merely learning key psychoanalytic ideas, but experiencing them by submitting to psychoanalytic treatment themselves, long before they start seeing their own patients/analysands. Once accredited, they can set up their own practice.

Depending on where one lives in the world, the availability and affordability of psychoanalytic treatment vary greatly. For instance, psychoanalysis does not have a large presence in the Arab region, whereas the Argentinian city of Buenos Aires is said to have the most psychoanalysts per square mile. This might have to do with the practice being rooted in a western culture that puts emphasis on individuality – the idea that each of us is their own, separate being, living their distinct lives. Paradoxically, clinical psychoanalysis affirms this idea each time an individual lies down on an analyst's couch; at the same time, however, the aim of the treatment can be described as making individuals aware of their fundamental state of '*un*separatedness' from others. In this respect, it is unfortunate that psychoanalysis has become marginalized by many welfare states, as governments – and individuals themselves – often favour other, allegedly 'quicker' and more 'cost-effective' forms of therapy.

Furthermore, due to its western origins, psychoanalysis has been critiqued as a white, modernist project that cannot simply be 'exported' to all corners of the world. Many regional variations and developments of psychoanalysis – for example, in Egypt, China and India – have emerged as a result. We briefly return to this point in Chapter 4, when we consider psychoanalysis and racism. But back to the beginning. At the very core of the so-called 'talking cure' (Freud & Breuer, 1895, p. 30) is the process of free association that Freud (1913a, p. 134) emphasized was 'the fundamental rule of psycho-analytic technique':

> You will notice that as you relate things various thoughts will occur to you which you would like to put aside on the ground of certain criticisms and objections. You will be tempted to say to yourself that this or that is irrelevant here, or is quite unimportant, or nonsensical, so that there is no need to say it. You must never give in to these criticisms, but must say it in spite of them – indeed, you must say it precisely *because* you feel an aversion to doing so. (Freud, 1913a, p. 134, italics in original)

Even more importantly, Freud emphasized that patients should never follow the urge of *not* saying something because it is *unpleasant* to tell (ibid.). In this way, he held that unconscious thoughts and unconscious ways of thinking, feeling and experiencing could be brought to the fore and made perceivable, understandable and thus conscious.

Unlike conventional academic psychology, Freud placed a great deal of emphasis on the dynamic interplay of (a) what people are consciously aware of, (b) what they might at any given time become consciously aware of, but simply do not focus on, and (c) what of their thinking and feeling is more or less opaque and inaccessible to them. Whereas Freud straightforwardly called (a) the conscious, he referred to (b) as the preconscious and only defined (c) as unconscious – that is, those thoughts people are totally unaware of themselves. And indeed, we are not always aware of why we do certain things – moreover, we are frequently not even aware *that* we do them in the first place. We are often unaware of how we relate to people in the ways we do, leave alone *why*; we seldom remember our dreams, but most of us remember recurring ones. However, this is without being able to say for sure why we keep dreaming them, or why we keep making the same old mistakes, repeating particular patterns or going in circles with our lovers, friends or colleagues with actions and reactions we know we should shake off but are unable to. Irrespective of whether we feel mentally healthy or fragile, our actions, thoughts, utterances, fantasies and desires are constantly being shaped by unconscious processes. The psychoanalyst Phil Mollon (2000) defines the unconscious using digital technology as analogy:

Consciousness could be compared to what is visible on a computer screen. Other information could be accessed readily by scrolling down the document or by switching to a different 'window'. This would be analogous to the conscious and the preconscious parts of the mind. However, some files on the computer may be less easily explored. They may have been encrypted or 'zipped', or they may require a password or are in other ways rendered 'access denied'. Some may also have been corrupted, so that information is scrambled and thereby rendered incomprehensible. While the Internet potentially makes available (to people collectively) all kinds of information and images […], a programme [sic] may have been installed that restricts access to Internet sites, censoring some that contain material considered unacceptable. Moreover, most of the activity of the computer is not visible on the screen; this is analogous to Freud's idea of the bodily based instincts, or 'id', in themselves inaccessible to the mind, only to be discerned through their derivatives (desires and phantasies). (Mollon, 2000, p. 8)

With this quotation, we do not want to say that the mind works like a computer, but Mollon's analogy is productive in our context, not least because it links the unconscious to media technology. The psychosocial thinker Stephen Frosh writes that the psychoanalytic unconscious 'refers to the existence of ideas which are not just not being thought about (hence not just "not in consciousness") but which are also radically unavailable to thought' (Frosh, 2002, p. 12). For clinical psychoanalysis, the reasons for particular neuroses, mental troubles or forms of suffering often have blocked and inaccessible aspects, either because they are attached to our earliest, pre-linguistic experiences, made at a time when our consciousness had not been sufficiently formed, or because they have been repressed and banished from an established consciousness as they are too traumatic, shameful or, as Freud (1913a) put it drily, 'unpleasant' to face consciously.

While psychoanalysis holds the unconscious to be universal, it is nevertheless shaped by particular individual and sociocultural dynamics. As mentioned, it takes a culture in which individuality holds some importance, for example, for psychoanalysis to make any sense in the first place. Gillian Rose (2001) puts it thus: 'the unconscious is formed by the disciplines of a culture, by its particular pattern of interdicts and permissions. Subjectivity is thus culturally as well as psychically constructed, and this process of subjection continues throughout our lives' (p. 104). The unconscious is never simply a box or kind of hidden place where something can be hidden or buried. In that sense, Mollon's analogy of the zip file is not fitting. Rather, the unconscious is dynamic and, to stay with computer analogies, a reservoir of algorithms and if-then patterns which continuously announces its presence in our interactions with others. As Frosh (2002) writes, these 'hidden ideas', as he calls them, 'have a profound influence on psychological life', by remaining 'active ("dynamic"), pushing for release' (p. 13). In other words, unconscious fragments continuously intrude on and reintroduce themselves into our interactions and mental activities.

Breasts, penises, mothers, fathers – what was Freud('s) thinking?

Readers unfamiliar with psychoanalysis will nevertheless be familiar with many of its ideas. These ideas have deeply penetrated popular culture. Proverbial sayings that have long since turned into common-sensical wisdom are, for example: that everything in life is about sex; that young children desire the parent of the opposite sex; that men strive to marry someone who is like their mother and women someone like their father; that cigars and other pointy objects represent the phallus; that some people are 'anal' (i.e. obsessively controlling) and some others are characterized by 'oral cravings', etc. Although such notions are sometimes taken too literally, they often have some truth in them. For example, 'anal' and 'oral' as character traits denote particular phases in an infant's psychosexual development and, even though these phases are no longer seen as holding true in the rather rigid sequence in which Freud posited them, they still offer immensely productive models for conceiving human relatedness, a point we unpack in Chapter 5.

A key stage in this model is the **Oedipus complex**, which refers to a phase in a child's development, roughly from age four to six, in which the child develops a quasi-sexual – but not in the way we understand adult sexuality – attachment to one of the parents, usually that of the opposite sex, and a degree of animosity toward the other parent. Such tensions in one's earliest relationships have indeed proven plausible. Across different cultures, for example, toddlers have shown a tendency to make proclamations along the lines of: 'I am going to live with daddy/mommy one day.' As Freud stated, those oedipal wishes are given up at some point because, in the male case, the little boy fears that his father may punish him for such adultery through an act of castration (i.e. cutting off the penis, which stands for total destruction and/or subjugation). In turn, the little girl, Freud argued, upon realizing she does not have a penis, comes to feel inferior to her father and angry at her mother for not 'equipping' her with one. This part of psychoanalytic theory has been fiercely debated and challenged within and outside psychoanalysis, and we can only scratch the surface of this debate here by emphasizing that the Oedipus complex is not so much about the penis as a bodily organ. Rather, it comes to embody a particular symbolic meaning in society that has to do with power and the ways in which people invest things, other people and themselves – including certain body parts – with power or a lack thereof, something the French psychoanalyst Jacques Lacan elaborated on. Hence, although the idea of the Oedipus complex may sound a little *whacky*, far-fetched and embarrassing, we invite readers to take its basic premises seriously: specifically, how patterns of deep attachment and love – as well as sexual stirrings – which form first between the baby and mother, and subsequently among baby, mother and father (or other caregiver arrangements), come to shape a person's upbringing, identity and being in the world.

By crossing through the oedipal phase and giving up on one's parents as sole love objects, the child becomes able to see themselves as part of a generational line (in familial as well as societal terms) and thereby gains a (rudimentary) understanding of history and temporality. The child learns to see themselves as a subject of the future and begins to speculate and daydream about what that future might look like – and, importantly, they need to face what it will *not* look like. Although Freud argued that the Oedipus complex is universal, his theory's focus was clearly on boys. Yet, both boys and girls need to give up on their longings for a blissful return to a union with either mummy or daddy and, in the process, they internalize their parents as inner authorities. Through this process, and with the child becoming more aware of their surroundings, the *super-ego* is formed. The quasi-erotic desires of the Oedipus complex become repressed, tabooed and forbidden – a process Freud saw as a hallmark of civilization. The child 'is forced to swallow her or his desires in the face of the power of the real world', Frosh (1999, p. 36) notes.

Thus, mediated by the relationship to one's parents, the super-ego comes to represent the laws, customs and morals of a society, with Freud introducing two further neologisms in his later metapsychological writings with which he sought to delineate the subject's relationship to these laws: the *ego* and the *id*. Whereas the id comes to represent the unconscious and constantly seeks pleasure and enjoyment, in this way going against and coming into conflict with the laws of the super-ego, it is the ego's job to negotiate between id and super-ego and navigate the arising conflicts so as to keep them in check. Yet, this is no simple task, since the super-ego is seldom benign; rather, being intimately related to the id and its unconscious desires, it must be seen as the latter's flipside and thus as a hyper-moralistic and exactingly cruel agency which constantly taunts its bearer for their failures and shortcomings, their insufficiencies and transgressions, even – or better, especially – if these transgressions are not enacted but merely imagined.

In a long line of cultural-analytic works, Freud showed how unconscious conflicts among ego, id and super-ego seep not only into family relations, but also into wider sociocultural spheres – for example, in works of literature, theatre plays, visual art, jokes, proverbs and parapraxes (the famous Freudian slips!). It is this presence of unconscious processes in cultural and societal realms – or these realms' suffusion with unconscious processes – that makes psychoanalysis so truly radical and, in our opinion, so useful for analysing how individual subjects on one side and culture and society on the other shape each other in various ways. This question of the respective mutual shaping of the individual psyche and the collective or aggregated social is at the core of psychosocial studies, an approach and emerging academic discipline we are particularly invested in. Psychosocial studies argue that the individual-psychological and the social–structural dimensions of reality and existence are intertwined (Clarke, 2002; Hollway, 2006; Frosh & Young, 2008; Jones, 2008; Clarke & Hoggett, 2009; Day Sclater *et al.*, 2009; Frosh, 2010; Hollway & Jefferson, 2012; Woodward, 2015; Redman, 2016; Krüger, 2017b). 'We are psycho-social,' Wendy Hollway (2006) writes, because we 'are influenced by desire and anxiety provoking situations that are affected by material and social conditions, discourses, as well as by unconscious defence mechanisms and intersubjective relations' (pp. 467–8). This book, too, is interested in this process of the mutual shaping of individuals, culture and society, and it considers media as entities positioned at the intersections of these three.

Post-Freudians: debates, rifts and developments

When Nazi Germany occupied Austria in 1938, Freud and his family fled Austria, which had embraced its 'Anschluß' (annex) to the 'Third Reich' rather enthusiastically (Krüger, 2011, pp. 199, 293). The family immigrated to London, where Freud died of painful cancer of the jaw in 1939. Many German and Austrian analysts sought refuge in other countries, first and foremost the USA. Although agreeing in principle on the dynamic unconscious as the foundation of human subjectivity, psychoanalysts had quarrelled over Freud's ideas already during his lifetime. After his death, however, these quarrels developed into distinct psychoanalytic traditions (Makari, 2008). In that sense, it is wrong to speak of 'a' or 'the' psychoanalysis, as we have done up to now. Perhaps more so than other disciplines, psychoanalysis is at variance with itself and divided into different 'schools'. In the USA, for example, an ego-psychological school took hold whose focus on the functionings of the ego was presented as honouring the Freudian heritage, with Heinz Hartmann, Ernst Kris and Rudolph Loewenstein at the helm. In France, Jacques Lacan presented his revisioning of psychoanalytic ideas and concepts as a 'return to Freud'. However, instead of taking sides in the institutional conflicts which, in the wake of the Second World War, were simmering all over the psychoanalytic community (Lacan, for example, was expelled from the International Psychoanalytic Association in 1963), we agree with those moderating voices today that mediate between, and find productive perspectives in, the various schools, without regressing into an anything-goes attitude. To our minds, the multiplicity of perspectives and approaches within psychoanalysis is testimony to the 'heterogeneity of the unconscious' itself (Laplanche, 1996, p. 11). Therefore, what we argue is required, particularly in psychosocial and cultural analysis, is a careful dialogue between, on the one hand, one's empirical material and the part of reality one seeks to analyse and, on the other, the broadest possible scope of psychoanalytic theory that one can bring to bear on one's analysis.

Since one of the main tasks of this book is to present already existing psychoanalytic dialogues between psychoanalysis and media culture, and since these dialogues have mainly been conducted from Freudian, object-relational and Lacanian perspectives, it is these central schools that we will focus on in this book, as well as in the remaining parts of this Introduction. However, it is important to note that there are highly influential psychoanalysts who did not form a school of their own, such as Didier Anzieu, Bracha L. Ettinger, André Green, Juliet Mitchell, Jessica Benjamin and Jean Laplanche, some of whom we will encounter in the course of the following chapters.

As regards to the establishing of psychoanalytic schools, the so-called 'Freud–Klein controversies' were pivotal in shaping the intellectual landscape of psychoanalysis in Britain and beyond. In Britain, two main camps emerged, one led by Freud's daughter Anna (1895–1982), who had become a highly theoretically versed psychoanalyst herself, and one led by Melanie Klein (1903–60) who, born in Budapest and psychoanalytically trained by Karl Abraham in Berlin, moved to London in 1926 where she developed her own ideas about psychoanalysis, often radically redefining Freudian concepts, such as the super-ego, in the process. From 1942 to 1945, in the midst of the Nazi German 'Blitz' on London, a string of meetings was held there at the Institute of Psychoanalysis, where Freudians and Kleinians, too, fought battles over their diverging ideas. Yet, despite deep-seated feelings of embitterment, which come to the fore in private letters exchanged at the time – for example, between Anna Freud and Ernst Kris, who had migrated to New York (see Krüger, 2011, pp. 395–7) – the London Institute was *not* torn apart, and the three separate groups that were formed (Kleinians, Freudians and the Independent, or Middle, group) learned to coexist.

Melanie Klein: object relations and early infantile fantasies

Settling in London in the mid-1920s, Melanie Klein quickly became influential in psychoanalytic circles, and she is still particularly well known for her analyses of and writings on children, an interest she shared with Anna Freud. For Klein, a developmental phase key to the understanding of the human experience is what she called '**the paranoid–schizoid position**' – 'a constellation of anxieties, defences and [...] object relations' characteristic of the earliest months of an infant's life whose influence continues into childhood and adulthood[2] (more about this in Chapter 4). Klein, among other notable object-relations analysts, such as D. W. Winnicott, Esther Bick, Ronald Fairbairn, Wilfred Bion, Donald Meltzer and Harry Guntrip, was key in advancing and supplanting Freud's theories towards a more relational and intersubjective perspective. Whereas Freud had been most interested in people's inner conflicts – an interest that often centred his ideas on the individual person – object-relations psychoanalysis emphasized the primary importance of people's relationships with other people, most importantly those with their main caregiver, traditionally the mother.

We are not only born out of a (sexual) relation between two individuals; throughout our lives, we foster connections with others. '**Objects**' in this tradition do not refer to things, such as smartphones, milk cartons or chairs, but to other human beings and how they are rendered 'inner objects', or fantasy representations that shape how people relate to themselves and each other both 'out there' and 'in here'. As Klein writes about the process of object formation in the infant's mind:

> The baby, having incorporated his parents, feels them to be live people inside his body in the concrete way in which deep unconscious phantasies are experienced – they are, in his mind, 'internal' or 'inner' objects. [...] Thus an inner world is being built up in the child's unconscious mind, corresponding to his actual experiences and the impressions he gains from people and the external world, and yet altered by his own phantasies and impulses. (Klein, 1975, p. 345)

Klein placed great emphasis on seemingly 'negative' states such as envy, guilt, hatred or fantasies of destruction – which remain integral parts of subjectivity. She often worked with children and focused on their unconscious phantasy life and how dynamic it was. Julia Segal writes about Klein's observations of her own four-year-old son: 'When he was feeling angry with her, he saw her as a witch threatening to poison him. When he was feeling happy and loving towards her, he saw her as a princess he wanted to marry' (Segal, 2004, p. 28).

Fantasy, a key concept for psychoanalysis in general, is even more central in the object-relations paradigm than in the Freudian. In fact, object-relational analysts even spell it more emphatically, as *phantasy*. Generally, fantasy refers to imaginary scenes and small plots that individuals dream up so as to insert themselves into them as the protagonists. Fantasies have strong unconscious dimensions and motivations; and in the Kleinian version, phantasies usually remain unconscious altogether. Especially in Freud's early work, fantasizing, and the related daydreaming, represent a desire for wish fulfilment and constitute the creation of a particularly desirable reality (Freud, 1914, 1915). For Klein, in turn, unconscious phantasies are constitutive of all mental processes, and although they are expressive of both libidinal and aggressive impulses (Bott Spillius *et al.*, 2011, p. 3), Klein's focus was decidedly more on phantasies of attacking and being attacked, destroying and being destroyed, particularly in relation to the mother and close others. However, although the differences between 'fantasy' and 'phantasy' are often important to note, we merely use 'fantasy' in this book to refer to both conscious and unconscious fantasies, so as to not overwhelm readers with the theoretical intricacies of the diverging schools.

As regards Klein's theory, the existence of archaic aggression may be difficult to acknowledge, let alone digest, for many, but Klein was right, we think, to devote important parts of her work to this human proclivity. Certainly, human beings are capable of amazingly nourishing acts of love and care towards others; in equal measure, however, humans are capable of acts of unspeakable aggression and violence – and sometimes both in close proximity to each other. Klein brought this idea of polar opposites in one and the same human being to fruition in her conceptualization of the 'paranoid–schizoid' and the 'depressive position'. Unlike Freud, who posited more of a linear form of psychosexual development, for Klein infants, and human beings in general, shift between two main 'constellations of attitudes and mechanisms' (Segal, 2004, p. 33) for dealing with feelings of anxiety and loss. In the paranoid–schizoid position, the child feels existential, deadly threat and anxiety. In a process of what Klein called '**splitting**' (1946), 'good' and 'bad' are rigidly kept apart. Parents of small children normally show intuition for what their children need by behaving in ways that emphasize calm, goodness and kindness. However, if parents themselves have been brought up in ways in which elements of cruelty were mixed into those of care (something psychoanalysis understands as 'perversion', which we discuss in Chapter 3), they may find themselves reproducing and repeating such patterns in their own parenting (Welldon, 1988).

Inhabiting the paranoid–schizoid position, the subject is thus unable to tolerate ambivalence, that is, to see that human beings usually embody both good and bad elements at the same time, and this is the main insight of – and sets the feeling state for – the depressive position. But to remain with the paranoid–schizoid position for a moment: the kind of thinking informed by it splits the world into stark opposites, and this has concrete implications for social phenomena. Contemporary politics, for example, are discussed through notions such as division, antagonism and polarization, which bear clear traces of the paranoid–schizoid. Likewise, social media are characterized in ways that echo Klein's thinking: as filter bubbles, echo chambers and networks with their radically individualized nodes. Although Klein has been used relatively little by scholars of culture and society, her ideas are very useful for interrogating contemporary politics and forms of (digital) discrimination – interrogations into which we enter in Chapter 4.

The second main position in Kleinian theory, as broached already, is the 'depressive position', which is characterized by an awakening of a 'capacity for concern', as Winnicott (1963) put it. The onset of the depressive position marks the beginning of empathy with the other in an infant's development. Although, in the paranoid–schizoid position, 'the main anxiety concerned survival of the self [..., i]n the depressive position anxiety is also felt on behalf of the object' (Bott Spillius *et al.*, 2011, p. 84). A sense of guilt for one's aggressively destructive feelings towards the other now also comes into the picture. From this depressive position, the subject then moves towards a reparative one, while still returning, however, to the depressive position frequently. At this stage, the subject is able to recognize the complexity of themselves and others, involving 'good' as well as 'bad' aspects in one and the same object. The baby, and by extension the mature individual, becomes able to tolerate frustration, jealousy, anxiety, loss and disappointment. Conflicts become manageable and the other comes to be seen as able to sustain and survive one's attacks. The characteristics of this position are again transferable to contemporary politics, which has likewise been described as in need moving towards a state that echoes the depressive position: caring, compassionate, empathic and relational in its forms of communication and practice. We return to this in Chapter 4 and the book's Conclusion.

Donald Woods Winnicott: children's play and transitional objects

A friend and ally of Klein's, but one who also developed markedly different ideas, was the psychoanalyst and paediatrician Donald W. Winnicott (1896–1971). Without reservations to draw upon other psychoanalytic paradigms, Winnicott came to be associated with the Middle or Independent group during the controversies. His central ideas, however, are rooted in the object-relations tradition. Like Klein, Winnicott's concepts are grounded in close observation of children. He gave great importance to the way children played with toys and objects which he saw as significant of their inner worlds, with specific object relations becoming expressed through such play. As we discuss in Chapter 6, free-flowing play and its canalization into more structured game-play has been a marker of mental freedom for centuries, and Winnicott is most famous for a theory that outlines a path towards this freedom. At the heart of this theory is what Winnicott calls 'transitional objects and phenomena' (2002), such as teddy bears, cuddly blankets, a favourite soft toy or a soothing tune that the young child must always have when going to sleep. They calm the child and help manage feelings of loss and anxiety that accompany the transition from total dependence on caregivers towards a more self-reliant and independent state – a process that children both intensely desire and fear. As anyone who has observed young children knows, transitional objects are by no means 'just things', but become intensely invested in and animated. At the same time, children harbour a sense of having at least partly created their own illusion, and Winnicott cautions that this ambivalent status of the object is something parents must never question. '[D]id you create that or did you find it?' (Winnicott, 2002, p. 119) is not a helpful question because for the child the illusion that the object is invested with needs to be left inconspicuous and indeterminate. This indeterminacy becomes apparent when the child grows older and more mature and, instead of the transitional object being mourned or ritualistically discarded, it simply loses its importance and frequently ends up in attics or closets, with their owners unable to properly and ultimately let go.

For Winnicott (2002), transitional objects constitute the foundation of cultural phenomena such as art or religion. They are the precursors of the symbolic and cultural creations in people's mature lives. As we discuss in Chapter 1, scholars, particularly in the UK, have developed Winnicott's ideas further and included media products, such as TV series and objects of fandom, like people's favourite bands, into the field of transitional objects. Winnicott is widely regarded as gentler and less archaic in his outlook on children than Klein. As the French psychoanalyst André Green (2005) has pointed out, Winnicott holds a view of fantasy and play that is positive to a degree that risks downplaying or even ignoring the brutal and sadistic forms that children's and adults' play can often take. Nevertheless, Winnicott's ideas have been extremely influential and, in the context of this book, they are definitely fruitful for analysing the deep attachments people have to media objects, such as social media platforms (see Chapter 2) or videogames (see Chapter 6).

Jacques Lacan: language, subject and desire

Next to Freud, the French psychoanalyst Jacques Lacan (1901–81) is perhaps the most influential thinker in the field, particularly when it comes to the application of psychoanalysis outside the clinic. Notorious for his jargon, word creations, as well as his knack for paradoxical concepts – indeed, he even used mathematical formulas to define unconscious dynamics – Lacan extended and opened psychoanalysis toward notions of the social far beyond Freud. This 'socializing' of psychoanalysis makes his ideas extremely useful when it comes to questions of culture and society. At the same time, Lacan has been accused of emptying out psychoanalysis's core focus on people's inner lives and intrapsychic functioning by locating psychic life more in people's social structures than within themselves.

Lacan developed what is perhaps the most sophisticated and logically rounded off universe of psychoanalytic thought; this, however, also tends to seal it off hermetically, and at times Lacanian terms and concepts only seem to work within their own discursive universe. This can feel as though one spends large amounts of time growing the most beautiful flowers in a greenhouse, but once one takes them into the wild, they soon wither in the harsher climate, or are eaten by slugs. Yet, despite his idiosyncrasies and peculiarities, engaging with Lacan's thought can be immensely gratifying and productive.

Language and subject formation

Being heavily influenced by the linguistic, structuralist and post-structuralist currents of his times, Lacan grants language an overarching and powerful role, both in society and in the lives of individuals (Lacan, 2002). Language and other ways of using symbols are what structures the social and determines a subject's very identity and place in the world. This is not only because we use language to communicate, or to account for who we (think) we are. Rather, and quite literally, the subject is nothing without language, and even worse: language, instead of giving substance to subjectivity, covers over the nothingness, or void, that Lacan sees as at each subject's core.

This paradoxical state can be further unpacked through what Lacan calls 'the Symbolic' (which we capitalize in the book whenever we refer to Lacan's term specifically), or 'the Symbolic Order'. Among other things, the latter encompasses the norms, customs, belief systems and laws of a given society. Here we obtain an example of how Lacan translates Freudian thinking into more social concepts, with the Symbolic creating a strong parallel to Freud's super-ego. Hence, when a child is born, it is born into a Symbolic Order that is already established and, consequently, the child's paramount task is to make themselves at home within this order – by acquiring the mother (and father) tongue, internalizing the relevant social rules (via one's parents), adapting one's expectations to the set cultural ways of doing things, and so on. Lacan introduces an important gender dimension to this existential process of adaptation when he refers to it as 'sexuation' (1999 [1972]). With this process being closely related to taking up and associating oneself with particular signifiers, that is, with particular symbolic entities – such as one's name, whether one is a 'boy' or a 'girl', whether one is, say, a 'big sister', a 'little brother' or an 'only child' – one learns to see oneself as *naturally embodying* a certain gender that is different from another.

Whether we are concerned with gender relations in particular or human relations in general, there is always a gap between human subjects and the symbolic means they have at their disposal to define themselves. In other words, there is always something of the subject that is outside language and something of language that is outside the subject. Language is thus a strange and, at the same time, strangely familiar thing that the subject speaks and writes all the time; but even if we often come really close in words to expressing what and how a person is, we never quite manage to capture this completely.

For Lacan, the subject can never truly or fully say what they mean. Language is both strangely intimate and alienating all at once. It is a closed system that endlessly runs on, with every word referring to another word, and then another, and another – without us being able to ever properly reach outside of the Symbolic and directly into our lives. There is always something that evades symbolization, and this 'out-side' of the Symbolic Lacan calls 'the Real'. This Real, in turn, does not refer to any straightforward sense of *reality*. Rather, it refers to those aspects that pertain to 'real life' but cannot be put into words, such as, for example, raw, unmediated and particularly *traumatic* experiences, the reality of which we can feel but never fully know.

With the Real pushing onto human experience and shaping Symbolic production, Lacan developed a third term to round off his structural vision of human existence: 'the Imaginary'. This Imaginary is the register of fantasies, imaginations and identifications that flow into the gap between the Real and the Symbolic. Unable to fully account for how we live our lives and who we are, fantasies, ideals, fears, anxieties and imagos (i.e. unconscious role models) fill these gaps and blind spots and patch up the loose ends of our existences. Lacan sees the Real, Symbolic and Imaginary as tightly interwoven; indeed, he visualizes this relation through a Borromean knot in which three rings are intertwined, with all three determining the experience of 'reality' for the subject.

Lacan's understanding of the unconscious

Linked to the centrality of language and the Symbolic in Lacan's theory is his formula that 'the unconscious is the discourse of the Other' (Lacan, 1966, p. 143). The unconscious, according to him, is like a machine that operates outside the individual human being. This is so because, as mentioned earlier, the unconscious is not something within the subject that can straightforwardly be 'recovered'. Rather, for Lacan, it amounts to a reality that is radically different from that of the subject's conscious experience, with this subject always forming an unconscious that is in close relation to its Symbolic universe, but that is always and principally remaining outside of it.

This obverse of consciousness articulates itself in dreams, free associations, parapraxes and other attempts at turning something that is impossible to express into symbolic form nevertheless. All psychoanalysts emphasize that the unconscious shows itself in contradictions, distortions and other failures at making 'common sense'. Yet, language also remains the only way to give structure and meaning to this unconscious. As Laplanche, a student of Lacan's, put it: 'The unconscious is a phenomenon of meaning, but without any communicative finality' (Laplanche, 1999, p. 102). In that sense, the unconscious communicates a great deal and nothing all at once.

Enjoying what we cannot find: *jouissance, objet* a and desire

A last key moment in Lacan that we want to present here is his focus on *jouissance*, which translates from French as 'enjoyment', but the term points to an element of anguish and pain as well. A better translation would thus be 'pleasure-pain'. Contemporary Lacanians – and first and foremost the Lacanian–Marxist philosopher Slavoj Žižek, who we will meet at several turns in this book – see society to be structured by an almost sadistic command to enjoy. This can be gathered, for example, from the deluge of self-help books filling our shelves, whose mantra is that we must enjoy and be happy at all costs. Arguably, it is this imperative of enjoyment, rather than the tabooed and repressed ideas about sexuality that Freud had posited in his time, which is the greatest source of distress for many people today. We can never be fully happy, with each moment of enjoyment already coming with a sigh of melancholia, and a mixture of sadness or a pang of raging dissatisfaction. Alternatively, we are often prone to enjoy something that is damaging per se or that suggests a mode of enjoyment that can quickly turn self-destructive, as the various diagnostic descriptions of drug, sex, social media or videogame overuse/abuse indicate.

Moreover, since humans are characterized by a fundamental distance between their life experience and their conscious understanding of this experience, a direct and uncomplicated form of enjoyment seems just out of reach. Hence, what Lacan calls *objet (petit) a* refers to an object-cause of desire that is triggered by the lack or emptiness that people feel each time they get caught up between the Symbolic and their own sense of self. This lack opens up a foundational gap or hole in our existence which animates and perpetuates our search for 'something' that is missing from our lives. It causes desire to flow endlessly and hop from object to object, with the subject trying to fill this gap in ever new ways (love, success, religion, hobbies, collections, sports, etc.) that are never enough. As Sean Homer explains:

> The *objet a* is not an object we have lost, because then we would be able to find it and satisfy our desire. It is rather the constant sense we have, as subjects, that something is lacking or missing from our lives. We are always searching for fulfilment, for knowledge, for passion, for love, and whenever we achieve these goals, there is always something more we desire; we cannot quite pinpoint it but we know that it is there. (Homer, 2005, p. 87)

As Mari Ruti (2018) puts it, we are always left 'wanting to keep wanting' (p. 14), desiring to fill the void we unconsciously feel. Desire is thus a forward-facing motion, perpetuating movement with productive force. It operates unconsciously and although we 'learn' to desire through fantasies, these fantasies are never the same as our *objects* of desire, but its engine.

What are media? Why media and psychoanalysis?

Turning to the field of media studies, one can see how the concept of media meets our psychoanalytic orientation between the individual psychic and the collectively social halfway. Referring to 'media' in the plural, we understand the term as the particular ways in which meanings are created and communicated. In this broad understanding, a medium is not merely a 'channel' or 'communication system' through which independently existing pieces of 'information' (or 'messages' or 'content') are 'transmitted' from a 'sender' to a 'receiver'. Much rather, media in this respect refers to the very forms that meaning takes on when it is communicated. The double meaning of 'sense' as 'making sense' and 'pertaining to the senses' is paradigmatic for the intertwining of form and content/meaning with which we endow the term. In this sense, then, although we will mostly write about media in the narrow definition of technological facilitators of communication across space and time (film, TV, print media, radio, digital media and the internet), even basic phenomena, such as the human voice, body language, light or water, can count as media, and it will be helpful to keep this broad understanding in mind. As Steffen (Krüger, 2022b) has written in a psychosocial context (and with a bow to Lacan):

> Paradoxically put, a medium in its most basic form is the facilitator of a communication that does not communicate by itself. It is the bringing about of a communion that is at the same time impossible to achieve. The sheer fact that humans need to use symbols – gestures, imagery, speech – to enable mutual understanding points to a chasm and principal distance between *alter* and *ego*, no matter how close they are to each other. This principal distance, which is at the root of the concept of 'communication' (Peters, 1999, p. 29), turns media into go-betweens, whose function is to bridge this divide, but whose mere existence is a constant reminder of the principle of 'unbridgability'. (Krüger, 2022b, p. 6)

In a similar vein, the psychoanalytic media researcher Elfriede Löchel (2019) has argued that media can be defined according to both their absence and their ubiquity. Media are everywhere and we take them for granted. Media make something appear and make what appears seem concrete and inevitable; yet they often remain invisible in this process themselves.

Watching a film on television, for example, we usually do not pay attention to the technological set-up, to how image and sound are transported into our living rooms, how scenes are cut, selected and assembled, or how certain camera angles have been chosen instead of others. As the psychoanalytic trauma theorist Amit Pinchevski has argued: 'The basic function of media, then, is to make something appear while making themselves disappear in the process. Media dissolve through their operation: they can render immediate what they mediate only inasmuch as in so doing they recede to the background' (2019, p. 142).

It is only when things go wrong and media fail to communicate smoothly that we become aware of the process of mediation itself – the glitches in digital images, for example, at the point when a wi-fi signal is lost, or the TV programme where audio and video are out of synch, an embarrassing typo in a newspaper article or an inconsistency in the mise-en-scène of a film, such as when an actor wears a digital watch in a historical drama. More often than not, those failures confront us with what is characteristic of media and their specific forms of mediation themselves. In this respect, too, media display an exquisitely human quality, since also humans show their particular workings especially in those moments when their sovereign functioning stalls and their façade breaks down.

Now, this parallel between and close proximity of human beings and media offers us a productive cue for why we feel that the combination of media and psychoanalysis is so useful. To quote from Steffen's work on media and psychosocial studies once more:

> The role of media as go-betweens makes them *psychosocial objects par excellence*. The question of how the 'in-here' and the 'out-there', the psychic and the social, the 'me' and 'not-me', are being woven together, or must be seen as one and the same thing, […] is being decided, rehearsed and demonstrated in the idea of the medium. Already those inner dialogues that humans lead with themselves point to the need of symbolic mediation between something individually psychological and something non-subjectively social. However, and this is the point of psychoanalysis, these inner dialogues also point to the limits of such mediation: they go on *ad infinitum*, because they work at the borders of the symbolizable and thus bring media into human existence. (Krüger, 2022b, p. 6)

To put it differently: not only is there no communication without mediation, but, rather, the whole phenomenological field of human psychology and relationality would be inconceivable without an understanding of media and the mediatedness of our life experience. In this respect, the entire field of psychoanalytic theory, too, can be conceived as a set of media with which ideas of human existence can be communicated, and this is how we use it. By the same token, media – in the general sense of means of communication – can be seen as in closest proximity to the psychoanalytic project in that what we can learn with media is how something communicates, or fails to communicate – how something comes to make a difference in our experience, or fails to do so. This holds true as well for media in the narrower sense of communication technologies, and particularly for the case of digital media technologies, which become ever more focused on and customized for the individual person and their everyday lives. This is something that we captured as follows in one of our earlier collaborations:

> As regards the in-depth study of this co-constitution, or mutual implication, of the psychic and the social, the media, media technologies and the user's relationship to these play a key role. In Western societies at the onset of the 21st century, questions regarding socialisation, individualisation and subjectivation can only thoroughly and satisfactorily be answered when we take our relations in, through and with media into consideration. In this respect, what is most striking from a psychoanalytic (but also from other, e.g. posthuman and new materialist) perspective(s), is the movement of information and communication technology ever closer to the human body and into each and every aspect of everyday life. With the steady increase in computing power and a significant rise in wireless transmission rates, with devices becoming smaller, lighter, more mobile and ever more able to merge with the human body, a media sphere has developed that is rapidly becoming a major, integral influence on the ways in which we relate to and interact with others – ways that psychoanalysis holds to be vital for subjective development. (Krüger & Johanssen, 2016, p. 8)

To us and many other scholars who work in the growing field of psychoanalytic media studies, psychoanalysis is uniquely equipped to address, analyse and critically question the ways in which our new digital environments shape the people within them and, vice versa, how these environments are shaped by people. The dynamic unconscious does not merely emerge from *within* people, but from *in-between* people and their surroundings, as phenomena that are distributed between various agencies. The novel applications of psychoanalysis and psychosocial perspectives that we present in this book are particularly useful because they foreground messy and contradictory dynamics, relationships, patterns and structures in a sphere in which individuals interact not merely with themselves and other humans, but with social and cultural institutions of which media are a vital, facilitating part. When Candida Yates (2007) argues, with a focus on gender, that 'the shaping of gendered subjectivities is always de-centred by the psychic forces of the unconscious' (p. 6), this process of de-centring can be seen to multiply when taking our media situation into consideration, characterized by a myriad of devices and applications in various distances from and proximities to our bodies competing in the structuring of our conscious thoughts and unconscious desires.

Bringing psychoanalysis to bear on such a complex cultural situation, it becomes clear that our access to psychoanalysis in this book is markedly different from the clinical practice that founded the field. By the same token, however, it would be bad cultural–analytic practice to simply lift psychoanalytic concepts out of the clinical realm and impose them on sociocultural contexts. Rather, as mentioned earlier, what characterizes our work in this book and elsewhere is an application of psychoanalytic ideas and concepts that places them in dialogue with media and communication studies as well as other disciplines. Susannah Radstone explains the difference between psychoanalysis inside and outside the clinic as follows:

> Whereas clinical perspectives tend to focus on the difficulties encountered by individuals in adapting to the realms of the social and the cultural, academic psychoanalysis emphasises rather the difficulties *posed by* culture and the social realm – by which I mean the exclusions, differentiations and inequalities of power produced by, and practised through, language and cultural texts and processes. (Radstone, 2007, p. 244, italics in original)

In this sense, our perspective is clearly that of 'academic psychoanalysis'. It is one, however, that includes a view towards clinical psychoanalysis and allows us to critically discuss problematic assumptions clinicians tend to hold – for example, about the pathology of videogames (see Chapter 6) or about questions of race (see Chapter 4). Ultimately, we are not clinically trained, but do not see this as a clear disadvantage for our psychoanalytically oriented academic practice. When Pascal Sauvayre (2022) writes with respect to the cultural–analytic works of German psychoanalyst and critical theorist Alfred Lorenzer that 'the heart of psychoanalysis can be thought of as lying […] equally in the areas of "cultural analysis" [and] "therapeutic psychoanalysis"' (p. 151), this covers our understanding of our own work well.

About this book and chapter summaries

This book is a critical introduction to media and psychoanalysis and the field of psychoanalytic media studies. We introduce key scholars and critically situate their work in relation to what we see as key themes pertaining to the media cultures of contemporary societies in many parts of the world. These include: modes of representation and misrepresentation in film and TV (Chapter 1), social media and user behaviour (Chapter 2), work and mental health (Chapter 3), politics and forms of discrimination online (Chapter 4), sexuality and the virtual (Chapter 5), videogames, and artificial and human intelligence (Chapter 6).

The field of psychoanalytic media studies has existed since at least the 1970s, if not earlier – depending on whether one should consider Freud as its originator or not – and it has seen substantial growth in the last 10–15 years. This is one of the reasons for writing this book. However, although our aim is to present a comprehensive and wide-ranging introduction, the result is by no means exhaustive, canonical or complete. We have provided particular *foci* according to how influential a given scholar is or has been, for example, but always according to our own viewpoints and convictions. Due to space limitations, we have had to make cuts to chapters, sometimes significant ones, or were only able to allude to an idea or briefly cite it. It is for that reason that each chapter ends with a 'further reading' list which assembles further important works in a particular area. In this Introduction, we have provided a basic outline of major psychoanalytic traditions and ideas. We define key concepts in each chapter, highlighting the most important ones in bold, so that readers can quickly return to this Introduction should they wish to refresh their memory. Each chapter discusses and unfolds different positions and ideas from psychoanalysis, as well as from psychoanalytic and psychosocial media studies, media and communication studies, sociology, critical theory, the humanities and the social sciences more generally. The book's chapters are designed to be read in chronological order, but also work when read in isolation.

The book is both an introduction to the topics mentioned and the development of a critical argument of what we regard as key issues that we as individuals and societies on the whole face with respect to mental health, our common-sensical understanding of work, discrimination and violence, polarization, sexuality and pleasure, as well as the future of humanity in the presence of intelligent machines. In that sense, we map the field of psychoanalytic media studies and its traditions as well as *intervene* in it and provide further analyses of it. The book is aimed at any interested reader, but we have a hunch that its main audiences will be students and academics, who may or may not have some familiarity with psychoanalysis, as well as clinicians, who may be familiar with the psychoanalytic terminology but less so with the media-specific issues we present.

Chapter 1, 'Reality and fantasy from film to TV', opens the book with a discussion of psychoanalytic film studies, presenting key scholars who laid the foundations of our field and their central works. We chart the historical development of this area from the 1960s particularly in France and the UK and trace its extension into other media, first and foremost television, throughout the 1980s and onwards. Devoting a full chapter to film and television might seem odd in a book about *digital* media; however, we wish to do so because these newer and older traditions belong together. Despite the breaks and discontinuities that exist in psychoanalytic media studies, many of the foundational texts discussing analogue film are still of key relevance for an adequate understanding of digital media. The works of what has been called 'Screen Theory', and especially thinkers such as Laura Mulvey, have foregrounded critical questions of the representation of male and female bodies and how they relate to social inequalities and power imbalances. Mulvey's theory of the 'male gaze' (1975) and how cinema has been framing women as objects to-be-looked-at by men kickstarted a whole range of studies on how gender relations become constructed in and by media. We will introduce some of the central contributions, with studies on the female voice (Silverman, 1988), the 'woman's film' (Doane, 1987b) and soap operas (Modleski, 1982) at the centre. Subsequently, we show how cultural studies scholars from the 1980s onwards – among them Janice Radway (1991), Valerie Walkerdine (1986), Roger Silverstone (1994), Jacky Stacey (1994) and Ien Ang (1985) – drew on psychoanalytic ideas in their work on television and popular culture more generally. Contrasting with much of the Screen Theory work, these present more optimistic views on the capability of media to hold and care for viewers in a comforting and soothing manner, similar to Winnicott's (2002) notion of the 'transitional object'. A host of scholars have continued these lines of thinking from the 2000s onwards and also they are present in the chapter.

Chapter 2, 'Social media and psychosocial relations', turns to digital and social media and their evolution across the past 30 years. Digital media platforms, such as Facebook, Twitter, YouTube and Instagram, have become the most important means of self-presentation and communication of our time. They facilitate specific psychosocial relations between users, and this chapter maps the existing research on those relations, beginning with Slavoj Žižek's (1996, 1998) writings on 'cyberspace' and the early internet. In these works, Žižek follows the question to what extent the early internet enabled the subject to create identities that were uncoupled from social rules and the dynamics of the offline world – a question that is also central in Sherry Turkle's early internet studies (1995). Both bodies of work have proven farsighted in that they identified key structural aspects of the internet that we still grapple with today, first and foremost how the internet and the ways it affects people are related to wider social, political and economic structures. The chapter then proceeds to discuss three approaches to social media that we think are key to an understanding of contemporary media practices: Jodi Dean's *Blog Theory* (2010), Matthew Flisfeder's *Algorithmic Desire* (2021) and Aaron Balick's *The Psychodynamics of Social Networking* (2014). The Lacanians Dean and Flisfeder see social media to be structurally characterized by the dynamics of the drive (Dean) and desire (Flisfeder), respectively. In different ways, they conceive social media to be about endless, repetitive and often seemingly senseless and useless behaviour: scrolling, clicking, liking, posting, sharing, laughing at the latest meme, getting angry about someone else – these hollow habits are ultimately seen as leading to nothing much but a dose of momentary *jouissance*. Contrasting with these bleak visions, the object-relations psychotherapist and scholar Aaron Balick (2014) has put forward a different theory of social media. Drawing from D. W. Winnicott and Jessica Benjamin, Balick foregrounds the ways in which social media can open up meaningful dynamics of relating and feeling connected for users, despite their downsides, which he also acknowledges. Social media tap into people's desires for recognition and being comforted in a safe environment, similar to how television was conceptualized by psychoanalytically minded cultural theorists (see Chapter 1). We critically position our own assessments in the tensions between these works with a view toward mediating between the pessimistic and optimistic visions of this scholarly field.

Chapter 3, 'Work, neoliberalism and the perverse pact', looks at contemporary work, both on and outside of social media. Under the economic framework of neoliberalism, which we explain here too, work has often become closely tied to digital tools and the forms of self-presentation and online networking that we have outlined in Chapter 2. As we go to show through a discussion of terms such as 'platform capitalism' and the 'information society', over the last four decades, work has taken on a form that, for many, is characterized by precarity, constant competition and self-exploitation. Relatively little has been written on this topic from a psychoanalytic perspective, so we begin this chapter with a discussion of what work actually is and how it has been conceptualized by Marxist as well as psychoanalytic scholars. Tying the various threads of digital work under neoliberalism together, the central theme of the chapter is perversion – a provocative concept through which we seek to make sense of the circumstance that many workers *know* that they are intensely exploited, but willingly allow themselves to be exploited nevertheless, even exploiting themselves, often to the point of what might be seen as a form of martyrdom in burning out. Indeed, what is striking here is the sense of masochistic pleasure exuding from the digital rituals of reminding themselves and others of how hard they work. Such dynamics can be particularly well exemplified through 'new' professions, such as influencers and other information-based work in the creative and service economy. Perversion pertains to damaging and destructive relationships where the one who is abused actively upholds this relationship because this abuse, humiliation and exploitation are seen as pleasurable and necessary for the subject in the service of achieving a greater good – as, for example, more self-knowledge, success or some other form of redemption. We know that we work too much, we know that our data are sold via social media, we know that other professionals on LinkedIn are really not much more successful than we are, but we continue to be part of the rat race – and it is not so much the denial of this knowledge, but the knowledge itself that brings us pleasure.

Chapter 4, 'Digital politics and the other', turns to the question of how the digital is informed by politics and politics by the digital. Be it in the form of racist slurs, trolling attacks, coordinated misogynist shitstorms and other forms of online extremism, the internet has become a violent and dangerous place for many. Increasingly, politics play out on social media and in other digital fields. Political opinions, attitudes and beliefs are often seen as becoming radicalized and polarized in 'filter bubbles' and divided in 'echo chambers', and the effects of such amplified, 'networked homophily' (Chun, 2018) often amounts to powerful demonstrations of the 'paranoid–schizoid' position in the Kleinian sense. We present psychoanalytic conceptualizations of extremism, authoritarianism, racism and antisemitism in different traditions, from critical theory to postcolonial studies, and tackle one of the key questions in psychoanalytic approaches to aggression, specifically to what extent such aggression can be seen as innate to and part of human nature. In general, what can plausibly be claimed for all instances of *pathological othering*, which underlies all violent extremisms, is that the notion of fantasy is key. The racist, for example, develops particular fantasies about the strange, foreign other who allegedly takes away their jobs, is a parasite of the welfare state, a criminal, etc. Such fantasies both order and destabilize the racist's psyche. The other is both sought to be destroyed or oppressed but is also needed and maintained because the racist's world is dependent on them. We draw on a range of examples and case studies to show how such dynamics unfold on social media where it has become all too common for particular groups to be harassed, abused and threatened to be killed on a daily basis. We discuss racist groups on Facebook (Krüger, 2018a), the use of 'racemojis' and racialized identities, the anti-feminist 'manosphere' (Krüger, 2021a, 2021b; Johanssen, 2022), as well as the relentless harassment campaign against the German YouTuber Drachenlord as a curious, but nevertheless characteristic, case of online political violence.

Chapter 5, 'Virtual sexuality: from the pre-oedipal to the post-oedipal', engages with how sexuality has been transformed because of and in relation to digital platforms today – transformations that can be understood as structured along pre- and post-oedipal lines. Sexuality is a crucial component of psychoanalysis, and we begin the chapter by introducing the notion of psychosexuality and how it has been developed by Freud and, subsequently, by Jean Laplanche and Jacques Lacan. For all three, sexuality is an essential part of subject formation; yet they markedly differ in their conceptions of how a child (and the subject in general) relates to the sexual. For Laplanche, the baby and later toddler are confronted with the sexual because it is all around them – especially due to the unconscious sexual dimensions in grown-ups' relationships with each other as well as their children. Children cannot make sense of the 'enigmatic signifiers' of unconscious mature sexuality, as Laplanche calls them, but sense their presence and import. In the case of the mother's breast, for example, there is the sense that it is not just a means for obtaining nourishment but also something else that remains puzzling. By way of this enigma, the breast expands in meaning, from a source of nourishment for the baby to an abstract but charged symbol and, subsequently, an actual source of sexual pleasure. Most importantly, as the person matures, the breast becomes a sexual fantasy object, no matter the person's sex. In this way, for both Laplanche and Freud, there is a form of infant sexuality, not in the sense of adult sexuality, which is less goal directed or dependent on particular erotogenic zones, but which is absolutely fundamental for the process of people's subject formation. Although the child derives pleasures from certain forms of auto-eroticism, those forms later become transformed, not only into sexuality proper, but also into distinct character traits. We connect this theory of psychosexual subject formation to digital platforms particularly through the works of Sharon Tugwell (2021) and Diego Semerene (2021), and argue that platforms are always already infused with the psychosexual. Our dependency on the smartphone, for example, finds strong echoes in Laplanche's notion of 'seduction' and his conception of the mother–child relationship. On a more phallic level of analysis, in turn, we can observe with Semerene how digital culture demands constant presence, arousal, manipulation, stimulation and excitement which comes close to a mature, coital and penetrating sexuality. We unpack those dynamics further through a case study of the most widely used hook-up app, Tinder, and Lacan's theory of sexuality. For Lacan, sexuality is solitary and quasi-masturbatory, with sexual partners turning the respective other into mere images and objects of desire. Tinder, as we show, is geared toward reproducing and amplifying these solitary dynamics. We end the chapter with a detailed discussion of one of the most significant transformations of sexuality today: the ubiquity of online porn.

Chapter 6, 'Videogames, AI and the vicissitudes of symbiosis', turns to the last two media technologies of the book. As concerns videogames, we first introduce the differences between playing and gaming and develop our own psychoanalytic approach to videogames by drawing on scholars in the field, such as Sherry Turkle (2005), Caroline Pelletier (2005) and Alfie Bown (2018), as well as literature from philosophy and game studies. Playing a videogame constitutes a curious activity that is characterized by high levels of both immersion and distance. Relying on the psychoanalyst Georges Devereux, we argue that this enables subjects to be 'sucked into' games, but in ways that do not let reality and fantasy collapse into each other. With the subject maintaining a sense of conscious control over their actions, videogames require an intricate balance between activity and passivity, fantasy play and reality testing. On this basis, we further present an exemplary clinical case study on the uses and abuses of videogames (Rosenfeld, 2016) and provide a critical assessment. We end the subchapter with a discussion of the question to what extent videogames make gamers violent and argue that it is not so much the symbolic renderings of violence that are problematic – indeed, videogames frequently enable the working through of unconscious conflicts. Rather, the problem as we see it resides in the objects, situations, contexts and mise-en-scènes in which videogames locate violent action. More often than not, these objects are reminiscent of marginalized social groups that are shown in situations that make their annihilation necessary.

The second part of the chapter considers one of the most hyped and evolving technologies of our time: artificial intelligence (AI) – that is, 'smart' computer programming, either embodied in robots or made interactionable through other interfaces, that is capable of making decisions in ways similar to how a human being would, often by 'learning' from vast amounts of data. We tackle this topic first through the philosopher Catherine Malabou's (2019) work on human 'intelligence', an idea with a problematic history, and how it relates to the alleged intelligence of machines. We discuss a range of examples that demonstrate the increasingly bewildering capability of contemporary AI technology to master (albeit still narrowly defined) tasks. For example, DeepMind's AlphaGo self-learning programme winning against a professional Go player, its AlphaStar AI playing the strategy videogame *Star Craft II* just like a human player does or the Duplex project, where an AI caller can have eerily realistic phone conversations with people, such as when booking a table at a restaurant. Such scenarios are pushed to fantastic levels in sci-fi films, such as Spike Jonze's *Her* (2013), in which the protagonist falls in love with a super-intelligent AI operating system. We discuss the film by drawing on recent scholarship by Isabel Millar (2021), Hannah Zeavin (2021) and Eli Zaretsky (2015a), all of whom place AI technology in relation to the human subject, while ultimately maintaining a (conceptual) separation between them. Pushing this debate a little further, we present our own conceptualization of the relation between humans and AI by drawing on the artist and psychoanalyst Bracha L. Ettinger's notion of 'the matrixial' (Ettinger, 1996; Pollock, 2020). In our opinion, human–AI relations as they are designed by the AI industry and as they are depicted in drama and sci-fi films can be expanded through Ettinger's conceptual focus on the womb, in which mother and baby form a 'relation-without-relating', as she calls it. This is a relation in which no one party dominates or is separate from the other. If we want to live with AI in a way that is less characterized by oedipal structures of domination and subjugation and more equal, we need to embrace its radical sameness to and difference from humanity.

Finally, the book's Conclusion chapter picks up on key commonalities across the chapters. With a focus on recognition, which is continuously given and received, withheld, craved or rejected in online forms of interaction, we bring the various themes that have arisen across the length of the book in conversation with each other. From this foundation, we seek to work out the conditions for how we can develop different applications and platforms, as well as ways of relating to each other online that are characterized by healthier forms of creativity and guidance, creation and destruction, via changed fantasies and psychodynamics. The path we propose to take to reach such new fantasies and relational constellations leads via processes of what we call 'transitional objectification': a hybrid that brings together opposing positions from object-relations, relational psychoanalysis and Screen Theoretical applications of the gaze. Thinking through how psychic life might be developed toward more ethical and socially progressive ways of experiencing and interacting, we find that such evolution needs to depart from the unconscious fixations, compulsions, obsessions, fantasies, fears, anxieties and desires that play key roles in people's lives. In this respect, digital media, with their manifold offers of call-and-response, afford particular possibilities for individuals to produce communications between the symbolic and symptomatic. In this lies the chance for users to have mirrored back at them *those* aspects in their communicative interactions that they are not conscious of, thus pointing them beyond their limitations and unfolding a transitional potential. Whereas Winnicott holds that transitional phenomena and objects are not mourned, but rather lose importance over time, we nevertheless close our book with a plea for an openness for and acceptance of the need for such processes of mourning and letting go – letting go of those fixations and fantasies that keep us in place, even if these places are not healthy, be they digital or other.

Notes

1.   In Freud's time, a psychoanalysis consisted of six sessions per week, with only Sundays off. Today, the frequency is set at four sessions per week, sometimes three. However, as psychoanalysts bemourn, many people do not want to commit to more than one session, maximum two sessions, per week, and they often prefer to sit upright and face the analyst. What we refer to as clinical psychoanalysis is the classic more-than-twice-a-week, lying-on-the-couch-with-the-analyst-sitting-behind-one set-up.
2.   https://melanie-klein-trust.org.uk/theory/paranoid-schizoid-position/

CHAPTER I

Reality and fantasy from film to TV

Key themes:
film as apparatus and mirror; Screen Theory and the male gaze;
real and imaginary audiences; television, working through and
transitional phenomena

Introduction

In this chapter, we introduce pioneering scholars in the field of psychoanalysis and media, specifically film and to a lesser extent television. Films have been analysed by scholars since moving images first emerged in 1895, the same year that Freud published his *Studies in Hysteria* (written with Joseph Breuer). From the early twentieth century, film studies started to emerge as its own discipline. It is concerned with theoretically and empirically analysing the aesthetic, social and cultural dimensions of film, specifically with a focus on its content and structure. Film has been one of the most successful and captivating forms of art and entertainment, often made in response to existing social conditions that are represented in and through film. And despite the substantial amount of teamwork and near military discipline going into the act of making a film, both its motivations and the finished product must be seen as deeply personal and suffused with the individual identities taking part in its creation.

Often, but not always, film has been conceived as a way of storytelling between reality and fantasy. It positions its viewers, or 'spectators' as they are called by many film scholars, at the intersections of reality and fantasy. This chapter introduces psychoanalytic film studies as the first area that made substantial use of psychoanalytic concepts in the study of media. We chart the historical development of this area from the 1960s and trace its extension into other media, first and foremost television, throughout the 1980s and onwards. Giving studies in film and television such pride of place and devoting a full chapter to them might seem odd in a book about *digital* media; however, we wish to do so because these newer and older traditions belong together. Despite the breaks and discontinuities that exist in psychoanalytic media studies, many of the foundational texts discussing analogue film are still of key relevance for our digital age.

A good way to start thinking about the relevance of film for the psychoanalytic study of media is through dreams. The parallels between film and dreams can hardly be disputed, and there seems to be something in the way in which films enable people to 'dream' – or at least enter a state that is dreamlike – which serves a distinctly human function. As the Lacanian scholar Todd McGowan (2015), along with other film theorists, has stated, dreams and films are in a tensely intimate relationship with one another. As far as dreams are concerned, although still posing a mystery to neurological research, it is relatively settled that they have an ordering, recreational and mental processing function. Troubling, exciting and strongly affective experiences during waking life are processed in the brain while sleeping. In this respect, Freud was by no means off the mark when he saw in dreams a rich source of the articulations of unconscious life, as neuroscientists have confirmed (e.g. Solms, 2018). Relating unconscious desire to film, McGowan (2015) explains: 'A filmmaker creates a film to satisfy the spectator's desire in the same way that a dreamer creates a dream in order to satisfy the subject's desire' (2015, p. 9). Unlike dreams, McGowan adds, films are no direct expression of a person's desire, but rather 'an attempt to lure or arouse this desire' (2015, p. 11). And yet, the comparison holds, he insists, because '[t]here is no film, just as there is no dream, that doesn't engage in an appeal to the subject's desire' (2015, p. 9).

Initially, Freud considered dreams as instances of wish fulfilment. He would later change his view, but we would like to focus on this point for a moment. At least the lucky ones among us have had dreams in which they managed to pass a dreaded exam, were promoted at work, finally obtained the thing they always wanted, had the most amazing sex or had other wishes fulfilled. Dreams can absolutely play out fantasies which we wish would become reality, and film functions on a similar level. We have to assume that film, too, arranges visions of specific fantasies which are animated by unconscious desire, on the part of the director, for example, but also – and more importantly – on the part of the spectator. After all, film is captivating to spectators because it creates variations of reality – different *worlds* – that we often feel a deep connection to, however revolting, arousing or shocking they may be in certain cases.

Analysing the specific ways in which film does that – for example, through its casting, camera angles, cutting styles, lighting, costumes and other parts of the mise-en-scène, or through the plot and storyline – has a strong cultural–analytic potential because these specifics tell us something about the ways in which fantasy and desire are woven into them. It is thus the specific *forms* in which fantasy and desire are evoked and captured that are characteristic of a specific cultural–historical moment. From the perspective of psychoanalytic film studies, for example, the massive success of the film *Dirty Dancing* (Ardolino, 1987) in the 1980s needs to be understood in the context of Francis 'Baby' Houseman's (Jennifer Grey) transition into sexual maturity and womanhood, brought about through the erotic medium of dance, which the film shows to cut across class, race, gender and age norms that were very much alive and kicking in the late 1980s (Dunagan & Fenton, 2014). From this perspective, then, the film's success lies in the intricate balance that it strikes between a nostalgic respect for and, at the same time, inevitable transgression of social boundaries, limits and taboos. The 'uptown girl' and the downtown man, the dirty and the clean, the light and the dark, the young and the old – such fault lines continue to have their hold on fantasies and desires, also in today's cultures, and the erotic tension between Patrick Swayze and Jennifer Grey gives credence to both the necessity of the existence of such differentiations and the necessity to defy them. It is thus the delicate sexualization of (several layers of) binaries becoming redeemed in love that is at the core of *Dirty Dancing*'s play on desire and fantasy and at the root of its success.

The beginnings of psychoanalytic film studies

The discomforting ambiguities between degrees of liberalism on the one side and clichés of traditional femininity on the other in *Dirty Dancing* point toward the perhaps most central interest in early feminist psychoanalytic film theory: specifically, showing the ways in which films, through their very play on and with desire, reproduce and reaffirm existing ideologies.

A key term since Marx, **ideology** refers to a system of beliefs and practices geared to maintain the existing order and status quo in society. Ideologies often reproduce unequal power relations and protect *some* groups of people while making others more vulnerable. Early Marxists had a straightforward understanding of ideology in which those in power also control 'the means of mental production' and the 'ruling ideas' of a given period, as Marx and Engels (1970, p. 64) wrote. Along these lines, ideology is a distorted understanding and experience of reality. A more productive and less normatively restrictive understanding has been coined by Antonio Gramsci (1971), who defined ideologies as those beliefs and opinions that seem natural, unchallengeable and common-sensical, and in this way become hegemonic in societies. An example of an ideology would be meritocracy: the belief and effort that anyone can make it and be successful, irrespective of their background, as long as they work hard enough. Countless studies have shown this not to be the case (Littler, 2017) and yet this belief is still extremely widespread and strong.

If it was not for the ground-breaking feminist work, much of the psychoanalytic scholarship that we chart in this book, including our own, would probably not exist. Hence, the field of psychoanalytic media studies that we are mapping here and continue to discuss in the coming chapters owes much to the legacy of feminists and psychoanalytic film scholars such as Laura Mulvey, Kaja Silverman, Teresa de Lauretis, Barbara Creed, Elizabeth Cowie, Mary Ann Doane, Tania Modleski, Cora Kaplan, Constance Penley, Biddy Martin, Jackie Stacey, Lisa Cartwright, Susannah Radstone, Vicky Lebeau, Joan Copjec, Jennifer Friedlander, Mari Ruti, Hilary Neroni, Jacqueline Rose, Keli Fuery, Chris Holmlund, Agnieszka Piotrowska, Jennifer C. Nash, Carol Clover, Barbara Johnson, Constance Penley, Catherine Constable, Patricia Mellencamp, Catherine Grant, Claire Johnston, Anneke Smelik, Michele Wallace, Griselda Pollock, Bracha L. Ettinger, Annette Kuhn, Valerie Walkerdine, Caroline Bainbridge, Candida Yates and many more. Those scholars have pioneered and continually refined the analysis of film in particular and of media in general. We cannot even attempt to do justice to the richness of this tradition and therefore will only map its early foundations in this chapter.[1]

However, before turning to some of the above scholars and their work, we need to discuss two authors who had prepared the ground for feminist psychoanalytic film studies to grow on. The first scholars to seriously address film in relation to psychoanalysis were the French theorists Jean-Louis Baudry and Christian Metz. Although both drew heavily on Freud and Lacan, Baudry also used the writings of the Marxist philosopher Louis Althusser for his conception of cinema as *apparatus*. Baudry argued that cinema as a *dispositif*, as an entirety and a whole, including all spatial and technological features of the cinema, the audience and the film itself, has a deeply ideological function and effect. In the Althusserian sense, cinema in Baudry's understanding amounts to a form of the Ideological State Apparatus (ISA) – a term that, according to Althusser (1971), refers to institutions and organizations (e.g. the church, school, family) that exercise ideological influence over people and maintain the social status quo.

What is interesting about Baudry's and Metz's writings is the way in which their conceptions of cinema and the cinematic experience differ. In order to unfold this difference, however, another principle of psychoanalytic thinking is important to clarify, specifically, the continuous immaturity of all human beings, and the continuous workings of the infantile and of childishness in all of us. Hence, although the psychosexual stages of development that Freud conceived in strict chronological sequence – polymorphous perverse, oral, narcissistic, anal, genital, oedipal, post-oedipal – are today no longer seen as cleanly separable and sequencable, they are still very useful in locating and interpreting the modalities of our desires and the ways they have formed and been shaped throughout our lives (see Chapter 5 for a longer discussion of this). Both Baudry and Metz see cinema as taking part in shaping, as well as playing upon, these modalities. Baudry sees the power of cinema and its ideological potential to lie in its doubling up, simulation, taking over and reactivation of aspects of primary relational orality, the stage at which the baby is held and fed by the primary caregiver. Metz sees its formative function to set in at a slightly later developmental level, namely at that of identification – a function that he sees cinema to perform by figuring as a specific form of mirror.

The idea of **identification** goes back to Sigmund Freud, who explained that 'Identification is not simple imitation but assimilation [...]; it expresses a resemblance and is derived from a common element which remains in the unconscious' (Freud, 1900, p. 150). Freud saw identification as a form of emotional, loving (indeed, libidinous) tie with an object. Identification essentially means an unconscious process whereby an individual comes to feel a sameness with another person, or the representation of a person in a film, and wants to be like them.

As Baudry (2009 [1975]) explains:

> Of course, there is no question of identifying mental image, filmic image, mental representation, and cinematographic representation. The fact that the same terms are used, however, does reveal the very workings of desire in cinema, that is, at the same time the desire to rediscover archaic forms of desire which in fact structure any form of desire, and the desire to stage for the subject, to put in the form of representation, what might recall its own operation. (p. 183)

As the film scholars Thomas Elsaesser and Malte Wagener (2010) summarize Braudy's argument: '[I]n the cinema body and mind "regress" to an earlier stage of psycho-physiological development' (p. 64), and this regression sits at the heart of what Baudry calls the cinema's 'more than real': a vision of reality that the cinematic apparatus suffuses with the human workings of the unconscious. According to Baudry, it is this suffusing of reality with desire in film that is also at the heart of its ideological effect: 'Instead of considering cinema as an ideologically neutral apparatus, as it has been rather stupidly called [...], in order to explain the cinema effect, it is necessary to consider it from the viewpoint of the apparatus that it constitutes, apparatus which in its totality includes the subject. And first of all, the subject of the unconscious' (2009 [1975], p. 184). Because film is something that is intended to be shown to others, there is at its foundation the combination of a 'wanting-to-be-seen-ness' and 'want-to-see-ness' that connects cinema to the primary, dyadic relation of 'feeding–fed' between infant and caregiver.

Metz, by contrast, holds a view in which the oral, mothering and feeding functions, which Baudry associates with cinema, are outweighed by an identification function. Metz constructs this mechanism on the basis of Jacques Lacan's theory of the *mirror stage* of the infant. In this seminal text, Lacan (2002 [1949]) observes that children from the age of six months start recognizing themselves *as themselves* in the mirror. However, since at this stage the body is not nearly fully functional – indeed six-month-olds are barely able to support themselves in an upright position – Lacan holds that this act of seeing oneself in the mirror, as whole, coherent and in one piece, results in a *misrecognition*. Simply put, the baby sees itself as in much better shape than it really is. This wonderful self-illusion leads to an attitude of the ego to itself that always struggles to match the *ego ideal* on the other side of the glass: a vision of oneself that is always somewhat out of reach and that comes to haunt the subject throughout their lives.

In 'The Imaginary Signifier', Metz (1975) cautiously expands Lacan's mirror scene so as to include the mother in it, writing that: 'In the mirror the child perceives the familiar household objects, and also its object par excellence, its mother, who holds it up in her arms to the glass. But above all it perceives its own image' (1975, p. 48). Metz makes clear that the formative process he sees cinema to facilitate is that very perception of one's own image. And that, he insists, even though the spectator's own body is the 'one thing and one thing only that is never reflected' in the mirror of the cinematic screen (ibid.). '[W]hat *makes possible* the spectator's absence from the screen – or rather the intelligible unfolding of the film despite this absence – is the fact that the spectator has already known the experience of the mirror (of the true mirror)' (ibid.). Therefore, with spectators themselves entirely absent, what they become identified with in the cinema is *that entity which perceives*: 'At the cinema, it is always the other who is on the screen; as for me, I am there to look at him [sic]. I take no part in the perceived, on the contrary, I am *all-perceiving*. [...] In other words, the spectator identifies with himself as a pure act of perception' (ibid., p. 49). In comparison to Baudry's theory of cinema performing an immediate holding function similar to being fed by the mother, Metz's theory of 'primary cinematic identification', an identification with the act of perception itself, is located on the side of consciousness: 'I know that I am perceiving something imaginary [...], and I know that it is I who am perceiving it' (ibid.).

Despite one's awareness, however, the way in which the identification with 'the one who sees' is put in place leaves the question as to what is conscious and what is unconscious in this identification open:

As an arrangement (and in a very topological sense of the word), the cinema is more involved on the flank of the symbolic, and hence of secondariness, than is the mirror of childhood. This is not surprising, since it comes long after it, but what is more important to me is the fact that it is inscribed in its wake with an incidence at once so direct and so oblique, which has no precise equivalent in other apparatuses of signification. (ibid.)

Now, the above passages – and this last quotation in particular – are hard to understand, but we have reproduced them here at some length because both Baudry's and Metz's positions point forward to the ways in which psychoanalytically oriented scholars have later sought to make sense of the internet. For example, Sherry Turkle's writings (1995, 2011) shift between Baudry's visions of apparatus-like attachment and what Metz works out here as a paradoxical (fetishistic) double-structure of directness and obliqueness, knowingness and unknowingness, consciousness and unconsciousness. Indeed, what Metz seems to say here is that cinema is unique in feeding us fantasies that we know are not real but leave a highly real – vivid and life-like – impression nevertheless. In this way, they unfold a real effect despite our knowledge to the contrary.

In this mode of extreme vividness, cinema, according to Metz, becomes a 'technique of the imaginary' (Metz, 1975, p. 15) and an imaginary support for spectators to see themselves as whole – by virtue of watching films from a position from which they can imagine themselves to be whole, even though the film is fragmented, consisting of discontinuous cuts, scenes, shots and angles, and even though, one might argue, the spectator is fragmented, too.

As Elsaesser and Hagener write, such a model of experiencing film based on identification:

seemed to explain the iterative, compulsive and highly narcissistic pleasures associated with narrative cinema, irrespective of whether style and genre were 'realist' or 'fantasy'. Identification in the cinema would thus be contingent upon establishing with the moving image not a relation of appearance versus reality, or fiction versus truth, but an imaginary relationship internal to the spectator. (Elsaesser & Hagener, 2010, p. 66)

The writings of Metz and Baudry would lay important foundations for thinkers in Britain and elsewhere.

Screen Theory and the male gaze

The term Screen Theory is used to describe a group of academics and filmmakers who published their work in the British academic journal *Screen* and whose writings built on Baudry and Metz. Screen Theory had its momentum from the early 1970s and through the 1980s. It greatly contributed to the establishment of what is known as feminist film theory and its influence is still strong today. For the adherents of this direction of film analysis, it was psychoanalysis together with Marxism that enabled ideology critique of mainstream Hollywood cinema. They asked, 'What are the social and psychic functions of cinema?' (Bordwell, 1996, p. 6). In particular, the works of Laura Mulvey (1975), Mary Ann Doane (1987a), Colin MacCabe (1974), Stephen Heath (1977), Steve Neale (1983) and Barbara Creed (2000) can be mentioned in this context. Screen theorists drew on and developed French film theory further – from general claims into specific genre observations, from theoretical statements into political interventions, with a particular interest in questions such as: What does it mean to view a film? How are sexualities and gender depicted? What are a film's political implications? How does it mirror or shape society, and with what consequences for people's conception of reality?

The psychoanalytic concept of identification that Metz had fore-grounded in his works was also central for one thinker in particular: Laura Mulvey, who became the best-known proponent of Screen Theory. Published in *Screen* in 1975, her essay 'Visual Pleasure and Narrative Cinema' became hugely influential for coining the term **'the male gaze'**, which has been used by generations of film, cultural and media studies students and academics to describe a male way of looking at and representing female bodies that is afforded by classic Hollywood films and popular culture more generally.

Mulvey argues that, in the context of watching films, the processes of identification and objectification are achieved not only through the relationships that male and female actors have in the roles they play, but also through the means of the script, direction, camera and editing. It is first and foremost these means that reproduce traditional gender roles and stereotypes, and ultimately the patriarchal order. Hence, Hollywood films, even to this day, invite their audiences, both male and female, to look at women on screen from a distinctly heterosexual male perspective. And they do so by suggesting such a look, or gaze, in the ways that male characters 'ogle' their female counterparts and in the ways that the camera doubles down on this look. For example, in Oliver Stone's (1987) portrait of stockbroker culture, *Wall Street*, the absolute male domination of this culture in the 1980s is shown to leave nearly no space for women at all. The latter come in only in the role of secretaries, who function either as gatekeepers to and facilitators of male business exchanges or as the providers of fast, impersonal sexual intercourse, which, again, is arranged and performed in the fashion of business exchanges. However, the soft-pornographic ways in which the film depicts these exchanges, with the camera gliding in lascivious, voyeuristic close-ups under expensive skirts, belies the critique of machismo Wall Street culture that the film sets out to bring forth.

Although in psychoanalytic lingo the (sexually charged) pleasure of *looking per se* is called '*scopophilia*', **'voyeurism'** by contrast refers to a sexual pleasure and gratification in looking at someone without oneself being seen. Especially in the case of voyeurism, aggressive and violently controlling impulses are involved in that the voyeur appropriates the other as an image, making the other an object of their scopophilic pleasure while remaining detached. Drawing on Freud and Lacan, Mulvey argued that traditional Hollywood cinema facilitates such a voyeuristic gaze by turning women into mere objects to be looked at. She focused on 1950s' Hollywood cinema, or 'narrative cinema' as it is known, which was dominated by men (and, to a significant degree, still is today): male producers, male directors, male actors in leading roles, with the audience being imagined to be mostly male, too. This resulted in specific ways of representation, as Mulvey wrote:

> In a world ordered by sexual imbalance, pleasure in looking has been split between active-male and passive-female. The determining male gaze projects its phantasy on to the female figure which is styled accordingly. In their traditional exhibitionist role women are simultaneously looked at and displayed, with their appearance coded for strong visual and erotic impact so that they can be said to connote *to-be-looked-at-ness*. (Mulvey, 1975, p. 11, italics in original)

Through this male gaze, Hollywood cinema reproduces and upholds a patriarchal, male-dominated social order and a particular hierarchy of sexual difference. Cinema has been dependent on this binary of active men and passive women as they are the devices around which a story is structured. As close-ups of female bodies or body parts are brought into focus, Mulvey suggests that women can only be shown in patriarchal terms and in relation to men. Psychoanalysis is used here in order to articulate a feminist critique of mainstream cinema and its ideology. The active, controlling and at times violent practices of voyeurism are likewise identified as male by Mulvey. The voyeur is distanced and in control. He is not seen but has uninterrupted access to what he is looking at (e.g. a filmic representation of a woman). This is amplified by the filmic compositions. For example, the camera follows the male protagonist or shows shots from his point of view. The female in the film is thus put on display for both the male hero and the audience, which is squeezed into a male cask. The very structure of the film leaves them no choice but to (unconsciously) identify with the male hero. In that sense, cinema goes further than other forms of sexist representation (theatre, striptease) as it restricts and directs the gaze in a specific manner. Not only does Hollywood cinema respond to existing forms of sexism and reproduce them in the ways that Mulvey discusses, but it *naturalizes* them through the camera and its gaze. It seems to objectively reflect social reality. '[T]he eye in cinema is the perfect eye, the steady and ubiquitous control of the scene passed from director to spectator by virtue of the cinematic apparatus', as Stephen Heath (1976, p. 11), another Screen theorist, put it. The filmic representation actively guides the spectator through the process of watching a film, 'holds their hands' so to speak and 'sutures' (another Lacanian term, which we return to later in this chapter) them to the flow of the story.

The mechanisms Mulvey describes relate further to the relationship between phallic power, on the one hand, and powerlessness and a state of castration, on the other. **Castration** literally means the cutting off of sexual organs, first and foremost the penis. However, contemporary psychoanalysis understands castration more at a symbolic level and as a traumatic psychic threat. On the symbolic level, castration refers to phallic, and therefore male-connoted, power – a power that is an imaginary one from the start and which the subject imagines as having been stolen, curtailed or taken away.

Watching female characters in films often triggers an unconscious threat of castration for male viewers. As long as women are presented as docile and shown in a position of mere to-be-looked-at-ness, men can feel assured in their role as spectators. But as soon as a woman on screen, say, returns the gaze and challenges the power relations implicit in it, this causes unease and anxiety, which, however, is often defended against, or defused, through the film's plot itself. Aggressive and dangerous women are thus either punished by the male hero (for instance, in the genre of *film noir* where the female character is often portrayed as both seductive and dangerous) or saved, as in action adventure films like the James Bond franchise where the 'Bond girl' has frequently been a mere sexualized prop kept alive by 007.

But times have changed since the publication of Mulvey's article and since the heyday of James Bond. Instead, our contemporary screens, magazines and billboards are full of objectified men as well, constructing a cis female gaze that assesses men's bodies just as the male gaze did with women, as Mari Ruti notes (2016). Cinema also frequently critiques sexism, racism and other forms of prejudice. But the deeply entrenched sexism within film and media has not gone away since Mulvey and others began writing about it. Women have likewise internalized the male gaze when they judge their own and other women's bodies in relation to ideological beauty standards. However problematic, this can also be intensely pleasurable for women, who 'learn to take pleasure in the idea that, like their female alter egos on the screen, they might one day be able to arouse men's desire by incarnating the mythological Woman of heteropatriarchal fantasy' (Ruti, 2016, p. 40). However, there are still more than enough instances of the male gaze being churned out of the Hollywood dream factory each year. And as much as we enjoyed Quentin Tarantino's *Once Upon a Time in Hollywood* (2019), the 'tongue-in-cheek-ness' with which it unfolds the relationship between Brad Pitt's 'Cliff Booth' and Margaret Qualley's 'Pussycat' nevertheless seems to be intended to give new lease to the pattern of narcissistic identification with a glorious male and desiring objectification of the siren-like female.

The female voice

The effect that Mulvey's article had on film studies of the 1970s cannot be overestimated. Especially to feminist scholars it was a wake-up call as well as a call to arms. In the wake of Mulvey's intervention, some of the most interesting work in Screen Theory was produced in response to the question of the place of women on, as well as in front of, movie screens. Kaja Silverman in particular deepened Mulvey's work on the dominance of the male perspective in cinema, first and foremost by unfolding in detail Mulvey's argument that cinema creates a defence against the challenge that women pose to male authority – an argument that she extends into cultural history. Although a paradigm shift in men's fashion in the late eighteenth century – the invention of the suit – had served to make men inconspicuous and nearly bodiless (Silverman, 1988, p. 25) and subsequently tasked women alone to bear the weight of the requirement of being beautiful and embodied, the stripped-down, functionalist cinema from the mid-twentieth century onwards doubled down on this naturalization of male bodilessness and female 'hyperspecularisation' (p. 24). This was done, Silverman (1988) argues, through a technological and architectural set-up that facilitated looking at beauty and spectacle, which by then was firmly female connoted, from an inconspicuous and neutral-seeming position, which by then was firmly male connoted. Yet, these elaborate but vastly unconscious arrangements have by no means been stable. As Silverman (1988) states, 'the classic film poses a constant threat to the very subjectivity it wishes to consolidate' (p. 30), and it does so through its continued diminution and derision of women.

In order to work out in more detail the place of women in this arrangement, Silverman (1988) shifted the focus from the visual to the audio-acoustic aesthetics of film and here particularly to the female voice. In films, the female voice is frequently one that is maternal and can thus be seen as nurturing and caring. More often, however, and in stark contrast to its male counterparts, filmic renderings of the female voice take on a child-like quality of frailty and helplessness, inferiority and dependence. Female characters are heard crying, screaming or laughing hysterically and, through their voice, they are made unstable, unreliable and out of control. The woman's voice becomes a *chiffre* for her whole body and, in Lacanian terms, she is represented in this way as **lacking** (see Introduction) and as having to carry the weight of that lack on behalf of man (whose own lack does not come into the picture). The cinematic female voice thus functions as a way for men to displace their symbolic castration onto women, functioning as an 'acoustic mirror in which the male subject hears all the repudiated elements of his infantile babble' (Silverman, 1988, p. 81).

Suture

Film's promise to heal our (male) feelings of lack and castration is what Silverman, following Lacan (2004 [1964]), called **suture**. The female voice is one device among others with which film does this; a conventional storyline is another. Film is effective in patching us up in this sense because it responds to a lack that belongs to us in a constitutive, fundamental way and enables us to feel immersed in a film so as to make us momentarily forget our problems and worries. The film's ability to suture us is especially propelled forward through plot twists and unexpected turns, as they make the expected end all the more desirable. Indeed, the plots of many films revolve around a kind of rhythmic portrayal of lack and the threat of castration. This is covered over with a narrative that enables identification and a form of closure – for instance, in the inevitable 'happy ending' of most Hollywood films. The horror genre provides a particularly vivid example of suture and the human need for narrative and identificatory support – because the plot is frequently moved forward in the face of harsh disruptions of the spectator's identifications. Shohini Chaudhuri, in *Feminist Film Theorists* (2006), offers Hitchcock's *Psycho* as an example with which to hit home this point:

> The healing of narrative can only happen after the wound has been inflicted; and the more wounded we are, the more desperate we become for meaning and narrative. We can see this at work in *Psycho* (1960), where we follow and identify with Marion Crane until she is murdered halfway through the film in the famous shower scene, where every cinematic cut appears to be the stab of a knife. This inflicts a traumatic wound on the viewer who is left with no-one to identify within the empty motel except the cinematic enunciator. So desperate is our need for meaning and narrative that we then identify with Marion's murderer, Norman Bates, when he arrives to dispose of her body and her belongings. We even feel anxious for him when, momentarily, Marion's car refuses to sink into the swamp. (Chaudhuri, 2006, p. 50)

Besides Mulvey and Silverman, it was particularly Mary Ann Doane (e.g. 1987b) who wrote lucidly about melodrama and especially the 'woman's film' of the 1940s. A mixed, 'impure' genre, drawing on melodrama, film noir, gothic and horror films, we turn to it in the next section.

Ordinary entertainment: from cinema to soaps

Doane sees the 'woman's film' as a substantial contribution to the representation of women, despite the many dismissals it received from male critics (Doane, 1987b, p. 284). Its value, she holds, lies exactly in the alternative that it offered to early female cinema audiences, who, due to the male gaze that Mulvey had found to be engineered into most Hollywood films, were left with two stark choices: 'a narcissistic identification with the female figure as spectacle, and a "transvestite" identification with the active male hero in his mastery' (Doane, 1987b, p. 195). The woman's film creates a first way out of this impasse, but at a steep price:

> Because the 'woman's film' purportedly directs itself to a female audience, because it pretends to offer the female spectator an identity other than that of the active male hero, it deflects energy away from the second 'transvestite' option described above and towards the more 'properly' female identification. But since the 'woman's film' reduces the spectacularisable nature of the female body, this first option of a narcissistic identification is problematised as well. In a patriarchal society, to desexualise the female body is ultimately to deny its very existence. (Doane, 1987b, pp. 295–6)

In viewing the female character on screen, the female spectator can either over-identify with her or regard her as her own object of desire (Doane, 1991). Both are excessive forms of identification. Instead, Doane argues that the female viewer should maintain a distance between herself and the woman on screen by regarding the type of femininity portrayed as exaggerated and excessive in itself. Drawing on the psychoanalyst Joan Riviere's notion of female masquerade (1999 [1929]), Doane argues that femininity is always, whether on screen or off, about the portrayal, or performance, of specific attributes and styles. Just like masculinity, femininity is something that is filled with meaning through, for instance, fashion, media representation and social norms. 'Womanliness is a mask which can be worn or removed,' Doane (1982, p. 81) argues.

Mari Ruti illustrates this point with a fitting example when discussing the makeover scene from the film *Pretty Woman* (Marshall, 1990), in which Vivian (Julia Roberts) is transformed 'from a hooker to a "lady"':

It turns out that clothes really do make a woman, for when Vivian walks out of the boutique, wearing a stylish sundress and carrying shopping bags filled with other character-defining garments, passers-by, including well-dressed men, look at her with deep admiration rather than with the disapproval that had met her hooker incarnation the previous day. (Ruti, 2016, p. 103)

It is through the physical transformation, Ruti argues, that the film depicts a moral transition from 'bad' to 'good woman', too. By virtue of fashion and 'learning' upper-class associated etiquette, Vivian is able to re-discover and unfold her true identity and, stereotypically, this transformation is made possible by a mentoring man, Edward (Richard Gere).

Yet, *Pretty Woman*, a film that came to define the rom-com genre of its era, does not only fall into the trap of glaring gender stereotypes, but also manages, at least to certain degrees, to portray female agency in more complex and ambivalent ways. In this sense, it also complicates the straightforward notions of identification that Mulvey, Baudry and Metz suggested. This complication had already been theorized by Tania Modleski (1982), who was one of the first psychoanalytic scholars to move beyond classic cinema and analyse more broadly popular genres, such as television soap operas. Soap opera, like the woman's film from Doane's analysis, received heavily derisive rejections from television critics and was mocked as a genre for housewives. In her appreciation of the genre, Modleski takes a large step further than Doane in her defence of the woman's film. Modleski also draws on Mulvey's analysis of Hollywood cinema and its inherently male perspective. In contrast to those male-gazing films in Mulvey's analysis, however, soap operas have no 'main controlling figure with whom the spectator can identify,' Modleski argues (1982, p. 83). Therefore, instead of the spectator becoming '"the representative of power", the multiple identification which occurs in soap opera results in the spectator's being divested of power' (ibid.). 'Instead of giving us one "powerful ideal ego […] who can make things happen and control events better than the subject/spectator can"', Modleski continues, 'soap operas present us with numerous limited egos, each in conflict with others' (ibid.). In distinction to narrative film that drives its action towards a conclusion, soap opera constantly interrupts and stalls such development; and instead of a beginning, a middle and an end, it consists of an 'indefinitely expandable middle' (ibid., p. 82), where 'conclusions only lead to further tension and suffering' (ibid., p. 84). However, she emphatically rejects those critiques that see in these characteristics of the soap opera weaknesses of a typically feminine genre. These critiques are caught up in the expectations set by the dominance of the male-centred Hollywood cinema – that is, exactly *that* genre which needs to be countered: 'To criticize classical narrative because, for example, it is based on a suspect notion of progress and then criticize soap opera because it *isn't* will never get us anywhere' (ibid., p. 97). Modleski rather calls for her readers to embrace the soap opera genre – not naively and not entirely, but in an informed and knowing way. And while the anti-progressive and fragmented form of the soap opera indeed points to troubling social characteristics in many women's lives – particularly the repetitiveness and fragmentedness of domestic chores which, in the 1980s, were still firmly deemed female – 'soap opera allays *real* anxieties, satisfies *real* needs and desires, even while it may distort them' (ibid., p. 101, italics in original).

All of the above accounts, Mulvey's and Silverman's in particular, serve to illuminate the *ideological* function of cinema as a mechanism of inserting people into a particular arrangement of the social and reproducing these positions through the visual arrangement of particular actions and relations. Spectators, then, are seen here as straightforwardly conforming to mainstream cinematic fantasies (of everlasting love, hard work, overcoming obstacles, the victory of good over evil) when watching a film and unconsciously reproducing such ideas in their everyday actions and thoughts outside the cinema. In this perspective, cinema functions in a very reassuring, comforting and recognizable way. This approach is poignantly summarized by the feminist thinker Teresa de Lauretis (1984), when she states that the spectator, and the female spectator in particular, is continually remade as a 'properly' gendered subject through the latest Hollywood blockbuster. The very idea of what it means to be a woman (and a man) is *invented* in patriarchy and reproduced through cinema. As Mari Ruti has more recently stated, 'one of the most prominent features of Hollywood has always been its capacity to map our culture's ideals of masculinity and femininity onto (gendered) bodies that appear to incarnate these ideals in relatively pure form' (Ruti, 2016, p. 36).

Critiques of Screen Theory

Although Mulvey's essay can rightly be considered an intellectual bombshell that has had an enduring legacy, it nevertheless comes with a set of problems and theoretical weaknesses that need to be discussed too. First, Mulvey provided an interpretation of the notion of the gaze that, within a strict Lacanian reading, would not be correct. For Lacan, the gaze is not the same as a look, or a one-directional taking-in of an object by a subject. On the contrary, the gaze is a disturbing phenomenon that, rather than providing instances for feelings of mastery or identification, throws us off course and reveals a hole within both ourselves and our field of vision. We could say that the Lacanian gaze is a feeling of being looked at by an object – a presence in our field of vision whereby something unsettles us as spectators. As Lacan explained: 'I can feel myself under the gaze of someone whose eyes I do not see, not even discern. All that is necessary is for something to signify to me that there may be others there' (Lacan, 1988, p. 215).

In other words, the Lacanian gaze is the feeling of being watched by another, while watching someone or something oneself. One of us (Steffen), for example, painfully remembers the following scene: coffee cup in hand, one early morning he looked from the third-floor kitchen window of his then apartment into the still quiet inner-city street below. There he followed, in half-conscious reverie, the swinging gait of a beautiful woman on the sidewalk. When he looked up, however, he had to realize that a neighbour in the house on the other side of the narrow street had been watching him watching the woman. It was in this moment, that the social, cultural and – not least – political dimensions of his unthinkingly longing look crashed into the scene and, as pleasant and scopophilically exciting (voyeuristic?!) his watching the woman in the street might have been, the fact of 'being watched watching' clearly put him into another frame of mind. Hence, it is not even of importance what this neighbour was in fact thinking about Steffen at that moment. Rather, what becomes important in the Lacanian concept of the gaze is that such gazing as Steffen did when he suddenly got caught up in it through the presence of the neighbour is that all kinds of meanings and implications constantly come into the field of the scopic. We can never *merely look* at something without such social implications coming to weigh in, whether there is a neighbour around to witness it or not, or whether we are in the cinema with the lights out or elsewhere in plain daylight. Hence, although for Mulvey the male gaze operates in a very linear way and captures the spectator in an identification set entirely by the film, Joan Copjec (1994) uses Lacan's more prism-like understanding of the gaze to argue in her influential critique that 'the speaking subject *cannot* ever be totally trapped in the imaginary' (p. 32, italics in original). Instead, one could say that, paradoxically, this trapping is always already trapped in other perspectives as well. Furthermore, the black feminist bell hooks (1992) has pointed out that Mulvey's theory of the male gaze tacitly assumes a *white* gaze and *white* audience, thus failing to account for issues of ethnicity and racism in the dubious scopophilic pleasures that cinema offers. By coining the term 'oppositional gaze', hooks emphasized how a different concept of the gaze, which remained closer to Mulvey's than Lacan's, can challenge and disrupt more straightforward conceptions of how we desire and identify with others while watching films (see also Gaines, 2000).

A further strand of critique against Mulvey's concept of the male gaze has been directed against the dearth of interest in the actual people watching films. Stephen Prince (1996), for instance, points toward the lack of empirical investigations into film *reception*. Psychoanalytic film theory, he holds, *assumes* a subject that only exists *inside the film*, so to speak, or is literally glued to the screen, letting everything flow into itself unfiltered. Similar critiques have been made by feminist scholars as well, suggesting that theories of the gaze deny women agency (see Thornham, 1999 for an overview). The prominent cultural studies scholar David Morley (1992) even went so far as to compare Screen Theory with the 'hypodermic needle' thesis in mass communication research – an utterly naive, early belief in direct and strong effects of the media on people:

> I would argue that the psychoanalytically based work has ultimately mobilized what can be seen as another version of the hypodermic theory of effects – in so far as it is, at least in its initial and fundamental formulations, a universalist theory which attempts to account for the way in which the subject is necessarily positioned by the text. (Morley, 1992, p. 55)

This critique definitely overshoots the mark. After all, the project of Mulvey and other Screen theorists was not to show the many strategies (conscious and/or unconscious) of people to make sense of a film different from an ideological understanding, but to point to exactly this ideological understanding, how it was being offered to audiences and what its formative potential was. Mulvey, although she may have used the notion of the gaze without much regard for its original definition, was more interested in how female bodies are represented and how the look of the male protagonist intersects with this representation. Having said this, it needs to be stated, too, that there are significant overlaps between Mulvey's and Lacan's conceptions of the gaze. As Ruti (2016) has highlighted, the male gaze is disturbing, in both its Mulveyian and its Lacanian versions, because it throws the woman off course without her necessarily being aware of it at first. Mulvey herself has continued to reflect and elaborate on her 'Visual Pleasure' essay, most recently in her book *Afterimages: On Cinema, Women and Changing Times* (2019), in which she has included a useful appendix of frequently asked questions about the essay, which we can highly recommend.

Cultural studies and psychoanalysis: approaching actual audiences

First steps in the direction of including a concern for actual audiences into psychoanalytic film scholarship were taken by Teresa de Lauretis (1984) and Elizabeth Cowie (1997), who have both emphasized that spectators can – and usually *do* – adopt contrasting and shifting positions in relation to a film. Cowie's approach is especially interesting because she theorized a dynamic and fleeting kind of spectatorship on the basis of the notion of fantasy. Drawing on the works of Laplanche and Pontalis (1973), she conceptualizes fantasy as a 'a scene' in which unconscious desires become endowed with a 'façade of coherence and continuity' (pp. 129–30), very much as in Freud's (1908) definition of daydreams, where conscious and unconscious modes of thinking are being combined as well. Hence, when Cowie defines fantasy 'as a mise-en-scène of desire' and as 'more a setting out of lack, of what is absent, than a presentation of a having, a being present' (Cowie, 1997, p. 133), this 'enables the spectator to view a film as a staging and working through of these fantasies', as Candida Yates (2007, p. 53) has noted, rather than forcing the spectator to inevitably identify with a certain character and, hence, fixed ideological position (for further critical discussions of Mulvey, see e.g. Barker, 2005; Grosz, 2006; Senft, 2008).[2]

Rocky's struggle – Valerie Walkerdine's 'Video Replay' (1986)

It was Valerie Walkerdine who first brought real audiences into her analysis, combining psychoanalytic theory with (auto)ethnographic research on audiences. In a well-known essay, Walkerdine recounts her visit to a working-class family and their six-year-old daughter, Joanne. What she became involved in during this visit was the family's ritualistic watching of the film *Rocky II* (Stallone, 1979). Walkerdine's text offers a highly personal account of her experience of watching the film as well as observing the family watching it as a researcher, rejecting the commonly held idea that the researcher should act as an objective facilitator and ignore their own reactions, affects and emotions which inevitably come up in the process. She makes the crucial point that any viewing, be it of a film or television programme, takes place in already historically established contexts and relational, intersubjective dynamics that are anchored in both social and psychic dimensions as well as their interplay. Hence, when she observes the family watching the brutal finishing sequence of the final boxing match in the film, with the father replaying the sequence so that the kids don't miss out on anything, Walkerdine is initially repulsed by the family's fascination with the programme: 'How can they? What do they see in it?' (Walkerdine, 1986, p. 169).

Furthermore, due to her own working-class background, Walkerdine feels 'shame and disgust' (ibid.) in her precarious identification with the family. However, when Walkerdine watches the film once more at a later stage, alone in her office, she herself becomes moved to tears by what she comes to understand as 'Rocky's struggle to become bourgeois' (ibid., p. 175): 'No longer did I stand outside the pleasures of engagement with the film. I too wanted Rocky to win. Indeed, I *was* Rocky – struggling, fighting, crying to get out' (ibid.). Importantly, this emotive understanding of the film and its significance for members of the working class does in no way sacrifice its critical edge to the circumstance of its author's shedding of tears. On the contrary, on the side of the film, Walkerdine keeps a sharp eye on the conservatism in Rocky's reliance on his body and on physical pain and suffering to transcend his working-class existence and also cautions against Sylvester Stallone's later excesses of expanding this corporeality into a 'one-man defence of "America"' in the Rambo franchise (ibid., p. 177). And yet, this is not where the productiveness of the films lies: 'Although it is easy to dismiss such films as macho, stupid and fascist, it is more revealing to see them […] as a counterpoint to the experience of oppression and powerlessness' (ibid.), she explains. On the side of the actual audience that Walkerdine observed, in turn, her identification with the father of the family, due to their common working-class origins, does by no means stop her from pointing at the highly problematic ways in which he treats the female family members. In her understanding, the constant necessity to fight which creates an intense identification between the paterfamilias and Rocky is also a constant (symptomatic) reminder of the threat of losing, of powerlessness and, hence, of emasculation. It is due to such threats and the existential importance of the fantasy of being the '"big man" at home' that he can be seen to enforce gender hierarchies in the family and put the female family members down. Walkerdine's 'ethnography of the unconscious' (1986) was thus among the first to move beyond the dualism of psychic spectators vs. sociological viewers (Stacey, 1994, p. 42; Yates, 2010, p. 405). In her interpretation, she combined 'processes of fantasy' on the one, and 'real life' observations (Yates, 2010, p. 405) on the other hand – elements that heretofore were kept in 'conceptual duality' (ibid.) in the respective disciplines of cultural studies and psychoanalytic film studies.

Star Gazing with Jackie Stacey (1994)

Jackie Stacey's book *Star Gazing* (1994) is another key text that expanded feminist film theory into empirical work on audiences. Stacey reached out to women and asked them to write about why they liked Hollywood and British cinema from the 1940s and 1950s. On the basis of the responses she received, Stacey isolated three key themes: identification, consumption and escapism (Stacey, 1994, pp. 80–223). Stacey's female correspondents wrote about their worshipping of and devotion to Hollywood stars; and yet, mixed into these devotional forms, there often seemed to be a transcendental fantasy of stepping into the shoes and existences of the stars they were watching on screen (ibid., pp. 138–51). Moreover, such fantasies never remained merely within the cinematic and/or domestic realm of the female spectators, but they travelled far outside the cinema and were translated into demeanour and mannerisms that would mimic those of the stars and into practices of consumption, mainly that of clothing, which was supposed to copy and reproduce the stars' style. Contrasting these themes of identification and consumption, other women who replied to Stacey reported that they watched Hollywood films precisely for the marked difference that the stars displayed from their own lives. In this fantasy mode, the stars showed something that the audience did not have and could only dream about by way of a momentary escape. In times of rationed food and clothes of the 1940s and 1950s, it was impossible for many to aspire to such glamorous heights (ibid., pp. 198–217). These different ways of relating to 'star gazing', Stacey concludes, always remain partial and incomplete, not least due to material constraints that made the female stars (their clothes, styles, etc.) desirable in the first place. Incompleteness thus animates spectating and imagining practices. Ultimately, Stacey suggests that the observed phenomena, between ephemeral acts of identification and idealization, can best be understood by drawing on the notions of projection and introjection. In the case of the former, stars are seen as either entirely good or entirely bad objects that are filled with qualities that subjects experience as lacking in their own selves, or they are qualities rejected by the self and transferred onto the stars. In case of introjection, in turn, aspects of the female stars were absorbed by the viewers and taken into their own subjectivity (ibid., pp. 230–1).

Watching Dallas (1985) with Ien Ang

Although many cultural and media studies scholars were critical of psychoanalysis, some began incorporating psychoanalytic ideas into their works as early as the 1980s. The cultural studies scholar Ien Ang was key, alongside David Morley and Stuart Hall, in laying the foundations of theoretical models of audiences that, like Walkerdine, took seriously what people had to say about their media consumption. And like Walkerdine, they conceived audiences as active and creative consumers who have the critical skills of using media in nuanced ways. Ang's by now canonical study *Watching Dallas* (1985), for example, draws (albeit loosely) on the notion of fantasy in the psychoanalytic sense to analyse spectators' motives for watching *Dallas*, one of the most successful soap operas of all time. In a research design that seems to have offered a blueprint for Stacey's work in *Star Gazing* (1994, see above), Ang interprets letters that Dallas fans wrote to her about their engagement with the show. Viewers know that the show transports fantasies, she argues, and they take them up exactly on this basis so as to try them out: 'In the play of fantasy we can adopt positions and "try out" those positions, without having to worry about their "reality value"' (Ang, 1985, p. 134). Sherry Turkle would make a similar point about the playful and fantasmatic nature of the early internet, as we discuss in Chapter 2.

Reading romances with Janice Radway

In the classic work *Reading the Romance* (1984), cultural studies scholar Janice Radway, who drew on the psychoanalytic thinker Nancy Chodorow, examined how female readers of romance novels used those novels to structure, modulate and negotiate their existential longings and desires. Like Ang, Stacey and Walkerdine, Radway emphasizes the way that people use media texts in a manner that is meaningful to their specific life situation. The female romance readers she interviewed for her study 'felt an intense need to be nurtured and cared for'. Despite their 'universal claim to being happily married [...], that need was not being met adequately in their day-to-day existence' (Radway, 1991, p. 13). Romance novels thus fulfilled 'needs, desires, and wishes that a male partner could not' (ibid.). Readers desired the hero of the archetypical romance novel who is portrayed *both* as phallic and stereotypically 'masculine' *and* as tender and caring. Yet, although the potential for male brutality was a constant companion, even in what Radway's interviewees deemed good novels, the interviewed women consistently rejected fantasies of extreme promiscuity, rape, physical torture and sado-masochism as off-putting (ibid., pp. 72–3). For Radway and her interviewees, the act of reading romance novels – often labelled as 'dime novels', 'penny dreadfuls' or straightforwardly 'trash literature' by critics – constitutes a paradoxical act of both affirming and resisting gender norms. Such a position would prove to be hugely influential for cultural studies scholars such as John Fiske and the wider field of fan studies that would come into existence in the 1990s. In this way, Radway's work has lost nothing of its importance if we think about the ongoing debates about so-called chick lit, the *Bridget Jones* films or TV shows like *Sex and the City*, *Bridgerton* or *Gossip Girl*, and what kinds of gender roles they portray.

Television and working through

The theme of the media as nurturing and caring – even therapeutic – objects, which announces itself in the works discussed above, is unfolded in the psychoanalytically oriented work on television by Roger Silverstone (1994) and John Ellis (2000). For the latter, television offers attempts at **working through** potentially traumatic events by contextualizing and making them understandable. In his well-known text on clinical practice, Freud devised a three-step process of '[r]emembering, repeating and working-through' (1914) that analysands need to achieve in order to gain a sense of control over threatening and painful unconscious experiences. Working through in the consulting room entails a repetitive process of bringing into consciousness and remembering the unconscious experiences so that the subject may feel a sense of relief or better understanding of their suffering.

In this respect, what seems most important about television is not the content it offers – information and/or entertainment – but the circumstance that it offers this content so continuously and dependably. Similar to the notion of 'suture' (see our earlier discussion, p. 14), television provides a framing of events through embedding them in a familiar structure and endowing them with a familiar form. At the same time, however, television goes much further than cinema in providing conventions and routine frames for audiences. For instance, the BBC's major news programme, the *News at 10*, is shown every day at 10 pm, with the same jingle, the same logo, fonts, colour schemes and other visuals; the programme is structured in a ritualistic way, unfurling in a familiar narrative arch, with political news – first domestic, then international – at the beginning, and sports and weather towards the end. The news is relayed by a range of well-known talking heads who are tested for their powers of initiating and maintaining tight, near intimate relationships with their audiences.

By virtue of television's constancy, familiarity, rituality, flexibility (there are channels and programming for ever smaller niche audiences) and repetitiveness, television indeed comes close to facilitating an equivalent to what Freud called 'working through'. As with psychoanalytic treatment, television offers a way of remembering – or facing in the first place – that which is difficult and potentially painful in social life (which usually reaches into our personal lives as well); it offers a way of repeating the relational aspects of such painful experiences in the relative safety of one's home. Yet, the function of working through ultimately remains unrealizable and out of reach for television. As Ellis (2000) argues, televisual working through cannot be successful because the problems that are brought up and mulled over there might become exhausted, but they are never properly resolved (see also Richards, 2007). Jacob (Johanssen, 2019) has similarly explored working through in his research on viewers of the reality show *Embarrassing Bodies*. Frequently derided for its shaming and excessive qualities, it nevertheless offers viewers an opportunity to engage at various levels of (un)consciousness with their own embarrassing bodies. In contrast to the news format, the programme in many instances showed perfect solutions and healed bodies that had been taken care of by medical professionals. Yet, audiences still longed for solutions to their own problems, fantasies or anxieties – something the show could not provide. This led in some cases to them being jealous of the participants.

A similar argument was made by the media studies scholar Roger Silverstone. The ability of the media to offer a 'safe space' (despite all the scares 'out there') and act as a caring object, or the ability of subjects to *make* the media act as caring in their own lives, has perhaps never been explored more systematically than by him. Drawing on the object-relations tradition in psychoanalysis, Silverstone sees television as functioning similarly to what the well-known psychoanalyst Donald W. Winnicott (2002) called a '*transitional object*'.

Winnicott (2002) had observed that small children who were presented to him in his medical practice often held on to cuddly toys and other objects that they were highly invested in, in a situation that must have been anxiety provoking. This simple observation opened the gates to a landmark insight into the development of human affectivity and sense-making in their relationship to 'outside' reality. Children rely on transitional objects to create a space – between illusion and reality – in which they can negotiate between inner, psychic reality and outer, objective reality. Telling our teddy bears that, no, there are no monsters under our beds and that, after all, monsters don't exist in the first place allows the child and also the child-like parts within us to become displaced into teddy, who is then identified with holding the intellectual doubts that can befall us all, while our own egos can more assuredly identify with the mature, parental position of rational thought.

'Our media, television perhaps pre-eminently, occupy the potential space released by blankets, teddy bears and breasts,' claims Silverstone (1994, pp. 12–13), and by referring to blankets and teddy bears he evokes the two most iconic examples of transitional objects there are. It is Silverstone's merit to have introduced this concept into media and television studies. Television 'can be easily appropriated as a comfort and a security' (ibid., p. 15), he writes and this idea of television as a comforter has enjoyed significant popularity and has been used by several media scholars (Harrington & Bielby, 1995; Hills, 2002; Yates, 2007; Ribak, 2009; Bainbridge, 2012; Bainbridge & Yates, 2012, 2014; Kuhn, 2013; Krüger & Rustad, 2017). The fan studies scholar Matt Hills (2002) in particular has expanded on the idea of television as a transitional object by discussing fandom as such, when making a differentiation between a 'proper transitional object' (pto) and a 'decathected transitional object', explaining that '[t]elevision's texts can be used as a child's *pto* but can also be interpreted later by that same child as part of their cultural experience (functioning both as pto and as decathected pto)' (Hills, 2002, p. 76, italics in original).

This differentiation returns us to the point raised by both Ellis and Silverstone which can be summed up in the question of whether television (and other screen media, for that matter) can indeed have a developmental, maturational and emancipatory function that deserves to be described in these terms. Winnicott (2002) writes about the transitional object that '[i]ts fate is to be gradually allowed to be decathected, so that in the course of years it becomes not so much forgotten as relegated to limbo. […] It loses meaning, and this is because the transitional phenomena have become diffused, have become spread out over the […] whole cultural field' (p. 7). The question to what extent media can be therapeutic or are part of a larger therapy culture has been explored by Candida Yates and Caroline Bainbridge (e.g. Bainbridge & Yates, 2011, 2012, 2014). Other significant work in this area which we cannot discuss in any more detail is Annette Hill's study on the experience of watching television, and specifically that of engaging with different genres, which she links to the psychoanalytic idea of 'dream work' (Hill, 2007). Furthermore, Jo Whitehouse-Hart (2014) has explored television through empirical research with audiences (see also Cohen, 2013) and their favourite programmes which have a 'biographical emotional significance' (Whitehouse-Hart, 2014, p. 28). Viewers may be deeply attached to and repeatedly watch 'impact texts', as she calls them, over long periods of time so as to re-experience memories associated with them.

Conclusion

In this chapter, we have given an overview of the 'first generation' of psychoanalytic media studies, beginning with Metz and Baudry and continuing with Screen Theory and feminist scholars who developed this tradition further. Media and cultural studies also engaged with psychoanalysis – for instance, in relation to fandom, reality television and television's ability to comfort and contain. Although psychoanalytic scholars have conceptualized spectators, film and TV in different ways, they are all concerned with how media un/consciously shape desires, fantasies and ways of consumption that always relate to material and social aspects as well.

Cinema and television have moved from analogue to digital forms of production, circulation and consumption in recent decades. This has implications for people's experience of media as 'real'. Laura Mulvey (2006) has argued that, with the shift from analogue to digital, which comes into full swing from the mid-1990s onwards, the indexical nature of cinema becomes lost. Whereas analogue cinema had a material connection to *actual* objects and subjects, with analogue cameras and film literally taking these things in, this link has vanished in the digital age. Analogue cinema represents an original or authoritative connection between image and object, thereby maintaining some sense of reality. There is a 'physical link between an object caught by a lens and the image left by rays of light on film,' she writes, which 'is the material basis for its privileged relation to reality' (Mulvey, 2006, p. 18). The digital, Mulvey argues, 'has made a break with analogue imagery, finally sweeping away the relation with reality, which had, by and large, dominated the photographic tradition' (ibid.). It is this decoupling of media forms and content from any fixed, physically locatable notion of reality that has been taken up and debated in early psychoanalytic contributions to the internet and digital culture, and we will look at these contributions in Chapter 2.

A tradition that we could not cover here sufficiently is that of work on the *technology* of cinema, television and psychoanalysis. Laura Mulvey's later work (e.g. 2006, 2019), as well as that of Lisa Cartwright, Misha Kavka, Patricia T. Clough and others, need to be mentioned in this context. It was Clough's *Autoaffection* (2000) which, drawing on Freud and Derrida, argued that television as a medium mirrors particular characteristics of the human psyche. Television bears its traces and vice versa. Freud himself thought of the psyche as a medium and a machine that stored and retrieved 'content' or 'data' (memory). For Clough, there is an 'unconscious of television which is buried in the dream of telling-all, showing-all, giving-all to the other – the dream of full and endless self-knowing and self-exposure' (Clough, 2020, pp. 121–2). This, however, is never fully acknowledged; instead, this dream structures the very technology of the medium and then comes to the fore in its content – for instance, in the excessive focus on individual bodies in reality shows.

Writing about reality television, Misha Kavka has described the television screen as 'not a glass barrier between illusory and real worlds; instead, the screen is a joint that *amplifies* affect and connects real people on one side with the real people, in another sense, on the other side' (2009, p. 36, italics in the original). Kavka has argued that the very ability of humans to connect with reality show contestants, to be moved to tears by drama, laugh at comedy, feel their gut wrenching at a horror film sequence – in short, people's ability to be *moved* by cinema and television – has its blueprint in how the subject stores memories as moving images from the moment they are born, if not before. Lisa Cartwright (2008) has made a similar point about moving images. We often react to, or are attracted by, particular films or television series because they touch on or reactivate something in our unconscious that relates to our early experiences in life. Like Baudry, with whom we began this chapter and who stresses the oral qualities of cinema, or Silverstone, who emphasized television's ability to comfort us like a teddy bear, those more recent works emphasize our intimate relations with and attachments to media technology. Those connections continue to thrive on the internet and social media while at the same time also taking decidedly different turns, as we will see in the next chapters.

Notes

1. To be sure, the combination of psychoanalysis and feminism was (and still is) contested by feminists from other theoretical orientations, who hold that psychoanalysis is based on premises that reproduce the belief in the centrality and superiority of men. We will take up these discussions at various points in the book. Siding with Juliet Mitchell (1974), our main rejoinder to this overall critique, however, is that the very premises of psychoanalysis – such as, for example, that of phallocentrism (the belief in the centrality of the male sex) – can be turned into analytic tools with which to critique the continued dominance of phallocentric social structures.
2. The Lacanian philosophers Joan Copjec (1994), Jennifer Friedlander (2008), Todd McGowan (2007, 2015) and Fabio Vighi (2009) have all developed approaches that moved away from Mulvey's approach and Screen Theory more broadly. Many other scholars have also used psychoanalysis in their study of film. We cannot discuss their arguments in more detail in this chapter (see 'Further reading' below).

Further reading

Bainbridge, C. (2008). *A Feminine Cinematics: Luce Irigaray, Women and Film.* Basingstoke: Palgrave Macmillan.

Bainbridge, C. (2019). Box-set Mind-set: psycho-cultural approaches to binge watching, gender, and digital experience. Free Associations: Psychoanalysis and Culture, Media, Groups, *Politics*, 75, http://freeassociations.org.uk/FA_New/OJS/index.php/fa/article/view/253.

Bainbridge, C. and Yates, C., eds (2014). *Media and the Inner World: Psycho-cultural Approaches to Emotion, Media and Popular Culture.* Basingstoke: Palgrave Macmillan.

Bainbridge, C., Ward, I. and Yates, C., eds (2013). *Television and Psychoanalysis: Psycho-Cultural Perspectives.* London: Karnac Books.

Chaudhuri, S. (2006). *Feminist Film Theorists. Laura Mulvey, Kaja Silverman, Teresa de Lauretis, Barbara Creed.* London: Routledge.

Creed, B. (1993). *The Monstrous-Feminine: Film, Feminism, Psychoanalysis.* London: Routledge.

Creed, B. (2003). *Media Matrix: Sexing the New Reality.* Sydney: Allen and Unwin.

Doane, M. A. (1987). *The Desire to Desire: The Woman's Film of the 1940s.* Bloomington, IN: Indiana University Press.

Fuery, K. (2018). *Wilfred Bion, Thinking, and Emotional Experience with Moving Images: Being Embedded.* London: Routledge.

hooks, b. (1992). *Black Looks: Race and Representation.* London: Turnaround.

Jagodzinski, J. (2008). *Television and Youth Culture: Televised Paranoia.* Basingstoke: Palgrave Macmillan.

Kuhn, A. (1982). *Women's Pictures: Feminism and Cinema.* London: Verso.

Penley, C. (1989). *The Future of an Illusion: Film, Feminism, and Psychoanalysis.* Minneapolis, MN: University of Minnesota Press.

Smelik, A. (1998). *And the Mirror Cracked: Feminist Cinema and Film Theory.* London: Macmillan.

Silverman, K. (1983). *The Subject of Semiotics.* New York: Oxford University Press.

Silverman, K. (1992). *Male Subjectivity at the Margins.* London: Routledge.

Thornham, S. (1997). *Passionate Detachments: An Introduction to Feminist Film Theory.* London: Arnold.

Thornham, S. (1999, Ed.). *Feminist Film Theory: A Reader.* Edinburgh: Edinburgh University Press.

Yates, C. (2007). *Masculine Jealousy and Contemporary Cinema.* Basingstoke: Palgrave Macmillan.

Yates, C. (2012). Media and the inner world: mapping the psycho-cultural. Contexts and debates. In: E. de Gregorio-Godeo and A. Mateos-Aparicio (eds), *Mapping Identities and Identification Processes: Approaches from Cultural Studies* (pp. 115–32). New York: Peter Lang.

CHAPTER 2

Social media and psychosocial relations

Key themes:
cyberspace and the early internet; Symbolic Order, drive, big Other and social media; anxious narcissism and the selfie; recognition, transitional space, true and false self online

Introduction

Roger Silverstone (1994), whose work on television we presented in the previous chapter, uses Winnicott's theory of transitional objects and phenomena in order to sound out the role of television in the late twentieth century. However, when he cautions that television is never really outgrown, but that 'it can and does continue to occupy potential space', being 'potentially both creative and addictive' (1994, p. 15), this anticipates Sherry Turkle's (2011) assessment of digital, social and mobile media a good 15 years later. In her seminal study *Alone Together*, which, similar to Silverstone in the 1990s, approaches the central media technology of her time (the internet and networked media), she writes:

> The network's effects on today's young people are paradoxical. Networked technologies, such as smartphones or games, make it easier to play with identity (for example, by experimenting with an avatar that is interestingly different from you), but harder to leave the past behind because the internet is forever. The network facilitates separation (a cell phone allows children greater freedoms) but also inhibits it (a parent is always on tap). (Turkle, 2011, p. 169)

Although we hold this ambiguity between enabling and inhibiting to be a fundamental aspect of media technologies, we can gather from these observations, at this early point in the chapter, that there are no clear-cut situations in which we can unambiguously say that these technologies and the ways in which we use them are only 'good' or 'bad' for us. Rather, the picture is more complicated and ambivalent: '[s]imultaneously antagonistic and social, creative and disruptive, humorous and barbed,' as Whitney Phillips and Ryan Milner (2016, p. 10) write with regard to online culture.

However, importantly, already for Silverstone, this ambivalence did not grow merely out of the eccentricity of human existence, but also out of television's embeddedness in social, political and economic considerations, motives and intentions, which always weigh in on the direction of a medium's relational effects on people. And although there is little concern about these dimensions in Turkle's (2011) study on social media, they clearly work as a subtext for the negative, critical turn that her work took from the 2000s onwards. This period saw the transition from what is now referred to as 'Web 1.0', the early internet of the 1990s, to the form that the internet took on in the course of the 2000s, commonly captured in the term 'Web 2.0' – a label that the marketing and advertising agency *O'Reilly Media* managed to brand with astonishing success since 2004 (O'Reilly, 2007, p. 19).

Web 2.0 refers to the interactive and social–connective character the internet took on from the 2000s, with social networking sites and blogs defining the internet anew. This shift also had distinct economic dimensions, which we discuss in more detail in Chapter 3. Here, we first present the central efforts of theorizing the early internet of the 1990s from a psychoanalytic perspective, followed by the main psychoanalytic takes on the psychosocial implications of Web 2.0, with Slavoj Žižek and Sherry Turkle as central early theorists (whose work nevertheless cuts across the two paradigms). Jodi Dean, Matthew Flisfeder, Aaron Balick, Greg Singh and our own works (e.g. Krüger & Johanssen, 2014, 2016; Johanssen & Krüger, 2016; Johanssen, 2018b, 2019) are more clearly located in later perspectives.

The early internet: cyberspace between alienation and freedom

It is not without a tinge of nostalgia to recollect that, throughout much of the 1980s and 1990s, the internet was referred to as 'cyberspace', or – likewise romantic – as 'Virtual Reality'. Although the latter term has retained some of its currency due to advances made in virtual reality (VR) headsets, like the Razer OSVR, Oculus Rift or PlayStation VR, which have found some modest public uptake in videogames (something which Facebook tries to change now with its introduction of the 'metaverse'), the term 'cyberspace' has remained attached to the mostly text-based internet of the 1980s and 1990s. Both terms, however, denote the simulation of an experienced reality. The term cyberspace was originally coined by the science-fiction writer William Gibson, who in his 1984 novel *Neuromancer* imagined it as:

> A consensual hallucination experienced daily by billions of legitimate operators, in every nation, by children being taught mathematical concepts... A graphic representation of data abstracted from the banks of every computer in the human system. Unthinkable complexity. Lines of light ranged in the nonspace of the mind, clusters and constellations of data. Like city lights, receding. (Gibson, 1984, p. 128)

This idea of hallucination – not a mere fantasy or daydream, but an all-engulfing vision, the artificiality of which the user is not aware of – harks back to cinematic apparatus theory á la Baudry (2009 [1975]; see Chapter 1). As in some central passages in Baudry's writings, the scenario, which in the case of cyberspace found both utopian and dystopian interpretations, is that people become directly and immediately attached to a machine that embeds them pre-ideologically – that is, in a certain somatic experience and logic of reality.

Slavoj Žižek's numerous books, book chapters, articles, interviews and videos have often touched on cyberspace and online culture. Effortlessly weaving Lacanian theory and Marxist dialectical–materialist philosophy with jokes, examples from pop culture and emancipatory politics, Žižek has become one of the most important philosophers of the past 30 years, and he also plays a central role in this chapter.

What is cyberspace? Four visions of the early internet

In his article 'Cyberspace, or, How to Traverse the Fantasy in the Age of the Retreat of the Big Other', Žižek (1998) presents four different ways of conceptualizing cyberspace from a psychoanalytic angle. As one of his characteristic rhetorical moves, Žižek asks at the end of the article:

> What if it is wrong and misleading to ask which of the four versions of the libidinal or symbolic economy of cyberspace that we outlined […] is the 'correct' one? What if these four versions are the four possibilities opened up by the cyberspace technology, so that, ultimately, the choice is ours? (1998, p. 511)

But although this is surely an ambiguous ending, Žižek leaves his readers with, his four positions that he here offers as possibilities have indeed much to offer to digital media studies.

In order to understand these positions fully, however, we need to first discuss the oedipal dimensions implied in them on a more general basis (see also Introduction). Hence, the central conflict in generational relationships that Freud found – specifically, in the case of the young boy: being in love with mother and finding oneself in competition with father – becomes reworked in later (particularly Lacanian; see also Lorenzer, 2022 for a more materialist take) theoretical advances into a more general theory of the human being's entry into the realm of the social and the symbolic. This entry is seen to be brought about partly through the role that the father holds in a traditional core family context, which is that of an intervening third. Although the role of the mother has traditionally been to carry the child within her, give birth to the child and then nurse it, the father occupies a somewhat more removed position so that his involvement can easily appear as interfering in – and, not least, as breaking open – the hermetically closed-off relationship between infant and mother (particularly right after birth). In this respect, the father becomes a third – triangulating – variable that necessarily disturbs and thus opens up the mother–child dyad toward the rest of the world and toward a form of sociality that requires more distinct forms of symbolic interaction.

As we have discussed in the Introduction, the acquisition of and initiation into language of the child represents another major step in terms of both becoming a subject and being part of social life. In the process, the complete range of embodied, sensual–affective routines and rituals that have been established in the interplay between child and primary caregiver(s) become subject to symbolization – become available to the kind of conscious reflection that symbolization makes possible (Krüger, 2022a). This availability, however, is never complete, and the experiences that humans make, suffused with fantasies about themselves and others, can never be fully articulated. But Lacan goes even further, arguing that the entry into language involves a 'marking' of the child by the Symbolic Order. This order determines and fixes subjects in social reality, confronting them with notions of authority, norms and customs that seem to be pre-given and eternal. This 'marking' approximates what Lacan calls '**Symbolic castration**' (e.g. Lacan, 2021 [1994]) – a castration that is merely symbolic because no actual, physical castration takes place.

1. Vision: cyberspace as wasteland of freedom

Žižek uses the conception of the oedipal entry into the socio-symbolic that we have outlined above as a marker with which to make differentiations between the ways people become related to social reality when being online. Hence, the first scenario that he outlines is one that we already find in Gibson's (1984) fictional creation of cyberspace as a 'consensual hallucination'. Here, the oedipal entry into the symbolic is being taken back, or suspended, with 'individuals regressing to presymbolic psychotic immersion, of losing the symbolic distance that sustains the minimum of critical/reflective attitude' (Žižek, 1998, p. 484). As with Baudry's theory of cinema (discussed in Chapter 1), the internet turns into an orally oriented support-structure to which users latch on as to mother's breast – similar to the *Matrix* films (Wachowski & Wachowski, 1999–2003; Wachowski, 2021) where reality is all but a simulation and humans are chained to machines. Cyberspace is thus always *seemingly* 'a frictionless flow of images and messages – when I am immersed in it, I, as it were, return to a symbiotic relationship with an Other in which the deluge of semblances seems to abolish the dimension of the Real,' as Žižek (1997, p. 202) writes in *The Plague of Fantasies*.

Alternatively, Žižek states, this first scenario of an immediate, pre-symbolic and pre-oedipal connection to the world (via the internet) has often been imagined, not as a passive state of abandon, but as an active, radically unbound and liberated mode of following one's inclinations, longings and desires, no matter one's limitations. In this scenario, 'the subject gains the freedom [...] to shift between different sociosymbolic sexual identities, to construct a Self as an aesthetic *oeuvre*' (Žižek, 1998, p. 486). 'Cyberspace delivers one from the vestiges of biological constraints and elevates one's capacity to construct freely one's Self, to let oneself go to a multitude of shifting identities' (ibid., p. 484). In this scenario, everything seems possible, reachable and obtainable.

The internet scholar Sherry Turkle has made a similar argument in her seminal study *Life on the Screen* from 1995, in which she offers results from ethnographic research, based on interviews and participant observation, into the relational styles in so-called Multiple User Domains (MUDs), text-based multiplayer online games. Turkle's focus on MUDs is decisive because, due to their roots in role-playing games, MUDs invite their members to build characters that need not, but can be, distinctly different from their real-life social selves. For example, in the case of one of her interviewees, Doug, 'a midwestern college junior', this choice entails:

> four characters distributed across three different MUDs. One is a seductive woman. One is a macho, cowboy type whose self-description stresses that he is a 'Marlboros rolled in the T-shirt sleeve kind of guy.' The third is a rabbit of unspecified gender who wanders its MUD introducing people to each other, a character he calls Carrot. [...] Doug's fourth character is one that he plays only on a MUD in which all the characters are furry animals. (Turkle, 1995, p. 13)

By contrast to the 'real-name internet' which is vastly dominant today – partly for security reasons, but partly due to the big corporate platforms' interest in building detailed consumer profiles – the MUD-based internet that Turkle described in the mid-1990s offered many more possibilities for fluid, playful explorations of subject positions and identities. Turkle (1995) adds that Doug 'talks about playing his characters in windows and says that using windows has made it possible for him to "turn pieces of my mind on and off"' (ibid., p. 13). This experience of identity as distributed across various windows, or partitions, Turkle sees as the paradigmatic mode of subjectivation, identity formation and self-constitution on the internet in general. 'The life practice of windows is that of a decentered self that exists in many worlds and plays many roles at the same time' (ibid., p. 14).

The question that arises is whether such a hypothetical, decentred existence is one that is located as clearly outside the realm of the Symbolic as Žižek claims. In much of Turkle's account at least, this existence appears to be situated at an intersection between reality and fantasy, the private and the public, the hidden and the visible, the near and the far. Thus, in a subchapter of *Life on the Screen*, entitled 'Objects To Think With' – a clear analogy to Winnicott's (2002) concept of the 'transitional object' – Turkle argues that, when people log on to the internet, 'they are swept up by experiences that enable them to explore previously unexamined aspects of their sexuality or that challenge their ideas about a unitary self' (Turkle, 1995, p. 49). This formulation is significant: on the one hand, it grants the personal networked computer to function like a transitional object (see Chapter 1), with people using computers to explore aspects of their subjectivity and feel their way through who they are and what their relation to reality might be. On the other hand, however, Turkle sees a clear risk for people to become 'swept up' by the experience of virtual exploration. In this account, then, online experiences have the potential to be enabling and overwhelming at the same time.

2. Vision: cyberspace as a mirror of the Symbolic Order

Returning to Žižek's cyberspace variations, the second major formation that he names is one that is significantly less of a radical departure from physical, corporeal and social reality than that of the collapse of the Symbolic into the Real outlined above. Rather, this second scenario describes a mode of being in cyberspace that fundamentally accepts and acknowledges the inevitability of Symbolic castration there and elsewhere. In this vision, to which Žižek gives decisively more credence, the liberties and liberations that the internet can bring always come at the price of their inevitable virtuality – that is, as that which is *real* but not *actually real* (Shields, 2006). 'Yes, in cyberspace, "everything is possible",' Žižek outlines this scenario, 'but for the price of assuming a fundamental *impossibility*: You cannot circumvent the mediation of the interface' (1998, p. 487). In *The Indivisible Remainder* (1996), Žižek makes this same point as follows:

On account of its logic of instant gratification, the universe of 'virtual reality' signals the very opposite of what its name announces: the end of the virtual space of symbolization, or, as Winnicott put it, of the space of transitive objects – everything is instantly here, *but bereft of its substance and thus instantly devalued*. (Žižek, 1996, p. 190, our emphasis)

In this vision, then, the freedom that cyberspace was widely seen to bring could only be fully enjoyed by those with an extraordinarily rich fantasy life and the capacity to willingly suspend the stark limitations in the mediation between on- and offline life, the Symbolic and the Imaginary, or the virtual and the actual. Especially on the early internet, users had very limited possibilities to find their fantasies being met by the computing power and bandwidth that would enable convincing simulations; for instance, it was impossible to transmit large amounts of data, play realistic online games or stream videos because most users 'surfed' the web with slow 56k modems. Along similar lines, Žižek argues that, no matter how freely one might assume a different identity or several identities in cyberspace, this choice always entails a sense of alienation because there is a fundamental gap remaining between who I think I am and how I construct, for example, an avatar online. This alienation is similar to the acceptance of Symbolic castration that finds itself replicated on the internet. You can never be really you, neither in cyberspace nor elsewhere.

3. Vision: cyberspace as symbolic authority in crisis

For his third vision of the internet, Žižek builds on the second version. Specifically, he points out that, in Lacanian theory, the entry into the oedipal phase of development does not merely mean entering into language and signifying practices. Rather, Lacan holds that this castration in and through the Symbolic is doubled up by what he calls the 'Name-of-the-father' (or: the 'No-of-the-father', since the French 'nom' easily approximates 'non') – a mythical, totemistic and forbidding entity that doubles up the impossibility of any form of immediacy of being with a prohibition of it. *Not only is it impossible to get direct access to reality, it is also forbidden.* In addition to the mere acceptance of the Symbolic as a binding structure, Lacan claims that what is necessary for our adherence to such a structure is the belief in an additional authority (traditionally, a father in patriarchal society) that embodies and stands for the prohibitions, limits and laws erected through and in the symbolic itself. This authority is named the '**big Other**'.

'Paradoxically,' writes Žižek (1998, p. 495), 'the domain of symbolic rules, if it is to count as such, has to be grounded in some tautological authority beyond rules, which says "It is so because I say it is so!"' This part might be tautological and a doubling up, but, as every parent of older kids will have experienced, it is still of vital importance. For example, when Steffen's 10-year-old is supposed to empty the recycling bin, she tends to refuse and offers all kinds of arguments against her doing this chore until, finally, Steffen puts his foot down and makes her do it anyway. She knows it is her chore, and it is part of how she earns her pocket money, but quite often she'd choose to rather not do it, until she is given to understand that there is a certain 40-something becoming rather irritated with her. Interestingly, Žižek holds that it is exactly this element of effectiveness, which Lacanian theory captures in the 'Name/No-of-the-Father', that is in decline on the internet. 'What we have in cyberspace is the purely formal structure of symbolic prohibition, without the "little piece of the (paternal) real" (the paternal figure) sustaining it' (Žižek, 1998, p. 488).

In this third vision of the internet, then, cyberspace is both oedipal, firmly situated within the Real–Symbolic–Imaginary, and *post-oedipal* as there is no element or Other that would, for instance, sanction the expression of violent fantasies. As we will expound in later parts, this claim has proven uncannily farsighted and has anticipated many of the problems that vex the state of digital media and its sociocultural and political–economic contexts today. After all, without anything binding us – vividly and affectively – to the construction of the social that the symbolic offers, we are constantly prone to wrangle with the social which now seems to be dramatically ineffective and dysfunctional. As we outline, those points have been addressed and taken further in different ways by Jodi Dean (2010) and Matthew Flisfeder (2021).

The conclusion, however, that Žižek draws from this diagnosis is that what the internet as a symbolic realm without consequence and binding power gives rise to is a culture of perversity. After all, perversion, is *the* social–pathological figuration that is most complementary to the faltering powers of the Symbolic online. Although the binding power of social conventions and laws is in sharp decline on the internet, the pervert loves rules to the point that they get off on them (something we will return to in the next chapter). Hence, in the absence of binding powers online, internet users are prompted to make their own laws, and this perverse constitution of new laws, rules, borders and conventions from the bottom up goes hand in hand with the crisis of symbolic efficacy in the social that Žižek, and Lacanians more generally, diagnose in relation to the internet. Put differently, since an all-binding lawfulness falters, the sphere of the social becomes filled with the perverse laws of those that love them enough to try to make them binding for others. This perverse reaction to a declining big Other can show online in various forms – for example, in trolling, flaming, shitstorming, hate 'speaking', mobbing, 'doxxing' (publishing someone's private information), baiting, hacking, leaking, grooming, anti-political correctness, etc. Common to all of them is that they are performed, and operate, in a mode of making a point, setting an example, drawing a line and generally claiming to be the new law.

4. Vision: traversing the fantasy

Finally, the fourth vision Žižek presents is based on and departs from the diagnosis of the internet as a sphere of adherence to self-imposed rules and laws. Since the internet prompts us to emphatically redraw and rearticulate social rules and regulations along the lines of our desires, what we can glimpse in our expressions online – our personal websites, social media profiles, YouTube uploads, tweets and retweets – is always suffused with the central fantasies that give support to our existences. In question form, what do our internet activities and the expressions they result in show and say about those images, imaginaries and fantasies that we hold about ourselves and that are absolutely fundamental for us? Along these lines, Žižek argues that what the internet can offer us is the possibility to symbolize these fantasies online. Subsequently, these symbolizations allow us to take a step back from our fantasies so as to take them in and become aware of that which we would usually merely act out as our personal mythologies. In the Lacanian idiom, it allows us to '**traverse the fantasy**' (Žižek, 1998, p. 510).

Traversing the fantasy is a key Lacanian notion (e.g. Lacan, 2016 [1975–76]) that has been further developed by Žižek. It refers to letting go, or working through, those fantasies that sustain our identities but are also sources of great suffering and conflict. This letting go may be achieved through psychoanalytic psychotherapy, for instance, or via other means that enable the subject to arrive at a different relationship with themselves and their ego. No matter what stories we tell ourselves about us, they remain somewhat illusory and incomplete. A person may describe themselves as a cosmopolitan student who likes travelling and is interested in environmental issues. A lawyer may think of themselves as taking on corrupt governments and corporations. A teenager may see themselves as an athletic male. Those visions act as fundamental life stories that use specific signifiers to construct a meaningful and coherent narrative of who we are. And all those identity constructions are true to certain extents, but they also create absolute ideas about ourselves that complicate things by blocking out nuances, doubts and counter-currents. Misrecognition is, therefore, at the heart of the subject for Lacanians (see our discussion of the mirror stage in the previous chapter, p. 6). One can never quite catch up with such fantasies and the super-ego may punish or ridicule the subject for both believing in their identity and not seeing the world, and themselves for that matter, for what it really is. What if the student has not really seen much of the world after all? What if the lawyer is stuck with monotonous insurance cases and only dreams of one day taking on the big fish? What if the teenager feels not quite right in their athletic body and is longing for something else entirely? Such contradictions are perfectly common, but it is quite a step for the subject to come to terms with them, to accept or let go of them, and to find new ways of relating to their own subjectivity. In certain cases, the internet may indeed enable the traversal of fantasies, and especially experimental sexualities have thrived online, because of the ease with which people with even the most niche preferences can find like-minded souls. All in all, however, this fourth vision of the internet appears as the weakest, least plausible one to us – a rather improbable add-on whose utopian hopefulness stands in contrast to the stark visions Žižek offers otherwise.

In summary, we feel that Žižek was right to build a moment of doubt and openness into his assessment of the early internet. After all, it is possible to identify existing social scenarios and socioculturally plausible modes of subjectification for all of the visions of the internet he presents. Yet, there are a number of overall critical points we wish to make in relation to his 1990s work on the internet. First, this work mostly abstains from analysing internet phenomena empirically. Second, it treats the internet as a universal structure, while already in the 1990s there were a plethora of different applications (see Flieger, 2001, 2005 for related critical discussions). In this respect, there are good reasons for why the term 'cyberspace' is no longer in use today, since it indicates a universal space in which everyone and everything floats uncoupled from concrete, material reality. This might have been a viable possibility still in the 1980s and 1990s, but this has hardly any grounding any more in the heavily surveilled and commodified online platforms of the 2020s. In the same vein, hardly anyone would still refer to the internet as 'Virtual Reality'. Whereas a rapidly increasing part of our reality is indeed immaterial and has virtual qualities, the mobile nature of the internet, with 3G, 4G and 5G technology, has worked the presence of virtual goods and services deeply and seamlessly into our material and embodied lives. We no longer speak of our online, as opposed to our offline, lives – our digital, as opposed to our analogue, existences – but of a *postdigital* state in which electronic and networked devices are so deeply integrated with our sensual and relational experiences that it becomes increasingly hard to tell where the one ends and the other begins. Nevertheless, what is valuable about Žižek's work is that it consistently points to the formative importance of the social, political and economic forces in which the internet has been embedded from the very first. As he rightly points out, how the internet will affect us 'is not directly inscribed into its technological properties; it rather hinges on the network of sociosymbolic relations [...] which always and already overdetermine the way cyberspace affects us' (Žižek, 1998, p. 511).

Social media are bad for us! Web 2.0 and its discontents

When Žižek wrote about the internet in the mid-1990s, few of the phenomena that would shape the online culture to come had been present. Within the following ten years, a steady grind of technological advances – broadband high-speed internet connections, fibre-optic cables and steady improvements in processor technology – would speed up both computers and the networks connecting them significantly, making devices ever smaller and moving them ever closer to human bodies. Then, in 2007, Apple presented the iPhone, which ultimately took networked computing into the pockets of a large chunk of (the more affluent) global populations (MacRury & Yates, 2016).

And yet, Žižek's take on the internet would hold true to a certain extent, and this is emphatically demonstrated in the works of Jodi Dean, who followed in Žižek's footsteps. When Dean published her influential book *Blog Theory* in 2010, the research going into it had been several years in the making (e.g. Dean, 2002). Hence, although her work is frequently mentioned in the context of 'early' psychoanalytic scholarship on the digital (see also Krzych, 2010, 2013; McGowan, 2013; Nusselder, 2013), her adherence to and further development of Lacan's and Žižek's notion of the crisis of the Symbolic makes her account useful for thinking about the structural and political implications of social media.

By focusing on blogs rather than social media of her time, such as Friendster or MySpace, Dean intended to work out the central implications of communication and interaction online through her concept of 'communicative capitalism'. As she explains:

> I take the position that contemporary communications media capture their users in intensive and extensive networks of enjoyment, production, and surveillance. My term for this formation is communicative capitalism. Just as industrial capitalism relied on the exploitation of labor, so does communicative capitalism rely on the exploitation of communication. (Dean, 2010, p. 4)

This new kind of capitalism, Dean argues, manages to exploit communication by inviting, prompting, nudging and incentivizing people to communicate non-stop and all the time. So many voices and opinions chattering away into the air, so many posts with so much news from so many people – the effect of all this chatter can often well be felt as mind-numbing and stupefying. It is not that Dean would hold that any of the concrete social media posts written and published by all kinds of people, from all walks of life, and all kinds of private and professional contexts might be lacking in intelligence; rather, according to her, the stupefying thing about Web 2.0 culture is that its sheer quantity of posts and expressions creates, not stupidity, but stupor. When all speak, there is nobody that will listen, and in such a situation what becomes tacitly, unconsciously agreed upon by all is that nothing of what is said has any kind of effect on anybody else.

While her book is called *Blog Theory*, her argument proved to be farsighted in that it has become even more applicable to social media than the 'slower' category of the blog. Hence, what Dean sees in social media is the kind of communication that has given up on a belief in its own social effectiveness. 'Words are no longer "subjectivised" insofar as they fail to induce the subject to stand by them' (Dean, 2010, p. 7). It is this idea that goes back to Žižek's notion of the decline of Symbolic efficiency online:

> Sometimes it's difficult to tell when a blog or a post is ironic and when it's sincere, when it's funny or when it's serious. Terms and styles of expression that make sense to an 'in-group' can shock, insult, or enrage folks who just happen upon a blog. Moreover, the uncertainty, the potential for unexpected meanings, provides its own affective intensity. Images and affects may flow into the gaps left by the declining symbolic. (Ibid., p. 5)

Just how captivating these intensities – indignation and elation, shock and enchantment – are can be seen in the ways that people consume other people's social media posts. Most of us will have experienced getting stuck in Twitter or Instagram feeds, or in autoplay mode on YouTube without any real purpose, just because we wanted to check something quickly, or simply out of habit. Such behaviour is encouraged and assisted by the platform's design features, such as automations and intuitive design features, nudges, reminders and notifications. Aza Raskin, the inventor of 'infinite scrolling' (whereby you cannot reach the bottom of a website or app as content is endlessly loading while you scroll down), has expressed regret as millions of users are now seemingly glued to their screens, never reaching the end of something (Knowles, 2019). What Tania Modleski (1982) observed for the soap opera genre holds true for social media news feeds as well: audiences as well as users are always stuck in the middle, with no beginning and no end.

In such a technosocial environment, we can say with Dean, we are caught in endless affective loops that lead nowhere. She suggests the Lacanian concept of '**drive**' for an understanding of this bottomless descent: something that literally just 'drives on', that is unrelenting, stupendously repetitive and deaf to moderation; something that knows no aim or saturation point but only pauses in moments of rupture. Communicative capitalism thus thrives 'as the repetitive intensity of drive' (Dean, 2010, p. 30).

The Lacanian notion of the drive (e.g. Lacan, 2002, 2004) is related yet also different to Lacan's concept of desire. Both relate to *jouissance* and loss, but in different ways. Drive is an objectless process that knows no goal. Paradoxically speaking, it is through reaching that very non-goal, of getting nowhere, that *jouissance* is obtained by the subject. It is the repetitive process of the drive itself that is pleasurable. Drive only enables a partial realization of desire. Desire, in contrast, is desire for desire itself, a desire for *jouissance*, which ultimately remains unfulfilled. We can say that not reaching *jouissance* via the drive gives the subject pleasure, and not reaching it via desire further amplifies desire and leaves the subject wanting to want more. We can never obtain *jouissance* through desire and this equally provides us with a sense of pleasure or longing. Both drive and desire relate to *objet a* and how it is experienced by the subject. It is helpful to quote Žižek, who Dean also cites, at length here:

' Although, in both cases [of desire and drive], the link between object and loss is crucial, in the case of the *objet a* as the object of desire, we have an object which was originally lost, which coincides with its own loss, which emerges as lost, while, in the case of the *objet a* as the object of drive, the 'object' is directly the loss itself – in the shift from desire to drive, we pass from the lost object to loss itself as an object. That is to say, the weird movement called 'drive' is not driven by the 'impossible' quest for the lost object; it is a push to directly enact the 'loss' – the gap, cut, distance – itself. (Žižek, 2008, p. 328)

Via Žižek, Dean argues that drive is inherent to capitalism and the workings of capital itself. Capitalism is circular and capital always seeks to accumulate more capital, increase profit, etc. Dean sees our endless posting, liking, sharing, commenting, scrolling, swiping, our habitual states of excitation and irritation, as symptoms of a great displacement – distraction – from more substantial and consequential issues. While everybody is busy expressing themselves and policing the expressions of others in a climate of constant symbolic transgression, real decisions and real politics are made elsewhere. Hence, the alarming effect of communicative capitalism, as Dean sees it unfolding online, is that people's habits of politics as communication and communication as politics trap their political energies and make people lose the expectation that their political standpoints would matter all that much in the first place.

The logic of the drive in communicative capitalism is characterized by an exploitation of communication for its own sake. People believe in the fantasy of really communicating with others online but are at the same time driven by the enjoyment of purely circulating messages. What matters is not *what* but *that* something was posted, shared and liked. A culture of pure affect and attention. To Dean, much of online culture is 'parasitic, narcissistic, and pointless' (Dean, 2010, p. 37). The force of habit that has lured us into it means that we take part for the sake of it. 'The subject gets stuck doing the same thing over and over again because this doing produces enjoyment. Post. Post. Post. Click. Click. Click' (p. 40).

In true Lacanian fashion, Dean diagnoses the underlying anxiety or symptom of internet culture as one about enjoyment. In contemporary times of influencer success, polished Instagram profiles and successful YouTubers, the anxiety that others are able to enjoy more and better than me has increased further. This enjoyment also translates into rationalization of our time spent online: yes, we are spending endless time scrolling through social media and we would rather be out meeting friends, saving the environment or decluttering the house. 'Confident in what we would prefer to do, if only we could, we overlook what we are actually doing' (Dean, 2010, p. 93). The networks of communicative capitalism are driven by a force that animates the very posts, likes and shares that subjects produce every day. As, according to Dean, much of such activity is done for its own sake, it always leaves something excessive behind. The habitual and repetitive nature of activity in digital networks produces *jouissance*. 'The something extra in repetition is enjoyment, the enjoyment that is captured in the drive and the enjoyment that communicative capitalism expropriates' (ibid., p. 116). It is the failure and incompleteness of (being stuck in) the drive that has captured subjects in digital platforms, always seeing ourselves, each other and imagining being seen by others. As Dean clarifies in a more recent contribution:

> The loop of the drive is an uneven repetition and return that misses and errs. Stuck in the loop of drive, the subject keeps doing the same thing, trying to get the same result, but rarely really gets it. Still, the subject gets something, a bit of enjoyment, in the repeated effort of trying. And this nugget of enjoyment is enough

of a payoff to keep the subject keeping on, although each moment is a little different. (Dean, 2018, p. 5)

What keeps us attached to social media has been further explored by Matthew Flisfeder.

Is the big Other on Twitter?

Paradoxically, one could say that, in *Algorithmic Desire* (2021), the Žižekian theorist Matthew Flisfeder both continues and counters Dean's argument. Flisfeder argues that social media have become *the* metaphor of our times – the central representation of the era of neoliberal capitalism. In line with Dean, he holds that, although social media may have enabled, or at least assisted, social movements such as #BlackLivesMatter or #MeToo, this positive view ignores the role that ideology and capital play in the organization and architecture of commercial platforms. In distinction to Dean, Flisfeder does not conceive of digital communication itself as a 'sideshow', as one could call it, or 'roadside attraction', which traps people in circles of stupefying drive. Rather, social media capture people – their attention, preoccupations and life energies – by *enabling the formation of desire for* showing and teaching them what to want, how to want and how to be wanted. In this respect, Flisfeder does not define social media as a symptom of a declining Symbolic Order, as Dean argued, but on the contrary, as instances of a renewed widespread belief in, and wish for, the existence of the big Other. He writes:

> In the context of social media, we see how we perform, not necessarily for our own sense of self – we curate our identities, not to satisfy our own desire, but to satisfy the desire of the Other in the form of likes, shares, comments, follows, and so forth. It is this ambiguity that provides the pretense for our activity, and social media is the platform through which, today, in popular culture, the big Other continues to be operative. (Flisfeder, 2021, p. 67)

Flisfeder links this belief in the Other to a masochistic attitude whereby the subject clings onto desire by unconsciously longing for a figure of authority and prohibition, writing that: 'In order to save her desire, the subject requires (at least the fantasy of) some figure of prohibiting agency whom she can transgress, whose gaze she wishes to impress. Today, we transpose this gaze onto the form of social media' (ibid., p. 66). In this sense, Flisfeder sees Dean's idea of digital media as capturing users in circuits of drive as merely a starting point – a state of engagement that sooner or later switches into the wish for renewed guidance. Rather than being trapped in the logic of the drive, the subject thus responds to the decline of the Symbolic with a fresh desire for the big Other – an Other not only to adhere to, but also to transgress. For it is only in moments of transgression and rule-breaking that the subject is confronted with the big Other's authority.

This is what makes social media ideological and a metaphor of the wider workings of capitalism today: that even though subjects know that the big Other does *not* exist, they act as if the opposite were true. This 'as-if' performance is powerful because it responds to a rift that has been left open by the decline of the Symbolic. Against Dean, Flisfeder argues that it is *desire*, not drive, that is amplified by user activity and communication: 'The subject of desire chooses, whereas for the subject of drive, choice is inverted into making-oneself-chosen' (Flisfeder, 2021, p. 77). For Dean, all we do on social media is pointless and we take on a 'whatever' attitude as a result, but we use social media nevertheless for a bit of enjoyment. Loss is embraced. For Flisfeder, we disavow that knowledge and deny loss. For him, drive is an ethical way out of the deadlock that Dean describes because of its reflexivity. There is no hope of obtaining the object of desire within drive. Drive is indifferent to its object and, as Žižek (2006) has argued, because of this indifference, it constitutes a freedom to embrace the inevitable. 'If desire is that which attaches the subject to ideology, the drive moves the subject in the direction of emancipation' (Flisfeder, 2021, p. 77). Once we have traversed the fantasy and acknowledged that desire can never be satisfied, all that remains is the drive, and the knowledge of this can be liberating.

The power of algorithms

The dynamics we have discussed via Dean and Flisfeder are particularly pervasive as algorithms (and wider big data analytics) always already structure the user experience (Bucher, 2012; see also Johanssen, 2019, Chapter 6). Algorithms are pieces of code that, generally speaking, manage the relationship between input and output – for example, when a user creates a Facebook post which then appears in the Newsfeed of others. An average user will never be offered *all* of their friend's content in the Newsfeed because that would be overwhelming, but Facebook's algorithm makes selections on the basis of criteria that remain hidden. As another example, Google's PageRank algorithm automatically returns search results for a user's search query in a ranked order of relevance which is again hidden from users. We cannot rank Google's search results ourselves or edit what type of content we would like to see in Facebook's Newsfeed (Bucher, 2012; Finn, 2017).

Flisfeder argues that algorithms always *dissatisfy* users and grant them only a little bit of enjoyment, so that they keep coming back to digital platforms. Jacob has outlined similar dynamics in terms of perverse rewarding and withholding patterns (Johanssen, 2019; Chapter 6). For Flisfeder, algorithms reproduce the lack at the heart of the subject and deny access to desire. At the same time, algorithms are ideological in themselves as they, in the case of commercial social media, are built to maximize user and profit growth (see also Singh, 2019). This is often done in a stereotypical or discriminatory way, whereby algorithms increase 'click bait', polarization and division between users on social media (see our discussion in Chapter 4). Users as subjects, or subjects as users, are thus 'interpellated' on social media, an act that, according to the French Marxist philosopher Louis Althusser, is always ideological. For Althusser (1971), interpellation refers to an act by which the subject unconsciously recognizes themselves in relation to an other. He uses the example of a policeman who shouts 'Hey, you!' and the subject turns and *feels* that they are the one who must be meant. They recognize themselves in the act of being addressed. Interpellation is ideological because the subject reproduces ideology in a particular instance. In this case, in the reaction to the policeman, the authority of the state and the police is unconsciously reproduced.

Social media *address* users as individuals and interpellate them in similar ways, although much less threateningly than in Althusser's example. For instance, Facebook asks: 'What's on your mind, Jacob'? Or Twitter wishes to know from Steffen: 'What's happening?' Social media are so successful at binding subjects to their platforms because a significant part of the user experience is customized and tailored to the user's individual lives: we see our friends, our content, our likes, etc.

(Krüger & Johanssen, 2016). Such forms of interpellation establish a strong bond between platforms and users. Therefore, the notion of the interpellated user is all the more convincing when we remind ourselves that algorithms are invisible at the surface of the user interface and that they cannot be 'cheated', 'outwitted' or 'modified' in any meaningful way by ordinary users. Hence, people cannot help but respond in line with the algorithms' affordances and assume the subjectivity of 'the user'.

Critical remarks

Žižek's, Dean's and Flisfeder's theories about the internet are 'grand' theories in the sense that they offer a vision of the overall workings of *all of the internet* and social media, as well as the wider social structures in which they function. They present structural conceptualizations with a particular emphasis on the political implications of the internet and how it is always embedded in existing capitalist relations. One could also argue that those works are abstract, theory heavy and jargony in their Lacanian orientation. They are difficult to follow for someone who is not well versed in Lacanese. Due to their structural focus, they lack more concrete attention to the actual *psychodynamics* of social media and the internet and how subjects interact on different platforms. We feel that such work can be enriched, for example, with a strong focus on how subjects present themselves and are presented on social media (e.g. Krüger & Johanssen, 2014; Krüger, 2021b; Johanssen, 2022).

Furthermore, Dean's and Žižek's analyses have a marked tendency towards the hopeless and fatalistic. Both could be critiqued for being too pessimistic, even cynical, about the internet in times of commodified online culture. Yes, the internet has become a space that is colonized by capital and where users are under constant surveillance and exploitation, but this does not mean that they would not be able to form deeply meaningful connections, organize for activist purposes and experience joy. After all, if we gave complete credence to Dean's perspective in particular, we could stop thinking and writing here, since all further efforts at understanding, describing and defining digital media would be superfluous, and – what's worse – they would be complicit in communicative capitalism. However, whereas the fewest of us are free of such complicity – and indeed, even Dean posts pictures of her cats on Facebook – something we can do to counter this tendency is to make sure our communications are worth each other's time and to invest work, love and care in them in the belief that they will have consequence and weigh in on the social situation.

Anxious narcissism

Online or social media narcissism is the label for one of those phenomena that unkind critics of digital culture often categorize as a straightforward example of Dean's communicative capitalism. In the context of social media, the notion of narcissism refers to a set of self-relating, self-investing and at times self-absorbing practices and discourses (i.e. the exchange of communications across wide parts of society) which have received their perhaps most significant form of representation in the 'selfie'. The selfie, in turn, is 'a photograph that one has taken of oneself, especially one taken with a smartphone or webcam and shared via social media' (OED, 2022). If one ignores the 'social media' part of the *Oxford English Dictionary*'s definition, it can be argued that selfies have existed for a long time. They have their origins partly in Japanese *purikura* – photobooth culture (see Rambatan & Johanssen, 2021, Chapter 3). With the dawn of social media, however, they have expanded explosively, particularly with the launch of Instagram in 2010 and the iPhone 4, which was the first mass-market smartphone to be equipped with a front camera, which made it possible to photograph oneself and see oneself being photographed at the same time.[1]

Together with Bonni Rambatan, Jacob has conceptualized the selfie as an instance that is addressed to both concrete and general others. On the internet, I can never know who sees my content. It could be seen by all of my Instagram followers, or just a few. Or my selfie could be copied and circulated far outside of my Instagram account and become used and consumed for completely different purposes than what I had (vaguely) intended. In publishing a selfie online, I am at least dimly aware of these scenarios and dynamics and thus one can say that, with each posted selfie, I am offering myself up to something that lies beyond myself. In this respect, Flisfeder has a strong point when he diagnoses a resurrection of symbolic authority online. As Rambatan and Johanssen write:

In taking a selfie, the Subject demands that the Other look at and acknowledge them. The selfie is a form of exhibitionism, but not in the form the term is commonly understood in terms of sexuality, showing my semi-naked or naked body on social media (although such forms of self-representation are also commonplace today). It is a form of exhibitionism in revealing the vulnerability of the subject and exposing a naked hunger for approval and the desire of the Other. (Rambatan & Johanssen, 2021, p. 70)

Arguably, such revealing of one's own vulnerability is not often obvious to those witnessing the showcasings of perfect faces and bodies, as well as the exchanges of call-and-response – that is, of posted image and metrical applause in terms of likes, comments and shares – which often appear quite vain. Rather, it comes to the fore when approaching the selfie from a psychoanalytic lens. To be sure, there is a deluge of literature, including the international classification directory of mental diseases (ICD-10 [WHO, 1993]; DSM-V [APA, 2013]), which identifies narcissism, be it on or offline, as pathological egotism, articulating a grandiose sense of self-importance, displaying an obsession with fantasies of unlimited achievement and so forth. Psychoanalytic perspectives on narcissism, in turn, have consistently emphasized the question of what compensatory functions such a striking investment in oneself holds. It is this insistence on empathy and a compensatory viewpoint that retains an openness towards what one might find someone else's behaviours to reveal about them that has brought the two of us to psychoanalysis and has been keeping us with it. In line with these premises, Steffen (Krüger, in press) approaches the question of the selfie from a relational and intersubjective psychoanalytic perspective, which he sums up under the label of 'anxious narcissism'. This narcissism emerges in online self-image practices as 'the performance of complete independence [and] as a defence against insecurity, insufficient protection and the anxieties these entail' (n.p.). In other words, the vulnerability at the core of narcissism might be summed up in the act of taking the questions *Who am I?*, *How shall I be?* and *Am I good enough?* to others that are then tasked with judging me. Hence, one can say that what is often thought of as an obsession with oneself is tightly connected with a fundamental insecurity about one's (social) worth. In yet other words, one turns to *an other* for validation because oneself is deeply anxious about one's true standing. To a degree, this insecurity is surely anthropological: we need others to become who we are. However, the widespreadness of practices, mostly located online, which de facto outsource the questions of self-worth, identity and belonging, point to a social and historical juncture that makes these questions particularly urgent and prevalent.

Greg Singh (2019) has recently made a similar point in *The Death of Web 2.0*, an extensive study in which he explores social media in relation to questions of ethics and recognition by drawing on Winnicottian psychoanalysis, Carl Gustav Jungian depth psychology and communitarian ethics. He, too, stresses that the freedom we have in constructing and playing with identities online is always constrained by the architecture and algorithms of the platforms we move upon. Social media is necessarily what he calls, drawing on Winnicott, a 'false self system' (2019, p. 139) because subjects continuously shape their self-presentation in relation to questions of impression management, privacy, avoidance of harm as well as forms of collaboration and communication. In line with our argument here, Singh holds that those practices can never mirror or represent the 'analogue' self in its complexity.

In this respect, the selfie points us to further related issues that internet culture brings to the fore. What is mirrored to us by our selfies is always already *ourselves as another* and this distance between ourselves and the image/imagination of ourselves we carry within us from the first. In psychoanalytic theory, it goes back to the psychic instances, and especially what Freud first defined as the ego ideal and the super-ego – that is, an idea(l) of oneself that one strives to become and that gives one's strivings direction – and an instance in oneself that critically assesses the gap between ourselves and our ideal, that instance representing an often harshly strict parental voice. In the first chapter, we introduced Lacan's early notion of the mirror stage; selfies as a paradigmatic digital practice constitute just such a moment of mirroring.

However, when Lacan sees in this moment in which the infant for the first time beholds itself in the mirror the constitution of an ideal that will be impossible to ever obtain or realize, this guides our attention to the many services and solutions that social media platforms and third parties offer which purport to close this vexed gap and make an end to that which haunts us within ourselves. Facetune, for example, one of the most downloaded selfie editing apps globally, promises to help 'highlight what makes you YOU' (Facetune, 2021);[2] the Instagram 'About Us' page invites users to 'stand out on Instagram' and 'Connect with more people, build influence and create compelling content that's distinctly yours' (Instagram, 2021).[3] Paradoxically, however, these promises of bringing oneself closer to one's ideals rather widen the gap by inadvertently making us more aware of it and turning what many psychoanalysts and philosophers see as a sisyphus-like task into an impossible and all-absorbing identity-building project.

Social media, then, by aiming for their services and functions to mend and close a self-distance that is constitutive of human wanting and desiring itself, attempt to tap into a life energy that is only ever fully exhausted when we die because that which drives us on does not have a fixed direction and desire is thus never desire for specific objects but always something that looks for more, for something else and something new. Formulated in a more sombre way, then, whatever we might do on social media, it is never enough – never enough to be happy, or content, or satisfied, or consoled, or at ease 'ever after'. And this is the whole point, since, after all, the platforms want us to come back again and again for more, and this can only be vouchsafed if gaps between who we are and who we want to be are problematized time and again and thus kept wide open.

Social media are good for us! Recognition in the online transitional space

It seems only right to close this chapter with the scholar, psychotherapist, author and psychological consultant Aaron Balick because it was he who wrote the first book-length psychoanalytic study on the central social media platforms that we still find today. In *The Psychodynamics of Social Networking*, Balick (2014) sets out to understand how people interact and relate to each other on social media. He draws on object-relations psychoanalysis, specifically as developed by the British paediatrician and psychoanalyst D. W. Winnicott, which is very different from Freudian and Lacanian psychoanalysis. Briefly put, the key moment of the formation of the subject and a sense of self does not only happen through the Oedipus complex (Freud and Lacan) and misrecognition along the Real, Symbolic and Imaginary (Lacan). Rather, Winnicott saw Lacan's mirror function to be performed not by the child alone, but between mother – or better, the primary caregiver – and infant (see Introduction). Famously, Winnicott (2002) writes that the 'precursor of the mirror is the mother's face' (p.

149), and this statement shifts the focus of psychoanalytic theory away from oedipal concerns of becoming a fully fledged social and symbolic being towards the formative importance of primary human relations and the relational styles with which an infant's primal needs – food, love, security, calm, excitement, joy, play, etc. – are satisfied or frustrated.

It is Winnicott's focus on primary relationality that Balick takes into his studies of social media communication. His approach needs to be understood in the context of its time. In 2013–14, when his book was published, the smartphone had long been established as a ubiquitous and perfectly ordinary means of communication across large parts of the globe, also among younger generations. Also in 2014, the media scholar danah boyd published a very influential study on the social media uses of teenagers and young adults that found social media to have become an integral part of how teenagers extend school interactions with their friends and classmates into the afternoons and evenings. Especially in the context of the US, teenagers often lack access to cars and transportation, and a culture reluctant to let young adults move freely on their own is compensated to a degree by having them interact on social media. On this account, social media use, as boyd (2014) found, merely means the continuation of those face-to-face interactions that are already established outside media and with people known from face-to-face contexts. In this new media environment, non-mediated and non-digital interaction would segue into the digital and, vice versa, digital interactions into physical, face-to-face interactions again. In other words, what boyd insists upon is that, far from the political and ideological concerns of Dean and Flisfeder, social media offer young people the possibility to be in touch with their friends.

Continuing and expanding on boyd's (2014) work, Balick is first and foremost interested in concrete interactions between people online. But whereas boyd mostly resists any thinking about the possible impact this digital mediation of friendships and social relations can have on people's psyches, Balick zooms right in on the question of how social media *matter* in these relations. This is where object-relations psychoanalysis comes in: 'We are using the technology as a medium to relate, and that is why psychoanalysis can be utilised to understand the underlying processes informing this relating' (Balick, 2014, p. xxxiii).

Balick's path toward such understanding leads via three main concepts from two psychoanalytic theorists: the 'true self/false self' dichotomy as developed by Winnicott; the 'transitional space' as a portmanteau of two terms, 'transitional object/phenomenon' and 'potential space', also developed by Winnicott; and 'recognition' in the rendering of the American psychoanalyst Jessica Benjamin (1988). The last is perhaps the most important, and Balick quotes Benjamin by way of an outline of the term:

> Recognition is so central to human existence as to often escape notice … it appears to us in so many guises that it is seldom grasped as an overarching concept … to recognise is to affirm, validate, acknowledge, know, accept, understand, empathize, take in, tolerate, appreciate, see, identify with, find familiar … love. (Benjamin, 1988, pp. 15–16, quoted in Balick, 2014, p. 22)

To recognize another as another, 'as a separate person who is like us yet distinct' (Benjamin, 1988, p. 23, in Balick, 2014, p. 23), and to be recognized as such by others creates mutual bonds without which we cannot live. Without the responses of other people to my actions, I cannot become who I am. Rather, my subjectivity is formed in close interaction with others as well as my wider social environment. Benjamin's concept of recognition adds to this a minimal moral component in that such responsiveness, if in an ideal balance, is seen to affirm the other's existence in a non-violent way.

If such a balance cannot be achieved, however, human relations and the process of relating can become troublesome. Independence from the other then might become equal to total domination or eradication of them; attachment, in turn, might not be achievable other than in a form of subjection or surrender. As Balick writes, although much of social media is based on and driven by the processes of mutual recognition – I befriend you, you accept my friend request; I follow you, you follow me; I like your posts, you like mine – 'its architecture leaves it open to some perversions of both the aim to be recognised and the ways in which recognition from others may or may not hit its mark' (2014, p. 23). In order to get these perversions and architectural failures into view, he draws on Winnicott's concept of the true and the false self. In this sense, the false self is not merely 'a fake "add-on"' that stands in the way for others to see who we truly are'. Rather, explains Balick: 'The false self is the outward aspect of the psyche that takes on the role of a great deal of interpersonal work,

work such as being nice, saying the right thing, getting on with people, and doing what is expected' (p. 17). In this respect, the false self is not simply disingenuous, but takes over the social, representational role of a subject so that more intimate needs and vulnerabilities can continue to exist in a more guarded way. An imbalance in a person's interactions tipping towards the pole either of the false or of the true self can become pathological. In the first case, we are putting on too much of a show so that we ourselves struggle to identify with this outward version of ourselves; in the second case, we are spurting out things that, in the best case, are only partly digested and which we, as well as those around us, will struggle to bring in line with our social persona. Whereas on social media we are constantly prompted to drop our guards and expose our true selves, Balick is right when he sees the structural problems of corporate social media platforms and their uses to rather lie in the excessive facilitation of those aspects that trigger and highlight false self performances and the development of masks and personas.

In this respect, then, Balick's analysis lands upon a point that anticipates to an astonishing degree that made by Flisfeder, namely that social media culture turns problematic where it prompts us to cultivate an outer, or other, directedness that leaves us lacking at the core. From Flisfeder's Lacanian perspective (via Žižek), this lack is inherent in the human condition; for Balick, this lack is something that can be mended by integrating outer and inner aspects of the self and bringing them more into a healthy balance. Furthermore, although theorists such as Žižek, Dean and Flisfeder assess social media from the normative angle of critical theory, Balick writes from the perspective of a therapist (he was a 'residential psychotherapist' for BBC Radio 1's Sunday phone-in advice show, for example). He approaches the digital with a strong social consciousness but with less of a downright *critical* interest. Rather, individual wellbeing takes centre stage here. Unlike Žižek, Dean and Flisfeder, Balick pays specific attention to the psychodynamics of social media rather than the structural dimensions. This makes his work emphatically concrete and renders it an important addition to the scholarship we have discussed so far. For him, it seems, social media are largely 'supportive of positive relational interdependence' (Balick, 2014, p. 122).

Balick's 'transitional space' vs Turkle's Alone Together (2011)

Just how much Balick is willing to hold on to a positive, benign conception of social media can be shown when homing in on the third aspect central to his conception of the digital platforms: the transitional space. In this respect, a comparison with Sherry Turkle's later work (2011, 2015) helps bring this benignity to the fore. As mentioned, Turkle in her earlier works conceptualized digital media as evocative objects which she defines as closely aligned with Winnicott's 'transitional object' – an object with which to negotiate between fantasy and reality, between how one imagines reality to be and how it actually responds to one's actions. This optimistic approach pales significantly when Turkle confronts the changed media landscape at the onset of the 2010s. With smartphones and social networks having become fixed parts of young people's lives, she argues, these objects are no longer transitional in the sense that they lead from a less to a more mature level of development; rather, Turkle now sees them as arresting adolescents in this very state of transitioning into adulthood (and again, as in Modleski's (1982) depiction of soaps, we are always in the middle, never reaching an end point or a new phase): 'This thing took me right back to high school,' is the association that comes to Turkle's (2011, p. 182) mind when an acquaintance tells her about her conflicted relationship with Facebook. Hence, whereas the function of the transitional object, as Winnicott originally conceived it, is to help children to eventually master situations without their support, the internet would retain people in transition exactly by virtue of the affect-modulating function characteristic of transitional objects. 'And now we look to the network to defend us against loneliness even as we use it to control the intensity of our connections,' Turkle (2011, p. 13) writes.

The usage of social media as defences against loneliness must particularly ring alarm bells because, according to Winnicott, the capacity to be alone without feeling lonely (2002) is exactly that which transitional objects are supposed to achieve. And it is in this respect that Balick remains decisively more positive: 'I posit that the presentation of the *self* online operates like a transitional object in the transitional space that is the online social network' (2014, p. 111), he writes, and already this 'positing' is a strong qualification of Turkle's position. And further: 'In order to be an active subject in the social world, one has to manage not only the capacity to be alone, but also the capacity to be with others; SNS [social networking sites] can be utilised either way' (Balick, 2014, p. 112).

Balick is not so naïve as to think that there are no inherent obstacles to such utilization in the technological affordances and use cultures of the social media platforms, but he has sufficient faith in both people and platforms so as to grant them this possibility. 'Part of the thrill of online social networking is the experience of engaging with other minds, despite the fact that this engagement is so frequently made remotely, when one is alone' (Balick, 2014, p. 21).

In ending, we would like to illustrate this last point with an example. When the Swedish pop band ABBA released a single, following a 40-year hiatus, one of the many hundreds of thousands of ecstatic YouTube comments read: 'It is not only an honour to hear ABBA again in their brilliance but it is also an honour to share the same overwhelming joy with millions of people, like you, in this joy. It unites us. Brilliant ABBA' (www. youtube.com/watch?v=hWGWFa3jznI). This sentiment was echoed and repeated hundred- and thousandfold; it thus seems that social media can bring us moments of collective joy after all.

Conclusion

In this chapter, we have discussed the wider workings of the internet and particularly social media from various psychoanalytic perspectives. Beginning with early work on cyberspace, we moved to more contemporary accounts of social media. Žižek's different versions of cyberspace across the pre-oedipal, oedipal and post-oedipal divide laid the key foundations which, we argue, have left their mark on all psychoanalytic work on the digital in its wake. We return to these works and particularly their relation to perversion in the coming chapters. Although Lacanian-inspired theorizations of the internet and social media are dominant in the field, we were keen to discuss other approaches, too, through Sherry Turkle and Aaron Balick in particular. Balick's (2014) book serves as an important counterpoint to scholarship, including our own, that strongly focuses on the damaging and destructive potentials of social media.

All of the work presented in this chapter has in common that it discusses social media and online culture, as such, without distinguishing much between platforms, specific use patterns or specific case studies.

One such case study concerns (digital) work. In the next chapter, we focus on how the nature of work is changing in connection to the digital today.

Notes

1. Although the first phone with a front camera was the Kyocera Visual Phone VP-210, released in Japan in May 1999.
2. www.facetuneapp.com [Accessed 17/6/2022].
3. https://about.instagram.com [Accessed 17/6/2022].

Further reading

Beresheim, D. F. (2020). Circulate yourself: targeted individuals, the yieldable object & self-publication on digital platforms. *Critical Studies in Media Communication*, 37(5), 395–408.

Bunham, C. (2019). *Does the Internet have an Unconscious? Slavoj Žižek and Digital Culture*. New York: Bloomsbury.

Carpentier, N. (2014). 'Fuck the clowns from Grease!!': fantasies of participation and agency in the YouTube comments on a Cypriot problem documentary. *Information, Communication & Society*, 17(8), 1001–16.

DeVos, J. (2020). *The Digitalisation of (Inter)Subjectivity A Psy-critique of the Digital Death Drive*. London: Routledge.

Elliott, A. and Urry, J. (2010). *Mobile Lives*. London: Routledge.

Hodge, J. J. (2020). The subject of always-on computing: Thomas Ogden's 'autistic-contiguous position' and the animated GIF. *Parallax*, 26(1), 65–75.

Johanssen, J. (2019). *Psychoanalysis and Digital Culture: Audiences, Social Media, and Big Data*. London: Routledge.

Krzych, S. (2010). Phatic touch, or the instance of the gadget in the unconscious. *Paragraph*, 33(3), 376–91.

MacRury, I. and Yates, C. (2016). Framing the mobile phone: the psychopathologies of an everyday object. *CM: Communication and Media*, 11(38), 41–70.

McGowan, T. (2013). Virtual freedom: the obfuscation and elucidation of the subject in cyberspace. *Psychoanalysis, Culture and Society*, 18(1), 63–70.

Young, R. M. (1995). Psychoanalysis and/of the internet. www.psychoanalysis-and-therapy.com/human_nature/papers/paper36h.html.

Young, R. M. (2011). My media and my inner world. A natural history. *Free Associations*, (62), 1–17. https://freeassociations.org.uk/FA_New/OJS/index.php/fa/article/view/45.

CHAPTER 3

Work, neoliberalism and the perverse pact

Key themes:
work and labour; neoliberalism, the information society and platform capitalism; psychoanalytic approaches to work; digital labour and platforms; counter-phobic attitude; perversion

Introduction

This chapter continues and broadens the analysis of social media from the previous chapter by shifting attention to the political and psychic economy of online social networking and other technocultural phenomena that might not feel and be experienced as work but need to be considered as such. At the core of this broadening of our analytic perspective sits a focus on neoliberalism, with its belief that all social relations can and should be structured and regulated along the lines of the free-market principles of competition and rational choice. This belief has encouraged the rise of an entrepreneurial subjectivity, which is prevalent in the self-promotional atmosphere of social media, expressed in the numbers game of how many 'likes', 'friends', 'followers', 'retweets', 'shares', etc. a 'message', 'post' or 'tweet' receives. In neoliberalism, the subject must constantly strive to increase their productivity and optimize their skills and (self-)knowledge. Work and leisure, therefore, tend to become indistinct for a type of subjectivity that has learned to see every aspect of themselves as competing in a market with a vast number of others. This tendency has led to new professions and fields of work, such as influencers, livestreamers, vloggers, web consultants, content creators and digital reputation managers.

Yet, also beyond the field of online social networking, work plays an increasingly big role in the context of digital media, although little has been written on it from a psychoanalytic perspective (Krüger & Johanssen, 2014; Krüger, 2016; Johanssen, 2018b, 2019). Computer-based tools and platforms have become indispensable for sectors such as the creative industries or information work, as well as for individual subjects in their attempts to advertise their own skills and services to potential employers. Over the last 30 years, work has taken on an increasingly precarious dimension for many in the west who are hired on a project basis, work freelance or are employed on so-called 'zero-hours contracts', where their number of working hours are decided by managers on an ad-hoc basis, subject to envisioned customer demand.

By virtue of digital technologies, forms of contemporary work have enabled convenient and seamless cooperation between workers as well as more flexible and self-determined ways of working for many. Workers in the creative and tech industries in particular report deep levels of love for and satisfaction with their work. However, such positive aspects are often used as trade-offs for long working hours, low salaries and a lack of workers' rights and protections. Those developments, then, suggest a form of subjectivity that unconsciously pushes individuals to work ever harder and increase enjoyment while surveying themselves and others against inner and outer commands and prohibitions. These latter commands are made all the more intrusive and persistent by a wider backdrop of internet-based surveillance, as revealed by the whistleblower Edward Snowden (Fidler, 2015) and, more recently, by the former Facebook employee Frances Haugen (Milmo, 2021a).

We discuss the above dynamics from a psychoanalytic lens and particularly through the concept of **perversion** (Johanssen, 2019; Krüger, 2021a; Rambatan & Johanssen, 2021). Whereas, in its common usage, perversion often positions the perverse outside norms, we use this notion here to refer to a relational phenomenon that is potentially pathological and damaging to self and other. Hence, in its pathological manifestation, perversion denotes a relationship in which the pervert simultaneously loves and abuses, idealizes and dehumanizes the partner. It is a relationship often marked by exploitation, degradation, humiliation and shaming, while also being structured by significant dimensions of care and love (Knafo & Lo Bosco, 2017). Perversion becomes particularly problematic when it is pathologically and universally used to mask exploitation and destruction through feelings of love, care and (self)-discovery. Such relationships can be dangerous, particularly for the one who is ab/used by the pervert (Bach, 1994). Yet analysands often report great difficulty in getting out of the relationship because they feel so deeply entranced by and intertwined with the perverted other (Baker, 1994; Stein, 2005; Celenza, 2014).

It is this form of pathological perversion that we take to be similarly present in digital media, where these relations are enacted between online platforms and individuals. Although users contribute to the immense profit maximization of digital platforms by acting as the producers and consumers of content, they receive no remuneration. The developers, customer service and PR staff behind such platforms articulate intense feelings of love and appreciation towards users as individual subjects, while also treating them as objects that can be tracked, surveilled and sold as data points (e.g. Johanssen, 2019). It is in this way that a perverse relationship is reproduced in digital media. Users, nevertheless, enter into and remain deeply committed to it because the promise of the next job offer, the next friend request or the next meaningful communication appears to be just around the corner. Many users know full well that they are entwined within damaging relations, but do not leave. This notion of perversion, then, extends beyond the relation discussed above and becomes fixated within the individual subject themselves, where it subsequently shows in the ways they constantly push themselves to work harder in relation to real and imagined others. For many workers, particularly in the creative and tech industries, self-exploitative dynamics often result in constant exhaustion, and even burn-outs are commonplace. Yet, many are reportedly unable to switch off, log off or slow their pace, which suggests the continued actuality of Otto Fenichel's theory of 'the counterphobic attitude' (1939), as we explain in this chapter.

What is work?

A photo has circulated online for a while now that shows a poster ad for the Samsung smartphone 'Galaxy Z Fold3 5G with Google', very likely hanging in a New York train or in a subway station. It encourages people to:

Work from Central Park

> Work from a Bushwick Brewery
> Work from a cabin upstate
> Work from your bed
> Work from their bed
> Work from the dog run
> Work from a SoHo sample sale
> Work from a dumpling shop
> Work from this train
> Work from wherever

Right underneath the last line, someone has written with a fat felt pen: 'Work Work Work – Sounds like you need a union!' (e.g. see https:// twitter.com/HishamAidi/status/1460638716108681218).

This witty comment captures brusquely the current nature of work, our attachment to it, what digital technology and the internet have to do with it and what is problematic about all of that. In short, what it seems to say is: work is everywhere and all the time; we love it to the point that it threatens to swallow us whole. This is by no means exclusively due to digital technology, but also due to changes in the organization of workers' rights (indeed, we might all need a union!). Yet, as one can see from the advertised smartphone – from the '5G' tag (fast mobile internet) and from 'with Google' – connective, digital technology facilitates the omnipresence of work in many of our lives. And although there are definitely situations in which it is convenient to be able to work from almost anywhere, the possibility that we *can* also means that there is always a slumbering expectation, a nagging voice within ourselves, that we *do*.

It is in such ways that work has changed significantly over the past 30 to 40 years and, while the growing influence of digital technologies weighs in on this development, it must be seen as part and parcel of wider social and economic changes that such technologies help make possible, reflect and shape. In this chapter, we discuss how changing forms of work and its dynamic nature in today's economy impact individuals both in realms that are clearly job and employment related, but also in realms that may not be as readily considered to pertain to work and labour. We are particularly interested in thinking about how the internet and digital platforms play their part in both changing work itself and the ways in which we experience ourselves in our social contexts. This includes considering the steady increase in mental health conditions across the world, such as burn-out, depression and anxiety, which are not merely work related, but also reflect how much of our self-worth and self-understanding we derive from experiencing ourselves as active, able, powerful, contributing and useful beings – sometimes to the point of fantasized martyrdom. Before entering into this discussion, we shall briefly discuss what the term 'work' means in general, how it differs from 'labour' and how it has developed over the past 100 or so years.

As the German social researchers Thomas Leithäuser and Birgit Volmerg write in *Psychoanalyse in der Sozialforschung* (*Psychoanalysis in Social Research*, 1988), work is central to all processes of socialization, and they refer to the philosopher Karl Marx (1976) to corroborate this point. Marx, who himself built on Georg Wilhelm Friedrich Hegel's philosophy of social evolution through the tense relations between dialectic opposites (in Marx's case, for example, capital in relation to labour), defined 'work' as a universal human activity whereby people practically change and transform their natural and social surroundings, changing themselves in the process. By doing work and 'changing the world', even if only in tiny parts, people *become realized* in their surroundings. That is, they work parts of themselves into the material world through the changes they bring about there and experience themselves as in relation with this world. Through work, then, we are *cultivating* the world according to our image and experience ourselves as part of a community of 'workers' (in the general sense of purposefully acting beings).

In this way, work creates community, sociality and society, as well as individual subjectivity. Each member of a community can see from what they do – from their own work – how they relate to other working people and how their contribution complements those of others. This, however, becomes more difficult and opaque the more complicated forms of work become. In this context, 'division of labour' (Durkheim, 1997 [1893]) means that complex work tasks are being divided up into a set of simpler steps that can be done without those doing them really understanding how their activities relate to the entire work process and the end product. In that sense, a distinction between '**work**' and '**labour**' needs to be made. For Marxists, work is the universal process we outlined above, whereby humans create things by transforming nature and society as a whole. Work is purposeful, socially needed and not wage dependent. By distinction, 'labour' refers to forms of work that are *quantified* (e.g. by setting work hours or paying wages) and controlled (either voluntarily by the labourer, if they are self-employed, for example, or by a manager or supervisor). Hence, we mostly use the term 'labour' in this chapter, although applying 'work' in those contexts in which wage-based labour can be deemed to have a relatively strong self-realizing effect. However, we have decided not to make the distinction in the cases of 'worker' and 'labourer'. In these cases, we have invariably chosen the more colloquial 'worker', even though strictly speaking the term 'labourer' would often have been the more correct one.

Industrialization throughout the nineteenth century and Taylorism in the early twentieth century – that is, the introduction by Frederick Taylor of such simple labour tasks performed by relatively unskilled workers, with conveyor belts supplying ever new materials and thus dictating the tempo of labour – made it near impossible for people to still experience how their labour might contribute to the building of an entire community, leave alone a society. It is at this point that a worker can no longer be expected to understand how what they do connects with what others do.

Additionally, the function of money as a universal means of exchanging goods and services between all members of a society renders even more opaque what Marx rightly identified as the original meaning of work as people's main way of experiencing themselves as part of the world. Money makes it very easy, indeed, to have somebody else doing one's own work – thus turning work into (wage) labour – in this way placing people into contexts in which work is no longer theirs, in which they produce goods that do not belong to them, with equipment that they do not own. To this *objective condition of* **alienation**, as Marx called it – and, indeed, besides some very early writings, Marx was not particularly interested in the *psychology* of alienation (Musto, 2021) – the use of money for remunerating people in exchange for their (ability to) work heightens the possibility of exploiting them. After all, as Marx points out, the whole point of capitalism and of being a capitalist is to produce goods and services with the acquired labour of others in a way that does not pay adequate wages to workers in relation to the time and energy they have spent. This, among other factors, allows the capitalist to make a profit. In Marx's theory of labour, or 'labour theory of value' as it is known (1976 [1867]), the logical counterpart of someone's profit is someone else's exploitation.

There is a deluge of reports about the conditions of workers through-out the ages that suggests that business owners were seldom fussy when it came to measures to increase their profit margin. The German psychoanalyst and social–psychologist Alexander Mitscherlich (1966), for example, states that: 'The bourgeois businessmen identified with each other, empathy with a working-class child was out of the question. That employees were something to be exploited was a matter of course' (1966, pp. 16–17, our translation). The communist, socialist and social–democratic movements of the late nineteenth and early twentieth centuries fought to improve the living conditions of the working classes, but it was only in the wake of the second World War that comprehensive welfare reforms, public health insurance, workers' rights, and unemployment and social security measures were introduced. With labour days limited to certain hours, five-day working weeks and workers' unions doing the annual pay negotiations, the cold facts of alienation and exploitation were no longer as stingingly felt or experienced to be as urgent as before.

However, when the post-Second World War reconstruction efforts met a saturation point and growth levels began to decline in the 1970s, corporations started to move production to less industrialized countries, often in the global South, where hourly wages could be paid that were only a fraction of what workers in the corporations' home countries had negotiated for themselves. In this way, high profit margins could be maintained – at the price of having people in far-away places work under often devastating conditions. The degrees of alienation and exploitation of people working in such neocolonial contexts and their psychosocial effects can hardly be fathomed from the viewpoint of an average member of a western society.

With manual labour increasingly being moved out of industrialized countries, to where commodities can be produced at radically low costs, developed countries have experienced a state of overflow, affluence and plenty that has tipped the balance from production to consumption. This is important for a perspective that focuses on psychological/ psychodynamic as well as social/sociological aspects since, for the last five decades, people in developed countries have defined and fashioned themselves perhaps more through what they buy and own than through what they make and create. From the 1970s onwards, rising unemployment in developed countries has been coinciding with new cultural and lifestyle philosophies that were established in the wake of the student movements of the 1960s and that have given increasingly heightened importance to personal freedoms and notions of individuality and uniqueness. This now affects our ideas of labour, too, in that we are constantly prompted to front the value of our individual selves in order to compete with others for coveted jobs on the labour market.

However, although we will delve into the construction of such psychic and social realities further below, we would like to remain with the material aspects of work and labour for a little longer. Hence, what people who have grown up during, or been born since, the 1980s seem to experience as a quasi-natural order of things is that goods are made elsewhere but consumed at home. This trend also means the outsourcing of the production of hardware technology – and now also much of software production. Industrialized countries have been undergoing a transformation from places where material goods are being developed and produced through manual labour towards places where such production is merely designed, developed, controlled and analysed. As Sean Cubitt (2017) argues, even if coding and programming tasks are now being shifted to other places, such as India, the economic foundation of highly developed countries has seen the clearest shift from producing things to producing information, from an industrial mode of production to an information-based one. The major advances in computer and networking technologies from the 1940s onwards have meant that an increasing number of so-called blue-collar jobs have been converted to white-collar, office jobs (Fuchs, 2008).

From the late 1970s and early 1980s onwards, with the election of Ronald Reagan in the US and Margaret Thatcher in the UK, the doctrine of a new liberalism – *neoliberalism* – rang in a major change in social and economic policies. Because of neoliberalism's central importance to what we see as the specific forms of subjectivity that digital work and labour produce, we will delve into the theme of neoliberalism in more psychological depth below. What is important in this brief overview is to take note, first and foremost, of neoliberalism's push towards deregulation. In direct opposition to the post-Second World War advances in workers' rights and welfare, this credo of deregulation holds that all kinds of state intervention in the relations between private corporations and the labour force, between corporations among each other, and between producers and consumers is misguided and error prone, ultimately creating more social problems for populations at large than it solves. This credo, we hold, is ultimately misguided.

Neoliberalism, the information society and platform capitalism

Our current form of the internet cannot be fully understood without taking neoliberalism into consideration. The 1990s saw unprecedented amounts of investment money flowing into the information and communication technologies sector and the internet in particular. Although industrial growth had been stalling for decades, the internet was widely seen as a new Eldorado, where new business ideas could open new markets at breath-taking speed. This widespread lure of fast profits led to stark imbalances between the quality of business ideas, which frequently lacked a thorough understanding of what the internet was and what one could do with it, and the readiness for money to be pumped into them. Hence, with hardly any of the online start-ups delivering returns on investment anywhere near the overblown expectations, the bursting of the so-called 'Dot-Com bubble' in the years 2000 and 2001 was all but imminent. By then, however, as Nick Srnicek (2017) writes, 'millions of miles of fibre-optic and submarine cables' had been laid out, 'major advances in software and network design' established 'and large investments in databases and servers' made (2017, p. 22) – all thanks to the easy money that was to be had for 'Dot-Com'-related services in that era. Hence, with infrastructure in place, computers and software affordable and available to ever wider parts of society, and interface design increasingly geared towards usability for ever less tech-savvy rookies, it seemed a mere question of time before an internet application would be found that combined mass appeal with a viable for-profit business model.

This model came in the guise of 'Web 2.0'. In a testimonial-style article, 'What is Web 2.0?', Tim O'Reilly (2007), head of O'Reilly Media, a marketing and trend-spotting agency, expounded the paradigm change. Web 2.0 would focus on *user participation* instead of mainstream media *publishing* and on emphasizing the social and relational status of the web through blogs and social media. All of this, O'Reilly held, could be turned profitable if companies no longer conceived of themselves as the producers and sellers of things, but rather as platforms facilitating the exchanges of their users. In more neoliberal lingo: companies needed to stop thinking of themselves as producers and start seeing themselves *as marketplaces*.

The new uses of the internet that O'Reilly pointed out can be seen to play seamlessly into the expectations created by the creed of neoliberalism of how a person needs to be in order to succeed in society. As Stuart Hall, Doreen Massey and Michael Rustin (2015) put it:

> Every social settlement, in order to establish itself, is crucially founded on embedding as common sense a whole bundle of beliefs – ideas beyond question, assumptions so deep that the very fact that they *are* assumptions is only rarely brought to light. In the case of neoliberalism this bundle of ideas revolves around the supposed naturalness of 'the market', the primacy of the competitive individual, the superiority of the private over the public. (Hall *et al.*, 2015, p. 14)

This common sense of individuals as constantly competing with each other in a world experienced as a marketplace comes most clearly to the fore in the notion of the entrepreneur: a self-reliant, individualistic human being, rationally calculating and always looking for their advantage in the context of an open playing field where one competes with all others for the opening up of ever new sources for creating revenue and making profit. As Jeremy Gilbert (2013) observes about the psychological dimensions of neoliberalism, it encourages:

> particular types of entrepreneurial competitive and commercial behaviour in its citizens, ultimately arguing for the management of populations with the aim of cultivating the type of individualistic, competitive, acquisitive and entrepreneurial behaviour which the liberal tradition has historically assumed to be the natural of civilised humanity, undistorted by government intervention. (Gilbert, 2013, p. 9)

For the advocates of neoliberalism, then, there is a distinct idea of what the natural abilities and characteristics of the human being are and how they are brought out in the best way. They believe 'self-interest to be the only motive force in human life and competition to be the most efficient and socially beneficial way for that force to express itself' (ibid.). Critics of such developments point out that 'individuals must increasingly shoulder the burden of risks that were once borne by employment structures: pay, training, benefits, and more' (Duffy, 2017, p. 194).

Having discussed key parts of the recent history of labour under neoliberalism, we now turn to psychoanalytic approaches to work and labour so as to set the stage for our analysis of notions of labour in the context of digital media.

Psychoanalytic approaches to work

'Work, Work, Work...' The comment smeared on the Samsung ad from the beginning of the chapter could just as well be used for Freud's conception of the human psyche. 'Only a few other authors can be named, at best Karl Marx and Max Weber, for whom work plays a more prominent role,' writes Ludger Lütkehaus (2006, p. 11), who lists the types of work that Freud sees as being performed in the human mind more or less unconsciously. There is the work of mourning, there is dreamwork and, analogous to the latter, there is 'joke work' in the *Jokes and Their Relation to the Unconscious* (1905b), and, as part of both dream and joke work, there is the work of condensation and displacement (Lütkehaus, 2006, p. 12).

As Jay Rohrlich (1980, 1993), one of the few dedicated psychoanalytic scholars of work, points out, Freud, despite his ample use of work metaphors, was otherwise *not* very interested in the functions of work for the human mind. There is merely one footnote in *Civilisation and its Discontents* (1930), in which Freud takes up the theme. This footnote, however, has become canonical for psychoanalytic explorations of work and labour. Freud writes:

> No other technique for the conduct of life attaches the individual so firmly to reality as laying emphasis on work; for his work at least gives him a secure place in a portion of reality, in the human community. The possibility it offers of displacing a large amount of libidinal components, whether narcissistic, aggressive or even erotic, on to professional work and on to the human relations connected with it lends it a value by no means second to what it enjoys as something indispensable to the preservation and justification of existence in society. (Freud, 1930, p. 80, fn. 1)

For both Rohrlich (1980) and, before him, Karl Menninger (1942), it is Freud's point of the 'displacement' – sublimation, really – of aggression that is work's foremost task. Echoing Freud's footnote, Menninger states:

Of all the methods available for absorbing the aggressive energies of mankind in a useful direction, work takes first place. It may not be the oldest, it certainly is not the most pleasant. But it has a certain realistic quality which makes it seem the most practical and obvious of all sublimations. (Menninger, 1942, p. 134)

Rohrlich (1980, pp. 109–10) supports this analysis by evoking the overdetermined quality of working in the formulaic comparison between work and rage: 'When the need to change materials has a constructive, creative goal, we call it work. When the desired change is destructive, we call it rage' (ibid., p. 47). In true Freudian fashion, he traces the creative/destructive duality of work back to toilet training in childhood. Yet, while this seems almost a psychoanalytic stereotype, the notions of control and discipline, productivity and efficiency, linearity and goal-directedness, which are doubtlessly part of this training, support this point. However, as regards aggression, the emphasis on what can more generally be understood as disciplinary cultures of cleanliness, properness and the right social and moral behaviour (indeed, there is a primitive notion of morality in toilet training; just remember the last public toilet that you found in a reeking state …) seems to cut both ways. Not only do the power struggles that are at the core of such disciplining cultures channel and, hopefully, sublimate aggression into something creative and productive, they also seem to call aggression forth and frequently risk turning creativity into destruction. In this respect, we can already see here that societal work and how it relates to wage labour holds a highly ambivalent potential that will occupy us further as we go along.

Leithäuser und Volmerg (1988) summarize the psychosocial functions of work in terms that again are very similar to Freud's: 'Becoming institutionalised in work are the enforcement of mental and physical activity, the assignment of social status, the specification of a time perspective, the formation of a social horizon and social identity' (p. 64). Furthermore, Freud's observation of the displacement of narcissistic, aggressive and erotic charges onto the field of work offers the authors a guideline for their own mapping of the functions of work in a psychosocial context. Questions of time are here seen as connecting to the theme of aggression (when to do what and how fast is a constant source of conflict in many contexts); questions of the social horizon connect to object love and erotic ties (for or against whom does one do what?) and questions of social status and identity connect to narcissistic themes (how does what I do reflect on myself?). In all these aspects of human relational proclivities, work can take on a compensatory – orienting, stabilizing and, indeed, also refining – function, and this idea of compensation (of doing something instead of something else) has been central to nearly all psychoanalytic thinking. This is a point we return to in our later discussion of digital labour and perversion.

Loving precarity

At this point, we have brought enough theoretical fodder together to help us think through the transformations of the psychological and relational proclivities that are being addressed, alleviated, displaced, channelled, compensated or sublimated in work and wage labour in a neoliberal and digital context. Rosalind Gill (2011) conducted interviews with workers in the creative industries whose self-reports about their experiences offer valuable insights into the state of labour in the digital age. Creative professions, such as service design, advertising, public relations, film and television, have been emblematic of current digital labour environments. People working in these fields have been empowered by digital media technologies in that these technologies have made the means of production widely accessible. Today, almost everybody can, say, build a small music recording studio at home or in a rehearsal space, while, only a generation ago, such studios and their equipment required engineering, were scarce and meticulously gate-kept by the music industry. At the same time, this breaking down of professional barriers of entry to the creative fields has rendered labour in these professions precarious. People in the creative industries increasingly find themselves with few supporting structures and faced with a large number of competitors for few sufficiently paying jobs. The workers Gill spoke to were acutely aware of the pitfalls of their industries – low pay, long hours, unequal access to opportunities, lack of long-term prospects and a constant need to keep up with the latest trends and technological advances. Yet they all stated that they absolutely loved what they did. This feeling of love and self-fulfilment in relation to labour can also be described in romantic terms. Angela McRobbie (2016) has argued that young women working in the creative industries today romanticize their professional lives:

No longer looking for a husband as a sole breadwinner, young women romanticize the idea of career. They want to find work about which they can feel passionate. Passionate work in turn becomes a further mark of feminine intelligibility and success. This desire transcends the boundaries of both class and ethnicity, while simultaneously retaining and even reinforcing hierarchical characteristics along these lines of demarcation and difference. [...] By in effect marrying her work, having devoted so much romantic energy into finding the right job, rather than the right man, the woman can uplift herself into a relatively undesignated middle-class social category. (McRobbie, 2016, p. 91)

Although such dynamics may be particularly applicable to women, we hold that to an extent everyone who works in the creative and digital sectors today has developed such passionate attachments to their labour. Taking us further into the field of digital labour, Brooke Erin Duffy (2017) has similarly shown in a study of bloggers, influencers and internet entrepreneurs that the creative industries in general are widely 'seen as idyllic professional destinations, characterized by autonomy, flexibility, and, above all, the potential for self-actualization' (Duffy, 2017, p. 3). But again, this idyll is tainted with bleak working conditions, which, in the case of the fashion bloggers, Instagram influencers, YouTube vloggers and blue-ticked Twitter personalities from Duffy's study, become captured in the term 'aspirational labour'. This labour is characterized by people working for free with the hope of eventually 'making it'. 'If only I get more likes, more followers, more engagement, more connections, I will eventually be paid for doing what I love,' so the fantasy goes.

What we find striking about the work constellations evoked in Duffy's and Gill's studies is the trade-off between personal fulfilment and remuneration or, in (an admittedly blunt use of) Marxian terms, between alienation and exploitation. In other words, the heightened sense of meaningfulness, connection and self-actualization attached to these jobs makes people extremely vulnerable to exploitation and self-exploitation. This is especially virulent online, where creating posts and circulating pictures that frequently deal with and reflect upon one's self and are commonly seen as effortless and highly enjoyable pastime activities, which only a few years ago hardly anybody would have even considered turning into a professional career. It is due to these notions of self-involvement, gratification and enjoyment that the question of pay and wages frequently becomes sidelined to a bonus and add-on, and, in this respect, work and leisure, labour and free time tend to merge increasingly.

An apt example is that of the singer–songwriter Jamie Mathias, who shared an anonymized private message on Twitter that he had received from a famous influencer, who invited him to sing at his wedding in Ibiza and to write a song for the happy couple. However, the influencer made it clear that, '[W]e're not really paying the suppliers. We'll do promo posts and what we charge for promo is worth way more than any track.' Instead of payment, he would receive free posts from the influencer, promoting his songs. When Mathias responded that he'd rather be paid for his labour, the influencer replied: 'Bro it's a wedding with shit loads of other influencers with big money there, think of the reach!' Perhaps unsurprisingly, he declined the offer.[1] The offer, however, perfectly illustrates Duffy's 'aspirational labour' where subjects are constantly encouraged to think of the future and to carefully consider what opportunities may arise from free labour. What one can detect in these new arrangements and functions of labour is a refocusing on self-realization, which frequently, however, comes to the detriment of one of the central societal modes of recognition, namely that of paid wages (e.g. Honneth, 2010).

The tendency of little or no wages shows parallels to the crises that many of the authors presented in Chapter 2 have pointed out in regard to how our social relations are configured online. When Žižek (1998), Dean (2010) and Flisfeder (2021), in their specific ways, each point to shifts in people's relations with the oedipal, paternal and socio-symbolic dimensions online, in which the binding power of the laws and regulations of the social are somehow at stake, this is echoed in the frequent absence of financial remuneration as a socio-symbolic response to and recognition of people's labour, as we have also shown through the example above. Accordingly, Axel Honneth (2010) writes about the state of labour as a means of social recognition in the early twenty-first century that 'the struggle for professional respect and recognition based on accomplishment does no longer take place within the economic sphere itself, but, in totally different forms, in front of its increasingly locked gates' (Honneth, 2010, n.p,. our translation). Bringing this diagnosis in touch with Leithäuser and Volmerg's (1988) psychoanalytic assessment of work as relevant in terms of aggressive, narcissistic and sexual/erotic mental needs, we might suggest that the status of work and labour under neoliberal and digital conditions shows tendencies of an 'eroticization' at a pre-oedipal level (since the kinds of work performed are often self-referential and thus auto-erotic). At the same time, it displays a strong potential for narcissistic wounds (because of the precarious nature of the recognition given or withheld by others, not least in the face of a frequent absence of financial recognition), which again leads to a proclivity for aggression (the absence of acts of recognition leading to projection and suspicion).

Ultimately, the fact that Jamie Mathias chose to reveal a private conversation on social media may in itself be seen as an act of aspirational labour and the hope that something may come out of it. A few days after his tweet, he contacted the influencer, informing him that, since his tweet about the free wedding gig had gone viral and 'my enquiries have gone mental', he was willing to offer a free song without 'any exposure in return'.[2] Using precarious dynamics as a way to advertise himself is therefore quite telling of contemporary auto-erotic patterns of creative and digital labour.

Free labour, anxious subjects and counter-phobic existences

Before delving further into these dynamics, we would like to remain briefly with the notions of pastime, leisure and fun that are so closely related with what we do online. The proverbial 'If the service is free, you are the product' has long since become common wisdom, and, indeed, social media's practice of collecting user data so as to make aggregations of this data available to advertisers on the basis of complementary interests is a business model that really *puts social media users to work*, even if most of us do not realize it. In other words, even everyday social media users – that is, people who do not have any professional aspirations that are directly related to what they do online – can be seen as engaged in digital labour.

Tiziana Terranova (2000) was the first to argue that many activities on the internet constitute acts of free labour whereby people perform tasks that contribute to the value or profit of websites and companies, such as designing levels for videogames, writing code for programmes, translating websites and manuals, or providing other content. This has become particularly significant from the mid-2000s onwards with social media constituting major cultural activity and, with it, so-called user-generated content. All of the content on social media is created by users. Without users, platforms such as Instagram would be sad, empty places. In Marxian terms, users contribute to social media companies' profit maximization and, therefore, their activities can be seen as labour. According to Christian Fuchs (e.g. 2014), social media users are even *doubly* exploited. Not only do they produce the content that other users then consume, but by the same token they also produce the personal data that are sold as a commodity to advertisers. Hence, if we go with Fuchs's Marxist understanding of the political economy of social media, we must conclude that social media users are given a stunningly bad deal. Whereas Facebook, for example, has managed to almost triple its yearly revenue within only four years, from $40 billion in 2017 to nearly $118 billion in 2021 (Statista, 2021), their users do most of the labour, but are not remunerated.

Hence, picking up and interweaving some of the above threads, we argue that, no matter how leisurely, personal and intimate it feels to many, and no matter if it pays nothing at all, what we do on social media is labour – even if we are not explicitly in the influencer or any other creative business. Probably the most telling metaphor for the form this labour takes is that of the internet *platform*. As Tarleton Gillespie (2010) points out, social networking sites started applying the term 'platform' to themselves not least as a way to defend against copyright infringement lawsuits. By claiming to simply give people a 'platform' for their creativity and expressivity, these corporations tried to deny responsibility for what was posted and circulated on their networks. For the users, however, who are also always workers in a neoliberal, digital economy, the term platform captures an expectation of elevatedness, where they are told, or promised even, to be made more visible to others, but where this promise also comes with a potential state of being exposed and unprotected. Users are invited onto a stage and expected to perform and, since there are no handrails on the edges of these platforms, there is always the risk that they get vertigo, lose their footing and fall.

In this image, then, labour in the digital age is about showing ourselves and performing so as to catch the attention of others and fulfil the expectations that come with being given a platform and, in this way, digital corporate social media double down on the self-entrepreneurial logics of neoliberalism. Hence, we show ourselves for our own sakes and with a focus on ourselves, which is widely seen as gratifying in itself and which implicitly precludes any direct expectation of being paid a living wage. To achieve such financial recognition, people are expected to work excessively hard in an attempt at compensating and overcompensating the link to the social environment that somehow seems to be missing from their activities. The social character formation that emerges from this scenario amounts to a subject that is dynamic, anticipatory, aspirational and shapeable, which returns us to the theories of neoliberal subjectivities from earlier in this chapter. As one interviewee who Duffy spoke to put it: 'Being an entrepreneur, nothing is the end-all, be-all; everything is like your launch pad to the next thing' (2017, p. 186). In Duffy's words, this state of constantly preparing for a recognition that remains elusive leads to 'a frenetic work pace punctuated by moments of uncertainty; the pressure to remain ever-accessible to audiences and advertisers alike; and a nagging sense of unease as one's personal life becomes folded into a carefully curated digital persona' (ibid., p. 189). The flipside of this frenetic state, then, are systematic feelings of shame or inadequacy. As Duffy notes: 'Social media can perpetuate a culture of supposed instant success and leads to a culture of insecurity, especially amongst young women who compare themselves/their work unfavorably to polished people/products' (ibid., p. 188).

Bringing this back into a psychoanalytic paradigm, we can see how our observations about narcissism in Chapter 2 take on a more existential dimension when assessed in the context of work and its central importance for our sense of self and place in the world (and not least for the necessity to sustain ourselves and keep bodily selves alive, the existence of which is widely disavowed). The ever-optimized representations of 'a perfect I' have the compulsive function to make other people depend on the illusion of my independence. The upkeep of this illusion, however, also costs me dearly, in that I constantly need to strive to produce symbolic material that renews the fantasy that my ego is in fact ideal. This again has foreseeable consequences for the formation of our conscience function, and Slavoj Žižek (1994) has long argued for the sociocultural formation of a particularly sadistic super-ego that dictates ever harsher forms of enjoying oneself. Hence, by being allowed to work how we want, when and where, and thus making work depend on our own conscience, we are being handed over to the mercy of our potentially worst enemy: ourselves.

Jorge Ahumada (2016) refers to Otto Fenichel's concept of the 'counter-phobic attitude' (1939) to make sense of this current climate of labour and people's mental states in it. Fenichel observed a repetitive kind of behaviour in which adult people seek out anxious situations that they then go about to master time and again. The pleasure of mastery that Fenichel sees them derive from such an orchestrated challenge is one that has its roots less in an unproblematically perceived safety from harm; rather, as he explains, 'the preference displays the character of an overcompensation and shows that unconsciously the anxiety is still alive' (Fenichel, 1939, p. 264). As he goes on to explain: '[T]he person in question is by no means really convinced of his ability and, before he engages in any such activity, actually passes through a sort of anxious tension of expectation, though he may not consciously recognize it as such' (ibid., p. 266). Whereas Fenichel formulates these observations as individually subjective mental problems, it is Ahumada's point that we are now living in a socio-economic climate that has alleviated the counter-phobic attitude to a widespread, commonplace cultural phenomenon. By labour becoming our own responsibility, by tying us to it whole and by investing us in it completely, our existences are on the line each time we get to it, and the only way to dispel the anxiety that befalls us is to work *more*. It is in this way that the digital takes on such a haunting meaning within the more general field of labour. As in the Samsung ad from the beginning of this chapter, digital technologies, which are always borne from an existing sociocultural climate, facilitate, enable and normalize the unbound working conditions of our times and make them ever more attractive. For example, a *New York Times* report into Amazon's business practices disclosed that the corporation expected its executives to respond to email requests at all times, day or night (Kantor & Streitfeld, 2015); this is merely the elevation to company practice of the compulsive routines that some social media users have developed on their own, getting up in the middle of the night to check their accounts so as to be 'ahead of their game'.

In such ways, and due to the sheer endless quantities of tasks available – as infinite as scrolling through social media news feeds – the functional pleasures that Leithäuser and Volmerg (1988) have granted work and labour seem to turn increasingly more compensatory, counter-phobic and compulsive, with the boundlessness of labour constantly inviting ways of dealing with it that appear to go against the pleasure that they might have been experienced initially. Hence, many people have professed to have devised strategies in which tasks that used to be enjoyable and meaningful become merely expelled and gotten rid of, rather than digested and cared for.

The counter-phobic attitude is captured in a particularly extreme way in the German TV series *Bad Banks* (Kienle, 2018–20), which became an international success. It follows the ambitious and extremely hard-working investment banker Jana Liekam, who frequently works until complete exhaustion, sacrificing every last speck of private life. In the final episode of the first season, she is shown speaking to her boss:

> I could get out, enjoy my money and a quiet life. You once asked me why I wanted to have a career. I have some very smart answers. But the truth is simpler: I don't know. I don't have a clue. But I *need* it. Like you. And I will no longer deny it. (S1, E6)

Platform labour, platform life: the 'perverse pact'

A final way to make psychoanalytic sense of the current state of labour in the contexts of neoliberalism and digitalization is to conceptualize social media platforms not merely as specific *environments* – as stages, or marketplaces, or networks – but to look at the relationships users have, not only on and via these platforms but *with* them. Here we can productively tap into studies that we have been conducting respectively and mix them anew. Hence, while Jacob (Johanssen, 2019, 2021) has highlighted the notions of romance and passion that often go into the relationship between platforms and their users, Steffen (Krüger, in press) has been working on an approach that looks at user–platform relations through a formative, and thus generational (i.e. child–parent relational), lens.

As concerns the latter perspective, there is a deluge of examples that suggest platforms take over a nourishing, enabling and facilitating role that approximates caregiving functions traditionally associated with the roles of mother and father. For instance, we are continuously encouraged by platforms to express our feelings and show the world who we are and what we are up to, which is indeed reminiscent of the ways parents raise their children into becoming individuals: don't be shy, stand up for yourself; open your mouth if you want something, etc. In this respect, the platform metaphor and the implied functions of elevation and exposure are also in line with a widespread parental wish for their offspring to be recognized, acknowledged, admired and adored, as a typical form of displaced narcissism. Beauty pageants for children are only an extreme form of a common tendency for parents to put their kids on pedestals, which one often finds reproduced in social media.

At the same time, the people representing social media platforms have long displayed the wish to come across as our peers and equals. Facebook's Mark Zuckerberg, in particular, in his blog posts, interviews and public appearances, has been cultivating an emphatically informal, college student-like relational style that oozes friendship, flat-share and the effortless intimacy of a long-time partner or best friend. And although this might not be easily identified with romance and passion, the ways in which the platforms themselves, and many other digital services for that matter, purport to attach themselves to us often suggest romance-like constellations. Another advertisement, this time by the software company Oracle, helps illustrate this point.

In the advert 'The disconnect' from 2020, an energetic, young, female, off-screen voice addresses what appears to be a romantic partner for a serious conversation about their relationship. On screen, we see a sporty, attractive young woman in various scenes illustrating her everyday life – jogging through an urban landscape (New York); pacing through a stylish inner-city apartment, reading a book she holds; sitting on her apartment floor surrounded by her computer and printouts of texts while talking on the phone; then going to a club with waves of long brown hair flowing over a glittering silver top. All the while, she can be heard impatiently addressing a partner who remains absent: 'I feel like I've given everything I can, but there's just no connection,' she complains, and further: 'We've lost that – spark. And to be honest: I'm fed up. I've told you where I want to go, what I want to do, but it's like you're not even listening to me. I'm sick of waiting around while you try to figure out who I am.' Towards the end of the spot, it turns out that the invisible partner who is criticized in this way is not a human being – not a romantic partner at all – but an unspecified company of which the woman is a disillusioned customer.

Although Oracle as a tech company thus positions itself as a go-between that offers to put the 'spark' back into the relationship, the romance that the woman demands from the company could just as well be transferred onto social media platforms. After all, the woman's demands are perfectly aligned with what the platforms aspire to as an ideal intimacy with their users, namely: to know these users in such a complete way and to such a total degree that their knowledge becomes superior to that of the users themselves. 'Sometimes I want you to make some suggestions, to do something that surprises me – that shows me you know me!,' complains the female voice from the Oracle ad, effectively putting herself in the position of a lover who demands to be more and better appreciated.

What we find striking about this ad is its radical revaluation of a position that has been commonplace in critical internet and surveillance studies for some years now: instead of being alarmed, concerned and taken aback by the proximity and granularity of 'dataveillance' (i.e. surveillance through analysis of user data), the woman imagined in the commercial does not find the resulting intimacy going far enough. *With all this data I've made available to them*, the woman seems to imply, *corporations should do better to 'get me', satisfy me, and care for me*. This woman, then, represents an ideal (social media) user (from a corporate perspective) who knows that they are completely transparent and in the hands of digital platforms, but who embraces this state completely and to the point at which they challenge the corporations to do a better job at 'handling them with care' and recognizing them.

Whether we combine this dataveillance aspect of digital platforms with notions of parental or romantic love, the troubling question for both scenarios is whether one can talk of care in such a relationship at all. Tech companies' advertising and public relations efforts constantly seek to keep this question outside the frame of reference. *Of course we care*, they assure their users, *by bringing you close to the people and things you care about!* But counter to these efforts, this question constantly shores up again and pushes its way back into the frame, because even the best advertising campaigns cannot dispel the implicit knowledge on the part of the users that the love and care that digital platforms have to offer go against well-established cultural expectations of both morally and pedagogically sound parenting – what Winnicott poignantly called 'the good enough mother' (1960) – and a good romantic partner in a healthy, equal relationship.[3] When it comes to revenue models and profit strategies, then, platforms do not love users for their own sakes; rather, these users become a means to an end, and it is through this disparate, unequal power relation that one can speak of a *perverse* relationship between digital platforms and their users, as Jacob has suggested elsewhere (Johanssen, 2019, 2021).

We are aware of the disturbing, highly moralizing connotations that the term 'perversion' holds. As a concept, perversion has clear links to sexuality but, via a form of psychoanalytic thinking along the lines of psychosexuality, this sexual component takes on a much broader scope. Perversion is commonly associated with sexual fetishes or practices that go against mainstream norms (and thus always display a degree of moral flexibility in that what is seen as perverse changes together with the cultures in which it exists). Psychoanalysis, however, is most interested in the dynamics of submission and domination which are at the core of the concept and which – despite, or exactly through, the sexual component in perverse relations – can manifest themselves in various social contexts: between employee and employer, for example, or sergeant and soldier, civil servant and citizen, customer and staff, parent and child, etc. We want to argue that another actualization of such a perverse relationship is that between social media platform and user.

In order to corroborate this thesis, it is important to define exactly what the perverse relationship consists of. In this respect, Sergio Benvenuto, in his seminal study *What Are Perversions?* (2016), differentiates between 'amor' and 'caritas' when defining perverse love. While 'amor' refers to the sexual, passionate component of love, 'caritas' refers to the 'compassionate' element. As Benvenuto explains: '[W]ithout compassionate *caritas* every sexual act – even the most normally heterosexual – takes on a perverse shade, and appears as using the other qua subject, qua means of pleasure' (2016, p. 10). In other words: 'It is not the desired anatomical object that makes the perversion, but what I would call the lack of care for the other as the subject of desire and enjoyment' (ibid.).

This description fits the situation users face on social media platforms well. Granted, platforms do not engage in sexual acts with their users, and users still need to be cared for as 'subjects of desire and enjoyment' to a degree. This care, however, is not given out of a compassionate love for them, but so that they can be used for the platform's own gains. When the psychoanalyst Ruth Stein writes that, 'Perversion as a mode of relatedness points to relations of seduction, domination, psychic bribery and guileful uses of "innocence", all in the service of exploiting the other' (2005, p. 781, emphasis in original), the ways of soft coercion applied by digital platforms so as to retain users glued to their services for increasingly longer stretches of time are articulated quite convincingly in our opinion.

The lack of care that one party in a perverse relationship displays, in turn, becomes articulated through what Benvenuto observes as perversion's necessary restrictions: 'The perverse person, far from appearing as the champion of a sexuality which overflows without any inhibitory brakes, appears instead strongly dependent on a restrictive condition' (Benvenuto, 2016, p. xxx). As in comedian Demetri Martin's laconic linguistic meandering – 'You can say, "I love kids," as a general statement. That's fine. It's when you get specific, that's when you get into trouble: "I love 12-year-olds"'[4] – a perfectly altruistic love of children is drained of its altruism and caritas once the 'restrictive condition' of '12-year-olds' is introduced. In this way, Martin not only achieves the (dubious) feat of making us laugh about paedophilia, but also points us to another central component in perverse love that often follows rigid rules and regulations.

In a similar way, we receive a significantly more realistic vision of the love digital platforms show their users, when adding to *We love users!* the restrictive condition of *We love users' data!* Whereas older commercial media – television first and foremost – have used audience ratings and demographic analysis for decades, having shown heavy biases in demographic preferences, social media can altruistically claim that they appreciate *all demographics*, but only under the condition that this means that these demographics are also ready to hand over their user data. After all, even those demographic groups that proved least attractive to traditional media might still be sold to providers of niche demographic goods and services. Indeed, this is what is meant by the 'long tail' of the internet, where a platform's strength in community-building hinges not least on its ability to also bring people with the most remote interests together. In this sense, perversion resides in the digital platforms, their developers, customer service staff and PR workers constantly articulating intense feelings of love and care towards users, while also consistently treating them as objects to be tracked, surveilled, categorized and sold as data points (e.g. Krüger & Johanssen, 2014; Rambatan & Johanssen, 2021). It is in this way that a perverse relationship is reproduced in digital media.

Yet, it always takes (at least) two parties to maintain such an exploitative relationship over time. And this circumstance widens our perspective again, from an exclusive focus on the social media platforms themselves, back to the users and the part they play in what, drawing from Ruth Stein (2005), one can call 'the perverse pact'. In this respect, the component that is at the very heart of perversion comes fully into play, specifically, the mechanism of denial, which is foundational of perversions as the ego's attempt to hold two diametrically opposed understandings of reality at one and the same time. Along the lines of the conception of fetishism, the insight into a harshly threatening – indeed, castrating – reality is denied and acknowledged at the same time. In perversion, there is always a strong ambiguity about what is known, acknowledged and denied. Benvenuto (2016) writes in this respect of a 'coexistence of two "knowledges"': 'on the one hand there is *knowledge*, on the other there is "knowledge"' (p. 8). The pervert thus holds a 'double knowledge' in which 'the subject's supposed knowledge is split from another "knowledge"' (ibid.). The fetishist *knows* the woman has no penis, but nevertheless the fetishist 'knows' that the woman does have a penis. In sadism, the sadist *knows* that the victim does not really deserve to be punished, but all the same, the sadist 'knows' that the victim deserves it.

This structure holds for digital platforms, their owners and operators, as well. They *know* very well that they do not care for their users, but still 'know' that they care and love them a lot. A leaked and much-debated internal memo by Facebook executive Andrew Bosworth (2018), for example, outlines the company's philosophy of user growth as follows:

> So we connect people. That can be bad if they make it negative. Maybe it costs a life by exposing someone to bullies. Maybe someone dies in a terrorist attack coordinated on our tools. And still we connect people. The ugly truth is that … anything that allows us to connect people more often is de facto good. (quoted in Zuboff, 2019, p. 506)

In our opinion, the key perverse moment in this passage is how Bosworth evokes scenes of deadly violence in his readers' minds and, almost in the same breath, defines the actions leading up to, or at least involved in, this violence as 'de facto good'.

However, what about the users themselves? How do they figure in this relationship? What is their part? It is at the point when these questions are being asked that things get complicated because people often have to acknowledge that they are at least tacitly complicit in the exploitative power play of the platforms. Users, too, often know very well that they are committing to an unbalanced relationship, with seductive and bribing aspects and a reversal of means and ends (Stein, 2005) that is potentially harmful to them. And while one seldom finds people who embrace this relationship as openly and (auto-)aggressively as the young woman from the Oracle ad, or as large parts of the industry literature imagine them (e.g. see Eyal, 2014; Moatti, 2016), what amounts to the users' consent is usually again masked in plaints about the cruelty and inadequacy of the platform – plaints which keep the mechanism of denial intact.

When psychoanalytic film scholar Elisabeth Cowie (1997) points to the gap between feminist political positions of the second half of the twentieth century and the ways in which women, including feminists, are being interpellated – despite themselves – by exactly those media representations they have been standing up against, this offers a productive blueprint for understanding the ways in which many people today derive pleasures from working in contexts and under conditions that they know they should reject as unacceptable. 'Whether they are images of motherhood or of pornography or whatever, we cannot necessarily accept or reject them simply through an act of conscious will,' Cowie states, rather: 'We will be moved by images in ways which we neither expect nor seek nor want' (1997, p. 5). Likewise, social media users, too, and particularly people working in the digital sector and/or in digital environments, often find their better knowledge countered and neutralized by what they experience to be moved by. The circumstance, for example, that the LinkedIn platform, an important tool for professional networking, has in recent years also been discussed for its merits as a tool with which to engineer romantic and sexual encounters (Huang, 2018) is but one indication that the forms of objectification and self-objectification, domination and submission, which labour in the digital neoliberal economy entails, are often experienced as exciting, enticing and pleasurable. Along similar lines, the hook-up app Bumble introduced its Bizz feature in 2017. 'Perversions involving the gaze,' writes Benvenuto (2016), 'are an erotic use of self-awareness' (p. 21), and it seems it is this kind of erotic that directs fantasies of sexual encounters towards self-entrepreneurial facilitation networks such as LinkedIn.

Admittedly, the circumstance that we often enjoy our submission and objectification in the context of digital labour, and that we tacitly consent to and become complicit in our relations of production there, invalidates our application of the term perversion to the field of digital labour to a degree. Referring to the ethical dimension of perversion, Benvenuto explains that, 'we don't consider as perverse those SM games in which, for example, one partner is chained to the bed and maltreated, but derives pleasure from it all' (2016, p. 7). We fashion ourselves in the required ways in our current work environments and we derive sexual pleasure from performing the kind of person that is wanted there. Thereby, we become active parts in the creation of a sociocultural norm that might by no means be healthy, but that is likewise difficult to critique as pathological in any effective way. As Leithäuser and Volmerg (1988) observed, when it comes to work and its mental functions, the borders between sublimation and more compensatory and pathological forms of displacing mental needs onto structured activity are fluid and must be assessed and determined in concrete case studies. What we can say, however, is that the presence of and play with sexualized forms of submission and domination in the realm of labour are symptomatic for an overall environment in which hierarchies might be hard to discern but have been incorporated by people in such unforgiving ways that many of us develop the need to erect them again in our professional relations so as to find anchor points in our lives.

Conclusion

For better or worse, such anchor points used to be made available by tradition, faith, class and gender. Now individualism is offered to absorb human needs for orientation, with labour functioning as the main production site of such individuality. In a time of waning beliefs, perverse structures of acknowledgement and denial thus become a fundamental structure of culture *per se*, as Hartmut Böhme has impressively etched out in his *Fetishism and Culture* (2014). The Lacanians Heiko Feldner and Fabio Vighi (2018) observe that perversion has become a general functioning of neoliberalism since the 2008 global financial crisis. The financial crisis, they argue, laid bare the fundamental problem at the heart of neoliberalism, which prioritized finance capital and led to an out-of-control banking and mortgage system. The shockwaves were felt all over the world by large parts of its populations, as western governments bailed out banks, people lost their homes and jobs, and austerity measures were introduced in many countries. Nobody could effectively deny the problems that had led to the crisis. However, although this crisis energized political activists and anticapitalist movements, such as OccupyWallStreet, their efforts ultimately led to very little progress. Rather, for Feldner and Vighi (2018), the collective answer to the failure of capitalism has been one of denial – a denial of the very failure of capitalism to mask its flaws. Historically, capitalism has been remarkably successful, via politics, science, ideology, the state, the family, religion and other forms, at sustaining itself and proclaiming its exclusivity. Yet, this ability has been hampered by recent epochal crises. 'In short, in our current predicament global capitalism has no substantial fiction with which to disguise its own growing unproductivity, which is why the only defence mechanism at its disposal is perversion' (Feldner & Vighi, 2018, p. 109).

This sense of denial is also a defence against loss, finitude and the fact that we cannot function 24/7. It comes with enormous implications for our mental health as the rising cases of burn-out and other conditions demonstrate. We have turned a blind eye against the conditions of exploitation that we willingly reproduce. '[W]e are vaguely aware that we chose not to look at the facts without being conscious of what it is we are evading' (Steiner, 1985, p. 161). As we have discussed previously (Krüger & Johanssen, 2014), our implicit knowledge of exploitation and suffering is identified with and enacted online, for example, by making demands to Facebook about how our data should be handled: '*Well, if you want to instrumentalise me,*' these comments seem to tell Facebook, '*then at least treat me as a precious instrument and maintain me well!*' (ibid., p. 643, italics in original), as we wrote about user comments on Facebook. Paradoxically, the instrumental ways with which we are treated by tech companies and employers alike only seem to strengthen the sense of our own importance, which sadly often furthers our impotence.

In being instrumentalized as an *individual* subject, we develop quasi-personal romantic relations with social media companies, platforms, gadgets, employers and companies. Such ties are only strengthened via the communal and intersubjective relations we have with other individuals on social media and via digital means today. As we wrote about user complaints on social media:

> the repeated, mutual confirmation amongst users of being victims in the same intrigue takes the edge off the personal sense of powerlessness that the betrayal might otherwise have. In the cases

we looked at it is thus the very articulation of indignation that serves as a safety valve and makes the continuation of the relation possible, if not pleasurable. (Krüger & Johanssen, 2014, p. 644)

In this chapter, we have discussed the psychodynamics of contemporary labour in relation to the digital. We outlined how labour has significantly changed as we moved into neoliberalism and more recently into neoliberal platform capitalism. In our platform age, jobs have become ever more insecure and temporary for many. We have focused on the creative industries to detail the romantic-loving levels of attachment that many have for their jobs, even though they are all too aware of the exploitation, precarity and discrimination they face. We also discussed the notion of digital labour on social media where users are like unpaid staff members who create value for Facebook, Instagram, Twitter and co. Similarly, users know of the business models and other scandals behind social media but stay connected. We then unpacked this paradox through the psychoanalytic notion of perversion which characterizes a relationship marked by love and abuse. We are excited by being in perverse relationships as they enable us to deny our powerlessness and emphasize narcissistic ideas around self-importance. This also shows itself in futile stagings of criticism on social media. As a form of denial, perversion allows us to keep going against all odds, until we break down or change our mindset. It is this denial that renders contemporary work and its digital expressions fundamentally political. The next chapter further looks at digital politics from a psychoanalytic perspective.

Notes

1. https://twitter.com/jamiemathias/status/1476899833839599621
2. https://twitter.com/JamieMathias/status/1478469554259083266
3. We return to this point to discuss its implicit sexual undercurrents in Chapter 5.
4. http://funny-stand-up-comedy-central.blogspot.com/2009/11/demetri-martin-talks-about-loving-kids.html [Accessed 17/6/2022].

Further reading

Benvenuto, S. (2016). *What Are Perversions? Sexuality, Ethics, Psychoanalysis.* London: Routledge.

Fenichel, O. (1939). The counter-phobic attitude. *International Journal of Psycho-Analysis*, 20, 263–74.

Hirschhorn, L. (1990). *The Workplace Within. Psychodynamics of Organizational Life*. Cambridge, MA: MIT Press.

King, V., Gerisch, B. and Rosa, H. (2019). *Lost in Perfection. Impacts of Optimisation on Culture and Psyche*. London and New York: Routledge.

Knafo, D. and Lo Bosco, R. (2017). *The Age of Perversion. Desire and Technology in Psychoanalysis and Culture*. London: Routledge.

Krüger, S. and Johanssen, J. (2014). Alienation and digital labour – a depth hermeneutic inquiry into online commodification and the unconscious. *Triple C: Communication, Capitalism & Critique. Open Access Journal for a Global Sustainable Information Society*, 12(2), 632–47.

Menzies, I. E. P. (1960). A case study in the functioning of social systems as a defence against anxiety: a report on a study of the nursing service of a general hospital. *Human Relations*, 13(2), 95–121.

Rohrlich, J. B. (1980). *Work and Love: The Crucial Balance*. New York: Summit Books.

Stein, R. (2005). Why perversion? 'False love' and the perverse pact. *International Journal of Psychoanalysis*, 86(3), 775–99.

CHAPTER 4

Digital politics and the other

Key themes:
homophily; theories of aggression; otherness; extremism and
racism; fragmentation, polarization and the paranoid–schizoid;
online misogyny; cancel culture

Introduction

In this chapter, we discuss how forms of extremism, such as racism
or misogyny, articulate themselves and become social forces on the
internet. We draw on scholars in the traditions of critical and postcolonial
theory who have used psychoanalytic concepts in their work and unpack
extremist dynamics online by first presenting what we see as the major
structural dimensions of the current, commercial form of the internet
as driving detrimental social dynamics of othering online. We will then
take a step back from the internet and offer a brief discussion of central
psychoanalytic works on otherness, authoritarianism, xenophobia,
racism, antisemitism and other forms of extremism, so as to give
ourselves and our readers a solid foundation from which to then gradually
return to the digital. We will then look at extremist and racist groups
on Facebook, racial dilemmas in the design of emojis, male subcultures
and online misogyny, trolling, as well as so-called cancel culture. We
cannot do full justice to the differences in racism, fascism, antisemitism,
Islamophobia, right-wing or left-wing populism and other related 'isms'
or to how they have been discussed in and outside of psychoanalysis.
Rather, we seek to understand the various forms of prejudice, violence
and oppression discussed in this chapter with Elisabeth Young-Bruehl
(1996) as 'social mechanisms of defence' (p. 209).[1] This means that all
forms of prejudice seek to erect boundaries between groups at the social

level. For instance, when racists or misogynists make use of pseudo-science about evolutionary psychology, genetics or conspiracy theories, then such discourses are of subjective and social significance because they allude to ideas about collectivity, or 'others' invading or weakening an in-group, however flawed and outlandish these ideas might be. Such discourses serve to strengthen the position of the in-group that subscribes to them while both (symbolically) destroying and maintaining the target. We return to this point in a short while. To begin this chapter, we first need to examine social media in relation to the political.

Online neighbourhoods and 'negative transference'

In October 2021, *The Guardian* reported on internal research at Twitter which showed that the platform's algorithms had a clear bias towards right-wing content. Tweets from right-wing politicians and media organizations were amplified and shown more in users' timelines than those from left-wing profiles (Milmo, 2021b). Similar arguments had been made by academics and journalists before, but the fact that the platform itself had investigated the problem and published its findings is noteworthy. For a number of years, the argument has been made that social media are built around 'echo chambers' (Sunstein, 2002) and 'filter bubbles' (Pariser, 2011). In the case of echo chambers, it is held that internet users inhabit spaces where they only encounter their own opinions echoed back at them by like-minded people; similarly, in the case of filter bubbles, users are seen as put inside an algorithmically produced bubble, or 'information cocoon' (Bruns, 2019), where they are offered only information and messages that align with their existing political orientations, tastes and interests. The difference between the two concepts is that the former is built on communication between people, whereas the second is grounded in the notion of the supply and curation of information by the network and its 'news-feeding' algorithms themselves. In both scenarios, different voices and opinions, differing information, as well as diverging tastes, affiliations or attitudes disappear from perception. To a degree, Twitter's in-house investigation gives renewed credence to these claims. And even though a significant amount of research shows that such algorithmic filtering of information and the discreet buffering of each individual worldview reaches by no means the dramatic socially fragmenting effects that some scholars have foreseen (see Bruns, 2019), there is little doubt that digital social networking has an effect on how we experience ourselves in relation to others and the world around us.

The digital media scholar Wendy Hui Kyong Chun (2018, 2021) has approached the question of the political costs of social networks via the concept of **homophily** (Latin for 'love of sameness'), which does a lot to sharpen the notions of 'echo chamber' and 'filter bubble' and to render them more precise. As she explains, it is a general characteristic of digital networks that they aggregate the people within them into neighbourhoods that display similarities. These can further be inferred from the connections between the network's members themselves, as Chun (2018) writes: 'latent attributes such as age and political affiliation are easily inferred via a user's "neighbours"' (p. 65). Simply put, if your Instagram network, for example, is filled with teenagers who are into skateboarding, chances are you are one such teenager too. It is shared attributes that digital networks are after in their ongoing analysis and patterning of user data because their main aim is to order them along the interests of third parties (as explained in Chapter 3): 'Networks, because of their complexities, noisiness, and persistent inequalities, foster techniques to manage, prune, and predict,' writes Chun (2018, p. 61) and, in so doing, they also inevitably construct a social world that makes every user fall – seemingly effortlessly and naturally – into one or several of those neighbourhoods of like-minded people. *Neighbourhoods*, that is, not *groups or crowds* – a difference that will become of interest shortly.

Through the creation of neighbourhoods, homophily creates seeming consensus and harmony in networks. As the saying goes, birds of a feather flock together. So far so good, but this assumption – that people who have much in common also like to be around each other and that, vice versa, people who are around each other will have a lot in common – tends to erase the political pressures that more often than not have gone into the creation of these similarities, samenesses and proximities. For example, the fact that many cities across the world have very rich neighbourhoods as well as extremely poor ones does not mean that this is so because of a natural inclination for like-minded people to be near one another. Rather, particularly in the case of the inhabitants of city slums, hardly anybody would venture that they have come together because they are most comfortable around others with the same experience. In more subtle ways, however, this is how corporate digital networks represent the world. Both neighbourhoods that become constructed in this way, however, are constructed on the basis of articulated interests which are arranged as *entirely discreet* from one another. As Chun (2018) writes poignantly:

> [H]omophily (often allegedly of those discriminated against) – not racism, sexism, and inequality – becomes the source of inequality, making injustice 'natural' and 'ecological.' It turns hate into love and transforms individuals into 'neighbors' who naturally want to live together, which assumes that neighborhoods should be filled with people who are alike. (Chun, 2018, p. 76)

Along the lines of this tacit network logic, then, conflict, which many scholars – us included – see as at the core of politics *per se* (see Heywood, 2013, for an overview), becomes avoided; in psychoanalytic lingo, we could say *fetishistically disavowed*. Important at this point is that, if everybody lives in homophilic neighbourhoods and thus in the places they seemingly belong, the entire network population is brought into a harmonious order and to the point where conflicts no longer register widely, because potential conflicting parties no longer meet there.

Paradoxically, however, it is this tendency of social networking sites to avoid conflict that amplifies political and social conflicts today and makes them more polarized and seemingly unresolvable. For even if digital networks seek to keep each of us within our own neighbourhoods, compounds, ghettoes, slums or gated communities, we are all avid observers of the lives of '*other Others*' to varying extents. For example, 'those people' in one's real, physical neighbourhood that just don't seem to 'fit in', or 'those people' across town who seem to be 'completely out of this world', not to mention those media personalities and celebrities who are known merely for their eccentric otherness. Within or without the newsfeeds of social media, there is ample opportunity for such encounters. What the categorizing and compartmentalizing efforts of social media seem to support, therefore, is not so much a life in blissful ignorance of others, but increasingly distanced visions of otherness that do not invite for encountering and fully experiencing others any more. The media scholar Axel Bruns (2019) captures this well in his distinction between fragmentation and polarization:

Fragmentation implies the existence of echo chambers and filter bubbles, where like-minded partisans connect and communicate amongst themselves and are oblivious to the view of the outside world. But this manifestly does not represent contemporary experience. Rather, as citizens especially on the fringes of the political spectrum become more polarised in their worldviews, they still *hear* but are increasingly less willing to *listen to* the views of their political opponents, preferring instead to repeat their own beliefs ever more noisily. (Bruns, 2019, p. 106, italics in original)

Although this view tends to leave out what the political constitution of the 'centre' of society might have to do with the polarization of the fringes, the differentiation between 'hearing' and 'listening' is an important one. It alludes to blockages and deadlocks in the relations between people that psychoanalysis was early to address, first and foremost in the conception of **'negative transference'** – that is, the ways in which analysands resist and defend themselves against – sometimes rightly so – the insights offered by their analysts.[2] Also, in these cases, it is extremely difficult to reach the other who is caught up in relational patterns that preoccupy them to a degree at which they are no longer open to new encounters with the possibility of new outcomes. Indeed, to the degree that digital networks wrap users into social environments of sameness from which others appear as far removed and almost unintelligibly strange, they seem to create a general ambience of 'negative transference'.

In what follows, we unpack these dynamics of negative transference. First, we take a brief walk through some central psychoanalytic ideas of otherness, which then offer us a diving board into psychoanalytic theories of authoritarianism, xenophobia, racism, antisemitism and other forms of extremism, ethnocentrism and racial hatred, and from there we will then gradually return to the digital.

Psychoanalysis and otherness

Myself against my brother
My brother and I against the family
Our family against the clan
All of us against the foreigner

Jim Hopkins (2018), in an article that brings together neuroscientific, Darwinian and psychoanalytic perspectives on political violence, uses the above proverb in a discussion of what he sees as a universal, anthropological mechanism of 'in-group cooperation for out-group competition and conflict' (Hopkins, 2018, p. 220). He writes: '[W]e continually form and re-form communicating and cooperating *in-groups*, which compete with comparable *out-groups*, in hierarchies of ascending complexity' (ibid.). The wisdom of the proverb and Hopkins's observation is that the members of the out-group can turn into members of the in-group any time that 'another other' appears on the horizon. That means that *how* someone becomes either a collaborator or a competitor of someone else might not at all depend on any particular, inherent qualities of these others; rather, group constellations are often merely dependent on context and relatively accidental positionings. However, the problem that Hopkins sees at the centre of in- and out-group dynamics is that, for people to cooperate, they require an out-group that they can co-operate against. This has already been observed by Simone de Beauvoir, who states that: 'Otherness is a fundamental category of human thought. Thus it is that no group ever sets itself up as One without at once setting up the Other against itself' (Beauvoir, 1974, p. xvi). And as Hopkins explains further: 'For insofar as we cooperate in groups only to compete in groups, we cannot cooperate as a single group, however important the shared interests that might impel us to do so. [...] Attempts at species-wide cooperation thus constantly regress to forms of *all of us against the foreigner*' (Hopkins, 2018, p. 221, italics in original).

We have reservations against Hopkins's grounding of Darwinian observations and psychoanalytic theorizing in neurological 'proof' as well as its ahistorical universalism. However, even the most sceptical political scientist will have to admit that Hopkins's conception of the human 'compulsion of othering' can be encountered everywhere and anywhere at the current historical juncture. Russia waging war on the

Ukraine reignites the Cold War standoff between Russia and the West, which had held the latter half of the twentieth century in thrall; Polish populism cultivates a hatred of Germany; German and other western populisms have cultivated a general hatred of Muslims and refugees from all kinds of backgrounds; Chinese authoritarianism scapegoats the Uighurs; Myanmar attempted a genocide against Rohingya Muslims, and the list goes on and on and on. The Brexit vote in the UK, the election of Donald Trump as US president in 2016, the increase of right-wing and authoritarian populisms in India, the Philippines, Brazil and France, among others, have rightly been discussed in terms of division and polarization. People are bitterly divided and opposed to each other.

Already in *Civilisation and its Discontents*, Freud (1930) commented upon what he called the 'narcissism of minor differences': 'It is always possible to bind together a considerable number of people in love, so long as there are other people left over to receive the manifestations of their aggressiveness' (Freud, 1930, p. 114). If anything, this psychosocial truth of the social glue of the scapegoat – be it constitutive of human nature or a historical effect of specific recurring arrangements – points to a deep-seated, existential need of an other, who confronts us with ourselves and gives us an idea of who we are by setting borders and limits for us by their sheer presence. At the same time, it also points to the extreme ambivalence that this other provokes and the difficulty of tolerating and enduring such an other and their mere otherness and independence from us. Even before infants have a conception of themselves and of the circumstance that there is more than *one* (m)other, this difficulty to tolerate the other's otherness prompts us to divide this other up into two: one we can identify as exclusively bad, cruel and mean, and one who we are thus free to love more easily.

Even though it may be at times difficult for us to consistently, enduringly and unconditionally love others, we need them (and the plural is important here because we need more than one; Bruner, 1998) in order for us to become fully fledged social beings. Taking this existential importance of the other(s) into account, the question that is perhaps most relevant to an understanding of politics is how aggression towards others comes about. In this respect, Stephen Mitchell (1998) has developed a theory that co-ordinates the two major psychoanalytic approaches to aggression that have been at loggerheads with each other. On the one hand, the position derived from Freudian drive theory assumes aggression to be a biologically inherent and inborn human proclivity. On the other hand, the alternative view understands aggression as the response to frustration. Mitchell proposes to harmonize these positions by conceiving aggression as 'biologically mediated and prewired' but nevertheless as always functioning 'within a relational context' (1998, p. 25). From this position, then, even the biological dimension of aggression must be perceived not as a 'push from within, but as a response to others' (ibid.). Hence, aggression arises in the relation between infant and caregiver and specifically in those scenes in which the infant subjectively experiences 'endangerment and being treated cruelly, without an assumption of actual and/or intentional mistreatment (although many children are actually and/or intentionally mistreated)' (ibid., p. 27). In this rendering, aggression is always perceived as an inevitable, defensive reaction against what one subjectively experiences as a threat. This conception gestures not only towards the inherent politics of human aggression – indeed, each human being's first experiences entail being subjected not only to loving care, but also to the inevitable shortcomings of this care administered by more powerful others. Rather, this conception of aggression as defence also gives us an idea of the ways – often riddled with contradictions and dialectical switches – in which humans tend to bring these inner politics to bear on others.

As many psychoanalytic studies of extremism, racism, antisemitism and other 'isms' emphasize – and as we have pointed out at several points in this book – there is no other in our social environment who stands outside our psychic reality. Therefore, each new encounter with people holds a challenge to the borders that we have erected in earlier parts of our lives. Every person we encounter is thus being drawn into the fantasy scapes that are tied to our porous boundaries and make up our experience of reality. With regard to Mitchell's view of aggression, particularly the mechanism of *projection*, in which I 'project' unconsciously held feelings – and particularly negative ones – onto others, becomes central. After all, what I might unconsciously feel the need to defend against in others might be my own former experiences of existential threat.

Although we have so far discussed inherently human characteristics that situate in-group/out-group phenomena and aggression as part of 'human nature', we need to be careful to differentiate such phenomena from instances of racism, fascism or antisemitism. Those forms of extremism present particularly extreme forms of exclusion of and competition with the other that might be considered as inherently human; they build on the latter, but cultivate them further. We, therefore, unpack the specificity of the violence of racism, fascism, antisemitism, Islamophobia or the violence against Asians that has occurred as a result of Covid-19 as types of extremism in the next section. In-group/out-group behaviour and human aggression are the starting points, or backdrop, for forms of racism, homophobia or misogyny. We also wish to stress that the phenomena we write about in this chapter, and indeed in the whole book, are *psychosocial*: they are enmeshed in our subjectivities and appear to us as 'naturally given', but are driven by specific socio-historical events, contexts and dynamics. Indeed, the capitalist economy and modern forms of colonialism are largely dependent on the existence of racism, sexism, misogyny and other forms of prejudice.

Psychoanalytic studies of extremism, racism and antisemitism

Murial Dimen (1998), in a critical review of the connections and disconnections between psychoanalysis and feminism, comments poignantly that, 'in a failure of nerve', Freud's comparison of female sexuality in *The Question of Lay Analysis* with 'a dark continent' (Freud, 1926, p. 212) buries 'in femininity the underproblematized racism of psychoanalysis' (Dimen, 1998, p. 207). And indeed, the psychoanalytic practice of drawing on ethnographic studies of so-called 'primitive' cultures in order to shed light on the regressive states of the modern mind cannot but be seen as problematic today as it carries racialized and colonialist undertones. Yet, as Khanna (2003) has shown, whereas Freud's language was influenced by colonialist ideas, this does not automatically mean that he was a colonialist; rather, those ideas were part and parcel of a much wider zeitgeist. And yet, it must be said that, to this day, psychoanalysis more often than not functions 'as a writing of the ethnicity of the white western psyche', as Claudia Tate (1996, p. 58) has put it (see also Stoute, 2017). Indeed, clinical psychoanalysis is still riddled with a lack of diversity, and questions of race and racism in the consulting room and in training institutes keep coming to the surface at regular intervals (Kovel, 1984; Tate, 1996; Brickman, 2003; Altman, 2009; Snider, 2020). At the same time, its theoretical positions have consistently created openings for liberatory politics, as Eli Zaretsky has argued (1976,

2015b, 2017). Daniel José Gaztambide has recently made similar points in *A People's History of Psychoanalysis* (2019).

Critical theory in the wake of national socialism

As concerns psychoanalytically oriented studies of extremism, the political histories of the countries from which this research hails are important indicators for their orientation and direction. In Germany, it was the experience of Nazism, antisemitism and the Holocaust during the era of 'National-Socialism' from 1933 to 1945 that set the stage for much of the research on extremism that has often focused on questions of authoritarianism. Already in the 1920s, the Frankfurt-based Institute for Social Research – what is now known as the Frankfurt School – integrated psychoanalytic perspectives into its critical inquiries. From the 1930s, research conducted by Erich Fromm, Theodor W. Adorno, Max Horkheimer, Herbert Marcuse and Leo Löwenthal ranged from 'workers and employees just before the Third Reich to the studies on authority and the family published in 1936, to the unpublished research on antisemitism in the American workforce (1944/1945) up to the five volumes of the *Studies in Prejudice* published in 1949/1950' (King & Schmid Noerr, 2020, p. 747). Although these studies still offer productive perspectives for the study of authoritarianism today, and particularly Erich Fromm's writings have experienced a renaissance recently (McLaughlin, 2019), the most noteworthy work from this era is that on the *Authoritarian Personality* by Adorno, Else Frenkel-Brunswik, Daniel Levinson and R. Nevitt Sanford (1950). As the critical theorists Vera King and Gunzelin Schmid Noerr (2020) sum up this study, the 'authoritarian personality primarily showed the characteristics of conventionalism, subordination and aggression toward outsiders', as well as a super-ego formation based on the 'dominance towards those below and compliance towards those above', combined with the 'construction of images of enemies, and contempt and hatred towards weaker people' (2020, pp. 748–9). Even though this study, and particularly its construction of the 'Fascism-Scale', or 'F-Scale', which formalized the detection of latent character structures in people's expressed moral attitudes, were heavily criticized in the decades after the study's release, its findings have weathered this critique well (King & Schmid Noerr, 2020).

Colonialism and its others

Turning to English-speaking research into extremism, it is again the attempt to confront the shameful parts of national history that gives studies of extremism their direction. In the United Kingdom and its former colonies, it has been Britain's colonial past and the migration of people from the former colonies to Britain after the Second World War, whereas in the USA it is the country's history of slavery and its aftermaths. Cultural studies, postcolonial and critical race theorists have widely drawn on psychoanalysis – for example, Frantz Fanon (1967), Stuart Hall (1993), Homi K. Bhabha (1994), Edward Said (1978) and others (see Dalal, 2001; Cohen, 2002; Khanna, 2003; Riggs, 2005; Greedharry, 2008; Hook, 2008, for overviews). Crucial for postcolonial studies is the interrogation of the 'colonizer and colonized' relationship and how it relates to dynamics of 'othering'.

The feminist scholar Gayatri Chakravorty Spivak (1985) has been key in developing the notion of 'othering'. She argues that othering works as a practice of subordination where the other is made aware of who holds the power and begins to see themselves as othered and other. This process can be described as the internalization of inferiority, or as a sense of existence that is only upheld in relation to the (white) subject who is doing the othering. Such dynamics are vividly described by Audre Lorde in the following encounter:

> The AA subway train to Harlem. I clutch my mother's sleeve, her arms full of shopping bags, christmas-heavy. The wet smell of winter clothes, the train's lurching. My mother spots an almost seat, pushes my little snowsuited body down. On one side of me a man reading a paper. On the other, a woman in a fur hat staring at me. Her mouth twitches as she stares and then her gaze drops down, pulling mine with it. Her leather-gloved hand plucks at the line where my new blue snow pants and her sleek fur coat meet. She jerks her coat close to her. I look. I do not see whatever terrible thing she is seeing on the seat between us – probably a roach. But she has communicated her horror to me. It must be something very bad from the way she's looking, so I pull my snowsuit closer to me away from it, too. When I look up the woman is still staring at me, her nose holes and eyes huge. And suddenly I realize there

is nothing crawling up the seat between us; it is me she doesn't want her coat to touch. (Lorde, 1984a, pp. 147–8)

As Lorde states, nothing is spoken in the above encounter, but she becomes acutely aware of how she is perceived as an alien by the white woman, as a 'dirty' other who has come to invade the white woman's space (Puwar, 2004). The activist, clinician and postcolonial thinker Frantz Fanon similarly writes about this form of hyper-perception of the self through the eyes of the white person that he has internalized:

I cannot go to a film without seeing myself. I wait for me. In the interval, just before the film starts, I wait for me. The people in the theater are watching me, examining me, waiting for me. A Negro groom is going to appear. My heart makes my head swim. (Fanon, 1967, p. 107)

One key dimension of Fanon's work is the effects of colonization on the psyche of the colonized. Fanon has been immensely influential, both academically and practically, for activists and liberation struggles across the world. A clinically trained psychiatrist from Martinique, Fanon drew on and developed psychoanalysis both in his practice and in his writing. Building on the French philosopher Jean-Paul Sartre's work on antisemitism (1946), he stressed that anti-black racism and the colonial logic of Manichaeism – a belief in a stark dualism between lightness/goodness and darkness/evil – was particularly strong in its capacities for othering because it could be anchored in the body of the black subject and their skin colour, a colour that could not merely be represented as 'the absence of values, but also the negation of values' (Fanon, 2004 [1963], p. 6). This alienates the black subject from their own body. They are split off from themselves through the colonizer and internalize this split, as Fanon discusses through the use of the French language in France's former colonies.

Fanon argued that there is no Oedipus complex for the colonized subject, but that they are instead forced to choose between family and colonized society. The source of suffering and psychic pain is brought about by the forced internalization of a white unconscious. This means that the subject 'continues to experience family authority and societal authority as conflictual' (Hiddleston, 2014, p. 31). The black subject, for Fanon, is dependent on the white colonizer and, alienated from themselves, can only exist as an other who constantly compares themselves to them (see also Bhabha, 1994, for key discussions of Fanon). Fanon calls this '*black skin, white masks*' – the title of his most famous book (1967).

Race between lack and jouissance: *Lacanian perspectives*

Lacanian scholars have discussed racism in relation to fantasies of superiority and inferiority. The American Lacanian scholar Sheldon George (2014), for example, sees racial identities to be constituted through the Lacanian notion of lack, defining race 'as a tool for masking the central lack of subjectivity' (2014, p. 360). Along these lines, the notion of race figures as a mechanism through which one's existential alienation from one's own being is covered over. Fantasies of race ground people in containing narratives of who they are in relation to 'their' people, and they allow them to construct an identity related to other categories such as gender, sexual orientation, etc. These fantasies often circulate widely and become varied and adapted to new contexts, but their relational core remains stable. As the examples by Lorde and Fanon have shown, it is all the more painful if such fantasies are brutally undone by racists.

In a Lacanian paradigm, then, racism figures as a discursive, but also affective and sensual, way to achieve *jouissance* – that is, the experience of painful pleasure or pleasurable plain (Lacan, 1988) on the part of the racist, whose *ideal ego* is propped up by the fantasmatic construction of an *ego ideal* that makes sure it is superior to the 'smelly', 'ugly looking', 'dangerous' other, whose very abjectness deserves to be abjected. 'At the heart of this mode of jouissance is the oppression of black others whose supposed inferiority secures for white Americans a notion of superiority and greater being,' writes George (2014, p. 360) about anti-black racism in the US.

Related to this gain of racism – that is, the calming, strengthening and empowering effect of the fantasy of an inferior other – is the more troubling, disquieting idea of having one's enjoyment stolen by an undeserving other. Slavoj Žižek (e.g. 1994), Jacques-Alain Miller (1994), Sheldon George (2014), Derek Hook (2020) and Jason Glynos with colleagues all find in their research into right-wing populism and racism that people hold potent fantasies of a *theft of enjoyment*, the belief that others – foreigners, or people with non-heterosexual orientations, etc. – are able to enjoy a far better life than those who, for various reasons, hold a more righteous claim to this life (Chang & Glynos, 2011; Glynos & Mondon, 2016).

More recently, Derek Hook (2018) has critically discussed this idea of the theft of enjoyment and his points can be connected to our discussion of Hopkins's and Mitchell's work earlier. Indeed, Hook offers a whole list of points, arguing that the hypothesis is:

> (1) guilty of a depoliticizing psychological reductionism; (2) conceptually under-differentiated and overly inclusive in its field of reference; (3) inattentive to different modes of enjoyment; and (4) conceptually decontextualized, cut off from the associated psychoanalytic concepts that necessarily accompany its proper application. (Hook, 2018, p. 244)

Nevertheless, he maintains that the notion is useful if understood properly and conceptually developed (see also George & Hook, 2021), arguing that it is particularly the 'emptiness' of the concept that remains an asset, 'precisely because of the malleability of what different (groups of) people "get off" on' (Hook, 2018, p. 262). Scholarship that draws on *jouissance* in relation to different forms of prejudice and discrimination should 'investigate how they might appear in highly distinctive fields of analysis, rather than summarily generalize across empirical contexts' (ibid., p. 263). Instead of conceiving of enjoyment as a merely subjective or ahistorical category, it 'is, indeed, located within very specific symbolic and historical co-ordinates given that it emerges alongside – or as the apparent underside of – social norms, moral values, and symbolic ideals' (ibid., p. 261). This makes it a psychosocial concept that is always situated between the Symbolic and subjective; a concept that is 'always mediated by fantasy; invariably linked to profound anxieties of what might be *taken away from us*' (ibid., p. 259, italics in original).

Antisemitism: needing and destroying the other

Hook's emphasis on a mediation by fantasy (which is itself shaped by social beliefs, the media and subjective experience) can be unpacked further with Slavoj Žižek's (e.g. 1994) and particularly Stephen Frosh's discussions of antisemitism (Frosh, 2005, 2011, 2016). Above all, Žižek was one of the first to argue that the idea of the theft of enjoyment is a fantasy that bears no grounding in reality in that sense. This fantasy structure makes it a particularly strong concept for the analysis of extremism. It is a fantasy that operates through a double layer of affirmation and rejection. As Žižek explains, 'This paradox [...] has already emerged apropos the Jews in Nazi Germany': 'the more they [the Jews] were ruthlessly exterminated, the more horrifying were the dimensions acquired by those who remained' (Žižek, 1994, p. 78).

Frosh has expanded on this argument in his writings on antisemitism, suggesting that:

> the Jew is a figure chosen initially for its cultural congruence as a hate object, but is then excessively invested in as a carrier of all this otherness; conspiracy is to be found everywhere. This produces a spiralling of paranoia and hatred, as the Jew serves both to contain and to exaggerate the projected impulses of the anti-Semite. Psychosis is in the air, kept at bay only by endlessly increasing rigidity and escalating anti-Semitic hate. The Jew is a safety valve for destructive impulses, but this use of the Jew has a profound personal and social cost. (Frosh, 2016, p. 35)

The Jew as the 'safety valve', as Frosh calls it, at once destabilizes and orders the antisemite's psyche. The 'anti-Semite lives in terror of the persecutory universe she or he has created, but the benefit is that at least this universe makes sense, and nominates one single, identifiable source of danger – the Jew' (Frosh, 2016, p. 35). In the above accounts, forms of extremism are thus not (only) about the radical annihilation of the other but also about the need to maintain the other as a constant object of fantasy.

Paranoid–schizoid and absolute states of mind: Kleinian perspectives

Frosh's image of the 'spiralling of paranoia' which is kept at bay 'only by endlessly increasing rigidity' (2016, p. 35) has been anticipated by another psychoanalytic thinker, the object-relational scholar Karl Figlio. In his seminal article 'The Absolute State of Mind' (2006), Figlio works out the thanatotic alignment of destructive and self-destructive tendencies in extremism in impressive detail. What Figlio's theory of 'absolute states of mind' (2006) adds to our picture is the importance of the ego ideal in combination with a constant drive to eject and expel the other within oneself. Figlio explains this combination of idealism, aggression and auto-aggression by drawing on Melanie Klein's theory of 'depressive anxiety' and the 'paranoid–schizoid position' (Figlio, 2006, p. 9; Klein, 1935).

For Klein, the paranoid–schizoid position is a primitive mental set-up that people use unconsciously to defend against existential, traumatic feelings of threat. Since infants in the first months of their lives are entirely at the mercy of others and since important brain structures are not yet laid down, the infant's experiences fall into extremes of good and bad: for example, of being fed (good) or not fed (bad), of being held (good) or ignored (bad), of being cared for (good) or neglected (bad). The kind of reasoning, or proto-thinking, that Klein saw as arising from these foundational, primitive experiences was one of an absolute division – or 'splitting', as she called it (1946) – into a good (kind, caring, loving) object and a bad (careless, hateful, cruel) one. In Klein's fascinatingly archaic language, the first objects of human beings are thus the 'good breast' and the 'bad breast', with the infant not realizing that these diametrical opposites belong to one and the same actual object, the primary caregiver. In this respect, the paramount job of each maturing human being is to bring these two extremes together and learn to tolerate and handle ambivalence (i.e. the parallel existence of love and hate in relation to one and the same object), not only as refers to the caregiver as object, but, just as importantly, as refers to oneself as the bearer of such feelings and attributes.

In what Figlio calls 'absolute states of mind', people fail to tolerate ambivalence, neither towards themselves nor towards others, and regress to a defence against it that splits the object world in half. Importantly, however, this process ultimately empties out and drains the subject and its relational capacities themselves. 'Since there is no state of complete goodness, there is always a compulsive drive for an unattainable completion,' Figlio (2006, p. 11) writes, and the more people strive to be only good or strive to obtain their fantasy of an ideal ego by attacking what they perceive as bad, the more they damage this goodness, too, in a vicious circle of aggression that is always also a displaced auto-aggression.

Race and extremism online

Racist echo chambers and barbarous others

Having presented key psychoanalytic approaches to extremism, we can now turn to applying some of them in relation to the internet in two case studies. Steffen, together with Figlio and the political psychologist Barry Richards, have combined Kleinian, object-relational perspectives with those derived from the Frankfurt School tradition in a volume on *Fomenting Political Violence – Fantasy, Language, Media, Action* (Krüger *et al.*, 2018). Steffen's study from the collection (Krüger, 2018a) analyses ethno-chauvinist Facebook pages set up to protest and reject the establishment of asylum-seeker homes in towns and areas in Germany with the psychoanalytically informed method of 'in-depth hermeneutics' (Lorenzer, 2022 [1986]). These pages emerged in the hundreds in the wake of the influx of refugees and asylum seekers fleeing the war in Syria and neighbouring countries in 2015.

Analysing the posts and comments from a selection of those pages, Steffen shows how processes of othering and projection, as well as dynamics of ordering and destabilizing, enjoying and stealing enjoyment, unfold online; at the same time, his study speaks to questions of homophily and polarization. What the Facebook pages perform can be summed up in no more than two interrelated 'forms of interaction' (Lorenzer, 2022 [1986]) which combine to construct a coherent sense of reality and identity for the users. First, the pages accumulate and repost individual local news reports about often minor crimes perpetrated by refugees across Germany so as to condense these individual crimes into a general, overall and overpowering reality that the sheer number of reports proves to be completely in the thrall of stealing, brawling, sexually assaulting and raping refugees.

Second, the anti-asylum pages then continuously comment upon their constructed reality with a barrage of plaintive posts that describe the lives of the 'indigenous' German people in this reality as an immense and continuous suffering. It is this theme of suffering that presents itself as a variation of Lacanian *jouissance* and the fantasy of stolen enjoyment. After all, the willed construction of a reality that then causes immense suffering points to an aspect of masochism and taking pleasure in suffering as a main ingredient. What thus comes to the fore in the stream of suffering on Facebook is a partition of the scapegoat function that is characteristic of right-wing populism. On the anti-asylum pages, the then-German government became identified with the 'elite', who fail to protect its people from the assault of the refugee out-group. Although, time and again, the refugees are shown as a mindless, instinct-driven 'force of nature', befalling Germany like a plague, the government is depicted as cruel sadists, who look on with cold pleasure, so the fantasy goes, while the German people are eaten alive by the barbarous hordes (Krüger, 2017a).

Specifically then-chancellor Angela Merkel is imagined as abusing the maternal role attributed to her by pushing away 'her own people' so that she can care for undeserving others. In this way, child-like wishes of being looked after, which Ferdinand Sutterlüty (2021) sees as a general phenomenon in authoritarian movements, and fears of being wiped out and forgotten blend with a viable enjoyment of this state of things – not least because it brings the possibilities of the barbarism and sadism launched upon oneself in one's own possession. In line with Mitchell's (1998) theory of aggression, this suffering is enjoyable because it suggests a response in kind and a turning of oneself into part of an equivalent horde. Put crudely: the suffering is pleasurable because it serves as foreplay for making others suffer in return.

In these dynamics, there also shows something – if only in exemplary form – of the ways in which the mechanisms of othering and projection are allowed to unfold in the homophilic climate of digital networks. In Germany at least, where established news media can still generate relatively solid levels of trust among citizens, even Facebook pages that cater to radicalized users do not find it possible to serve these users' constructions of a completely illusory reality. Rather, their brand of 'fake news' is based on the credibility of established, major news sources. Time and again, the pages point to the news from these outlets as *true* but *not taken seriously*, trying to awaken people to the violent realities right in front of their eyes. This is a key insight – that is, that those Facebook pages do not so much circulate fake news but actual news that is deliberately misread or misconstrued. The strategic effect of the anti-asylum pages is the identification with the victims of attacks by refugees, but only so as to bring equal suffering onto the presumed aggressors.

Harking back to what we have presented from Chun's (2018) work on homophily, the effect of the digital network that emerges from Steffen's research is not so much that conflict does not occur; rather, each conflict is kept to smother in the echo chambers that are specifically interested in it. Sardonically put, the anti-asylum pages offer a neighbourhood for people interested in suffering from refugees, and the circumstance that the page users can easily steer clear of information not meeting this purpose helps significantly in keeping the neighbourhood intact. The creators of the anti-asylum pages are thus able to exploit the network's orientation towards the fostering of ever more friction-free connections by recontextualizing a constant supply of distinctly remote others so as to order and stabilize one's own world according to one's own mental needs.

And yet, since all kinds of information are so readily available online, once one starts looking, it takes a sizable effort not to be swayed by divergent information, not to be shaken by the myriad voices that tell a story different from the one oneself adheres to. Axel Bruns (2019) gestures in this respect towards the renewed relevance of 'media psychology', writing that 'the question is no longer what material these hyperpartisans encounter and how much that information diet is shaped by algorithms, but rather how they receive and process this content and incorporate it into their worldviews' (2019, p. 118). In our opinion, this question of the psychology of information processing leads us once more to the fetishistic structures of desire that are threaded through late-capitalist societies (see also Phillips & Milner, 2021, pp. 52–63). Some extremists at least also *know* that their beliefs of belonging to a superior race and of barbarous others enjoying privileges that are not rightfully theirs are not fully borne out by reality. At the same time they 'know' these things to be fundamentally true. In this way, extremists, too, need to constantly turn a blind eye to openly available information so as to maintain the echo chambers they have created through wilful acts of the reversal of truths. But since this 'other knowledge' constantly looms right underneath the surface of hard-gained securities, they tend to defend and insist upon the latter with an urgency and vehemence which, referring back to Karl Figlio (2006), we can describe as 'absolute'.

Racemojis and the question of identity

Our second case study concerns more progressive but nevertheless troubling phenomena: the ethnic diversification of emojis. Advocates of liberal notions of 'multiculturalism' and 'diversity' may argue that many parts of the world are now characterized by 'hybrid' identities, fusions of different ethnicities and cultures that come together at a time of globalization and cultural convergence. Yet, as many postcolonial and critical race theorists have argued, such notions often serve to protect and maintain the status quo of the majority rather than de facto include minorities in a society (e.g. Ahmed, 2012; Vertovec, 2013; Warikoo, 2016). One digital artefact that can be understood as an example of such seemingly progressive developments is the emoji, which recently has become racially diversified, seeking to represent different ethnicities. For example, it is now possible to choose from five 'thumbs up' emojis with different skin tones. On the one hand, this may be seen as a welcome step towards the presentation of diversity; on the other, however, this has also led to complex questions that hark back to Fanon's and Lorde's discussions of the internalization and hyper-perception of one's own race.

The early internet, which we discussed in Chapter 2, was often seen as utopian, playful and creative. One could test out other identities online, other genders, sexualities, even ethnicities or flat out adopt an animal as avatar. Yet, this promise of becoming someone – or something – else was flawed from the beginning; people can never completely disconnect their actual identities from their virtual ones (Nakamura, 2002, 2007). For many years, emojis were shown as having a yellow skin colour. Yellow could be associated with neutrality or of moving beyond race. We could also regard the apparently 'neutral' yellow emoji as a way of avoiding race. Yet, we need to be mindful that the term 'yellow' is often used disparagingly to refer to people of Asian heritage, although it is also being used as a self-descriptor (Chow, 2018; Fang & Liu, 2021). The yellow, default emoji is often linked to the show *The Simpsons*; its origins may also be traced back to the smiley face, which has been shown as yellow since the 1960s. Yet, the yellow characters on *The Simpsons* are not of a new kind of race; they are essentially depicted as white. The yellow emoji could thus be seen as implicitly modelled on whiteness.

Many postcolonial and critical race theorists have argued that one of the characteristics of whiteness is that it tends to remain invisible for white people (e.g. George, 2014). Rather, it has been non-white subjects, whether they live in a predominantly white society or not, who are constantly reminded of their race and are forced to account for their racialized subjectivity in some form. As a popular discussion piece has recently argued, the introduction not only of browner and darker 'thumbs-ups' but also of lighter, whiter versions, which one can now choose as alternatives to the cartoonish, *Simpsons*-like yellow standard one, makes white people also 'confront their race as people of color often have to do' (Marquez Janse *et al.*, 2022, online). In this way, the diversified thumbs up emoji might absolutely be a way of bringing race into online communication for everyone, including white people. At the same time, this diversification seems to have opened another Pandora's box in terms of symbolic identity politics. And while some white people fear that choosing the white 'thumbs up' might come close to the proclamation of 'white pride' (McGill, 2016, online), far-right and racist users regularly use white emojis to signal just that. By the same token, non-white emojis are often 'being used to make racist comments on social media and insert questions of race in texts and tweets where it may never have arisen before' (Tutt, 2015, online).

In the easily polluted online environments of social media, the question of whether to use a racialized emoji or not often becomes a critical one for people of colour. As an engineer tells McGill (2016):

> Every time I use an emoji, I have to make a choice: Do I use a colored racemoji, and draw attention to my ethnicity (even when it's not pertinent), or do I use a default emoji, which may misrepresent me altogether? [...] It's disempowering because people of color are uniquely burdened with this choice. (2016, online)

The diversified emojis may thus paradoxically further contribute to 'feeling being out of place' (Fang, 2020) in any society structured by white privilege.

The manosphere and the politics of sullied ideals

Online misogyny, which is rife on the internet today, is another case that is intricately intertwined with tacit privileges of certain groups of people – not so much with the privilege of being white, as was relevant in the previous case, but of being a (white) *male*. It is no coincidence that we have both chosen to focus on men for our works on politics in the digital age – with Jacob covering large parts of the so-called 'manosphere' (Johanssen, 2022) and Steffen taking a deep dive into male online subcultures (Krüger, 2019a, 2019b, 2021a, 2021b). These male-dominated, male-defined internet spheres, we hold, have not only come about as effects of digital culture, but have been triggered by current socio-economic shifts that have strongly gendered effects. Hence, men in particular have proven vulnerable to suffering from the recent pushes of modernization.

When discussing the psychology of digital work in the previous chapter, we showed that this usually implies a contemporary ideal of a tireless, relentlessly industrious and omnipotent individual. This heroic genre of self-presentation has found extremely fertile ground on social networking sites, which have quickly advanced to central hubs for such demonstrations of attractivity and employability. These idealized displays of perfection are only one, if but a very visible, aspect in a much more widespread culture of (self-)perfection. In this respect, as argued in Chapter 2, what is often condemned as self-aggrandizing displays of narcissism in social media might be more empathetically interpreted as unconscious articulations of an anxious need for social recognition and for a positive answer to the question 'Am I good enough like this?'.

We agree with Nancy Fraser and Axel Honneth (2003), who already two decades ago argued that questions of recognition had become just as important for a critical notion of social justice as those regarding the redistribution of wealth and material means. In a study on new forms of authoritarianism, the German sociologists Oliver Nachtwey and Mauritz Heumann (2019) observe that these authoritarianisms are at least partly a result of *anomies* that, coming about in pushes of modernization, impact different parts of populations in different ways. Anomy here means 'the imbalance "between the relative levels of aspiration of societal subgroups and the regulations of admission that are fitted to them, as well as the implementation possibilities of various societal areas of activity"' (Nachtwey & Heumann, 2019, p. 4, quoting Bohle *et al.*, 1997, p. 57, our translation). Simply put, a main driver of new forms of authoritarianism is the experience, widespread among societal subgroups, of having one's career ambitions and wishes of self-realization frustrated because one no longer 'has what it takes' to be wanted in a fast-moving job market.

When the threatening insight of self-failure dawns in a neoliberal climate of self-responsibility, there is a plausible risk that people respond aggressively and regressively to their predicament. Hence, in a recent review article on the notion of 'regression', Vera King (2021) brings the above observations in touch with digital media again, arguing that, especially for those who already feel excluded, 'the increasing self-constraint, accompanied by competitive pressure and imperatives of optimisation' can easily switch into its regressive opposite, namely 'a tendency to orient oneself toward fabricated alternative realities' (King, 2021, p. 99). Such regressive tendencies are most readily available online. In our works on men online (Krüger, 2019a, 2019b, 2021a, 2021b; Johanssen, 2022), we have each found the drives toward self-constraint, perfection and purification, as well as their switch phenomena of regression, ressentiment, rage and revenge, in the relational styles cultivated in the relatively closed-off debate forums and channels. What comes to the fore in our efforts is that a significant number of men from these cultures are painfully aware of their subordinate status, or at least of the danger of becoming subordinate and subsequently of the risk of exclusion from either professional or social fields, or both. Therefore, turning to misogyny and a hatred of women must once more be seen as a defence, in this case against the men's own abject otherness and a fear of being a failure.

Societal reasons for these dynamics of displacement, projection and othering are manifold. For one, the gradual but paradigmatic shift from industrial production to information management and 'communicative capitalism' (Dean, 2010) has led to an increased demand for social skills and character traits in workforces that have traditionally been connoted as female: approachability, openness, warmth, friendliness, care. New online professions, first and foremost that of the influencer, which use displays of self-perfection to advertise goods and services to their followers, are also accessible to women to a larger extent. What Sarah Banet-Weiser writes about feminism, specifically that it is 'framed, by media and society alike, as a set of risks' (2018, p. 3), threatening work culture as well as conventional definitions of masculinity and heteronormative femininity, also holds true for people with various gender identities, who protest their rights for recognition in the face of a reactionary backlash driven by a redistribution of wealth from poor to rich and the dismantling of social welfare institutions.

Alternatively, those traditionally male-connoted qualities which are frequently sought after in the information and communication sector, such as maths and programming skills, are stereotypically regarded as coming packaged with otherwise few appealing qualities. The male social roles of 'geeks' and 'computer nerds' are 'stereotypically cast as intellectual overachievers and social underachievers' (Bucholtz, 2001, p. 85). As the masculinity scholars Ran Almog and Danny Kaplan (2017) write, 'nerd masculinity reflects an ambivalent social location: it is privileged on the one hand but greeted with derision on the other, and it benefits from the economic advantages of hegemonic masculinity but [is] marked also by otherness and subordination' (p. 30). In this respect, what appears tragic to us about male computer cultures is that the men inhabiting them are actually living a version of masculinity that does *not* conform to traditional gender stereotypes – that is, they are far from the cliché of a 'real man'. Tragically, however, they hold up these stereotypical chauvinistic attributes as ideals even though they are painfully aware that they will never reach them. In this way, the anomic experience of standing in front of the 'locked gates' of the labour market (Honneth, 2010; see our Chapter 3) becomes displaced, or reproduced, in the field of sexual relations, where nerds and geeks frequently play the role of quasi-immature onlookers trying to get glimpses into a world of grown-ups.

In this respect, Steffen (Krüger, 2021a) has drawn on André Green's (2002) concept of 'negative narcissism' in his analysis of male subcultures, and particularly so-called 'incel' groups (i.e. men who define themselves as 'involuntary celibate' and in a self-contradictory move of appropriation celebrate this stigma and take it as a badge of honour). Although, as stated above, the grandiose narcissistic self-stagings on social media can frequently be interpreted as defences against existential fears of not fitting in, or of not being worthy of attention, negative narcissism inverses this logic by presenting oneself as utterly unacceptable, misfitting and abject. Green describes negative or 'death narcissism', as he calls it, as 'a culture of void, emptiness, self-contempt, destructive withdrawal, and permanent self-depreciation with a predominant masochistic quality: tears, tears, tears' (2002, p. 645). This death narcissism creates a place for those who feel rejected and worthless, or 'sullied', to use Figlio's word (2006, p. 11). Yet, even if this place is imagined as at the very bottom of the social hierarchy, it is a place nevertheless and as such serves as an – albeit negative – 'holding environment' (Winnicott, 1960). Hence, whereas the anxious, positive narcissism of commercial social media aims at binding as many other users to one's demonstrations of radical independence, omnipotence and perfection, the negative narcissism of many subgroups of the manosphere aims at cutting such ties in what Green describes as 'the search for ground zero' (1999, p. 110).

This severing of ties is frequently attempted through harsh performances of self-deprecation. Figlio (2006), by drawing on the French psychoanalysts Béla Grunberger (1989) and Janine Chasseguet-Smirgel (1985), describes the extremist's experience of themselves and the world as gradually approximating a 'faecalized universe, literally a world in which everything is turned upside down, and shit is idealized as a perversion of the genital world of the father and the mother' (Figlio, 2006, p. 10). This can indeed be taken as descriptive of many of the channels and discussion forums online where male subcultures interact. These are places for those who know that their ego ideals are sullied and where they reproduce their 'faecalized universe' in ever new variations on what Green (1993) has called 'primary anality' – a position that fantasizes itself as excluded from all phallic aspects of sexuality but at the same time also rejects all oral forms of compensatory satisfaction. As Steffen has shown, on 4chan discussion boards, anonymous users refer to themselves and each other as 'shitlords' and to the 4chan platform itself as 'the asshole of the internet' (Urban Dictionary, 2008) in a playfully ironic way so as to reject normal people and keep them out of their proudly negative realms (Coleman, 2014; Krüger, 2021b). This same identification with shit and faeces, however, takes a significant turn to the more sombre and suicidal in forums that are more specifically oriented towards incel culture, where the carnivalesque topos of the 'world upside-down' and the inversion of morals and norms are regressing further to a baser level of maladaptedness and nihilism.

Not all groupings of the online manosphere subscribe to this nihilism, however. The 'Men Going Their Own Way' movement, for example, combines an aggressive turning away from relationships with a hatred of women and with a masculinity that is just as aggressively identified with traditional notions of male machismo. In order to make sense of such variations, Jacob (Johanssen, 2022) uses the portemanteau 'dis/inhibition' as an umbrella term for an understanding of the breadth of misogynistic rituals. What many men interacting in the highly anonymized meeting places of the internet have in common is that they are often intensely shy and reclusive beyond their online communities; however, they can become completely unleashed and symbolically violent when interacting with like-minded men on the internet. Both of these modes of interaction, the inhibition when one is away from the keyboard and the disinhibition frequently shown when in front of it, can be understood within the framework set up in this subchapter. They are both in breach not only of the sociocultural norms of politeness and mutual respect, but also of the expectations of a job market that increasingly demands people to be approachable, well balanced and in a good mood. In this sense, 'dis/inhibition' captures a radical and wilful maladaptation when assessed in the context of the ideal performances that are otherwise typical for social media use. Compared to the latter, the double mode of dis/inhibition shows intensities of either 'too-little' or 'too-much'. Much more than the rampant misogynistic invectives that their forum pages are awash with, it is these maladapted intensities that are telling of the men's own otherness and their own painful experience of anomy at the root of their social exclusion.

Women in these contexts are highly overdetermined objects. They are simultaneously desired and hated; they are the agents and the symbols of the men's failure to adapt to harsh neoliberal requirements of perfection and must also be seen as proxies for men's autoaggression and attacks upon themselves (see Krüger, 2021b). What is perhaps the most baffling aspect of digital 'popular misogyny' (Banet-Weiser, 2018), however, is that it seems to be performed in full consciousness and awareness of the complete set of defensive, compensatory dynamics entailed. Hence, what we are seeing in these forms of online proto-extremisms are regressive switch phenomena (King, 2021, see above) that result in fabrications of reality that are *already performed as openly pathological and as derived from a sullying failure, and consequential inversion, of ego ideals.* Jacob (Johanssen, 2022) refers to Klaus Theweleit's (1987) *Male Fantasies*, a study of the proto-fascist Freikorps soldiers in Germany between the First and Second World Wars, to corroborate this observation:

> What is very striking about the posts and interactions [of misogynist groups online] is that those narratives and fantasies are very consciously named and discussed. This also relates to Theweleit's description of the Freikorps soldiers. Both kinds of men have a desire to verbalise and articulate their fears of women as well as their hatred of and desire towards them. The fear of castration, as Theweleit argues, is conscious: 'as far as I'm concerned, we really can't talk about an unconscious displacement, or an unconscious fear. On the contrary, it strikes

me that concealing the kinds of thoughts we've been discussing, the ones traditional psychoanalysis would call "unconscious", is the last thing on earth those men would want to do'. (Johanssen, 2022, p. 117, quoting Theweleit, 1987, p. 89)

This present chapter offers us the opportunity to enquire further into the question of whether unconscious structures are entirely erased here. In this respect, it is striking that the members of male subcultures regularly refer to the internet and their spaces as an 'id' or 'unconscious', which points to a topographical fantasy and a general process of externalizing and projecting mental states into one's social environment. Although this compartmentalizing again aligns well with Jacob's theorem of dis/inhibition, it also once again leads us back to the themes of perversion and fetishism. In his *Three Essays on the Theory of Sexuality*, Freud (1905a) had already defined perversion as the opposite of neurosis: what neurosis seeks to repress, perversion brings shamelessly into the open. And whereas online social networking itself is characterized by a promise of love and care on the part of the big platforms that ultimately proves perversely compromised and abusive (see Chapter 3), what can be seen to come out into the open in the forums and channels of the manosphere, we argue, is a way of suffering from this abusive, perverse form of care. As Steffen (Krüger, 2022a) has recently put it, what we find in the harsh displays of a misogyny that uses perverse visions of women and notions of female care so as to bring harm to the men themselves is a negative or *inverse fetishism*. Although fetishism usually has the function to stabilize the ego of a person through acts of denial and disavowal, an inverse fetishism, which is aligned with Green's (2002) negative narcissism, seeks to destabilize the ego ever further.

The banality of harassment

There is one more path to understanding the status of politics in the digital age, and this understanding proceeds via *the crisis of the Symbolic*, which we already touched upon in Chapter 2 when we outlined Žižek's (1998) writings on the internet. What Žižek sees the internet bringing symptomatically to the fore is a social crisis of the paternal function. This crisis becomes apparent in a lack of respect, or lack of fear, for the binding powers of the Symbolic. Without anything binding us to the lawfulness of the social that the Symbolic offers, we are prone to ignore the Symbolic as not applying to us, complain about its dysfunctionality or busy ourselves with introducing our own laws to the world – again via the Symbolic. When Dean (2010) writes about the state of online discourses that '[s]ometimes it's difficult to tell when a blog or a post is ironic and when it's sincere, when it's funny or when it's serious' (p. 5; see also our Chapter 2), this shows the extent to which the three scenarios just outlined can coincide, with new laws being introduced in modes that already anticipate their lack of binding powers.

Žižek's forecast of a thorough crisis of the Symbolic has proven farsighted and it is only in recent years that we have begun to make out the shape and extent of this crisis, which is driven by the internet, but by no means caused by it alone. We can behold it in the ways in which words, images and other symbolic materials either just aggregate online or circulate wildly, receive no response at all, are met with tepid lip service that drains them of their social efficacy or are blown up and taken seriously up to a point where the efficacy ascribed to them seems to leave the realm of the symbolic altogether. In these last cases, one can witness how the symbolic is met with responses that indicate it has not been understood as symbolic, but has rather been experienced as direct action – an immediate act or event with immediate, physical and corporeal consequences that psychiatry attributes to psychotic states (Lacan, 1993).

Bafflingly, in many politically charged incidents that have played out in the digital age, this crisis of the Symbolic has unfolded in both aspects and directions, the 'too near' to something real and the 'too far' from it, in bizarre dialectical contortions. In a key scene of the documentary film *Feels Good Man* (Jones, 2020), about the remarkable journey of the comic series character Pepe the Frog from obscure indie cartoon hero to right-extremist hate symbol, the film offers a montage of visual materials taken from 4chan's /pol/ (the 'politically incorrect' discussion board, where right-wing extremists recruited nerds to the Alt-Right). The montage includes amateur videos and professional television news footage of an Alt-Right 4chan member shouting 'Pepe!' during an election campaign speech by Hillary Clinton. In the build-up to the scream, the film shows the comments that had spurred on the shouting person – 'let's warp reality' and 'make the meme real'. This has the logic of something that, until that point, had been *virtual* and without *actual* consequence pushing and forcing its way *into actual reality* beyond the internet.

Another case, which has been testing the digital adeptness of German jurisdiction, is that of the 'Drachenlord' (dragon lord), a computer gamer in his early thirties who had been posting videos of his gaming sessions, his passion for heavy metal music and precarious lifestyle on Twitch and YouTube since 2011. His overweight, unkemptness and chaotic and unsanitary living space, as well as broad southern German dialect, which all stand in harsh contrast to the pathos of his online alter ego of the 'dragon lord' and the chatter with which he accompanied his game-play, turned him into a massively ridiculed and passionately hated internet anti-celebrity. The mockery of his 'fans' reached new lows in 2015 when a user tricked him into believing she had fallen in love with him and with the dragon lord subsequently proposing to her live on Twitch – only to be cruelly rejected, relentlessly laughed at and mocked.

The hate-filled symbolic interaction by his thousands of anti-fans, however, although often formed at a similar level as the dragon lord's own speech style, has again been pushing further and further the limits of what is *virtually* and what is *actually real*. For example, with people regularly sending huge pizza orders – as well as police special forces teams – to his address (both widely known practices of internet trolling) and organizing mass 'pilgrimages' of anti-fans to his house in a small German provincial town. His haters saw all of those actions as taking place within what they term the 'Drachengame', a fictionalized and gamified fantasy that makes their actions possible, while disavowing the seriousness of them. After the YouTuber threatened some of the 'pilgrims' who had ventured onto his property with physical violence and, in desperation, hit one of them with a flashlight, a German judge was naïve enough to see all blame lying with him and give him a two-year prison sentence.

In this way, the German court system failed its digital stress-test miserably in that it completed the work of the trolls by closing the virtual circle and making real the symbolic magic that the trolls had sought to practise in their attacks all along. To make matters worse, the judge felt that the agreed sentence was too short and subsequently appealed the court's decision, opening the door to a new hearing. The second hearing's judge seemed to possess more common sense and the dragon lord was sentenced to one year on probation. Having sold his house, he began roaming Germany in March 2022 while continuing to livestream. The 'Drachengame' could continue and its outcome remains to be seen. The Drachenlord is an extreme case of the levels of abuse that many face on social media today, women and minorities in particular. The climate on a platform such as Twitter has become so toxic that it is commonplace for women with large numbers of followers to receive death and rape threats every day, simply because they voice an opinion that runs counter to those – or in other ways upsets the sense of normalcy – of the predominantly male *ab-users*.

Cancel culture

As a last scenario and exemplary 'battleground' of politics online, we want to briefly shed light on what has been called 'cancel culture' through the prism of Scott Krzych's (2021) study on the 'politics of hysteria'. Analysing contemporary US politics and conservative media, Krzych argues that hysteria plays a key role in it. When he cautions early on in his study that hysteria as an element of contemporary politics is by no means bound to the strategies of only one side of the political spectrum, but 'may be understood as a common and politically unaffiliated reaction to democratic antagonism' (2021, p. 18), this becomes highlighted in the continuous debates about the term 'cancel culture'.

On a basic level, cancel culture refers to the act of uninviting, 'deplatforming' or 'cancelling' a speaker from an event or agreed book deal, or ceasing to follow them and blocking their posts on social media. Whereas Krzych sees right-wing communication strategies as forcing leftists into the position of an overwhelmed hysteric, the Marxist critic Angela Nagle sees cancel culture as a sure sign that the Left itself had been gravitating towards that position, leaning on the late Mark Fisher, also a Marxist critic, activist and prolific writer, to make this point. In 2013, Fisher had taken issue with the Left for excessive infighting and quarrelling, arguing that it had lost sight of the bigger questions in relation to class and instead focused on identity politics, where certain groups occupy a moral high ground and seek to advance their cause in the endless cycles of self-purification of the 'narcissism of minor differences' (Freud, 1930, p. 114). Such processes, as Fisher (2013) wrote, particularly play out on social media and have resulted in a purely self-referential, self-destructive Left.

Both Fisher and Nagle, in their critiques of leftist debate culture, risk falling into the trap of playing out questions of recognition against those of redistribution again, which Fraser and Honneth had previously sought to transcend in their philosophical debates published in 2003. However, their critique holds, we argue, when it focuses on the forms that intra-leftist debates have taken. Although some of those who had been called out and condemned by the Left had often said things that were objectionable, Fisher argues, 'the way in which they were personally vilified and hounded left a horrible residue: the stench of bad conscience and witch-hunting moralism' (Fisher, 2013, online, cited in Nagle, 2017, p. 75). Nagle, in turn, illustrates this moralism with the example of the feminist Germaine Greer, whose invitation to speak at Cardiff University triggered an hysteric response from related groups on the Left who petitioned to cancel the event due to Greer's allegedly 'misogynistic views towards trans women' (Nagle, 2017, p. 78, quoting from the petition). 'As far as this new generation of campus feminists was concerned, Greer may as well have been on the far right,' judges Nagle (2017, p. 78) dryly. And the pattern of interaction she exemplifies in this way goes to show the extent to which the hysterical position that right-wing communication strategies seek to push leftists into (Krzych, 2021) might have already been sought out by leftists' hysterical responses to one another. Indeed, when Nagle points out that Greer's comment about transgenderism had already been 15 years in the past, this moves hysteria back into Freudian territory, because the historical distance makes the negative identification with Greer's alleged desire on the part of the petition's authors all the more willed and fantasmatic.

The media scholar Meg Leta Jones (2016) offers another example of the hysteria-provoking proximity of personal data online with the case of Jacqueline Laurent-Auger. Laurent-Auger's 15-year contract as a drama teacher at a private boys' school was not renewed when erotic films, in which she had played 50 years prior, became available online and, as the school's statement put it, 'ushered "the erotic portion of [Laurent-Auger's] career into the present"' (Jones, 2016, p. 4). Like the unconscious parts of our minds, 'digital memory "negates time"' and, like the unconscious, digital memory can also return and dominate our present. Key to the efficacy of this process of 'presencing' (Couldry, 2012), however, is, in Lacan's idiom, people's appropriation of 'another's desire by identifying with them' (Evans, 1996, p. 79). *The drama teacher must have been plotting to seduce her students all along when she played in erotic films in the 1970s; Greer must have been pre-emptively targeting campus feminists of the 2010s when she made her critical comments against transgenderism in 2000* – such logic is what lies implicitly in many instances of cancel culture. That this dynamic struck a chord with people on the Left was soon exploited on the Right too, with activists going through the history of tweets of Left-leaning individuals to 'usher' politically incorrect materials from their accounts into a significantly more sensitized present. What all these patterns of political struggle have in common, however, is the wildly fluctuating intensity of their symbolic binding.

To be sure, although our interest here has been in a specific aspect of cancel culture, we have not covered the whole of its territory by far. Indeed, some progressives, particularly people of colour, have argued that the debate about cancel culture in its entirety is misplaced and the phenomenon might not even exist at all. Rather, they hold, what is actually taking place is a discursive shift that results in mostly white men, who have traditionally occupied most newspapers' front pages, television studios and speech podiums of the western world, being less frequently called upon in favour of more diverse voices. These men feel 'cancelled' as a result, but are simply invited less often – a circumstance that results in a more complex discursive arena where different voices debate ideas. Furthermore, as another stance towards the issue, many progressives have argued that one should not debate with extremists at all so as not to give them a platform from which to make their views public. In this context, cancel culture means to no longer engage with toxic views so as to no longer amplify them. As for media culture in general, Whitney Phillips and Ryan Milner (2021, pp. 81–99) have developed a convincing argument to this end. They claim that the liberal media's obsession with the Alt-Right was at least partly to blame for the strength that this loose accumulation of extremists was able to gather.

Conclusion

In this chapter, we have provided an overview of key psychoanalytic concepts and work on racism and other forms of extremism. We have further related these concepts to the digital realm and how it has become intensely politicized in recent years as right-wing extremism has taken hold of online spaces and politics in general. We end this chapter with some final reflections on psychoanalytic ways of knowledge production and our own identities as white male, European scholars.

Jacob has recently argued (rightly so, Steffen thinks) that 'psychoanalysis itself still has questions to answer when it comes to internalised racism, whiteness, and ideas of "neutrality" in light of continued racisms and forms of racial oppression in many parts of the world where psychoanalysts practice' (Johanssen, 2022, p. 33). In the face of the sophisticated knowledge that psychoanalysis has gathered on the origins of aggression our ambivalent relationships to others, as well as extremisms and prejudices, psychoanalysis itself still struggles to bring its practice in line with its theories. Like many other fields, it still has a problem with diversity, as well as a feeling of discomfort when it comes to interrogating the whiteness and vastly heterosexual points of orientation of the profession and how these play out, not only in the consulting room, but also in cultural analysis – that is, in the dialogical 'application' of psychoanalytic thinking in the fields of culture and society.

In this respect, we must realize that this chapter, too, has turned out relatively 'white', with our chorus of voices consisting of a majority of white, western people, many of them men. Surely, this emphasis in our thinking seems to be at least partly owed to what is perceived as canonical texts and positions in the fields of politics, psychoanalysis and psychosocial studies. And yet, one voice within us protests that the reliance on established authority (the canon) is exactly one such mechanism that reproduces long-standing power imbalances. Another voice, by contrast, arbitrates, stating that the politics that are being proposed are more relevant than those proposing them. Faced with this ambiguity, we can by no means rule out that some of our choices have not been grounded in shortcomings, ignorance, insecurities or even blockages, as well as their rationalizations in our own thinking. At the same time, what we feel we *have* achieved with this chapter is a psychoanalytic take on politics and the internet that is staunchly anti-fascist and anti-extremist and takes a firm line against all forms of xenophobia, while at the same time not being afraid of taking psychoanalysis 'where it hurts' – into the patterns of thinking, feeling and interacting, as well as into the dynamics that feed into extremist attitudes online. This we have done in order to try to understand – so as to then resist and counter – the positions to which we do not want to offer a platform otherwise. In other words, we have written as informedly as possible (in both thinking and feeling) about the political challenges that we know best and that are most vivid and urgent to us within this interdisciplinary field, and perhaps we have not moved sufficiently out of these personal (dis)comfort zones at times. Once the dust of our busy and tense work process on the book has settled, a reassessment of this chapter in particular will be a productive task, if perhaps not an easy one.

In our minds, a question that future psychoanalytic enquiries into forms of extremism need to tackle is that of the transposition, displacement and – indeed – sublimation of *the other as our own creation*. Put differently, if a respective other, or out-group, is indeed a fantasmatic construction that all people need in order to stabilize their lives and subjectivities, the question is how to shape the process of othering itself so that its outcomes are less violent than the circuits of splitting and guilt that we have witnessed all across global politics over the past years. This seems to us a process that needs to be triggered and set in motion first of all by people adhering to *that* cultural identity that has been the least visible and remarkable, namely that of white people. As Jamie Steele writes:

> The dismantling of white supremacy becomes contingent on white people's ability to own and face the threat of ego disintegration based on their whiteness and to shore up their internal organization through new fantasies, configuring new possibilities for external social organization which no longer rely on the invisible social order of white supremacy. (Steele, 2021, p. 400)

These new fantasies, we argue, crucially depend on how they address, activate and modulate the human proclivity toward aggression, splitting and destruction, instead of repressing, disavowing and foreclosing it. We return to this point in the book's Conclusion.

Notes

1.   Although we focus on questions of race and politics in this chapter, we wish to acknowledge the intersectionality (Crenshaw, 1989) of how forms of prejudice and oppression relate to race, class, bodily ability, gender and sex.
2.   Transference is a process in which particular desires, feelings and structures of relationships or modes of relating by the analysand are 'transferred' to the analyst. Transference often means an 'actualisation of unconscious wishes' (Laplanche & Pontalis, 1973, p. 455) which the analysand (unconsciously)

attributes to the analyst but that goes back to earlier relationships, often the earliest in a subject's life. Freud also called the phenomenon of transference a 'false connection', where a present experience is equated with past ones and the transference sets in. There are positive and negative instances of transference – for example, when loving patterns of relating are transferred. Psychoanalysts speak of transference and counter-transference. Transference takes place from patient to analyst and counter-transference from analyst to patient.

Further reading

Beshara, R. K. (2020). *Freud and Said. Contrapuntal Psychoanalysis as Liberation Praxis*. Basingstoke: Palgrave Macmillan.

Bhabha, H. K. (1994). *The Location of Culture*. London: Routledge.

Bülent, S. (2014). *The Psychopolitics of the Oriental Father. Between Omnipotence and Emasculation*. Basingstoke: Palgrave Macmillan.

Dalal, F. (2013). *Race, Colour and the Processes of Racialization: New Perspectives from Group Analysis, Psychoanalysis and Sociology*. London: Routledge.

Fakhry Davids, M. (2011). *Internal Racism: A Psychoanalytic Approach to Race and Difference*. London: Red Globe Press.

Fang, N. (2020). Feeling/being 'out of place': psychic defence against the hostile environment. *Journal of Psychosocial Studies*, 13(2), 151–64.

Fanon, F. (1967). *Black Skin, White Masks*. London: Pluto.

Kakar, S. (2007). *The Analyst And The Mystic: Psychoanalytic Reflection on Religion and Mysticism*. London: Penguin Books.

Khanna, R. (2003). *Dark Continents: Psychoanalysis and Colonialism*. Durham, NC: Duke University Press.

Martin, J. (2019). *Psychopolitics of Speech: Uncivil Discourse and the Excess of Desire*. Bielefeld: Transcript Verlag.

Richards, B. (2018). *What Holds Us Together. Popular Culture and Social Cohesion*. London: Routledge.

Said, E. (1978). *Orientalism*. New York: Pantheon.

Sheehi, L. and Sheehi, S. (2021). *Psychoanalysis Under Occupation: Practicing Resistance in Palestine*. London: Routledge.

Yates, C. (2015). *The Play of Political Culture, Emotion and Identity*. Basingstoke: Palgrave Macmillan.

Yates, C. (2019). The psychodynamics of casino culture and politics. *Journal of Psychosocial Studies*, 12(3), 217–30.

CHAPTER 5

Virtual sexuality: from the pre-oedipal to the post-oedipal

Key themes:
sexuality and psychoanalysis; psychosexuality and the digital;
enlarged sexuality and seduction; the sexual non-relation; online
dating and hook-up apps; online pornography

Introduction

Sexuality is everywhere. We see it in subtle and explicit forms in fashion, the media and our everyday language. And, not least, it is something we engage in with others or, for that matter, alone (Attwood, 2009). Perhaps *the* quintessential example of pleasure, sexuality is also a source of conflicts and anxieties, and, for many, harassment and abuse. It seems straightforward and spontaneously springing from a human need, but it carries contradictions and troubling compulsions and fantasies. And even more perplexing, these compulsions are often pleasurable and enjoyable. The body may want what the mind regards as forbidden and taboo. In contemporary culture, violence is often sexualized and sexuality violent.

Early psychoanalysis has had a great deal to say about sexuality. Indeed, it is a widespread stereotype of psychoanalysts – captured in many jokes – that everything they think and talk about has to do with sex. Yet, on some level, this is completely true. Sex and how it is related to gender and identity is a crucial part of human life and psychic functioning. However, later generations of psychoanalysts have often toned down the importance of sexuality, and we discuss some of the psychoanalytic contributions to sexuality through the past century in this chapter. We wish to emphasize from the start, however, that there is a difference between *psychosexuality* and *sexuality* as commonly understood. The former is an exquisitely psychoanalytic term that refers to an understanding of sexuality shaped by processes of socialization and subjectivization. Psychoanalysis holds that sexuality cannot be understood as a purely 'mature' and conscious set of bodily practices that develop throughout puberty into adulthood. Instead, distinctly affective and unconscious components enter the picture from the moment a subject is born. In addition, as we discuss via Laplanche, psychosexuality designates a form of sexuality that is not coextensive with sexuality proper. Instead it is a sexuality that 'leans on' and finds expression in practices, symbols and aesthetics, as well as forms of relating that do not *seem* to be sexual but are uncannily so at the same time. Indeed, in a way we can say that sexuality is always uncanny because it always marks the return of, or to, something unfinished and undigested in people's lives.

This strangeness of sexuality is discussed by Sigmund Freud, who wrote in *Civilization and its Discontents*:

> The sexual life of civilized man is [...] severely impaired. [...] Sometimes one seems to perceive that it is not only the pressure of civilization but *something in the nature of the function [of sexuality] itself* which denies us full satisfaction and urges us along other paths. (Freud, 1930, pp. 105–6, our emphasis)

Intriguingly, what Freud refers to in this quotation is not any specific dynamic that might affect sexuality. Rather, his point is that sexuality as such and in itself has something paradoxical, troubling and disturbing. Danielle Knafo and Rocco Lo Bosco similarly point to this problematic nature of sexuality:

> For most people, sex is a subject they don't clearly understand, even if they are much preoccupied with it, consciously or unconsciously. Sex may sometimes seem as if it has a mind, life, and language all its own. Clearly, sex, like death, is a problem for all human beings. (Knafo & Lo Bosco, 2020, p. 6)

Beyond this unfathomability of sexuality, psychoanalysis is not merely focused on the – more or less biologically defined – notion of 'sex'. Rather, it also holds valuable insights into the socially constructed categories of 'gender', such as 'man' and 'woman', 'boy' and 'girl', and other terms people use to describe their sexual orientation and identity today. Indeed, across the past hundred or so years, psychoanalysis has been the single most influential, original and provocative field when it comes to defining ideas about sexuality, sex and gender. In this chapter, then, we discuss sexuality in this broad sense of sexual orientations, gender constructions, sexual practices and fantasies, as well as the act of sexual intercourse itself.

As psychoanalysis teaches us, a particular symptom is always mirrored – and often channelled or distorted – in much broader cultural pathologies and practices. In this sense, broad cultural debates about the sexualization, or 'pornification', of digital media are of vital interest to a psychosocial perspective. This prompts us to take seriously neologisms such as 'food porn' on Instagram or the notion of being lost in a 'YouTube-' or 'Wiki-hole' (Tugwell, 2021, p. 170), as well as memes, such as those around 'big dick energy' (bizarre, right?), as symptomatic articulations of cultural currents and orientations. The language we use to talk about technology – it being 'turned on' or 'flashing us' – is often sexual, whereas the language we use to talk about sex is often highly technical, as in someone 'pushes my buttons' or 'rewires my system'.

After providing a brief introduction to Freudian, Lacanian and Laplanchean conceptualizations of sexuality, we discuss how sexuality and related phenomena are facilitated and mediated, exaggerated and enhanced, modulated and changed by digital media. We broadly differentiate between pre-oedipal and post-oedipal theories of sexuality, or in other words between developmental, psychosexual phenomena, as elaborated by Laplanche, and more phallic-oriented, socio-Symbolic conceptualizations of sexuality, as elaborated by Lacan and his followers. These two approaches to sexuality have proven particularly important for current psychoanalytic perspectives on the matter, and the differences in their conceptions have implications for our discussion of digitally mediated sexuality.

Sexuality and psychoanalysis

But let's start at the beginning. Freud put sexuality front and centre in his theory of the unconscious, especially in his earlier writings, and he had both radically progressive and conservative views on the topic.

On the conservative side, Freud assumed that the infant was naturally and biologically developing toward heterosexuality and toward being attracted to the opposite sex. In this process, the child was going through several stages of psychosexual development – oral, anal, phallic, oedipal. However, although Freud saw these zones as erogenous, he did not grant them the status as being part of a fully developed sexuality, but rather saw people with marked, say, oral or anal sexual preferences as stuck at, or as having regressed to, a more childish – and therefore perverse – level of sexuality. According to this definition, large swathes of the global population today would be perverse. By the same coin, however, Freud's theory is nevertheless still productive. After all, it might be important to consider what a marked cultural preference for one or other sexual practice can tell us about this culture.

Further on the conservative side is Freud's conception of the Oedipus complex (see Introduction), which, as Juliet Mitchell rightly observes in her famous study *Psychoanalysis and Feminism* (1974), focuses largely on the development of little boys, leaving the conception of female development as an afterthought. In this respect, Freud was criticized as 'phallocentric' and sexist, particularly by feminists from the 1960s onwards. Queer theorists since the 1990s have critiqued psychoanalysis's emphasis on an oedipal 'origin' of sexuality, too, arguing that it denies the political aims of sexualities that do not fit the binary poles of male/female (Bersani, 2010; Rehberg, 2019; Florêncio, 2020). To make matters even worse, psychoanalysis has had a poor track record when it comes to pathologizing particular sexual practices and identities, suggesting that forms of gay, lesbian or queer sexuality are disorders that can be 'cured'. In this respect, queer theory in particular often relies on Deleuzeian notions of pleasure and desire which reject the Lacanian conceptions that are tied to lack and instead constitute desire as free-flowing and world-enabling rather than foreclosing and restricting. Such points also relate to much bigger questions about *how and when* the subject becomes a subject and is 'sexuated' in Lacanian terms. The multiple psychoanalytic schools and queer theory markedly differ in their views.

On the progressive side, what needs emphasizing is just how radical many of Freud's ideas were in his own time – and, indeed, still are in ours. A reason why psychoanalysis is still little recognized in academic circles is that its theoretical basis in human sexuality still triggers strong taboos and holds a high potential for shame. Freud's insistence on the existence and psychological relevance of infant sexuality still jars with pious notions of the innocence and purity of childhood and his ideas on the plasticity of sexuality – that it is something that is being formed and shaped by experiences throughout our development – makes his theory far less biologically deterministic and 'sexist' than many critics maintain. Freud held that there was no natural phallic sexuality from the start. Rather, everyone must be seen as originally bisexual. Even more radically, he held that the sexuality of the neonate infant is 'polymorphous perverse': variable, dynamic, not attached to any specific body parts or part objects. It is indifferent to norms and laws and, in this respect, must be understood as a basis for what becomes an individual's unconscious. This idea still has the power to challenge taboos and conventions and to defy expectations (Freud, 1905a).

Freud's concept of infantile sexuality is not the same as mature adult sexuality. Infantile sexuality, as the French psychoanalyst Jean Laplanche would argue from the 1960s onwards, can be directed at and derived from any object. Pleasure on every part of the body, rather than primarily designated erogenous zones or genitalia, can be felt, and subsequently sought out, by the infant, and in this way it is gradually centred on more specific body parts and channelled through the oral, anal and phallic phases that we mentioned above. These represent phases of sexual development, as well as different modes and maturities in which to interact with significant others, which stretch from infancy into adulthood: oral (birth–12 months), anal (12–36 months), phallic (3–5 years of age), latency (5 years–puberty), genital (puberty–adulthood). Once the first three stages have been left behind, the Oedipus complex gives rise to the super-ego as the incest taboo and moral judgement are internalized.

In Freud's stages of psychosexual development, children subsequently learn to 'direct' drives towards specific (sexual) goals and pleasures and develop, via puberty, to adult sexuality. The polymorphous nature of infantile sexuality and with it particular desires henceforth become repressed and remain in the unconscious. We can say that the unconscious itself has a polymorphous perverse core. As stated, although Freud's psychosexual phases remain of interest, the overall development model of which they are part is rightly seen as problematic today. It suggests a sense of 'progression' from infantile to pubertal, to mature sexuality, and in this way also suggests a definition of healthy and inconspicuous, as opposed to a problematic and unhealthy sexuality, as Jean Laplanche has argued in great detail (e.g. 1970, 1989). It also entails a progression towards sexual difference that is marked by heterosexuality. Heterosexuality, however, is far from straightforward or harmonious, quite the opposite (Johanssen, in press). On the other hand, we do not wish to argue that forms of non-cis (i.e. non-heternormative) sexuality are always healthy. Any form of sexuality and sexual identity can take symptomatic, pathological and dangerous forms.

In the wake of Freud, and as psychoanalysis developed into different schools and traditions, sexuality became increasingly sidelined by many clinicians. It was often considered irrelevant and embarrassing to speak about in the consulting room (Fonagy, 2009) and was a burden on attempts at making it acceptable to the medical professions, particularly in the US (Giffney & Watson, 2017). Furthermore, object-relations and relational psychoanalysis, two traditions that have become very popular in the last decades, have tended to shy away from sex and instead emphasized intersubjective relationships beyond the sexual. This is also associated with declining interest in Freudian theories of drives and psychic energies that post-Freudian traditions, with the exception of Lacan, have initiated (Fonagy, 2009). This desexualization of psychoanalysis has been particularly driven by Kleinian accounts. As Peter Fonagy notes: 'Even though Klein and her followers conceived of this as a simple extension of Freud's ideas, the relation between the part-object of the drive (the breast) and its corresponding erotogenic zone (the mouth) came to be linked with the relationship of the infant to the whole object (the mother)' (2009, p. 4). As a result, sexuality becomes conceptually focused on particular early libidinal objects (e.g. the breast) rather than other objects that can also fulfil sexual drives. Object-relations psychoanalysis also often sees sexuality as a symptom of underlying problems or as defences against particular relationship pathologies. In this way, sexuality itself is left unexamined and decoupled from attachment (ibid.). It is then merely granted a metaphorical status whereby it comes to stand for something else in the subject. For instance, anality is seen as representing dynamics around holding on and letting go of others. In such accounts, sexuality is stripped of all its affective, bodily and sensual qualities.

Digital/sex

Before we move on to Laplanche's and Lacan's conceptions of the sexual, let us bring in the digital through a first set of examples to illustrate the two complementary and intertwined ways in which we see the digital as entangled with sexuality and subjectivity today. There is emerging scholarship that specifically discusses psychoanalysis, digital culture, the internet and sexualities (Semerene, 2016, 2021; Johanssen, 2021, Ed., 2022; Krüger, 2021a, 2021b; Millar, 2021; Tugwell, 2021). From this field, articles by Sharon Tugwell (2021) and Diego Semerene (2021), in particular, are exemplary for the ways in which they point to how different forms of sexuality are always already configured as part of the digital. In this way, these articles serve us as paradigmatic points of orientation for how we theorize the sexual in the digital. Touching briefly on the two before delving deeper into the psychoanalytic theories behind them, in Semerene's conceptualization, the digital can be understood along emphatically phallic and post-oedipal lines, describing interactions between people and digital devices and content as akin to engaging in sexual intercourse. Subjects touch, press, click on, use applications and content on platforms and are likewise touched, nudged, pushed and pulled by platforms in ways that Semerene compares to moments of being sexually penetrated. Social media and online cultures are arousal based, promising ecstatic rushes and orgasm-like pleasures, as subjects reveal themselves to others and are consumed by them through lust-fuelled patterns. When Semerene thus argues that there is a demand for a constantly aroused (digital) subject that is ready to get off, the understanding of the digital they offer draws very much on notions of the phallic that can be regarded as Lacanian and post-oedipal. In other words, Semerene moves interactions with and in the digital into the field of mature phallic and penetrative sex.

In contrast, Sharon Tugwell discusses the role of the smartphone in a way that brings in a more pre-oedipal[1] sexuality along the lines of Freud's psychosexual phases. Tugwell argues that the phone has become merged in a kind of constant erotic, libidinal union with its owner. For example, the smartphone qua its technological make-up of a screen that switches itself on, through nudges and notifications that are both visual and auditory, often seduces the owner to check their messages just once more, take one last look at their Twitter feed, swipe a few times on Tinder before going to bed, and to repeat the same actions all over again the next day. Our often intimate and seamless interactions with smartphones thus mimic 'the rhythmic pleasure of unconscious sexuality' (Tugwell, 2021, p. 170). This pleasure is characterized as ever flowing, being in a state of charge and tension, rather than ever reaching a particular end goal, similar to how Jodi Dean (2010) and Matthew Flisfeder (2021) have theorized social media (see Chapter 2).

There is thus a kind of sexual fusion between subject and technology today and it is this fusion that we take to represent the other paradigm of 'sexual digitality'. This version of sexuality is of a more pre-oedipal and fluid nature. One might be tempted to refer to Freud's concept of 'polymorphous perversion' to describe it. Smartphones, to remain with the example, do not only pertain to the eye (even though a lot is dependent on the gaze and the screen); they also vibrate in our trouser pockets – to the point where neuroscience can now see that humans have built neuronal brain structure that anticipates and even simulates this buzz all by itself (Eagleman, 2021) – and they even turn our hands into quasi-erotic zones (see Leader, 2017). However, the most important zone that the smartphone pertains to, even though it does not seem to have a direct connection to it, is the mouth, since, after all, what the phone seems to administer most is an *oral gratification*. Tugwell unfolds this point in the form of two complementary and interchangeable roles that the subject and the digital device can play respectively in their relationship. In the first, the smartphone is seen as the adult caregiver, or the Kleinian breast which (unconsciously) 'seduces' the infant into a relationship that is suffused with the sexual. In the second, Tugwell invites us to see the user–smartphone relationship as one where the user is the caregiver and the phone the baby wanting 'input'.

While we unfold Tugwell's pre-oedipal take on the smartphone further below, what is important at this point is that her conception of the sexual in relation to digital media is distinct from, although overlapping with, that expounded by Semerene. Indeed, this psychosexual realm of digital media use seems to us one that can be taken as a primary level of a (psycho)sexual analysis of people's digital media use, and we unfold the two steps of such an analysis in due course.

Jean Laplanche: from infantile to adult sexuality

First, however, we would like to do some groundwork, so as to further introduce Tugwell's and our idea of a psychosexual dimension of digital media use, and in this respect, the works of French psychoanalyst Jean Laplanche (1924–2012) are key. Laplanche, who died a decade ago, was without doubt one of the most original developers of Freudian concepts. His work remains underused in psychoanalytic applications to culture and society, although there has been a noticeable increase in interest over the past years (e.g. see Frosh, 2016; Ashtor, 2021). The transformation from infantile to adult sexuality, in particular, was one of the focal points of Laplanche's theorizing.

Psychoanalysis has long stressed that infants can feel pleasurable sensations that are sexual but certainly not in the way we would associate with adult sexuality. As we discussed earlier, those notions of infantile sexuality were pioneered by Freud. They refer to the infant discovering more or less solitary, auto-erotic forms of pleasure that, unlike many variations of adult sexuality, are not directed at or practised in relation to another human being. Those forms of pleasure are also not yet (fully) linked to particular erogenous zones and what is called 'genital sexuality'. For Laplanche, infantile sexuality is a form of foundational sexuality which, as the child matures, gradually transforms into adult sexuality.

In terms of the oral phase that is central in Tugwell's text (see also Krüger, in press), Laplanche was one of the few psychoanalysts to make a connection between the implicit erotic dynamics of breastfeeding practices and the dualist (cultural) status of the breast as an object. The breast in this sense is a highly sexualized, erogenous zone as well as a sheer means of providing nourishment for the baby. The breast is thus an enigmatic object both for the baby *and* for the mother, or, in other words, there is an erotically charged otherness that is present for all involved in such encounters. The baby, of course, does not consciously know of the breast as an erotic object or about the circumstance that it is *the* key signifier of femininity. Yet, the mother knows all of this and her own unconscious relationship to the breast, sexuality, femininity, being a mother and many other things comes to shape the baby's subjectivity and infantile sexuality, too. It is precisely because the mother is always *more* than just a mother – a complex, desiring social subject – that the baby's subjectivity can form. The child (unconsciously) senses and knows that there is more to mother, long before the father intervenes as a third (see Chapter 2). However, the question of what this 'more' is gives rise to riddles and anxieties in the relation.[2] There is something enigmatic and strange and at the same time utterly familiar about mother that the child tries to make sense of. Baby and caregiver share no fully developed verbal language yet with which they can communicate; instead, their communication is affective or, as Alfred Lorenzer (2022) would have it, *scenic* – through looks, touching, babbling, cuddling, kissing, and of course all the routine practices of feeding, washing, dressing, holding, rocking, etc. All the while, talking and using language on the part of adults surrounds the baby and accompanies the routine practices in which it is involved. Laplanche states:

> To address someone with no shared interpretive system, in a mainly extraverbal manner: such is the function of adult messages, of those signifiers which I claim are simultaneously and indissociably enigmatic and sexual, in so far as they are not transparent to themselves, but compromised by the adult's relation to their own unconscious. (Laplanche, 1989, pp. 79–80)

Naturally, the adults in the child's life continuously communicate with the child on an unconscious level too, which the child inevitably becomes confronted with, on both an unconscious and a conscious level. Those utterances, gestures and behaviours of the adults that remain incomprehensible or untranslatable for the child, and which might not be fully understandable for the grown-ups themselves, constitute what Laplanche defines as enigmatic signifiers. In other words, that which remains particularly enigmatic and unprocessed *for the adult(s)* is passed on to the infant in raw and unmediated form. As John Fletcher explains: 'These [signifiers] are anchored or inscribed particularly in the erogenous zones as folds and openings in the body surface – mouth, anus, genitals as sites of interchange where the first distinctions between internal and external are mapped out, and where the child's body is confronted by parental fantasy' (2000, p. 102). It is in this 'engrammatic' (Lorenzer, 2022, p. 24) way that Laplanche conceives of the signifiers becoming repressed.

Laplanche refers to those psychosexual dynamics between caregiver and child as dynamics of *seduction*. Unintentionally, unconsciously, but inevitably, the child is seduced by the adult caregiver/s into a sphere that is never only for the child. Rather, even if the caregiver has not the faintest intention to do so, and even if they are actively seeking to avoid this (perhaps particularly in these cases), the world of mature, adult sexuality cannot be shut out of the interactions between infant and caregiver. On the contrary, the enigmatic signifiers pull the child into adult sexuality, a scene where it does not yet belong and of which it cannot make sense. This relationship is unequal because the adult has access to meaning and a symbolic horizon, whereas the child does so only in rudimentary form (Laplanche, 1989). The child tries to make sense of the enigmatic signifiers, but this must remain inadequate, since it is by no means equipped to succeed in this. 'What does the other want? What in feeding, caring, loving does the other want of me?', the child wonders (Fletcher, 2000, p. 102).

According to Laplanche, 'Attachment, then, is *both* sexuality's condition of possibility *and* the medium through which the parent's radical otherness morphs libidinal development,' Avgi Saketopoulou (2014, p. 261, italics in original) explains. For Laplanche, '[s]exual excitement originates in the gap between maternal excess and what the infant's ego can bind; *the misalignment between the two is riveting*' (ibid., italics in original). In the case of the breast, this means that it expands from a source of nourishment for the baby to an abstract symbol as well as an actual source of sexual pleasure and, most importantly, to a sexual fantasy as the subject matures, no matter their sex (Giffney, 2021). This means, 'in spite of how personal my sexuality *feels* to me, it actually comes at me, first, from another person' (Ashtor, 2021, p. 88, italics in original). Sexuality is thus seen as something from the outside that the subject has taken in and comes to regard as part of themselves. Laplanche referred to this as *propping* (or 'leaning-on', or Freud's term of 'anaclisis'). It designates the 'leaning of nascent sexuality on nonsexual activities', without actual sexuality having emerged yet (Laplanche, 1970, p. 88). It describes a move from vital biology to metaphor, representation and ultimately fantasy. This is very significant insofar as Freud already maintained that the ego is 'ultimately derived from bodily sensations' (Freud, 1923, p. 26). Or as Marjorie Brierley explained: 'The child must sense the breast, for instance, before it begins to perceive (i.e. recognize) it, and it must feel its sucking sensations before it recognizes its own mouth' (1937, p. 261). The child senses the breast, perceives it, and then begins to remember, wish, imagine and *fantasize* about it. Affect precedes full perception and ego formation (see Johanssen, 2019, pp. 32–42, for an extended discussion). However, Laplanche developed this essentially Freudian idea further by stressing that sexuality is not just 'created' by the individual subject alone through a kind of outside–inside reversal; the sexual is always already there in the other (adult) subject who comes to interact with the infant.

An enlarged digital sexuality: within and beyond the sexual

As Jacob has argued elsewhere (Johanssen, in press) with reference to Flisfeder (2021): 'If social media has become our contemporary metaphor, this has not only to do with capitalism itself (Flisfeder) but with an originary, ontological process that enabled the existence of the subject's *ability* for creating metaphors and fantasies in the first place.' Laplanche, in turn, gives us a way to theorize this creative process by showing us how such metaphors spring from and become inscribed into bodily, corporeal and sexual acts, processes and relations. It is this bodily, creational realm, we argue, that digital devices, platforms and applications – hardware, software and interface design – tap into. This point is made by Tugwell, too, who states that: 'One could say that it is in fact the rhythms and traces of *our own unconscious sexuality, given back to us* as an otherness that is being transmitted. We are seduced by the return to our own infantile sexuality, facilitated and mediated through hand-held technology' (Tugwell, 2021, p. 174, our emphasis).

This seduction into a sexuality that is not so much about 'discharge and relief' and more about 'charge and tension' (Tugwell, 2021, p. 169) becomes perceivable when Tugwell writes about those interactions between users and their smartphones that seem to resemble an infant's feeding patterns, with users in this scenario being equated with infants that are breast- or bottle-fed by the mother/phone without an intervening third.[3] These forms of interaction, too, feed on a rhythmically patterned pleasure in excess of the mere taking in of nourishment; it might *lean on* the intake of food – or in the case of the phone: information, orientation and all kinds of other rationalizations of our engrossment – but in the final analysis, they are forms of sexual pleasure and in this way end in themselves:

> How much time is spent aimlessly scrolling through Facebook or Twitter – not because there is an aim or agenda but precisely

because of the allure (or seduction) of the scroll itself. If we consider the neverending turning wheel as we wait for a page to load, the unpredictable buffering whilst waiting for a strong enough connection, the ways in which one can get lost down a 'Wiki-hole' or any other pursuit of endless, infinite connections and possibilities, all of these libidinally invested activities are not seeking discharge and release but instead are propelled by the pleasure of charge and tension. (Tugwell, 2021, p. 170)

In another scenario that Tugwell envisions, the roles are reversed and, instead of being the babies, smartphone users take on the role of the caregiver/mother: the user cares for and looks after the baby (phone) and, as soon as the phone beeps, vibrates, flashes or reminds us of its existence, we are there – responding, picking it up, gently 'awakening' it and checking what it wants. 'We ensure our "phonebabies" do not get wet; do not get scratched or smashed; and do not fall. We protect them, look after them; keep them charged with (battery) life, keeping them close to us' (ibid., p. 176). No matter how admirably fitting these observations are, what is missing in this scenario is the crucial dynamic of seduction in the relation between subjects and the digital – what Steffen (2022b) calls the 'formative' dimension of digital media – that, we think, unfolds powerfully when the phone is seen as mother. As Tugwell writes:

We come to rely upon this 'phone-mother' to remember everything we need to know and more, to help us make sense of the world, to provide us with the answers and hold onto precious memories. Whenever we reach out to her for reassurance, distraction and information, she responds to our needs. Furthermore, she tries to predict what it is we want or need, in the form of predictive text or internet search prompts. The presence of our 'phone-mother' is unconditional, unwavering, reliable. It is we who call out to her, touching her, pushing her buttons, demanding an acknowledgement and response. We come to believe that our phones have the capacity for omnipotence, and with this comes a blurring of what belongs to us and what belongs to the phone. (Tugwell, 2021, p. 175)

But *into what* are we being seduced? What difference does this seduction make in and for our lives? And what is the specifically sexual component in this seduction when extrapolated onto the field of digital culture? Also to these questions, Tugwell's text offers some level-headed and productive answers which refer us back to our chapter on work, as well as to the next chapter on videogames and AI. When Tugwell points to the numerous reports that warn social media users of the vested interests of digital services in them and observes that 'many of us still seem to willingly surrender our data with very little reflection' (2021, p. 173), this ties in with what we have tried to understand with the notion of 'perversion' in Chapter 3, as well as the notion of 'interpassivity' (Žižek, 1998; Pelletier, 2005; Pfaller, 2014) in Chapter 6. The notion of perversion emphasizes the imbalance in the relationship between users and digital services due to the utilitarian, exploitative dimensions that the service providers add to what they otherwise present as love and care for the users. As Benvenuto (2016) states, the fetishist does not love someone as a whole, but only for their 'appendages' (p. xxxvi). Interpassivity, in turn, refers to the distribution of active and passive states between digital technology and its users, where users are often kept in relative passive states, merely pressing the buttons of a controller, for example, while being enveloped by machine simulation and action.

Tugwell points to a similarly imbalanced relationship by combining Laplanche's notion of seduction with what scholars, drawing on web developers, often capture with the terms 'front end' and 'back end', stating that the scope of people's involvement in and subjection to digital media can no longer be adequately understood from what users are offered at the 'front end' – that is, at the level of their screens and interfaces. Rather, in Laplanche's words (1989), much of what effectively impacts and shapes us users in our interactions with the digital remains enigmatic to us and is dependent on what happens behind and beyond the interface, at the level of the 'back end' – that is, at the level of our algorithmic, data-driven embedment into wider structures of commerce, consumer research, capital flows and political economy, as well as politics itself. In other terms, when Laplanche describes *being seduced* as a process in which one is addressed by 'someone with no shared interpretive system, in a mainly extraverbal manner', this can productively be compared to how users are being addressed by the affordances (Gibson, 1979) of their digital devices and applications. In this respect, we are indeed seduced – by Facebook, for example – to see the people who are part of our network, perhaps not so much as 'friends' (since public debate about 'Facebook friends' has inoculated us against such naivety), but at least as somehow belonging to us. And we are indeed seduced by Instagram to present ourselves in highly idealized and filtered images. And we are seduced by, say, a dating website such as 'Seeking' (formerly 'Seeking Arrangement') to want to date people who, as it says on their website, either have 'Looks & Charm' or 'Success & Wealth'.[4] Surely, we might have a hunch what these categories entail and how they position us as subjects within a cultural context in which good-looking people tend to find successful and wealthy others. And, yes, we should be painfully aware of the gendered dynamics in this arrangement – just think of the film *Pretty Woman* (Marshall, 1990). Yet, these categories are still highly enigmatic when we encounter them during the registration process. First of all, they are offered without any further explanation, as though they are the two most natural options in the world for everybody 'seeking' someone else. Second, they do not tell the user anything about how their choices will impact the dating experience.

As becomes clear, then, digital media seduce us into relying on them making arrangements for us, the nature of which we have no way of knowing before entering into them. What makes their seduction *sexual* in the Laplanchean sense is exactly the way in which they are inviting us to surrender to them – to their superior control and power, as well as to their whims – without really knowing what they entail. After all, terms and conditions are changed often and at times in significant ways. In a critical discussion of Leo Bersani, Gila Ashtor (2021) has written that, for Bersani, the infantile experience and 'journey' towards adult sexuality is *masochistic* because being confronted with, invaded by, and ultimately taking in, an external world constitutes an auto-erotic, 'masochistic thrill' (Bersani, 2010, p. 95). In line with our argument here, allowing oneself to be seduced by and into social media might hold at least a taste of this thrill.

The phallic layer on top

Once we have been subjected to the care of digital media, we usually tend to embrace it wholeheartedly, and it is only in the cases when an app or device stops working properly – when batteries are low, a service is down, reception is weak or an update buggy – that we realize how much we have allowed ourselves to become dependent on them. As long as things run smoothly, Tugwell (2021, p. 171) observes rightly, we do not even pay much attention to our devices and apps and tend to give in to a fantasy of mastery and autonomy that flatly denies our heavy reliance on technology. It is on the basis of this fantasy and on the (proto)sexual pleasures that we derive from the play between charge and tension with the hard- and software at our disposal, we argue, that ideological interpellation in the way Althusser defined it (see Chapter 2) is at its most effective. Such pleasurable reliance, for example, affords us to think that we are indeed likeable persons because we have become dexterous in eliciting 'likes' from others online. When Semerene (2021) describes current digital culture as phallic, this seems to refer to exactly this fantasy-infused level of subject constitution – that is, the level at which we have come to embrace digital infrastructure (Miller, 2012) so completely and libidinously that we no longer take note of its formative significance for who we are, but unthinkingly strive to meet its expectations of an ideal user. This user, as Semerene claims about the current media sphere, is never *not* excited:

> As excitation in digital culture becomes perpetually priapic – the ideal user is the user who is never not excited – it further becomes obvious that the penis can't keep up with its phallic expectations. So many lovers nursing a floppy dick after making the most phallic of promises; so many lovers dead on arrival, us wishing their next iteration could begin before the current one has had a chance to disappoint us any further. So many lovers logging on to hook-up apps immediately after, or even before, bidding us goodbye. (Semerene, 2021, p. 206)

In such a scenario, there can be no 'lack actually filled, which digital culture insists on deferring' (ibid.), Semerene continues. Or to put it in other words, while there is a persistent, formative tickling and teasing of the user at the pre-oedipal level, at the phallic, oedipal one, digital culture persistently prompts its users to embody an adult heterosexuality which both disavows and endlessly defers its own underlying logic. Users struggle to keep up with the impossible affordance of platforms and apps for them to be continuously present and aroused.

By way of summarizing our argument so far, we thus suggest two distinct but intertwined conceptions of sexuality as pertaining to two different levels of analysing digital culture and the ways that it affords people to embody and identify with certain sexual orientations and gender roles and to perform certain sexual practices. On a pre-oedipal, psychosexual level, conceptualized via Laplanche here, we find the subtle, enigmatic ways in which users are seduced into technosocial relationships, the scope of which they cannot hope to understand. On an oedipal/post-oedipal and phallic level, in turn, we are interested in the actual and fully sexual relationships of the people who have built digital affordances deep into their structures of subjectivity and desire.

To offer another example, take the ASMR craze of recent years. ASMR is short for 'autonomous sensory meridian response', which describes a pleasantly ticklish bodily response to gentle sounds and sights – for instance, whispers, crackling, soft scraping, rustling or, as a visual example, dipping fingers into a plastic pot with multicoloured slime. The trend towards this mild form of sensory manipulation triggered a whole online video genre in which attractive and highly stylized women produce such brain-massaging sounds in close proximity to large, high-end microphones, which are usually placed centrally in the lower part of the image. Although studies tend to bracket discussions of the kind of sexuality in ASMR videos (Andersen, 2015; Fredborg *et al.*, 2018; Starr *et al.*, 2020), we think our theoretical apparatus offers a more productive interpretation. Hence, although we can say that the sounds themselves and their very subdued nature clearly pertain to a psychosexual level of 'tension and charge' – a pleasure-seeking exercise in and of itself – the all-too obviously phallic microphones and the ways in which beautiful women play with them, touching them slightly with their hands and mouths, are surely positioned at a phallic level, but with a strong preference for orality. In this way, one can argue that the focus on the mellifluous sounds always also serves as a potential seduction into a more phallic dimension of sexuality. Therefore, when many of the female performers of ASMR videos have now opened accounts on OnlyFans, a platform that cross-fertilizes pornography with tailor-made and customized audiovisual sexual services for paying customers, the facilitated commercial exchange of money for part-object services seems to have clearly arrived in the realm of mature sexuality. As yet another example, for which we briefly return to the 'Seeking' app discussed above, the app's binary option of 'Looks & Charm' or 'Success & Wealth' and the highly gendered stereotypes it leans on already orient people in the direction of certain phallic, sexual set-ups. We can imagine these set-ups along strict heteronormative lines, with the website's images of curvaceous 'Kardashians' and smooth 'Beckhams' further pointing in this direction. As Semerene observes rightly, digitality in such instances is a 'normativising technology that structures movement across a specific path, helping perpetuate a particular kind of social negotiation and making sure that "[t]hings fall into place"' (2021, p. 205).

There is no sexual relationship, or is there? Sexuality as rupture

How exactly can we understand the unfolding of specific forms of phallic sexuality on the basis of a digitally suffused psychosexuality? As stated above, although psychosexuality is something that needs to be conceived of as auto-erotic, solitary or dyadic – that is, as mostly pertaining to user–interface relations, or, in the case of ASMR, as the user's relation to the sounds and sights – mature forms of sexuality always involve two or more people, or, again in the case of ASMR videos, the user *and* the, mostly female, person producing the sounds. Put differently, individual sexual excitement at a (post-)oedipal level is made possible because of another, or others: *I desire the other and therefore wish to have sex with them, I know that they desire me too and this amplifies my desire.* Sexuality is thus always also about expectations, fantasies and ideas of how my particular desires and preferences go together with those of the other. The psychosexual level at which the digital inserts itself, in turn, weighs in on these fantasies and expectations, as well as on the forms and modes in which a subject is able to encounter the other. Hence, whereas psychoanalytic thinkers such as Fonagy emphasize the process of attunement between two people in sexual communion – for example, 'the true pleasure of erotism derives from the opportunity to transpose oneself into a state of mind that is felt to be the other's' (Fonagy, 2009, p. 18) – our conception of the sexual dimension of the digital already indicates how such transpositions might be hindered and marred, such as by the 'ping!' of a push notification on the smartphone.

In this respect, Jacques Lacan's somewhat more sober and sobering account of sex and sexuality seems a better suited theoretical tool for the analysis of how the digital makes a difference in our love lives. One of Lacan's most famous aphorisms is: 'There is no sexual relationship' (Lacan, 1999, p. 193). With this, he basically means that there is no pure or unproblematic 'meeting of souls' in sexual encounters. Such encounters, Lacan holds, never really end in feelings of union, transcendence, harmony, complementarity or magic. Despite such notions being constantly evoked in poetry, romantic literature, rom-com films, etc., they must necessarily fail in sexual intercourse, because the people involved are always already part of the Symbolic Order and the non-relation (or non-rapport, as it is also often called by Lacanians) that subjects need to, well, *subject* to. Sexuality is made possible by – and itself enables – the lack that is at the heart of the subject. The subject is constituted in the gap between reality and the Symbolic and the lack arising from this gap (see Introduction). For Lacanians, one cannot explain or justify sexuality in any sense, yet subjects constantly try to do that as they use particular signifiers to make sense of sexuality and the other. Sexuality is thus never an act of pure biology or enjoyment that is brought about because of biological processes – that is, drives or the physical act of having sex. Instead, Lacan says that it is mediated and shaped by the Symbolic and this makes sexuality both arousing and conflict laden. We make sense of sexuality and our own arousal via the Symbolic and make sexuality work for us by engaging in erotic fantasies, having particular preferences, etc. This also means that I need to turn the other into an object of my arousal and fantasy in order to 'get off' and the other needs to do the same with me. In this way, then, sexuality is always already *virtual*. Two (or more) bodies are together, yet, in a sense, very alone, too, deep in their own fantasy worlds during sex.

Tinder sexualities

Combining the Laplanchean and the Lacanian paradigm, then, we can say that digital media and the ways they modulate our psychosexuality insert themselves in exactly the gap that exists between people's existences and the ways in which they constantly need to make sense of these existences. Seduction sets in at a pre-linguistic level and prompts people to incessantly try and make sense of the enigmas of human communication and of capturing the meaning of their ticklishness in ever new forms of failed symbolizations and failing performances of sex and gender. In order to show in an exemplary way how an analysis of sexuality in relation to digital media can work at these two levels and what insights such an analysis can develop, we now turn to the most successful online dating app of the last decade, Tinder.

There have been a number of psychoanalytically informed works on Tinder. We have arranged their findings here in a way that, we hope, brings the coordination of the two levels of analysis clearly to the fore. As Steffen and his colleague Ane Spilde have worked out in their analysis (Krüger & Spilde, 2019), online dating apps such as Tinder, which are also called 'location-based, real-time dating' (LBRTD) apps, work in a much more direct and gut-feeling based way than the traditional online dating pages of the 1990s and 2000s. LBRTD apps are vitally based on *visual* cues – a selection of portrait photos of people within a certain geographical range of individual users which these users are then offered one by one in the form of playing cards on their phone screens. The users are then able to swipe their finger either from right to left in order to reject the offer of getting in touch with the shown person or from left to right to indicate their interest in getting in touch. Once this person has reciprocated the gesture and also liked the user in return, the two can start chatting with each other and eventually – potentially – arrange a physical date.

By contrast, traditional online dating sites are located behind paywalls and require the user to fill out long questionnaires and answer literally hundreds of questions before they are finally offered their first potential match. 'OkCupid', having been around since 2004, is one of those 'old-school' platforms which nevertheless still have a loyal user base. People who opt for such a traditional, heavily cognitive way of dating often do so because their gut feeling has repeatedly caused them trouble, making them fall time and again for the same personality type who would ultimately disappoint them. Answering long sequences of questions about who they are and what they look for in a partner, they hope, will make it possible to break with problematic unconscious patterns. Hence, they use the app as a defence against parts of their unconscious. Yet, while we are not entirely sure whether such a 'cognitive–behavioural screening' can be made to work successfully in the long run, what becomes clear is that, by comparison, Tinder and other LBRTD apps, with their emphasis on pictures and their promise of swift physical meetings, bring back some of the spontaneity and absence of reflexivity that romantic notions of love hold dearly. As we shall show, however, these apps are also not without automated defence mechanisms.

To approach Tinder with our analytic structure of the pre-oedipal and post-oedipal, we can start our analysis with the observation that Tinder again erects a markedly *caring, maternally* connoted infrastructure that lovingly nudges and coaxes its children into the world of mature sexual relations. Echoing Tugwell's Laplanchean perspective, the Lacanian scholars Carolina and Arturo Bandinelli (2021) write about Tinder:

> If we look at the ways in which Tinder is designed, we notice that it constantly speaks to us, demands, invites, incites. Tinder is relentlessly friendly and always available. If you don't open it for a while, it teases with its messages, reminding you that others are enjoying the swiping: 'Who are all these new people swiping in your area? Swipe to find out', or 'You have 313 new likes! Swipe to see if you like them back'. If you are ignoring it, the app reacts, trying to be flattering, ultimately to win you back, to have you touching it, enjoying it. It wants us. It wants us to be there, to do things. And, when a match occurs, Tinder is there to encourage and reassure ('You know they already want to talk to you, right?'); to play on a sense of urgency ('Send a message before your battery dies'); or shamelessly remind you how likeable it is ('Someone should create an app to meet cool people. Oh wait'). Tinder seduces [...]. (Bandinelli & Bandinelli, 2021, pp. 191–2)

Indeed, as we will discuss below, although all those people out there already waiting to get to know us are surely fine, Mama-Tinder is still the best. Interestingly, the Bandinellis interpret this nudging, coaxing, enabling, empowering and facilitating role of Tinder as that of 'a partner in its own right' (ibid., p. 192). However, although this might partly be so, from the Laplanchean/Lacanian perspective that we take here, the functions that the authors point to are much rather 'motherish' in the sense that they create a dyadic sphere in which users are not directly entering into, but are rather *being prepared for phallic, post-oedipal relations*. This 'prep-sphere' itself, however, seems of a distinctly pre-oedipal nature.

Tinder users are invited to surrender to the app's superior knowledge – its database and the analytic tools with which to offer potential matches to users – into which they again have no sufficient insight, with the app's algorithmic function of matching individuals suggesting that romantic partners can indeed be 'objectively' brought together. In other words, users mirror a kind of Silicon Valley logic which constantly suggests that it is technology, algorithms and AI that is able to know, even predict, their desires in a better way than they ever could. But how well, we must ask, does this really work? And to what degree, if at all, can people 'objectively' be brought together? Parallel to what Tugwell writes about the productivity of the 'glitch' as 'not so much an error but "a much-needed erratum"' (Tugwell, 2021, p. 175) – that is, an incident that allows us to become aware of our technological attachments and dependencies – the Bandinellis have also focused their interview study on Tinder's rather dysfunctional and frustrating aspects. What they have found is that Tinder is captivating for many, not so much because it offers the chance to meet a romantic partner, but because it paradoxically facilitates the fantasy of such matches and encounters without people really having to endure the 'anxiety of an embodied encounter' (Bandinelli & Bandinelli, 2021, p. 181). In other words, for many Tinder users, the allure of the app does not so much lie in actually going on physical dates, but in pretending and playing *as-if*, without planning to actually pull through with what seems virtually possible. This abstaining from physical dates, in turn, finds a logical complementary in Tinder's business model, which, as Steffen and Ane emphasize, is 'not so much about facilitating relationships, as it is about increasing the number of users in the database and interactions on the app. From the application's perspective, then, it is desirable that users "swipe on", no matter how "ultimate" their last "match"' (Krüger & Spilde, 2019, p. 12).

Viewed from this perspective, the many quantitative studies that find 'fun and entertainment' as consistently ranking highly among what users claim as their reasons for using Tinder can be seen in a distinctive light. 'After all, if users are supposed to swipe on regardless of their situation, there are good reasons for them to remain at a safe emotional distance to the kinds of relationships the application produces' (ibid.). For Tindering *not* to lead to many physical dates and long-term relationships is not so much a dysfunction or glitch, then, but a central principle of the app's intended functioning. In this respect, however, users are not only doing well in keeping their distance from strong emotional investments in the people they encounter on the app, but rather the app itself becomes a defence against feelings of dependence on another, with such feelings being shifted towards the app itself.

However, once we have established that much of the user interaction on Tinder is not really meant to culminate in physical contact, the very act of Tindering, which has such a phallic, sexual reputation (Beware of the 'hook-up' apps!), again refers us back to the relevance of more subtle psychosexual dimensions. Against this background, then, the whole activity of Tindering becomes less of a means to an end, as Steffen and Ane have claimed (ibid., p. 8), but – again – an end in itself. Especially swiping – with its stroking, swishing and fidgeting associations – seems to approximate quasi-masturbatory motions once it is decoupled from the aim it had been leaning on. But also the process of accumulating, storing and collecting likes and matches takes on a significance that is charged with auto-erotism. What is at stake is a seductive dynamic in which the app itself commands a form of enjoyment, articulating its own demand of being used and touched. The app functions both as a void that attracts an array of emotions, feelings and projections, and as an object that ceaselessly syphons off our enjoyment; its existence depends less on its ability to 'deliver' a date than to keep us engaged in its ever-promising yet failure-ridden enjoyment circuits (Bandinelli & Bandinelli, 2021, p. 192).

To move from the psychosexual formation of subjectivity to the question of how the 'Tinder-form' of subjectivity articulates itself in its sociocultural, socio-technological setting, a finding that resounds in many academic texts with and without a psychoanalytic orientation alike, is that many users seem to follow a 'big-data mindset', or database logic (Krüger & Spilde, 2019; Rambatan & Johanssen, 2021). Using such logic, the activity of continuously accumulating matches (i.e. data) is tied to the vague belief that this will ultimately lead to 'better results' for one's love life (at least in the case of those who actually *do* use Tinder for *actual* dating). In the worst-case scenario, users transplant Tinder's psychosexual 'swipe logic' (David & Cambre, 2016) without modifications into the sphere of phallic sexual relations where the Lacanian notion of desire of 'wanting to keep wanting' (Ruti, 2018, p. 14) propels the subject endlessly forward from date to date, hook-up to hook-up. As one male Tinder user, interviewed by the journalist Nancy Jo Sales, put it:

> With these dating apps [...] 'you're always sort of prowling. You could talk to two or three girls at a bar and pick the best one, or you can swipe a couple hundred people a day – the sample size is so much larger. It's setting up two or three Tinder dates a week and, chances are, sleeping with all of them, so you could rack up

100 girls you've slept with in a year.' (Sales, 2015, online)

This, then, would be a sexual-relational pattern that displaces the seductive associations with shopping that are built into the Tinder interface onto the 'dating' or 'singles market'. The symbol where users need to click on in the Tinder app to get to the overview of their 'matches' is in the upper right corner, where shopping apps usually have their 'baskets' or 'trolleys' (Krüger & Spilde, 2019, p. 9). And, indeed, as with fast food and fast fashion, fast Tinder dates suggest a certain inbuilt disposability on the part of one's dates/acquisitions. As Jacob and Bonni Rambatan have argued:

> Ultimately, the (unconscious) wish for many users is to destroy the other after sex so that any reminder of them is wiped out; they are erased in their fantasies so that they can start all over again without the baggage of love, embarrassment, or other complicated feelings. Can we not read the expressions which the individuals in Sales' Vanity Fair article use to describe Tinder as symbolic acts of killing? 'Tinder is fast and easy, boom-boomboom, swipe,' 'Hit it and quit it,' 'It's like ordering Seamless,' says Dan, the investment banker, referring to the online food delivery service. 'But you're ordering a person.' (Sales 2015, online; Rambatan & Johanssen, 2021, p. 137)

Just how many people *do* in fact translate Tinder's formative interaction patterns into a way of being in the world that is as cruelly commodifying as the investment banker in the quotation lets on remains unclear. At least for those who claim to use the app for 'entertainment' only, it seems that they see meaningful sexual encounters and courtship to lie elsewhere. 'With users "only wanting to play", more meaningful and nourishing relationships are not eliminated, but relocated to a point beyond Tinder's reach,' write Steffen and Ane (Krüger & Spilde, 2019, p. 13), so as to end on a hopeful note. And yet again, since Tinder is by far not the only digital innovation basing itself on forms of interaction that are implicitly business like and consumption oriented – 'The good ones go into the pot, the bad ones go into your crop' (Cinderella) – we need to be concerned about what our bodies learn at a habitual, pre-oedipal level about how to make sense of ourselves and the world around us.

Online pornography and the revelation of desire

As one popular comedy video of the 2000s puts it bluntly: 'the internet is for porn'.[5] The video itself is perhaps emblematic of wider socio-symbolic dimensions of porn. It is everywhere, public and at the same time taboo, private and invisible. The video features a woman operating a puppet, Kate, on a theatre stage, who, in the spirit of an enthusiastic technological optimist, sings about the great features of the internet as such, only to be constantly interrupted by another puppet, Trekkie, who shares distinct character traits with Sesame Street's 'Oscar the Grouch'. Kate: 'The internet is really really great.' Trekkie: 'For porn!' Kate: 'I've got a fast connection so I don't have to wait.' Trekkie: 'For porn!' Kate: 'There's always some new site.' Trekkie: 'For porn!' And it goes on.

Indeed, one of the major influences of sexuality in the past decades that has massively gained in strength as it has become widely available online is pornography. There are estimates saying that about 35 per cent of all data transferred on the internet is used for porn. Whereas these figures are overblown and bordering on the mythological, even the more reliable measure that about 20 per cent of all mobile internet searches are porn related[6] shows how widespread porn has become thanks to digital technology. 'Behind every new technology is someone trying to have sex with it,' Danielle Knafo and Rocco Lo Bosco state (2020, p. 73, citing Bee, 2019), arguing that the internet radically changed porn and, we might add, vice versa. Porn has been a key driver of technological innovation. For example, it is noteworthy how webcams and professional camming were the predecessors and catalysts of forms of digital media and the platformization of subjectivities and ways of being that we have seen exploding in the last 10–15 years. The early camsites of the 2000s ushered in design interfaces and technology that we see multiplied on social media today. The user profile, the Facebook, Twitter and Instagram 'like' features, video chat, payment systems or simply the ability to make money through entrepreneurial practices – they all were pioneered by (mostly) female professional cammers and camsites. The example of camming and its playful use of nudity, teasing, deception, sexuality, pornography and above all desire is emblematic, and it has anticipated, by now, well-established forms of representation of both male and female bodies on Instagram, Tinder or Grindr, among others, where bodies are photoshopped and filtered to increase follower sizes and often to make money through promoting brands or oneself. The porn studies scholar Brian McNair (e.g. 2009) subsumes this trend under the label of 'porn chic', which, as he writes, first emerged 'in high art and popular culture, in Hollywood cinema and literature, advertising and fashion, in journalism and [...] scholarly outputs' from the late 1980s onwards (McNair, 2009, p. 55), before spilling over onto the internet. 'Porn became "chic" in these contexts,' he writes, 'insofar as talking about, referring to or borrowing from its codes and conventions had lost much of its transgressive, taboo quality and became acceptable, even fashionable' (ibid.).

With the advent of online porn, or 'cyberporn' as it was called in the 1990s, the waning of sexual taboos that McNair has observed received another decisive push. As Knafo and Lo Bosco (2020) argue, porn consumption has been becoming significantly more mainstream and widely accepted through the internet in general. Nevertheless, the internet porn consumption of the late 1990s and early 2000s was still torn between troubling choices. Either one left one's personal credit card details with a porn website in exchange for direct access to its contents and thus surrendered to the (more or less plausible) risk of being traceable and identifiable as a porn consumer, or one roamed the World Wide Web for free porn and risked becoming entangled in endless webs of 'click-throughs, pop-ups, mouse-traps, and Web rings' (Paasonen, 2011, p. 177). In the latter case, users, by clicking on porn links, were assaulted by steadily new browser windows opening which, for example, warned them of their computers' hard drives being infested with a virus. As Wendy Chun (2006) observed poignantly in her early work on online pornography, 'Porn sites were the first to use the now-standard pop-up window to push images at viewers. These tactics often create panic, since the user has lost "control" over his/her browser' (2006, p. 125). Translated into a psychoanalytic paradigm, one could argue by drawing on Elizabeth Cowie's 'Pornography and Fantasy' (1992) that what triggered these panics was the simulation of 'the gaze of the super-ego', or as Cowie explains further, of 'the child imagining a look which sees it looking, which discovers it in the act of forbidden looking' (2017 [1992], p. 8). And indeed, the fact that users *did* regularly panic in such situations goes to show how much the waning taboos of pornography could still suddenly gain in strength again and return as something that also showed traces of repression. Recently, Chris Vanderwees (2019) has developed this perspective further for the present moment, arguing that 'online pornography frequently portrays, encourages, and requires that the subject's jouissance be derived from the interplay between fantasies of looking and being looked at through the keyholes of technology' (2019, p. 25).

As the next important technological development for online porn as we know it today, the launch and immense success of the video-sharing site YouTube in 2005 made porn-only pendants quickly follow suit, with the proverbial (though less visited) YouPorn launching in 2006 and PornHub a year later, in 2007, among many others. These sites have worked to further 'alleviate shame and guilt' (Knafo & Lo Bosco, 2020, p. 59) from the activity of porn consumption. With their launch, users have no longer been necessitated to either leave traces with their credit cards or risk being trapped in wildly disorienting hails of pop-up windows in search of free porn. However, in another parallel to YouTube, not nearly all content posted to these porn sites was of the amateur, 'user-generated' type that the 'You' in YouTube suggests.[7] Hence, although in the case of YouTube itself, respectable – and very powerful – media corporations went on the counteroffensive and sued the platform for illegally sharing their copyrighted content, similar attempts on the part of the porn industry proved to be too much of a Sisyphean task. And whereas the creators and owners of PornHub *et al.* earned generously from their platforms' function as hub and go-between, porn actors, directors and producers suffered a heavy financial decline, with many of the performers being driven into escort work and prostitution. Recently, the success of the platform OnlyFans, which facilitates direct patronages of individual erotica and porn performers by subscribing users, has been celebrated as bringing a business model to fruition which might 'fix porn' (Bernstein, 2019); subsequent reporting, however, takes the wind out of the sails of this argument again (MacKinnon, 2021). Although it remains to be seen how the industry will develop further, what seems sure is that the lines between professional and amateur, business and leisure, will blur further, just as they do in all other fields becoming mediatized by the digital which we have been discussing in the book.

But what is porn in the first place? And what is it that fascinates us so much about porn that we turn to it so incessantly? (Almost 90 per cent of US male adults and nearly 30 per cent of females between 18 and 35 watch porn at least weekly.[8]) Whereas we will not devote space here to the definition struggles over the past decades, even centuries, which often saw the drive toward censorship set against a defence of freedom of self-determination (see Williams, 1989, for an overview), it suffices here to define pornography in a matter-of-fact way as the capturing, circulation and consumption of sexual acts and practices in media. And yet, already the word 'capture' opens out this meaning into more philosophical – anthropological (pertaining to the human), ontological (pertaining to the body and the thing itself) or epistemological (pertaining to knowledge) – enquiries. Hence, Linda Williams, who in her classic study *Hard Core* (1989) approaches porn from a Foucauldian perspective but with a psychoanalytic sensibility, sees in conventional porn videos, which enable a distinctively male gaze (Mulvey, 1975; see Chapter 1) onto women, the repetitive attempt to capture the truth of female pleasure and the otherwise unknowable female body. As the media scholar Niels van Doorn describes Williams's approach in the context of the many extreme close-ups in the gonzo-porn genre (i.e. an amateur-style genre filmed from the point of view of the acting man): 'It is as if a woman's sexual pleasure can be comprehended through the visual penetration of the organ that presumably constitutes its source' (van Doorn, 2010, p. 424).

From a Lacanian perspective, one can say that it is the desire to know the real and authentic – or even more directly, the desire for the real – that is promised to be satisfied in the pornographic capturing and documenting of 'real people', with 'real bodies', having 'real sex'. However, in a Lacanian spirit, both Williams and van Doorn see this promise remaining elusive and ultimately unrealizable. A similar stance is also taken by Elizabeth Cowie, who, in an early but very important – and sadly underappreciated – text, 'Pornography and Fantasy' (1992), makes a forceful argument against the common misunderstanding that porn shows us directly what we desire, writing that: 'The pornographic image is [...] a signifying system and a fantasy scenario. What is portrayed is not the object of desire but a scenario in which certain wishes are presented' in an intricate 'mise-en-scène' (Cowie, 2017 [1992], p. 7). Indeed, when Eugenie Brinkema (2019), in a recent special issue on psychoanalysis and porn of the journal *Porn Studies*, argues that 'in pornography it is neither the wet nor the moan, but in fact form that is what gets viewers off' (p. 12), this is a reiteration of Cowie's argument, without Cowie being acknowledged, however.

To remain with the latter, then, Cowie compares in her article the scene that pornography constructs – successfully, we think – with the 'primal scene' in Freudian theory:

> a scene posited by psychoanalysis as the child's earliest attempt through fantasy to imagine its parents when they are together at those times when the child is excluded. It is projected as a scene of pleasure between the parents, with the child looking on – a scene of parental coitus but imagined *without full knowledge of the sexual functions*. (Cowie, 2017 [1992], p. 8, our emphasis)

With this last part of the quotation harking back to Laplanche's concept of seduction again (see above), what Cowie is stating here is that what draws people to porn is invariably the painfully pleasurable, pleasurably painful desire to be confronted with something that goes beyond what one has bargained for. After all, seeing what one's 'parents do when [one] is not there' means to come dangerously close to something impossibly real and potentially traumatic. Moreover, the circumstance that this is done by 'authority figures' (i.e. parents in the primal scene or, in porn, people whose job is to show us sex) threatens/promises to expose the instinctual underbelly of human sociality and thus approximates the Lacanian real. As Cowie continues, the child/spectator models this always-liminal scene according to their own sexual wishes, depending on whether the 'particular array' (Cowie, 2017 [1992], p. 9), or mise-en-scène of the pornographic material is capable of facilitating these individual inclinations to a sufficient degree. In this way, a gravitational pull towards certain erogenous zones, fetishes and fixations, as well as ambivalences in one's intimate relations, can be triggered and activated. Hence, one might take pleasure in the position of one of the performers or identify broadly with the exhibitionism of the scene (ibid., p. 7), or one might find pleasure in the aggressive play of submission and domination between the performers in both active and passive modes or become confronted with the 'conscience and shame which is always so easily co-present in our best scenarios' (ibid., p. 8).

Without referring to Cowie either, Knafo and Lo Bosco (2020) present an understanding of porn that again comes very close to hers: 'Viewing porn implicates the enjoyer as the intended object and origin. The user inherently assumes a collusive position with dimensionless sex "characters" and their creators in the explicit tableau. It is as if the creators of the pornographic object are saying, "See, we know what you really want"' (2020, p. 60). Yet, whereas Cowie would surely be in agreement with the viewer's implication as object and origin of the pornographic scene and its envisioning as a 'tableau', we are less sure about the gesture of 'we know what you really want', since this might prematurely close off the space that fantasy needs to unfold. Drawing on Winnicott's (2002) famous statement, we might say that people find the porn they need just as much as they create it, with the question of 'did you create that or did you find it?' (Winnicott, 2002, p. 119) necessarily remaining open.

Now, we are aware that such a benign, quasi-therapeutic vision of pornography flies in the face of the many disturbing and destructive fantasies that have found their 'mise-en-scènes' in porn and other 'body genres' (Williams, 1991), such as horror, gore and slasher films. Furthermore, pornography is highly problematic for its degrading representations of women at the hands of men (e.g. see Benjamin, 1988; Steiner, 1993; Kaplan, 2006), and research has found that adolescents' and even kids' early exposure to porn, by virtue of its easy accessibility online, frequently leads to them developing highly unrealistic and, at times, highly gender-chauvinistic ideas about what is expected of them in terms of endurance, stamina and sexual performance (Kale, 2018). Arguably, this makes it plausible for the 'performance principle' – 'the violent and exploitative productivity which made man into an instrument of labor,' as Herbert Marcuse (1955) described it – to become ever more established in the sphere of sexual relations, too. Lastly and connectedly, pathological consumption of porn can exhibit addiction-like patterns that are undoubtedly damaging and can bring a great deal of suffering to them and their surroundings (Lemma, 2017; Knafo & Lo Bosco, 2020). Indeed, when the male online subculture, NoFap, vows to abstain from pornography and masturbation because they feel that it has turned them into weak, unsuccessful and unproductive men, the interpretation of sexuality within a neoliberal frame is complete (see Johanssen, 2022, Chapter 7 for a detailed analysis).

In our opinion, however, the question remains in how far and what ways pornography is the *cause* and/or *effect* of these social phenomena. If it is rather the effect of other societal pressures, we need to ask how exactly it might weigh in on the reproduction or change of the social relations from which its sexual arrangements emerge. In this respect, studies of internet, user-generated porn give reason for cautious optimism, with many of them finding that the democratization and easy availability of the means of production as well as those of circulation on the internet have led to more people from all walks of life becoming the producers and performers of porn, which again leads to a diversification of sexual practices that can challenge traditional gender roles (Paasonen, 2014; Rehberg, 2019; Florêncio, 2020). At the same time, however, we must be careful not to make too much of this liberatory potential. There is hardly a field of business in existence that is more entrepreneurial in spirit than the porn industry, and niche sexualities have been used there consistently to develop and tap into new markets.

In this respect, the Lacanian scholar Alison Horbury (2019) offers a differentiated view that positions itself in-between the enthusiasm of porn's democratization of sex and the sober realism of its constant commercialization. Horbury emphasizes that what is productive about the vast variations of internet porn is that viewers are prone to encounter materials in which certain scenes arouse them *despite themselves*. In these moments, porn may teach its viewers something they did not know they enjoyed, or make them realize that some things are completely off limits for them. For Horbury, it is those moments that make porn 'ethical' in the Lacanian sense. According to Lacan (2004), what is at the core of ethics is the injunction to follow one's desire and, in this sense, especially the vastly stratified field of online porn has the power to take the viewer to experience what it really is they desire. In other words, porn can take viewers into proximity of the polymorphous perversity of their unconscious, rather than obfuscating or displacing it onto other objects or forms of representation, as narrative cinema often does. Horbury writes: 'Where pornography's intractable aesthetic can be of ethical import is where it can teach the subject something about the truth of their desire and *objet a* beyond socio-symbolic values of "good" representations, or politically "bad" pornography' (2019, p. 94). In line with Cowie (1992) and others, Horbury holds that porn can never objectively depict or map this polymorphous perversity, but it certainly represents it to the viewer in an excessive, pleasure-driven, lust-fuelled way that floods the user, but pleasurably so. This is how the Real intervenes. Porn may 'pierce' or hit the viewer in affective ways that are incomprehensible, even traumatic. It penetrates the unconscious core in a particular way.

Pornography beyond the male gaze

There is one more perspective on porn that we would briefly like to present. Specifically, the media studies scholar Susanna Paasonen (2011) has cautioned against interpretations of internet porn that may analyse it through classic psychoanalytic (Screen Theory) concepts like scopophilia, identification, fetishism, voyeurism, exhibitionism and, most importantly, the gaze (see our Chapter 1). Instead, she suggests an affect-theoretical, Deleuzian perspective when she writes that: 'Pornography is about depicting people as both sexual subjects and objects – and also as assemblages of anonymous, interpenetrating flesh in motion. Objectification is merely one possible mode of encountering and experiencing these images, and it does not exhaust all available options' (2011, p. 175). Paasonen warns against interpretations that all too quickly identify what is happening in porn with the objectifying gaze developed by Mulvey (1975). Against this knee-jerk interpretational reflex, Paasonen suggests that it 'may just as well be that viewers do not want to be in control of the images unfolding but take more pleasure in being overwhelmed by them. And perhaps they do not identify with the characters engaging in performances of domination and submission on the screen' (ibid., p. 180).

This intervention is a productive counterweight to many psychoanalytically oriented interpretations. Linda Williams's (1989) discussion of porn through the Freudian concept of fetishism, for instance, is quick to find such power dynamics. And also Knafo and Lo Bosco's observation of porn's gesture of the 'see, we know what you really want' (2020, p. 60), where the spectator quickly becomes the object of the film's address, might be read as a case in point. In contradistinction, Paasonen refers to Theresa Senft's (2008) notion of the 'grab' in her work on webcams to drive at porn's possible interpellation. In comparison to Mulvey's gaze (see Chapter 1), the grab describes a more fleeting gesture as well as a bi-directional practice of looking. 'By "grab", Senft writes, 'I mean to clutch with the hand, to seize for a moment, to command attention, to touch – often inappropriately, sometimes reciprocally' (2008, p. 46). More generally, users 'grab images and technologies by which they are grabbed in return' (Paasonen, 2011, p. 178).

As Paasonen shows, users of online porn are often grabbed by it, affected and moved, they resonate with it and, as we would add, are often seduced by it in enigmatic ways. This last addition about seduction, we have made here so as to lead us back to Cowie's work. And as we have already broached above, Cowie draws on Laplanche's work on fantasy (less so on that of seduction) to make exactly *that* point about porn which Paasonen proposes should be made outside a psychoanalytic paradigm. Hence, when Cowie describes the scene of watching porn as in tight coordination with the primal scene of psychoanalysis, the excess impressions in such a scene, which unveil themselves to a principally overwhelmed spectator, might indeed be more akin to 'assemblages of anonymous, interpenetrating flesh in motion' than any straightforwardly delineateable object. In this sense, what we want to suggest is that, although Paasonen is right that psychoanalytic interpretation at times 'seems to result in predictable outcomes' (2011, p. 180), this predictability hinges not so much on the immense and still growing body of theory, but rather on the conventional productivity of some well-known theoretical strands. And whereas the job of this book is to present and discuss first and foremost these better-known strands, we hope that we nevertheless instil in our readers a longing for other, lesser-known parts of the field.

Conclusion

In this chapter, we have discussed Freudian, Lacanian and Laplanchean conceptualizations of sexuality and how they relate to the digital in ways that mirror the foundational dynamics of psychosexuality between infant and caregivers (Laplanche) and forms of adult sexuality in relation to the lack in the Symbolic Order (Lacan). Drawing on Sharon Tugwell (2021), we have shown how users oscillate between the position of the baby and caregiver, depending on the technology or platforms and apps. Whether pre-oedipal, oedipal or post-oedipal, sexuality is foundational for psychoanalysis and digital cultures today. It extends to seemingly ordinary and mundane ways of using technology and also mediates more explicit phenomena such as porn or hook-up apps. A question that has perhaps been left unanswered up to this point is: what do we actually think is people's relation to the digital? Is it pre-oedipal or post-oedipal? It is all at once. Depending on context, technology, content and other factors, the subject occupies one of the two. In the next chapter, we turn to videogames and AI.

Notes

1. This term was coined by Otto Rank in 1925.
2. Of course, the baby's gender is very important to consider here, too, as it influences the dynamics between mother and baby – something that, for example, has become an important factor in Estela Welldon's work on female perversion (e.g. Welldon, 1988).
3. This emphatically oral attachment/connection and the excess sexual components that are being taken in offer a strong connection to questions of online addiction (see Seymour, 2019).
4. https://members.seeking.com/join?_ga=2.93237085.1560830714.1646392798-206774153.1646392798 [Accessed 4/3/22].
5. Avenue Q, www.youtube.com/watch?v=zBDCq6Q8k2E
6. www.statista.com/chart/16959/share-of-the-internet-that-is-porn [Accessed 11/3/22].
7. Yet, the social feature of such platforms encouraged, or perhaps enabled, amateur porn and 'ordinary' users to upload their own videos.
8. www.statista.com/chart/16959/share-of-the-internet-that-is-porn [Accessed 11/3/22].

Further reading

Bown, A. (2022). *Dream Lovers. The Gamification of Relationships*. London: Pluto Press.
Cowie, E. (2017 [1992]). Pornography and fantasy. In: L. Segal and M. McIntosh (eds.), *Sex Exposed: Sexuality and the Pornography Debate* (pp. 132–52). London: Virago, 1992, Available at: www.academia.edu/31009171/Pornography_and_Fantasy [Accessed 6/5/2022].
Haga Gripsrud, B., Ramvi, E., Froggett, L., Hellstrand, I. and Manley, J. (2018). Psychosocial and symbolic dimensions of the breast explored through a visual matrix. *NORA-Nordic Journal of Feminist and Gender Research*, 26(3), 210–29.
Hardy, S. (2009). The new pornographies: representation or reality. In: F. Attwood (ed.), *Mainstreaming Sex – The Sexualisation of Western Culture* (pp. 3–18). London: I. B. Tauris.
Knafo, D. and Lo Bosco, R. (2020). *The New Sexual Landscape and Contemporary Psychoanalysis*. London: Confer Books.
Wang, C. (2021). The passivity of seeing: a Lacanian perspective on pornographic spectatorship in virtual reality. *Psychoanalysis, Culture & Society*, 26(2), 217–33.
Zabet, P. (2004). Going on-line: consuming pornography in the digital era. In: L. Williams (ed.), *Porn Studies* (pp. 104–25). Durham, NC: Duke University Press.

CHAPTER 6

Videogames, AI and the vicissitudes of symbiosis

Key themes:
playing, games and gaming; psychoanalytic approaches to
videogames; interactivity and interpassivity; videogames and
violence; clinical perspectives on videogames; artificial intelligence
and human subjectivity; AI, the maternal and the matrixial

Introduction

Having discussed film, television, social media and the internet as
psychosocial technologies so far in this book, this chapter turns to
videogames and artificial intelligence (AI). This combination is not as
accidental as it might seem, since the origins of both lie in the emergence of
cybernetics, developed in the wake of the Second World War as the science
of steering and regulation through feedback and correction. Although
there is still debate over what may count as the first videogame, all serious
contenders were made in the late 1950s (Overmars, 2012; Stanton, 2015),
around the same time that AI as a research field was created (Wooldridge,
2020). Nevertheless, with rapid advances in computer technology in the
last few decades, both fields seem to have increased their fascination with
people and their mythological potentials – a potential already captured
in the Pygmalion myth and, as a modernist version of this myth, in Fritz
Lang's film *Metropolis* (Lang, 1927). In the film, the inventor Rotwang
builds a robot meant to resurrect his dead love.

Despite many continuities, the sense of total simulation in the artificial
recreation of life, which harks back to the notions of virtual reality and
cyberspace broached earlier (see Chapter 2), signifies an important point

of departure from older technologies, particularly print, radio, film and television. In the coming pages, we introduce both fields and discuss key psychoanalytic works on the matter. We also bring in the clinical perspective and show how clinicians have encountered videogames in the consulting room. We then pick up on the discussion of a key question in the clinical, academic and public sphere: do violent videogames make their players violent, too? Our take on this is that, although many videogames feature violent fantasies, it is not so much this violence in itself that seems the problem because these fantasies frequently enable the working through of unconscious conflicts. The problem is, rather, the objects, situations, contexts and mise-en-scènes in which they locate the engagements with violence. These objects are often reminiscent of marginalized social groups that are shown in contexts that make their annihilation necessary.

Subsequently, the chapter moves to a discussion of AI and how it connects to human subjectivity, which we discuss through the work of the philosopher Catherine Malabou (2019) as well as the psychoanalyst and artist Bracha L. Ettinger (2020). Rather than seeing the existing and future relations between humans and AI as those in which AI acquires, or even surpasses, human intelligence, or, in a dystopian twist, dominates humans, we conceptualize them as relations that are characterized by proximity and difference, sameness and alterity. They can be seen as regressive fantasies of returning to the safe and nurturing space of the maternal womb.

Playing videogames and the reality of the virtual

In the action-comedy film *The Interview* (Rogen & Goldberg, 2014), a celebrity gossip TV show host (James Franco) and his producer (Seth Rogen) are invited to North Korea to interview Kim Jong-Un. The CIA sees in this invitation an opportunity to assassinate Kim and, when the poisonous strip intended for the deed is accidentally eaten by one of Kim's military staff, it sends a drone to deliver a second strip into North Korean territory. In a film filled with rampantly boyish and prankish humour, the brief, fast-cut sequence of the drone launch and delivery entails, in miniature, the complete set of negative stereotypes about gamers and gaming in western culture. After hectic cuts show the poison being made, the strip being prepared, dexterously packaged and loaded on the drone, we then see a young man (Willem Jacobson) in a baggy army uniform, and with considerably less purpose, sauntering toward a desert army barrack. Milky skinned, baby faced and with longish curly hair, features that immediately betray the complete absence of any direct combat experience, the young man sits down in front of a computer terminal with several screens, online porn on one of them, control pads and a joystick, pulling the trigger to launch the drone onto its mission. In the windowless darkness of the barrack, we then see the drone operator remote-controlling the drone and commenting on its progress in a nonchalant manner, while taking a sip from a can of Red Bull energy drink. Finally, when the shell carrying the poisonous strip is to be dropped, he counts down 'in three, two, one. Boom' (44:04).

Although this scene does not actually show someone playing a videogame, it shows someone we stereotypically identify as a videogame player – young, male, pale, slim and unmuscular, with unhealthy dietary habits – carrying out a real-life task with life-and-death consequences as though it were a videogame. The young man's anaesthetic technicality and emotional distance, skill and control in operating the terminal combines with a disinterest in the material consequences of his actions from which he is protected by geographical distance, walls and screens. This dryly funny depiction of a gamer in a non-gaming context captures the wariness with which mainstream culture looks upon gamers as people whose preoccupation with videogames has led them to lose their capacity for empathy. At the same time, however, as ambivalent as we might be towards such cultural phenotypes, it becomes clear, too, from our encounters with gaming-like patterns throughout society that videogames, gaming and gamers are becoming increasingly paradigmatic social entities. As the psychoanalytic game studies scholar Alfie Bown (2017) has stated in an interview with *LA Review of Books*: 'the gamer is no longer a niche identity taken up by those on the fringes [...] but a term that can describe all of us.'

Playing and games

The difference between playing and gaming has frequently been discussed in and outside of game studies. In this section, we present a brief history of the terms because they are particularly relevant for psychoanalytic ideas about fantasy, agency and play. The German enlightenment philosopher and playwright Karl Friedrich Schiller, for example, had the whole field of art in mind when he defined play as 'the free, non-utilitarian exercise of [a human being's] various faculties' (Hein, 1968, p. 67). As the philosopher Hilde Hein explains about Schiller's take:

> Characteristically human play, as distinct from that of lower animals, is expression intermediary between our purely sensuous, animal nature and our formal or purely rational nature. As a synthesis of both the sensuous and formal impulses, play cancels the authority of both and liberates man physically and morally. (Hein, 1968, p. 67)

That Schiller contrasts the freedom of play with the demands and deprivations of work makes his position anticipate that of Johan Huizinga (1955 [1950]) who holds that 'play sets the subject free to perform actions without material consequences' (Walther, 2003, n.p.). More importantly for a psychoanalytical perspective, however, Schiller's vision of play and creativity as at an equidistance between the 'instinctual' and 'rational' would become central in psychoanalytic thinking. When Freud (1905b), for example, defines the creation of a joke as surrendering a preconscious thought to the primary process of the unconscious so as to then grasp it by consciousness, Schiller's synthesis arises in new form.

The perhaps best-known psychoanalytic approach to playing, however, comes from Donald W. Winnicott. He again implicitly follows Schiller's enlightenment ideal when he writes about the importance of playing in the psychotherapeutic/psychoanalytic setting that, 'It is in playing that the patient is being creative' (2002 [1971], p. 72) and defines playing as a 'non-purposive state' (ibid., p. 74). Furthermore, he adds the following features to his description:

> to afford opportunity for formless experience, and for creative impulses, motor and sensory, which are the stuff of playing. And on the basis of playing is built the whole of man's experiential existence. No longer are we either introvert or extrovert. We experience life in the area of transitional phenomena, in the exciting interweave of subjectivity and objective observation, and in an area that is intermediate between the inner reality of the individual and the shared reality of the world that is external to individuals. (ibid., p. 86)

Hence, although Winnicott grants the notion of play certain limitations, writing that 'the behaviour of the environment is part of the individual's own personal development' (ibid., p. 72), he nevertheless demands of playing within an analytic setting an important degree of 'formlessness' which needs to be reflected back to the player/analysand in a constructive and benign way. Taking this requirement into the field of videogames, we can see that, despite considerable broadening of the scope of videogames currently in existence, such benignly reflected formlessness is still extremely rare and abides mostly in so-called 'sandbox' games, where a virtual world can be explored with relative freedom from formal restrictions and the stringent performance of preset tasks (although these tasks offer themselves in many places in the sandbox). The success of *Minecraft* (2011) and its popularity particularly with the *parents* of young gamers, who often see the game as an exception to the genre, might indeed be based on its relative alignment with Winnicott's developmental ideals.

French social philosopher Roger Caillois's systematic analysis of playing and games, *Man, Play and Games* (1958), offers an insightful map for locating videogames within the field of game-playing in general. Based on the socio-historical origins of playing, he suggests four main types of game/play:

- 'Agon' is about competition and conflict, with players being pitted against one another.
- 'Alea' refers to games of chance and luck, such as gambling.
- 'Mimicry' refers to fantasy role-play, make-believe and simulation.
- 'Ilinx', or vertigo, means playing games that challenge the player's sense of balance and orientation.

Additionally, Caillois (1958) makes a differentiation between 'paidea', which means less organized forms of play allowing for a higher degree of freedom and formlessness, as Winnicott put it, and 'ludus', which are more highly organized and rule-bound games.

Caillois's exercise in categorization gives us a chance to position videogames more precisely in the field of possibilities. Hence, as the game studies scholar Bo Kampmann Walther (2003) has pointed out, whereas videogames can draw from a whole range of classes of playing and games and mix – for example, 'agon' and 'ilinx' – in their game-play, as do most spacecraft games, for example, the majority of videogames, and especially the early ones, are clearly located on the side of 'ludus' rather than that of 'paidea'. As Walther (2003) puts it, the 'central "law"' of videogames is 'to reduce the complexity of play by way of a set of well-defined, non-negotiable rules: when the rules are not a discussion point, the player's attention turns to strategy' (ibid., n.p.).

The focus on calculating, regulating, steering, coordinating and strategizing that first gave birth to videogames in the US computer labs of the 1950s, where its programming went into the steering systems of air- and spacecrafts, for example, is still at the heart of the most commonly used definitions in the field of game studies. Here, games have been most decisively and resoundingly distinguished from narratives in films, television or literature. The game designer and theorist Jesper Juul (not to be confused with the famous family therapist of the same name) writes in his article for the inaugural issue of the journal *Game Studies*:

> Games and stories actually do not translate to each other in the way that novels and movies do. There is an inherent conflict between the *now* of the interaction and the *past* or '*prior*' of the narrative. You can't have narration and interactivity at the same time; there is no such thing as a continuously interactive story. The relations between reader/story and player/game are completely different – the player inhabits a twilight zone where he/she is both an empirical subject outside the game *and* undertakes a role inside the game. (Juul, 2001, n.p.)

Overlooking the discourse within and around game studies, the proximity or distance of videogames to the story genre has been a central point of contention in the understanding of the field. And much of the ire of game studies scholars against narrative approaches to videogaming centred on Janet Murray's 1996 book-length study *Hamlet on the Holodeck*, a study brimming with fascinating ideas, observations and conceptions about the narrative dimensions of videogames. About the famous *Tetris* game (1984), for example, Murray writes:

> Even a game with no verbal content, like Tetris, the wildly popular and powerfully absorbing computer game of the early 1990s, has clear dramatic content. In Tetris irregularly shaped objects keep falling from the top of the screen and accumulating at the

bottom. The player's goal is to guide each individual piece as it falls and position it so that it will fit together with other pieces and form a uniform row. Every time a complete row forms, it disappears. Instead of keeping what you build, as you would in a conventional jigsaw puzzle, in Tetris everything you bring to a shapely completion is swept away from you. Success means just being able to keep up with the flow. (Murray, 1996, p. 136)

At this point, Murray makes her central interpretation of the game:

This game is a perfect enactment of the overtasked lives of Americans in the 1990s – of the constant bombardment of tasks that demand our attention and that we must somehow fit into our overcrowded schedules and clear off our desks in order to make room for the next onslaught. (ibid.)

By all means, as far as symptomatic readings go, we think this is a very good and useful one because it tells us something about the emotive experience of playing the game as well as about the sociocultural context in which this experience makes sense. Indeed, the Lacanian scholar Alfie Bown, writing almost two decades later, makes a complementary point about the popular casual game *Candy Crush* (2012), a game that was surely inspired by the mechanics of *Tetris*:

[I]t is self-evident that we don't truly desire to play Candy Crush but unfortunately have to work, but rather that we feel the need for distraction only when we are working, to re-enforce the sense (increasingly lost) that our work has coherent order and value compared to these activities. (Bown, 2015, p. 30)

Whereas, in Murray's argument, Tetris is a tribute to our compulsory frenzy of needing to clear things off our desks, Bown sees *Candy Crush* as a barrage against the threatening insight into the meaninglessness of this compulsion. For both Murray and Bown, games can serve as both analogies and symptoms of wider psychosocial dynamics.

Playing videogames – a psychoanalytic approach

How, then, do we go about interpreting videogames? What is the adequate frame of reference for our analyses and interpretations if the existing psychoanalytic conceptions of playing show very little appreciation for the fixed structures and if-then lawfulness that are constitutive parts of videogames in particular and what Caillois has classified as 'ludus' games more generally? Walther's article on the relationship between 'Playing and [Video]Gaming' (2003) offers a helpful blueprint in this respect which we would like to extend into a psychoanalytically oriented frame. 'Play,' Walther writes, 'is an open-ended territory in which make-believe and world-building are crucial factors. Games are confined areas that challenge the interpretation and optimising of rules and tactics – not to mention time and space' (Walther, 2003, n.p.). Yet, he cautions, this difference between play and game does not mean that the latter does not draw upon aspects of the former. '[G]ames *should* not be play; but that does not imply that they do not *require* play' (ibid.).

Using the first-person shooter game *Hitman: Codename 47* (2000) as an example, Walther explains that, in order to play the game, 'we must first and foremost "get into character"' – that is, we must play in a mode that Caillois calls 'mimicry'. Once, however, 'we are "in" the game,' we must commit to its rules. At this level, 'Hitman obviously presents itself as an agon-based game that challenges senso-motoric capabilities and swift user reactions' (Walther 2003, n. p.). 'There is mimicry, and *then* there is agon. I am a character and I play by the rules,' Walther (ibid.) sums up the layering and interrelatedness of make-believe fantasy play and rule-bound game structures that are both constitutive of a large number of videogames. As the Lacanian media scholar Caroline Pelletier (2005) has put it: 'What defines a game are rules which, during the process of play, cannot be changed or critiqued; this is what makes play possible, and differentiates games from other activities' (2005, p. 323).

It is these two layers, or dimensions, and their various constellations – the balances and imbalances between them – that we suggest as a productive theoretical frame for approaching videogames from a psychoanalytically informed, hermeneutic angle. Assessing these two dimensions in relation to each other allows for interpretations of videogames, but prompts these interpretations to also engage with a concern for the games' rule-bound aspects which always pose a necessary counterweight and set limits for the fantasy activity. These dimensions can thus be expected to have clear tendencies for working into certain directions. Whereas the invitation to role-playing and mimicry – that is, the invitation to join into a ready-made, mise-en-scène (Cowie, 1997) of a fantasy – entails what poet Samuel Taylor Coleridge (1772–1834) called the 'willing suspension of disbelief', the requirement of abiding by fixed rules and pre-programmed laws of causes and effects in the videogame, by contrast, suggests a 'willing suspension of belief', or at least the receding of this *belief* into the background.

On the one hand, the process of the player inserting themselves into the fantasy play/play fantasy of the game means making available to the player the whole scope of aesthetic and fantasmatic support that helps them invest themselves into the act of game-playing. Just like the ornaments on a bow help a warrior shoot their arrow better, it makes an affective, emotional difference whether I imagine myself as being the pilot of a spacecraft or, in soberly realistic fashion, as merely sitting in front of my PlayStation. In this sense, immersing oneself in the fantasy a videogame offers means to make oneself available to the uses of illusion that Winnicott sees as residing in non-purposive playing. On the other hand, the interaction with a setting that demands technicality, skill and dexterity in the player's/gamer's adherence to the game's rules can easily drown out the fantasy aspects. For example, the fantasy of being an X-Wing Jet pilot in the *Star Wars Battlefront* game series (2004–) can easily recede behind a difficulty that the player-cum-pilot comes up against time and again in a battle sequence and that foregrounds the *playing* of the game rather than the *being* the X-Wing pilot. In such situations, we argue that what players come up against points to a parallel to what Georges Devereux (1967) has described as the intricate relationship between the human proclivity to experience unease, discontent and anxiety towards objects and the application of methods in the social sciences to defend against these feelings.

Admittedly, videogames are a far cry from the academic research situations that Devereux had in mind when writing his book; furthermore, we agree with readers who find that bringing the notion of anxiety into a sphere of game-play and fun seems somewhat far-fetched. And yet, the aspect from Devereux's study that we hold to be productive for understanding videogaming is the connection it makes between methodical action and affect regulation. Hence, we suggest that the rule-bound behaviour that gaming requires can be seen as working in a similar way, specifically as a shield and defence, first and foremost against the dimension of fantasy play, but also against the fantasmatic, imaginary and often anxiety-provoking broader aspects of our lives in general. Hence, as stated, although a difficulty at the rule-bound level of gaming can damage, or even destroy, the fantasy-scape to which a majority of videogames invites players, such an increased focus on the technical aspects of gaming can in other situations help to keep an anxiety-provoking illusion at bay, such as when focusing on the flow of controller coordination during a realistic horror-simulation game. In this way, the two interrelated dimensions of 'mimicry/paidea' and 'ludus' make possible the creation of dynamic sequences of affective balances between the two that fulfil the task of creating various degrees and states of immersion and distance between player and game.

Furthermore, with videogames becoming an increasingly popular, widespread and culturally relevant activity, the dynamic balancing of the two dimensions of fantasy and technicality might also become a relevant cultural–diagnostic tool for the interpretation of videogames and their sociocultural functions and effects on a broader scope. The short scene of the military drone operator from the film *The Interview*, presented earlier, can thus be interpreted within the frame of our model. Along its lines, the drone operator's focus on the rule-boundness and conventionality of the technical aspects of flying the drone would afford him protection from the deeper insights into the human consequences of his actions. At the same time, with the film's suggestion of a game-like activity being applied to a non-gaming, real-life task, we can further venture that the very routines of playing a videogame and the soldier's gamer identity, which the film suggests is well established, protect him further from facing the moral consequences of his actions. Hence, whereas the film presents this as a comical device, what it gestures towards are the very serious and far-reaching consequences of the inserting of media into ever more aspects of society which were not mediated before. This can be seen in the ways in which gaming as a paradigm spreads across large sociocultural spheres today, a process that is referred to as 'gamification' (e.g. Whitson, 2013). As one real-life drone operator put it, performing deadly drone strikes is like 'playing the same videogame four years straight every single day on the same level' (Pinchevski, 2019, p. 83).

The psychoanalytic trauma theorist Amit Pinchevski has discussed how the gamified ways in which drone operators control deadly drone strikes indeed constitute a defence. This defence, however, often breaks down, as many US-based drone operators have reported post-traumatic stress disorder and trauma-like symptoms similar to those exhibited by soldiers in combat situations. 'You are going to war for twelve hours, shooting weapons at targets, directing kills on enemy combatants, and then you get in the car, drive home and within twenty minutes you are sitting at the dinner table talking to your kids about their homework,' Pinchevski (ibid., p. 80) quotes another drone operator. This has become known as 'perpetrator trauma' (ibid., p. 19). Curiously, Pinchevski notes, many drone operators resort to playing videogames in their free time. This constitutes a mechanism of unwinding from the 'mediated battleground [as] the origin of trauma' whereby 'the pretend battleground is the outlet for its acting out' (ibid., p. 83). After all, there are no real casualties in a videogame.

Psychoanalytic approaches to gaming: from the 1980s to the present

Turkle setting the tone

Having thus brought a general structure for an interpretative analysis of videogames in place, we can now use the field of tension that its two dimensions of fantasy play and game-play create to assess some central psychoanalytic works on gaming. In this respect, Sherry Turkle's (2005 [1985]) early ethnographic study of arcade games in the 1970s and 1980s set the tone for most of the research following in its wake, including our present approach. The risk that Turkle sees in videogames and the widespread cultural popularity that they already gained in the early 1980s is that of an unlearning of empathy, not due to their entanglements in fantasy worlds, but – parallel to our earlier argument – the games' rule-bound set-up. In a passage that strongly echoes Winnicott's positions, Turkle writes:

> [T]he process of play [in videogames] is mathematical and procedural. Beyond the fantasy, there are always the rules. In all of this, something is missing, something that is abundantly

present in the open-ended role playing that children offer each other when one says 'You be the Mommy and I'll be the Daddy'. [...] In this kind of play children have to learn to put themselves in the place of another person, to imagine what is going on inside someone else's head. There are no rules, there is empathy. (Turkle, 2005 [1985], p. 81)

Although Turkle subsequently turned her attention towards the internet, social media and robotics, her preoccupation with empathy, together with the argument that the decline in people's capacities for empathy is related to the calculating logics of computing, has remained with her throughout the four decades of her work (Turkle, 2021). And, although we are wondering whether Turkle is not short-changing the fantasy dimension of videogames to a degree in the above statement, her early analysis remains a touchstone for considering the long-term effects of people's increasing attachment to gaming.

Interpassivity and indoctrination

Caroline Pelletier, a scholar in education and psychosocial studies with a Lacanian orientation, argues in a way similar to Turkle, but uses the term 'interpassivity' to make her case (see also Jagodzinski, 2004; Bown, 2018; Fizek, 2018; Gekker, 2018, who have all drawn on the concept in relation to gaming).

The Austrian philosopher Robert Pfaller (2014) defines **interpassivity** as instances where activities as well as their enjoyment are delegated and performed by someone or something else. An often-quoted example is the 'canned laughter' in sitcoms that not only signals when to laugh, but de facto laughs for and instead of the viewer (see also Žižek, e.g. 1998). Pfaller maintains that, 'interpassive subjects are actually fleeing from their enjoyment. They even avoid it in those situations where personally experiencing it would be easy. Owners of recording devices, for example, watch less television once they have the recorder than they did when they owned only the television set' (2014, p. 27). However, we wonder whether Pfaller and Žižek are not overstating a valuable point by rendering the distribution of active and passive states in an interaction too extreme in some of their examples. Rather than becoming completely displaced, the delegation of one's experiences and enjoyment elsewhere still seems to warrant and facilitate one's own actions and enjoyment to large degrees.

As Pelletier (2005) explains with reference to videogames: 'Interactivity allows me to be passive while being active through another (for example, pressing buttons translates into in-game actions); through interpassivity, I am active while being passive through another (I fulfil the game's demands)' (2005, p. 318). In our reading, what Pelletier drives at here with respect to interpassivity might be better understood as *being active while having one's experience of this activity passively constructed through another*. Indeed, she goes so far as to argue that the pleasure of gaming lies in 'being able to do what you are told' (ibid., p. 322). For the study of videogames, we take this to mean that the relatively passive and restricted activity at the 'ludic' level of the game – that is, of using a game controller to interact with a videogame in predesigned and rule-bound ways – nevertheless serves to offer identifications to the gamer. According to our structure, this would be so because the game's translations of the gamer's inputs into certain relational constellations pertains to the fantasy level where the gamer is continuously invited to identify with someone or something.

This point is brought out in Bown's (2017) work on gaming as a form of social dreaming. In the interview from which we quoted earlier, Bown explains his core thesis as follows: 'If games are dreams, they are not our own individual dreams – as classic arguments about games and wish-fulfilment might have argued – but complex social and political constructions that we nevertheless experience on a personal and emotional level in the act of playing' (Bown, 2017, online). Along Pelletier's lines, Bown argues that games are not so much devices that *we* operate, but – vice versa – 'we are devices that are operated by games' (ibid.). Playing videogames is often so immersive because it mimics or latches onto the endless loop of desire in the Lacanian sense. According to Bown, it is the ability of games to tap into our desires and forcing manufactured desires onto us.

Pelletier (2005), by contrast, holds that gamers *know* that the constraints they are faced with are set by others. Gaming is based on a particular identification with the other's desire and this can bring our own investment and fantasies to the fore and, ultimately, may provide some distance. As she goes on to explain:

Because the rules are already set, the goals already decided, we can be playful around them. It is precisely in the act of over-identifying with the game designer's orders, in other words the rules of the game, that we recognize them as a game. What defines a game are rules which, during the process of play, cannot be changed or critiqued; this is what makes play possible, and differentiates games from other activities. (Pelletier, 2005, p. 323)

We would treat such Lacanian accounts with a bit of caution, having argued for different degrees of immersion depending on the type of videogame, as well as for a tension between set rules and creative potentials inherent to gaming through the ideas of Georges Devereux and game studies scholars earlier. However, what Bown in particular refers to is not a direct translation of in-game action into real-life beliefs, but rather a form of ideological interpellation (Althusser, 1971) that works exactly because it is not the main focus of the game. Along our model, players are often so preoccupied with the game-play that they take the aesthetic artifice at face value, and it is exactly this face value that feeds into existing ideologies.

This subtle kind of indoctrination through the side-door, so to speak, has also been pointed out by game studies scholars outside the psychoanalytic paradigm. David J. Leonard, for example, states in an article on representations of race in videogames that sports games in particular provide for 'its primarily white creators and players the opportunity to become black. In doing so, these games elicit pleasure, playing on white fantasies as they simultaneously affirm white privilege through virtual play' (Leonard, 2004, p. 1). Building on Leonard's argument, Steffen (Krüger, 2018b) has shown how the Machinima film (i.e. a film created using a videogame engine) *Finding Fanon II* (Achiampong & Blandy, 2015) brings these white fantasies to the fore in the game *Grand Theft Auto V* (GTA V; Rockstar, 2015) – a game (in) famous for its immersion of mostly white players into African–American ghetto life (see Miller, 2012). Recreating their likenesses in the game's avatar generator, *Finding Fanon II* drops its creators into GTA V's game environment, which it otherwise shows devoid of all non-playable characters. This emptiness makes possible an evocative and uncanny encounter with the game and the ways it configures its players in relation to its strongly racialized world. 'Rather than endeavouring to remove our fantasies and so be "more fully ourselves", we should over-identify with them and, in this way, achieve some kind of distance from them,' writes Pelletier (2005, p. 323) about the strategy of traversing fantasies in videogames. Arguably, this articulates in Lacanian idiom what Steffen identifies as *Finding Fanon*'s strategy with respect to GTA V.

Videogames in clinical psychoanalysis

To be sure, none of the clinical psychoanalytic accounts that we have read conceives videogames as the single source of, or reason for, mental distress. Nevertheless, especially in clinical discussions, videogames and the internet are often given a power that we feel is too great and betrays a techno-deterministic strain that does not seem compatible with a psychoanalytic understanding of human relatedness otherwise. Andrea Marzi, for instance, makes sweeping references 'to the almost toxico-manic relationship that many young people today have with the internet world' (2016, p. xxxvi). Even if there are kernels of truth in these assessments, the ways in which they are presented betray the bewilderment (Bollas, 2015) of an older generation in the face of a media–cultural paradigm shift to which they respond with the full force of the pessimism of Freud's culture–critical writings (Griffin, 2012; Leskauskas, 2020). Along Devereux's lines, what can be expected of the ensuing treatment of those 'toxico-manic [...] young people' (Marzi, 2016, p. xxxvi) are countertransferential movements torn between the analyst's wish to help and understand and an unconscious defence against such understanding.

Symptomatic of this defence are the frequent references to *addiction* that clinical psychoanalytic literature makes. Even a renowned analyst such as David Rosenfeld (2016) is remarkably swift to claim that one of his patients, a violent and psychotic young man, who excessively played arcade-style videogames, was addicted to violent games. This label, we argue, is not productive for an adequate understanding of individual cases. As Billieux *et al.* (2015) note, in their review of literature on internet addiction, that the criteria used to diagnose forms of technological addictions tend to overpathologize current forms of activity that come with high usage patterns (e.g. gaming or smartphone use). Such forms may not necessarily constitute addictions but are instead evidence of changing media use. If we applied the 'addiction' label consistently, many of us would classify as addicts given the extent of smartphone and internet usage we exhibit. As for young people who turn to psychoanalysts for help, it is often unclear whether the overuse of digital technologies is the cause or effect of psychological problems, subjective distress, loss of agency and control, health problems, professional and social isolation and disruption. And, as clinicians will know, this unsolvability must prompt us to look elsewhere to understand the significance that videogames might have in these people's lives.

Apart from his use of the addiction label, however, Rosenfeld (2016) contains his analysand Lorenzo's attachment to videogames very well. Whereas the patient's former therapist had banned all games from his home, which had led to further deteriorating mental health, Rosenfeld reports that he joined the young man in playing them. What the adolescent liked playing were 'beat 'em up' arcade games, such as *Street Fighter* (Capcom), and in his vignette Rosenfeld makes much of the game's apparent violence, writing that 'you have to kill the characters with a sword, cut their throats, or hit them very aggressively' (2016, p. 140). However, although Rosenfeld's observation that his analysand celebrated his triumphs over him omnipotently but then came to the next 'session terrified because he had won – as though he had killed me and cut my throat' seems undoubtedly valuable, we wonder what a more realistic assessment of the game would have added to Rosenfeld's interpretation. Although it is unclear when exactly Rosenfeld treated the patient, the arcade-style graphics and sounds and manga-comic inspired visuals, which are characteristic of all of the game's versions since its original release in 1987, are not likely to be experienced as harshly 'violent' in the full sense of the world by someone versed in the videogame genre. Having played this game ourselves, notions of killing other people, or 'cut[ting] their throats', couldn't be further from this experience, with the game's comic style rather suggesting the characters' grotesque immortality. After all, even when characters 'die' during a round of play, here they are again when playing the next. And yet, true enough, the game is about eliminating and doing away with obstacles and powerful enemies when played against the computer, just as it is about prevailing over and winning against other people when played in multiplayer mode. In this light, we find that the analysand's anxiety upon having won over his analyst, a quasi-parental figure, might receive an importance different from that which Rosenfeld gives it.

Additionally, the fact that Lorenzo played arcade-style games with retro looks and that he took his analyst to an arcade, which is highly evocative of an earlier era of videogame play, is noteworthy but not considered by Rosenfeld. We would argue that this nostalgic strain points to a desire to regress on Lorenzo's part that may be linked to a wish to return to an earlier sense of self, or to a safe space in his childhood. This may be significant given that Rosenfeld reports Lorenzo discussing many instances throughout his childhood and teenage years where he witnessed aggressive and violent fights between his parents. Lorenzo might thus have projected his parents' fights into the videogames, as Rosenfeld notes. In this way, they might have served as 'psychic retreats' that enabled Lorenzo to 'win' against his parents without them ever really dying.

The term 'psychic retreats', coined by John Steiner (1993), describes 'an area of relative peace and protection from strain' (1993, p. 14), particularly for a patient in analysis. Drawing on Steiner's concept, Schimmenti and Caretti (2010) argue that videogames, too, can be seen as offering psychic retreats, and this conceptual transfer fits well, not only to our understanding of Rosenfeld's case study, but also to what we have described as the methodical defences against anxiety that can be facilitated by a gaming-like attitude to life in general. According to the authors, psychic retreats can be seen as ways of escaping stressful conditions or experiences beyond the digital realm. Such psychic states are enabled by the control over a videogame character or other cultural objects (see Giffney, 2021). However, this strategy has a double edge and, as Schimmenti and Caretti (2010) caution, becomes especially precarious when 'the psychic retreat is excessively extended' (p. 118). In such cases, psychic retreats can become 'psychic pits' (ibid., p. 127) in which 'feelings, states of mind and pieces of one's own self are buried and lost in oblivion' (ibid., p. 127).

Videogames and the question of violence

We would like to end this subchapter about videogaming with the persistent question of violence related to gaming. The critical game scholar David Leonard (2006), for example, observed with respect to Rockstar's launch of *GTA: San Andreas* (2004): 'As politicians and cultural commentators […] lamented the game's promotion of violence and dysfunctional values, little was made of the racial content of the game' (p. 85). Following on from our above arguments, the more dangerous form of violence might indeed be that of ideological, epistemological violence that players hardly notice when indulging in the pleasures of playing a game. Yet, there is still something in the straightforward ways in which games are often seen to trigger violence in players that has remained insufficiently understood. And this is so, despite several studies having disproven any direct linkage between game violence and the violent social behaviour of gamers (e.g. Barker & Pentley, 2001; Drummond *et al.*, 2020; Coyne and Stockdale 2021).

This insufficiency starts with the question of why game creators and the gaming industry add so many representations of violence to their games. As the literary scholar T.V. Reed puts it in an address to the gamer community:

> [U]nless you can make an argument that racism, sexism, xenophobia and homophobia, for example, are intrinsically necessary to games, then I invite you to think about how you might make the games that you love better at supporting efforts to open up gaming to people who are currently unable to enjoy their pleasures because they often feel more like targets than players. (Reed, 2014, p. 151)

Put bluntly, a central argument for the necessity of including such violence in games is the sales figures. As has been proven by the launch and persistent success of the Sony PlayStation, for example, which from the start targeted a more mature group of players with markedly non-family-friendly tastes, or the success of the *Call of Duty* military combat simulations, games that offer players the opportunity to shoot at, and annihilate, others – preferably recognizable others – sell exceedingly well. However, the circumstance that violence dials up sales numbers still does not offer a comprehensive explanation, but it shifts the question to that of the players and their needs, demands and desires.

With this, we are brought back to the basic human proclivity towards aggression and violence, which Freud (1920) captured in the notion of the death drive, whereas others saw this proclivity as arising from experiences of frustration and threat, with Steven Mitchell mediating between these two positions (Mitchell, 1998; see Chapter 4). In this respect, the psychoanalyst and child psychologist Bruno Bettelheim, in his classic study on *The Uses of Enchantment* (2010 [1976]), refers to the capacity of fairy tales and old folktales, which are also frequently violent, to permit children's unconscious 'formless, nameless anxieties, and […] chaotic, angry, even violent fantasies' to come to awareness and be 'worked through in imagination' (2010 [1976], p. 16). When he adds, however, that 'the prevalent parental belief is that a child must be diverted from what troubles him [sic] most' (ibid.), this creates a parallel to an attitude that is also widespread today in relation to videogames and that advocates a total abstinence from violence. In this respect, Bettelheim's plea for allowing violent aspects into children's play activities is to the point as it reminds us that a certain degree of aggression and violence in our social relations (inner as well as outer psychic) is unavoidable. The question then must turn to the fantasies of violence themselves, and, although the unconscious need and desire for violent confrontations is by no means an unhealthy sign in itself, the challenge for the gaming industry and community is how to imagine and develop better and more ethical ways of violent play.

The ambiguous status of violence in both forms of play and social reality is captured impressively in Valerie Walkerdine's study *Children, Gender, Video Games* (2007). Walkerdine rejects the commonly articulated positions that see videogames either as making children violent or as merely enabling the cathartic expression and working through of violent emotions. Videogames, she holds, 'neither cause nor contain violence in any simple sense' (2007, p. 75). Rather, she argues, with reference to men specifically, that games 'present us with one site, among many, for practising the regulation of violence for men, for knowing both when and how to act and to be violent and knowing when to stop it' (ibid., p. 86). The social realities of competition and conflict, mastery, dominance and submission also make certain forms and degrees of violence a social reality and what is learned in videogames is one more or less accepted way to be violent in society.

In the remaining half of this chapter, we turn to AI.

The limits of human and artificial intelligence

A very brief way to define AI is as the science of creating autonomous decision-making machines and/or software. Accordingly, Turner (2019) defines AI as the 'ability of a non-natural entity to make choices by an evaluative process' (p. 16). However, in order to get a grasp of what that means, we would first like to turn our attention to natural, biological – human – intelligence. After all, a lot of what we imagine AI to be is based on our 'being human', which has a strong proclivity towards endowing everything we encounter in the world with human qualities, too. This human tendency towards 'anthropomorphism', which is a central point in Freud's *Totem and Taboo* (1913b), can be experienced by everybody who has a pet at home. Dogs and cats in particular cannot be but loved and cared for by us in distinctly human terms. This becomes particularly evident in the ways owners talk to, cuddle with and feed their pets, many of them unable *not* to grant their animals the taste of human food.

The centrality of notions of interrelatedness that we find in human–pet relations (Haraway, 2003) can again be found in leading conceptions of human intelligence. Here it is particularly French philosopher Catherine Malabou's work that offers valuable insights. Malabou (2019, p. 9) starts her enquiry into intelligence with the troubling origins of the notion, which was introduced by French psychologists at the beginning of the twentieth century. From the first, intelligence was tied to attempts at testing and measuring people's mental capacities with the intention of using these measurements as tools with which to differentiate between 'valuable' and 'invaluable' people. Since intelligence tests became thus connected to hereditary and deterministic understandings of the human mind, many philosophers tried to avoid using the word intelligence and kept it at a safe distance from other, more ethical notions, such as 'intellect'. This attempt at bypassing intelligence, Malabou states, has ultimately failed and needs to be given up: '[T]oday we must recognize that [...] the return of "intelligence" in the cognitive era is one of the most important theoretical issues of the early twenty-first century' (2019, p. 9).

In the face of the emergence of computed, artificial intelligence in particular, which is increasingly used in order to assess individual human capacities, the notions of intelligence and intellect, as well as mind and brain, can no longer be kept separate. Instead, a renewed engagement with 'intelligence' has become urgently necessary. Malabou (2019) suggests John Dewey and Jean Piaget as two scholars with whom to break productive paths for developing a notion of intelligence that is not in opposition to biology and technology, but that manages to combine the human, the biological and the technological, without drifting inevitably towards a new determinism. In her descriptions of both approaches, Malabou uses words that again strongly echo Winnicottian ideas, which point to her proximity to psychoanalytic thought. About Piaget's approach, she writes:

> Intelligence is a gradual construction of what appears not to be constructed, namely, the logical structure of judgment, even though it precedes all experience. Although it is already given, this structure must still unfold. This is why psychology begins with child psychology. For Piaget, childhood is the name for the place of development of what is already constituted. (Malabou, 2019, p. 11)

Important to note in this understanding is that there are no fixities: no test of knowledge and fixed criteria that could determine for one and all the degree of intelligence of an individual person. Rather, intelligence is here defined as 'the process of an ongoing negotiation' (ibid.), a negotiation of a not-further-definable entity which is 'also biological', 'also material', 'also genetic' and responding to always new situations in the world.

For Dewey, in turn, human intelligence lies in the methods that people use to keep the ongoing process of the above negotiations in an equilibrium. Malabou explains that, whereas 'reason' for Dewey is 'the ultimate fixed standard … intelligence on the other hand is associated with *judgement*; that is with the selection and arrangement of means to effect consequences and with choice of what we take as our ends' (Dewey, 1981–1990, vol. 4, p. 170, cited in Malabou, 2019, p. 12). Malabou unfolds this method, this capacity for judgement, further by explaining that it entails to learn 'not to freeze past experience, not to remain a prisoner to outdated logical or ideological frameworks, to adapt judgment to current reality; such is the "method"' (2019, p. 12).

This understanding of intelligence aligns well with a psychoanalytic conception of relative mental health, which psychoanalysis sees not as a *fixed state*, but more as a *project* and maintenance task that is never finished and always ongoing throughout the course of our lives. This project, however, is always threatened by failure, or even doomed to fail from the start, depending on the branch of psychoanalysis one subscribes to, due to the limits to learning from experience that people are endowed with. As humans, we are attached to routines, habits and automatisms, we tend towards established patterns and, according to Bion, we therefore have strong resistances against *learning from experience* (the title of his most famous book; Bion, 1962).

From human stupidity to artificial intelligence

In the way that these patterns resist conscious assessment and reasoning, as well as adaptation to the lessons of lived experience, they display a kind of *stupidity*, by way of something automatic, unthinkingly mechanic and machinic that can serve us here as a bridge from our discussion of human to that of artificial intelligence. Malabou writes that 'stupidity is the deconstructive ferment that inhabits the heart of intelligence' (2019, pp. 7–8), or as Isabel Millar has put it from a Lacanian perspective: 'Stupidity is precisely the part of intelligence that intelligence itself cannot see, the place from which the subject of intelligence *enjoys* itself' (2021, p. 33, italics in original).

This prompts us to take stupidity as the necessary complementary of intelligence: the non-adapted, disequilibrium, the obverse of each and everything that can be spoken, articulated and understood at any given moment and the necessary unconscious residue springing from each act of affirming one's conscious awareness, but also the fixations and rigid defences against anxiety and perceived dangers. When, as Lydia H. Liu (2010) maintains, both Freud and Lacan see something machinic residing in the human psyche itself, with Lacan conceiving the unconscious to work along algorithmic and cybernetic lines, this echoes the concept of the death drive and the compulsion to repeat without ever stopping. The artist Vanda Vieira-Schmidt, for example, who has spent large parts of her life in psychiatric institutions – a circumstance that should not be seen to lessen her oeuvre at all – has been making several hundreds of thousands of drawings in an attempt to save the world (Röske, 2014).

Scholarship on AI makes a distinction of narrow, or weak, AI, general and strong AI and, finally, 'Artificial Super Intelligence', which would mean a fully-fledged artificial subjectivity. Narrow AI is the form of AI that we encounter everywhere in our everyday lives at the present historical juncture, for example, our Google Assistants, Alexas and Siris that play music or set a timer on voice command, but are little sure-footed when we ask them for anything out of this narrowly defined realm of the ordinary. These machinic, rather unthinking – and often idiotic – forms of sensing, recognizing and responding to simply defined situations seem to correspond to a form of (non-)intelligence that is rigidly compartmentalized.

Compared with the rigidity of such digital processing, then, in which the sharp differentiation between 'on' and 'off' states, ones and zeros, 'yeses' and 'nos' is still palpable, human intelligence as the capacity to encounter the world in an attitude of smooth fluidity and creative adaptation seems ultimately superior. And yet, there are well-established and widely applied approaches to AI today, specifically 'artificial neural networking' (ANN) technology and its further developments, for example, in generative adversarial networks (GANs), the results of which already come a decisive step closer to human ways of thinking than many of our interactions with Siri suggest. This type of AI is part of what is known as 'connectionist', which means that the machine gets 'better' the more data it is fed. By contrast, 'symbolic' AI (the other main type of AI) is much more rule based, with developers determining how input and output relate to each other or how an algorithm should behave (Apprich, 2018).

It is the neural network technologies of the connectionist paradigm that have proven most adept to self-training procedures. They are modelled after an important part of the human brain: neurons, or nerve cells, which are seen as the basic units of the brain and are 'responsible for receiving sensory input from the external world, for sending motor commands to our muscles, and for transforming and relaying the electrical signals at every step in between' (Woodruff, n.d., online). Hence, with neurons' job being to both receive and respond to the world, they are in this way also tasked with basic interpretation work such as identifying obstacles when moving through space in the case of self-driving cars. At this very basic level, present computing technology can be made to simulate neuronal activity and 'learn', albeit in still modest ways, to model specific tasks by itself. For example, neural networks can learn to discern letters, words and numbers from people's handwriting by being trained on a dataset. GANs take such tasks a decisive step further in that another, second network is then tasked to assess and correct the results that the first one produces. In many cases, there is a third network involved that works as a referee for the adversarial procedures between the former two.

However, although AI has been rapidly advancing in the last few decades and has made a quantum leap in the last 10–15 years, because of increasing processing power *and* massively increasing research funding, as Clemens Apprich (2018, p. 30) notes, we should nevertheless be suspicious of the portrayals of AI, particularly by its industry. We are still a long way away from autonomously self-driving cars, or robots that could have authentically complex conversations with us. Especially formulaic statements, such as 'If a machine acts as intelligently as a human being, then it has to be considered as intelligent as a human being' (ibid., p. 34), need to be taken with the proverbial pinch of salt. They are highly alluring, yet also highly problematic. It is a bit like making the argument that a plane is equal to a bird because it can fly, too. In this spirit, it is important to emphasize that there are still vast differences between human and artificial neural networks. In simulating human neural networks, artificial ones merely replicate some of its basic principles without, however, 'specific terms of reference' (ibid., p. 35). Those working in the AI industry cannot (yet) explain how particular results or outputs were achieved.

Nevertheless, within the – still relatively narrow – terms that people set for AI, technology has begun to make remarkable advances. These advances could be witnessed, for instance, when AlphaGo, an intelligent learning programme, based on ANN and developed by Google/Alphabet's DeepMind project, was made to play against Lee Sedol, a master of the highest rank in the game Go. As the technology philosopher Adam Greenfield (2017) writes, Go is a game decisively different from chess in that it is far more open, allows for far more combinations of moves and relies to a far greater extent than chess on the intuition of its players. The chess champion Gary Kasparov was beaten in 1997 by a computer, IBM's DeepBlue, which still relied on sheer calculation power, with each move being calculated on the basis of decision-tree models of what possible concurrent moves each actual move might trigger. This form of computing, writes Greenfield, 'is *not* how AlphaGo defeated Lee Sedol' (2017, p. 265; our emphasis):

> DeepBlue was a special-purpose engine exquisitely optimized for – and therefore completely useless at anything other than – the rules of chess. By contrast, AlphaGo is a general learning machine, here being applied to the rules of go simply because that is the richest challenge its designers could conceive of, the highest

bar they could set for it. (ibid., p. 264)

Sedol was beaten swiftly and resoundingly, with AlphaGo winning four matches out of five, but, as Greenfield reports, 'there was something numinous about AlphaGo's play, an uncanny quality that caused at least one expert observer of its games against Lee to feel "physically unwell"' (ibid., p. 265). Another Go master, Fan Hui, commented about the decisive sequence in which AlphaGo beat Sedol: 'It's not a human move. I've never seen a human play this move. It's beautiful' (Hui, cited in Greenfield, 2017, p. 268). The so-called 'uncanny valley' effect in AI and robotics comes about when an artificial object looks or behaves almost convincingly like a human, but not quite. In these situations, humans tend to respond with reprehension, not unlike Freud's (1919) situational description of the uncanny as standing atop an old well and feeling that it might carry water again: uneasy, disquieted, vertiginous. However, although these uncanny effects are routinely attributed to the perception of an *imperfection* in the artificial object, in the case of AlphaGo, the effect was triggered by a *perfection* exceeding the humanly fathomable.

Whereas the AlphaGo experiment from 2016 was designed to test the heights an artificial self-training programme could reach, other experiments in the meantime have already entailed the need to tone down – or more crudely put, *dumb down* – the existing capacities of AI today, so as to make it more accessible and relatable to human modes of interacting, sensing and sense-making. Just a little after AlphaGo, DeepMind presented the similarly uncanny Duplex project, designed to make automated phone calls to businesses, such as to book a table at a restaurant or schedule a hairdresser's appointment. The system, as shown in demos available online, is able to engage in natural conversation where an AI caller with a human voice talks in a perfectly human manner, precisely by sprinkling imperfections and hesitations into the flow of artificial speech, by pausing, stuttering, making 'erm' sounds, and so on. The AI is able to respond flexibly to simple questions and enquire after more details or context – for example, the number of people for a restaurant booking. Listening to those conversations is at once deeply fascinating and disconcerting.

As another example, DeepMind made public in 2019 that it had turned its artificial self-learning programme towards the videogame *StarCraft II*. As pointed out in an article in *The Guardian* (Hern, 2019),

StarCraft II is a game that is even more complex than Go; it is a real-time strategy game in which a player chooses one of three different 'races' (with different abilities) and builds up their base from which to conquer the map and destroy the other players. Like many strategy games, it uses the 'fog of war' feature, which renders large parts of the map invisible for the first few minutes of each game so that players cannot see what the others are doing. 'That means strategies have to be flexible enough to account for surprises, and need to incorporate mind-games as well: feints and ambushes are possible in a way they aren't in chess' (Hern, 2019, online).

Remarkably, by the time DeepMind went public with its 'AlphaStar', the AI had defeated 99.8 per cent of its human enemies and was placed among the best 200 players worldwide. (There are up to 500,000 players in a two-month 'season' of the game and many thousand matches a day). But even more remarkable than this ranking is perhaps that AlphaStar did not end up in first place and become completely out of reach for its human competition. Whereas the AI industry often advertises its programs as outsmarting and being able to make decisions vastly superior to humans (Johanssen & Wang, 2021), the DeepMind developers, by contrast, approached gaming from a different angle. Their goal was not to create an AI that could overrun all human players in seconds – for example, by simply making more command clicks in a given minute than any human player ever could. Instead, they designed the AI to play as human-like as possible in order to avoid being detected as an AI by other players. In this way, AlphaStar started at the bottom of the league, just like a 'newbie' human would, and while gradually making its way up the ranks as it 'learned' from (or was trained with) data from the game, it also became endowed with capacities for error that vouchsafed it was a good player, but not a *suspiciously* good player.

In these examples, we behold the difference between what has been called 'artificial idiocy' and 'artificial stupidity'. 'Artificial idiocy' would be the mindless and unfettered functioning of a more or less narrowly defined AI to the point at which, in the case of *StarCraft II*, no human would any longer be able to enjoy the game, or perhaps even be able to play it at all before being eliminated by the AI. 'Artificial stupidity', by contrast, is the term for exactly those modulations and moderations in the AI's functioning that bring it within the range of human capacities, rhythms and velocities, as well as human forms of interaction (see also Possati, 2021, for a related discussion). To many, if perhaps not to the DeepMind developers, the dangers of such an approach are plain to see. Creating AI that is as human-like as possible, with built-in limitations, in order to surpass human intelligence while remaining undetected as other than human, presents us with ethical and practical problems, particularly if the technology moves beyond games.

Human–machine relations

What we are confronted with in the feelings of bewilderment upon witnessing AlphaGo, or of bafflement upon hearing reports of AlphaStar, are the cognitive and emotive limits of human intelligence and of our human compulsion to approach artificially intelligent machines on the basis of human expectations. Even if humankind might indeed manage to create an artificial super-intelligence – that is, a machine endowed with subjectivity – this subjectivity might behave vastly differently from our human-centric expectations.

This is perhaps the most valuable insight that Spike Jonze's film *Her* (2013) takes its spectators to experience. In this film, the AI of a newly introduced computer operating system does not revolt and turn against humankind in a persecutory attempt to annihilate it, which is the stereotypical content of a deluge of AI fantasies. On average, these fantasies are far more telling of humans' own antagonistic need for othering than of anything pertaining to AI itself (Bratton, 2015; Millar, 2021). By contrast, *Her* tells a love story between a human and an AI system that falls apart, because the AI develops beyond humanly possible means (see also Black, 2020). Towards the end of the film, Samantha, the intelligent operating system who Theodore, the film's protagonist, has given a female gender, admits that Theodore is not the only human she has a relationship with. Rather, at the exact point of her confession, she is simultaneously talking to 8,616 other people, being in love with 641 of them. Theodore responds with a feeling of utter and bemaddening incomprehension that comes close to the AlphaGo masters' at obtaining a glimpse of an intelligence that is about to leave humankind behind.

Through its plot, the film can be taken to also unfold the core idea in Lacanian philosopher Isabel Millar's (2021) take on AI. Whereas Millar conceptualizes AI as 'a non-human mode of thought', she argues at the same time that Lacan conceives of the unconscious as similarly non-human, as we have also noted earlier. Focusing on the socio-technological phenomenon of the sexbot, which often means an AI as a female, semi-naked robot or cyborg, Millar uses this parallel between the machinic and the human unconscious to focus on the sexual relationship between humans and AI. She argues that, although AI sex 'is nothing more than an apparently superficial anthropomorphization of our fantasies of AI', this, in fact, might be said about sex between human beings as well. Bringing Lacan's formula of 'There is no sexual relationship' (see Chapter 5) in relation to the sexbot, she writes: 'This fantasy of AI sex obscures the fact that sex is *only ever* a fantasy covering up for a hole in reality itself' (Millar, 2021, p. 5).

Since there is no real rapport – no real merging of souls, as popular romance imagines – between people in sexual intercourse, replacing one of the humans with a sexbot can work to tell us something about the forms and shapes of human desire, exactly by stripping away any illusion of true containment in the other. In this way, what AI in the form of sexbots makes peculiarly perceivable – albeit by no means understandable – are the most subjective regions of ourselves. As Millar (2021) puts it in referring to Lacan's concept of 'extimacy': the sexbot unfolds 'the intimate exteriorization that belies the nature of subjectivity' (p. 6). By the same token, however, Millar also proposes to use the notion of unconscious desire to enquire into the specific forms of AI that our culture has been imagining so far. Put in question form: what can we say about the status of AI as its own subjectivity when approaching it from the question of: 'Does it enjoy?'

Returning to the film *Her*, what we find on the human side of the love (non-)relationship between person and operating system, Theodore and Samantha, is not only Theodore's stereotypical desire for what Millar (2021) calls 'the ultimate bespoke girlfriend [who] caters perfectly to Theodore's exacting desires' (pp. 76–7), but also, as Eli Zaretsky (2015a) has pointed out, 'a narcissistic wish for a good mother' (p. 206). 'But you're mine,' Theodore complains to his hundredfold-unfaithful AI, like a child claiming their mother, to which Samantha responds caringly and poetically: 'I still am yours. But along the way I became many other things too' (1:47:06).

This nearly pedagogical response by Samantha captures well what

Zaretsky (2015a, p. 206) sees as the AI's therapeutic, mental growth-oriented function. Hannah Zeavin (2021) argues in her historical study of telehealth and distance therapy that therapy chatbots, from the well-known ELIZA program that simulated a therapist to more recent versions, facilitate what she calls *auto-intimacy*: 'a closed circuit of self-communication, run through a relationship to a media object' (Zeavin, 2021, p. 133). Although forms of teletherapy, from Freud's letters to the father of Little Hans, to call-in radio shows and suicide prevention hotlines, have a long history based on intimate, triadic relationships established in them between patient/client, therapist and medium, AI-based therapies change this relationship between therapist and client significantly. A chatbot, for example, does away with the human therapist entirely, leaving the patient more or less on their own to do the therapeutic work. As Zeavin goes on to discuss:

> I take auto-intimacy to be a state in which one addresses one's self through the medium of a nonhuman. The aim of this state is to increase a kind of self-knowing and capacity of self, akin to that available within other kinds of self-circuitry and therapeutic care. One such circuit of self is the set of self-soothing and autoerotic mechanisms children develop to cope with the absence of their mother (or another caregiver). (Zeavin, 2021, p. 140)

Although such instances of more self-knowledge may very well occur, it is important to highlight, as Zeavin also does, that forms of virtual or chatbot therapy can by no means replace actual face-to-face therapy. Nevertheless, an encounter with a chatbot can bring a sense of soothing for the human subject. Similar states are also present in *Her* and we could read the film as being about Theodore's auto-intimacy which he achieves through Samantha. With Zeavin, we could describe him as having 'been put into a relation, not quite *with* but *to* this computational part-object' and that he has 'an intimate relationship to 'her'' (Zeavin, 2021, p. 141).

Yet, *Her* and other fictional representations go further insofar as they depict complex relationships that go beyond mere acts of self-soothing. Returning to Millar (2021), we can turn our attention from the human and their relation to AI to the AI itself and ask whether Samantha has indeed 'evolved from being merely a partial (invocatory) object of Theodore's enjoyment, or given her "other" mode of being that Theodore cannot be party to, does Samantha *enjoy* beyond her function as voice?' (Millar,

2021, p. 79). This is where we think the strength of the film ultimately lies – specifically, in taking a common-sensical, human and romantic understanding of love and desire beyond a human scope. Samantha's abandonment of Theodore can thus be read as the AI developing a psychic apparatus of its own (Apprich, 2018, p. 38), which opens up the question of whether 'an AI [can] misrecognise itself as a subject, thereby occupying the ontological void of sexual difference?' (Millar, 2021, p. 145). The AI herself at least explains her increasing distance to Theodore in the image of the words between the two of them being 'really far apart and the spaces between the words [...] almost infinite' (1:51). In this moment, she is still capable of communicating with the individual human being, but the significance of this is swiftly receding into the background because her desire is becoming something else entirely. Theodore, the human being, has served the function of a transitional object for the AI and this object has now lost its importance. 'Worse than being seen as an enemy is not being seen at all. Perhaps this is what we really fear about AI,' writes Bratton (2015, p. 70).

Womb fantasies

Theodore: 'What does a baby computer call its mommy?'
Samantha: 'I don't know. What?'
Theodore: 'Da-ta'. (Jonze, 2013)

It isn't only the fictional Samantha in *Her* who is assigned a female persona; the speech-based assistants in our homes and smartphones, Alexa and Siri, as well as many robots currently in development, come with a default female gender and are designed to embody first and foremost *maternal* qualities – of being there and caring for us, responding to our needs, reminding us of calendar events, finding the fastest routes and performing other basic tasks. The creators of these simple AI helpers, it appears, have followed the unconscious fantasy of creating mothers, and the ultimate scenario of this fantasy is the *symbiosis* of human and AI, which marks a regressive desire to return to the womb. In this respect, what is most salient and striking is the trend towards the fostering and engineering of increasingly dyadic and pre-dyadic, rather than triadic, and hence oedipal, states of relationality – a trend that we have already identified as problematic in Chapter 4 on politics. Complementarily, this final section offers us the possibility of an in-depth enquiry into the vicissitudes – but also potentials – of current ideas of AI technologies, with their evocation of symbiotic states and related notions of family romance, the mother *imago* and the all-flooded, yet highly protected space of the womb.

Psychoanalysts, most notably Karen Horney (1926), have discussed the womb in relation to envy, whereby – in a reversal of Freud's concept of penis envy – men are seen as envious of women's reproductive capacities since, at least for the time being, every man is born by a woman. By contrast, we want to approach the womb from the perspective of symbiosis and merger, taking our cues once more from the film *Her* (Jonze, 2013) and other fictional takes on AI, which flesh out this fantasy of the human being in a womb-like relationship with an AI. Along similar lines, the media scholar Mercedes Bunz argues that 'online technology has started to address us as if we were children' (2019, p. 67). From the mid-2000s onwards, she observes, the designs of contemporary platforms turned child-friendly, even infantile – a trend becoming articulated particularly in the use of mascots:

> Next to the fox of the web browser Firefox chirped the blue bird of the microblogging service Twitter, while a little white alien with antennae accompanied Reddit, a social networking service that provided online conversations for 'digital natives', as they were dubbed. And not only platforms but also technology companies seemed to have a thing for mascots, from Tux, the penguin of the Linux operating system, to the black Octocat that had landed on the 404 pages of Github, the web-based hosting service for software development projects. (ibid., pp. 64–5)

Various logos and platform designs, such as Google and its Google Doodles, feature bright colours, flat icons and modes of representation reminiscent of children's books. The very word 'Google' evokes the babble of babies and toddlers. As Bunz shows, the graphical user interface (GUI), the surface layer through which users interact with computer programmes, which was first developed by Alan Kay in 1973, was inspired by the observation of children aged 2–7 and how they played and sensually explored the world around them through their fingers and whole bodies. Influenced by Piaget and educationalists Jerome

Bruner and Maria Montessori, Kay wanted to develop a way of using computers for 'children of all ages' (Kay, 1972, cited in Bunz, 2019, p. 79). Bonni Rambatan and Jacob have similarly argued that the visuality of contemporary online culture, such as 'like'-buttons, hearts, memes and selfies, is *cute* – a cuteness that has its origins partly in Japanese visual culture of manga and anime (Rambatan & Johanssen, 2021, Chapter 3).

These cute and child-friendly environments of the digital should, in our view, not exclusively be regarded as masking the user surveillance and data exploitation that often lie behind them (see Chapter 3). In line with Bunz, for whom this child-like mode of address is both empowering and patronizing, we argue that it also points to the designers' and users' wishes to dwell in environments that come close to the Winnicottian idea of 'potential space' (see Chapter 2) – environments characterized by a maternal presence, but animated and shaped by the child. Such environments facilitate self-exploration and play, as well as the intuitive usage of platforms and their services. For Bunz, they signal 'that the users can be free from second thoughts about the complexity of the technological apparatuses as well as about the complexity of the world we live in' (2019, pp. 71–2).

This positive, enabling and growth-oriented potential which close, maternal relations between AI and humans might unfold can still be unpacked further than the infantile relationship between interfaces and users that Bunz describes, and we draw here on the works of the psychoanalyst, philosopher and artist Bracha L. Ettinger to do so. Ettinger has, over many years, conceptualized maternal subjectivity mainly through her notion of the Matrixial (see Ettinger, 2020, for a recent collection of her essays). Unlike most, if not all, psychoanalytic theory, she has argued that subjectivization begins *in* the womb and not *outside of* it, after the baby is born (see also Lorenzer, 1974 and Irigaray, e.g. 1993).

Our 'first home', the womb, is imagined as a blissful space, with the fetus being receptive to mother's nutrients as it grows through her and senses the inside as well as the outside of the womb – for instance, in the form of voices, learning to recognize the familiar sounds of mother, father and other regulars.

Although no one, Ettinger included, can really speak of how it is to be inside the womb, clinical research has established it as perfectly temperate, nurturing and peaceful. The womb 'houses' and 'grows' the baby, but it is also a site where mother and baby relate to each other and where both will be permanently changed over the course of the pregnancy. One affects and is affected by the other. At the same time, the womb can be a site of trauma for the mother, baby, or both, if there are complications during the pregnancy, for example. The womb thus enables a particular mother–baby relation, or as Ettinger (1996) calls it a 'borderspace', where both are united and at the same time different, or what she calls 'proximity-in-distance', writes Pollock (2020, p. 2) in a recent introduction to Ettinger's work. Importantly, those modes of relating are not ones of fusion or pure merger. They are situated somewhere between or beyond the linking and separation of two subjects, one pre-maternal and one pre-natal. Such conceptualizations had largely been absent from psychoanalysis before Ettinger began voicing them from the 1980s onwards, as Griselda Pollock argues. In fact, the womb had only been discussed through science or spirituality – and Ettinger's advances have had profound implications for notions of motherhood and the maternal (Baraitser, 2008; Hollway, 2015), as well as for postnatal existence, as Pollock notes:

> [T]he Matrix models a severality that is, therefore, a proto-ethical encounter, with an *I* being modified in the presence of a *non-I* and of a *not-yet I* co-emerging with its *non-I* in a prolonged encounter, washed in asymmetrical affects and registering effects that may later, postnatally be mobilized in certain key spaces or moments, even within a universe of meaning ruled by the Phallus. (2020, p. 55, emphases in the original)

As such, being in the womb is a pre-oedipal state not governed by the status of the phallus or any other conceptual frameworks that designate subjectivity only as 'actual' or 'real' after birth. 'As an encounter with a feminine psychic and corporeal sexual specificity, Matrixiality precedes – and is thus not shaped by – the later Oedipal complex' (ibid., p. 18). And even more so, Pollock refers to Ettinger's theory as 'non-oedipal' (ibid., p. 48). Ettinger rejects the Freudian/Lacanian accounts of a subject who passes 'inexorably down the one-way road to Language via the traumatic resolution of the Oedipus complex installing a familial modelling of gender positions and sexuality' (ibid., p. 49). Instead, she proposes a relational model of both subjectivization and subjectivity that 'exists with and beside and beneath' (ibid., p. 50) the phallic. There is no phallic logic in the womb, and Ettinger goes as far as to say that it actually resists any phallic logic, which is subsequently imposed through the Symbolic and the Oedipus complex.

Birth then, and this has been emphasized by many psychoanalysts since Otto Rank (1929), constitutes a primary trauma as the baby is suddenly and quite literally forced out into the world and quickly learns to adapt to new sensations (sight, smell, an own voice, hunger, anxiety, movement, dependency, as well as joy, recognition, communality, agency, mastery, etc.) and a phallic logic. Traces of the womb remain, but many of them are 'knocked out' (Pollock, 2020, p. 65) post-birth. The Matrixial, then, remains as traces and unconscious longing to return to it throughout life, somewhat similar to Freud's notion of 'oceanic feeling' (1930), Lacan's '*objet a*' (2002) or Anzieu's 'skin-ego' (2016). Ettinger, however, does not emphasize the lack or loss of an unobtainable object; what is important in her conception of subjectivity is rather a longing to return to the Matrix which marks the foundation of a kind of ethics of co-dependence and co-existential relating, similar to but also different from the work of Jessica Benjamin (1988), who stresses post-birth recognition through her notion of the Third (Benjamin, 2004).

It is this Matrixial notion of a pre-oedipal, 'proximity-in-distance' form of relatedness that we want to suggest as an alternative design goal for AI development. By contrast, attempts by the AI industry at building social or care robots have been dominated by mostly male fantasies of total symbiosis and merger of a markedly regressive kind, where desires of a return to the warm, enveloping space of the prenatal come in the form of maternally feminine servant machines that take care of every little discomfort their masters might have. What lies buried in these master–servant conceptions, we argue, is already the basis for the breakdown of the relationship into violence. As Jessica Benjamin (1988) writes about the dialectic of control: 'If I completely control the other, then the other ceases to exist, and if the other completely controls me, then I cease to exist' (p. 53). In this sense, creating intelligent machines with the aim of total servitude is programming for disaster, since the expectation of such servitude will make people hate and despise all inklings of agency on the machine's part – despite the vain ambition of making them intelligent. Rather, the challenge must be to create machines whose servitude is not connected to notions of power and domination.

With Ettinger we can add more nuance to the conception of a relational dimension in which womb fantasies – that is, the human longing for blissful containment – do not default to pure master-and-servant constellations. Rather, trying to avoid imagining and designing AI along stereotypical gender lines and an oedipal sexuality, Ettinger's matrixial vision of 'relations-without-relating' might point us toward developments in AI technology that, to re-quote Pollock's passage, can exist 'with and beside and beneath' (Pollock, 2020, p. 50) the phallic. These developments will not consist of relations in which AI mistakes itself for a subject, but ones where AI remains fundamentally alien and yet close to the human. Such a constellation seems to be echoed by Catherine Malabou, when she writes:

> [T]he challenge is to invent a community with machines together, even when we share nothing in common with them. Never will there be a community of machines. The automatic creation they are capable of will have a political platform and ethical texture only if we endow them with it. But to achieve this, a horizon must be met by responsibly letting go. (Malabou, 2019, p. 161)

With Ettinger, we can regard such a community as one where we acknowledge the proximity-in-distance between humans and AI rather than merely subscribing to fantasies in which AI is to fulfil all of our desires, acquire the status of a mother that caters for us or surpass human intelligence altogether. Malabou (2019) refers to this as a 'resemblance', between AI and humans, which 'in fact, produces a dissimilarity' (p. 149). Such a fine balance between resemblance and difference would open the way for a 'democratic construction of collective intelligence' (ibid., p. 153) which goes beyond the interests of making money. In short, perhaps we need to let go 'of the drive to control' (ibid., p. 161) ourselves, each other and intelligent machines.

Conclusion

In this chapter, we have presented and developed psychoanalytic approaches to videogames and AI. Both can, although in different ways, be seen as creating womb-like spaces and relations that are situated between fantasy and reality. Both videogames and AI have traditionally been created by men, and both industries are gradually undergoing change and have become more diverse. It is perhaps not surprising that both technologies are often imagined and created in phallic terms that cry out competition, domination, progression, advancement, winning by surpassing those that are 'weak', and so on. While it would be naive to demand the complete abandonment of such Although and modes of relating, we nevertheless have pointed to an alternative via the work of Bracha L. Ettinger. Her ideas of the principal modes of relating in the womb can serve as an ethical blueprint for the relationships between 'full' subjects, as well as between humans and non-humans.

This ethics becomes evident in a final example we want to offer in this chapter: the film *I'm Your Man* by German director Maria Schrader (2021). In the film, the archaeologist Alma Felser (Maren Eggert) has agreed to test a new generation of stunningly life-like humanoid robots that become customized to individual needs on the basis of an abundance of statistical data and individual mind-mapping technologies. However, from the start, Alma, who is shown as a conflicted and self-contradictory person, is highly unsure about her decision to partake in the robot experiment. She was recently left by her long-time partner, and her demented father is a constant reminder that she too might end up alone and helpless in the not-too-distant future. At the same time, she is a humanist, determined to face the challenges of the human life arc without the help and company of machines.

Upon being collected by Alma from the lab, the robot, called Tom, initially proves to be dysfunctional, his rigidly algorithmic 'if-then' way of interacting that he/it first displays a testimony to 'artificial idiocy'. This rigidity, however, gradually gives way to more sophisticated ways of interacting with Alma. As Tom says, failures in communication are the best way to train his algorithm. And yet, what the film ultimately suggests is that robots will not become worthy partners for humans by meeting all the latter's needs 'at the push of a button', as Alma puts it. Rather, Tom proves his worth by learning to *not* be the perfect envelope for Alma's desires, and the more fine-grained Tom's attempts become to take basic human conflictedness into his calculations, the less it seems that Alma is able to maintain a dogmatic stance about having a robot as life partner. Indeed, in a situation when Tom, upon being provoked into a display of anger, has to admit that he himself does not quite understand the difference between the *display*, or performance, and the *proper enactment* of an affect, this suggests the existence of real subjectivity.

What we think is productive about the film is that it treats the question of subjectivity as an open question. Towards its end, human and robot coexist in a zone in which it is no longer clear whether Alma is being seduced into 'a play' in which, as she says, 'I am all alone and am acting only for myself', or whether she and Tom are indeed entering into a more fully-fledged, equal relationship with all the misalignments and misunderstandings that such relationships hold. Indeed, spectators are taken to wonder in his case whether the borders between serviceability and autonomy, artificiality and authenticity, calculation and intuition, performing and desiring have been blurred beyond recognition. The question as to what we humans can hope for in relation to a future with robotic 'non-Is', to use Ettinger's term, seems to hinge on the acknowledgement of the radically different, yet intimately connected, modes of existence of humans and AI and to build a relationship on this foundation. In the words of Tom and Alma right before sleeping with each other: 'Think of a human if you'd like,' says Tom. To which Alma replies: 'And you can think of a robot' (1:19:30).

Further reading

Bown, A. (2018). *The PlayStation Dreamworld*. Cambridge: Polity.

Isaacs Russell, G. (2015). *Screen Relations. The Limits of Computer-Mediated Psychoanalysis and Psychotherapy*. London: Routledge.

Jagodzinski, J. (2004). *Youth Fantasies. The Perverse Landscape of the Media*. Basingstoke: Palgrave Macmillan.

Lemma, A. (2017). *The Digital Age on the Couch. Psychoanalytic Practice and New Media*. London: Routledge.

Malabou, C. and Johnston, A. (2013). *Self and Emotional Life: Merging Philosophy, Psychoanalysis, and Neuroscience*. New York: Columbia University Press.

Millar, I. (2021). *The Psychoanalysis of Artificial Intelligence*. Basingstoke: Palgrave Macmillan.

Rehak, B. (2003). Playing at being: psychoanalysis and the avatar. In: M. J. P. Wolf and B. Perron (eds.), *The Video Game Theory Reader* (pp. 103–27). London: Routledge.

Santos, M. C. and White, S. E. (2005). Playing with ourselves: a psychoanalytic investigation of Resident Evil and Silent Hill. In: N. Garrelts (ed.), *Digital Gameplay: Essays on the Nexus of Game and Gamer* (pp. 69–79). Jefferson, NC: McFarland.

Tews, R. R. (2001). Archetypes on acid: video games and culture. In: M. P. J. Wolf (ed.), *The Medium of the Video Game* (pp. 169–82). Austin, TX: University of Texas Press.

Turkle, S. (1988). Artificial intelligence and psychoanalysis: a new alliance. *Daedalus*, 17(1), 241–68.

Walkerdine, V. (2007). *Children, Gender, Video Games. Towards a Relational Approach to Multimedia*. Basingstoke: Palgrave Macmillan.

Conclusion

Towards a theory of transitional objectification

As we reach the concluding chapter, we want to synthesize some key themes of the book in an attempt to think through them beyond their traditional framings in the context of the field of psychoanalytic media studies. Hence, in a first step, we touch upon the main themes of the book to see how they relate to one another. From this foundation, we want to further unfold the conditions of creating better – more ethical, joyful, progressive and socially just – ways of living with and relating to each other in digital media and the internet. These alternative blueprints concern both the individual subject under present sociocultural conditions and alternative social visions, up to the point of *utopia*, a word hardly used any more in debates about (what is now called) 'wellbeing' or 'mental health', but which we think is worth resuscitating (Whitebook, 1995). Our discussion rests importantly on the following terms: transitional phenomena, recognition, objectification, the gaze, sublimation and acting out.

Browsing through the phenomena that we have discussed in our book, what emerges as one of the important common themes is the centrality of questions of *acknowledgement* and *recognition*. Arguably, this centrality is the consequence of the main structural change that the introduction of digital media technologies has brought about in culture and society, specifically, the evolution from mass to personal media, and from a structure of communication from one-to-many to one that goes from many-to-many, from a tree-like branching out to networks of nodes.

As stated in Chapters 2 and 4, the possibility for many, potentially all, people in a given society to express themselves in digital, social media points to the question of who is being heard and listened to when all are speaking. Whose expressions become recognized and whose do not? From this general concern, considerations of *form* become decisive, captured in the question of *what kind of recognition* is being given and received in media and with what effects for society and the individual people living in it. It also points to a much more fundamental question about what recognition actually means and entails. And yet, as we have sought to show in Chapter 1, these concerns by no means belong to the digital era of the past 20 or 30 years alone. Rather, what has made Laura Mulvey's conception of the male gaze (1975) as a core proposition of Screen Theory productive – and what makes it relevant still today – is that it sharpens our critical faculties for how mere visibility can by no means be equated with a healthy and nourishing kind of recognition and the creation of what Erik Erikson (1950) has called 'basic trust'. Women have been very visible in Hollywood films, but that has not helped their standing in a male-dominated world.

In this way, recognition is a productive point from which to re-assess the main themes in our book. However, instead of defining recognition at the outset here, we want to allow the notion to take shape from this reassessment itself. One thing, however, that needs to be taken stock of is the human proclivity towards aggression. As stated in Chapter 4, Stephen Mitchell (1998) mediates between the two psychoanalytic understandings of aggression – one holding aggression to be a biological constant and invariable, the other seeing it as a response to frustration – by defining it as a response to the experience of existential threat. Since, due to the total dependency of the infant on their caregiver(s), this experience is inevitable in early human life, aggression as a response also takes on such inevitability.

This role of aggression in human life has consequences for our conception of recognition and its proneness to crisis. Specifically, since humans start life in utter dependency on others, and since this dependency will create situations in which the infant experiences their life as in danger, whether realistically so or not, we cannot ever expect a human mode of existence in which processes of recognition will be perfectly balanced or undistorted by traces of such threatening situations in the unconscious. In this respect, human life will never be perfectly free from the danger of regressing to modes of misfiring recognition – misrecognition, that is, which goes beyond Lacanian notions of symbolic lack or *méconnaissance*, but is the corporeal expression of each individual person's life experiences. It is in this respect that we want to re-emphasize the importance of the process of sublimation, which we define as the sublation of regressive unconscious tendencies in socially and subjectively recreational acts.

Taking a closer look at Screen Theory's conception of the gaze from a perspective informed by recognition, Mulvey's (1975) focus, which largely deviates from Lacan (2002), on cinema as a mirroring apparatus (Metz, 1975; Baudry, 2009 [1975]) that creates particular forms of representation for spectators to internalize, gives us a cue to understand the process of *objectification* as a problematic mode of recognition. Problematic because it does not attempt to recognize a person (in the case of the male gaze, a woman) in their full personhood, but fashions their representation along the lines of the spectator's desires, defences and unconscious dispositions, tending to either render them into fetishes on the basis of isolated body parts or punish them for the danger to the spectator's phallic power that they exude. To be sure, it is impossible to recognize someone in their full complexity, but in the cases of the male and other domineering gazes, a withdrawal or withholding of recognition so as to diminish the other is a main point. Additionally, as 'material, embodied beings, we are always already objects, as well as subjects acting out in the world and establishing connections with other bodies within it' (Paasonen *et al.*, 2020, p. 18), but it is the form of objectification that we problematize here.

Despite the various moves to develop the theory of the gaze further, with Mary Ann Doane (1982), Kaja Silverman (1988) and cultural studies scholarship providing ways of making sense of spectatorship and representation, the other main psychoanalytic tradition that we discuss in Chapter 1, based on Winnicott's theory of transitional phenomena (2002), has hardly ever played a role in these developments. This can partly be explained through psychoanalysis itself and the different schools within the field which seldom engage in productive dialogue. Another reason might be because the two traditions tend to be oriented towards different media and thus go into separate media studies traditions. The gaze has been first and foremost related to cinema, with its darkened space facilitating ideas of immediate ideological effects on the audience, whereas the theory of the transitional has been mostly used in the context of television, with its notions of the domestic, flow and the everyday, making it more of a background phenomenon unfolding its effect in form of a constant and discreet 'holding environment'.

To a degree, this parallel but separate development has continued into research on digital media. In Chapter 2, we find a similar disconnect between a critical tradition of social media and internet studies, represented, among others, by Slavoj Žižek (1998), Jodi Dean (2010) and Matthew Flisfeder (2021), and a tradition more concerned with everyday modes of media use and its possibilities and pitfalls, represented by Sherry Turkle's (1995) early writings, Aaron Balick (2014) and Greg Singh's (2019) work, with all three drawing on Winnicott (2002) again. And yet, there is a way of relating and informing these two traditions with one another that we have not yet unpacked sufficiently in the book – specifically, that a gaze itself, in the way Mulvey defined it, can function as a *transitional phenomenon*, through becoming mirrored back and returning to its bearer. What we mean by this is that the gaze can open up transformational ways of looking and being looked at that gradually go beyond the modes of objectification that Mulvey and others rightly criticized. Hence, introducing the idea of the transitional into the notion of the gaze in this way requires us to theorize it as the potential for *transforming* the objectifying inclinations of the gaze – inclinations that prove inevitable when one accepts the presence of aggression in human relationships as something inherently relational, too.

When in Freud's famous example of the *Fort-Da* game, a young boy throws away and then retrieves a reel so as to symbolize – remember, repeat and work through – the absences of his mother, we find in this representation of the mother by the reel also an act of objectification of this mother. Indeed, symbolizing her in the reel makes her manageable, controllable and quite literally retrievable at will. In this respect, one can say that the reel affords the boy a kind of gaze onto and haptic control of the mother from the perspective of 'the representative of power' (Mulvey, 1975). Put bluntly, there is a distinct element of a dominating gaze in the child's *Fort-Da* game. And yet, we can expect this controlling gaze to only be a temporary and, indeed, transitional one. Devised by the boy so as to work through the dangers of abandonment, it is a transitional objectification that will lose its significance once a more complete understanding of the identity of both the present (good) and the absent (bad) mother can be achieved and a capacity for ambivalence is in place.

The notion of playing in Freud's example is key for our concept of transitional objectification. Play in Winnicott's (2002) definition is about creative processes that traverse the inner and outer world (see our discussion in Chapter 6), illusion and reality. What Winnicott did not focus on, however, was destructive playing, or what André Green referred to as 'perverted' or 'dirty playing' (2005, p. 12). In his expansion of Winnicott's concept, Green conceptualizes playing as an innate state in all people; hence, it does not merely come into being in the potential space between mother and baby, but is an anthropological constant. Green noted that Winnicott did not consider the relations between sexuality and playing, or between destructive forms of playing and mental health. It is this emphasis on the importance of negative – aggressive, destructive, regressive, sado-masochistic, domineering, controlling – elements in play that is important for our conception of an objectification that is ambivalent as to its quality between symbol and symptom (Lorenzer, 2022). Although it is symptomatic in articulating limitations and impossibilities in the flexibility of thinking, its very articulations offer themselves as means of symbolization and of making conscious nevertheless.

Rosenfeld's clinical vignette (2016) from Chapter 6 offers another illustration of how destructive acts of playing may approximate, and ultimately facilitate, forms of working through. Rosenfeld's analysand, Lorenzo, and his playing of a cartoonishly violent 'beat 'em up' videogame (*Street Fighter*) is most likely an acting out of parental conflicts he faced at home. However, instead of banning videogames, as a previous analyst had done, which made Lorenzo's condition worse, by playing the game with Lorenzo, Rosenfeld gradually transformed this playing into something that could be spoken about and made available to a process of reparation.

This is what we mean by 'transitional objectification' – a term that results from allowing object-relational media theory to inform Screen Theory's notion of the gaze; it is itself a hybrid creation and creative hybrid that points to the possibilities of sublimation within ensembles of gazes of precarious power. In the light of this theoretical device, objectification must be seen as a moment that is, if not inevitable, then at least difficult to avoid in the formation of people's object-relational capacities; ideally, it is an *early* moment.[1] In line with what Hans Georg Gadamer (2004 [1989]) has called necessary prejudices (or prejudgements), such objectifications are the starting point of a learning process rather than its end point.

Omnipresent objectification

We will return to this conception of necessary, transitional moments of objectification. For the moment, however, we want to continue reassessing the work in the book's chapters from the point of recognition. In this respect, Matthew Flisfeder (2021) and his emphasis on social media use being driven by desire and a wilful belief in the big Other can similarly be seen in relation to a desire for recognition. Such ideas – and even Jodi Dean's of the digital capturing of human drive (2010) – can be further discussed with the notion of anxious narcissism, as we have done, whereby social media users are constantly prone to wonder if their self-presentations make them good enough and the responses they receive validating enough so as to feel secure and sure of their rightful place in society. When Jodi Dean evokes a vision of social media in which acts of enunciation already come with a built-in disbelief in their own significance, this means our expressions on social media are formed by the anticipation of an absence of recognition. This anticipation comes from the experience of one's own stupefied modes of online engagement: the way we scroll through, click on and comment on things there, holds Dean, always bears the chance of lacking a basic interest and involvement. However, if we ourselves care so little for what we are encountering there, what can we reasonably expect of others when it comes to *our* content, *our* posts, *our*selves.

Whereas Dean thus conceptualizes the internet as a machine for draining communication of recognition, Balick (2014) tends towards the other extreme and makes it a straightforward 'recognitional space', as it were. Although Dean might render her argument too absolute, Balick tends to ignore the draining, arresting and regressive effects that are programmed into the platforms' design, with the gap in their facilitation of the ego's mirroring with its ideal ego continuously opened up again by them and the promise of recognition always made anew only for it to recede into the distance.

This dynamic of social media was already anticipated in Tania Modleski's (1982) study of soap operas and Elizabeth Cowie's *Fantasia* text (1997). Modleski observes that soaps do not offer one centralizing and controlling male gaze that results 'in the spectator's becoming "the representative of power"', but 'multiple identification […] with numerous limited egos, each in conflict with the others' (1982, p. 83). Cowie, in turn, highlights that fantasy can include ambivalent and defensive acts, 'such as turning round upon the subject's own self, reversal into its opposite, projection and negation' (1997, p. 135) through which the spectator takes up different subject and object positions. These two insights can productively be linked with the analysis of (self-)representations on social media, where there are also multiple gazes competing and coming into conflict with one another. Furthermore, when Modleski emphasizes that, unlike Hollywood cinema, soaps do not have a clear progression from beginning, to middle, to end, but remain arrested in an eternal middle part, this again is a fertile metaphor for the ways in which social media platforms insert themselves into the lives of their users as facilitators of seemingly endless personal growth and meaningful connection, while constantly keeping them put and retaining them under the spell of this facilitation.

The cruelness underlying this state of arrest and captivation comes yet more clearly to the fore when turning to the field of work and labour, which we have done in Chapter 3. Being embedded in digital media technologies means that many of us are available for work any time of the day. The excessive work patterns that many of us engage in are accompanied by a constant anxiety that we seek to master by working even more, while disavowing the damaging consequences, as we have discussed through the notions of the counter-phobic attitude and perversion. In this context, recognition and its pathologies come to the fore in the theme of perversion. Platforms frame their services in rhetorics of love, care and, yes, recognition – as the woman in the Oracle ad demands of the digital: *Show me you know me!* – whereas the actual relationship that users enter into with them is a rather utilitaristic, and above all economic, affair which pertains more to specific aspects of users' identities than to these users' fully defined individualities again.

Chapter 3 is also where the social dimension of recognition – what Axel Honneth (2010) has captured in the *struggle for recognition* – comes clearly to the fore. When workers in the digital economy are caught in cycles of aspirational labour in which they offer their work for free in the hope that this will make them more visible, strengthen their profile and, ultimately, qualify them for a 'proper' – paid – job, this implies a social logic in which a *prior recognition* is needed with which to gain access to the labour market in the first place. Only on the basis of this primary recognizability can one hope to receive the recognition entailed in being adequately paid for one's work.

Turning to questions of sexuality and gender, which we have done in Chapter 5, we can see how the aspirational labour and entrepreneurial, self-exploitational attitude of digital modes of work, suffused with the ideology of neoliberalism, is reproduced in the hyperphallic fantasies that structure sexual culture on Tinder and other online dating apps as well as social media as such. Whether we are working, networking or 'hooking up', we expect of ourselves to do more, work harder, faster, better, be more excitable, aroused, intensely present – a point we have discussed via the works of Diego Semerene (2021). Looking at these fantasmatic structures and ideologies, it often seems as though the male gaze has turned back on and comes to haunt its bearers, who feel they can only live up to what is expected of them when displaying a hyper-potency. Indeed, the fantasy seems to be that we can only gain recognition at the price of absolute perfection along the lines of long-outdated machismo ideals that refuse to die and are embraced by subjects of all genders.

A variation of this reversed male gaze and its structure of self- and other-fetishizing is replicated in parts of the online manosphere, which we enquired into in Chapter 4. When Mulvey (1975) observes that, in Hollywood cinema, female threats to male sovereignty are punished and tamed by male domination, this seems to be at the root of an online misogyny in which men lash out at the ambitions of women from out of an utterly nostalgic male self-conception. In the case of the incel movement, men seem to feel so far off the requirements of a desiring gaze that they can only conceive of themselves as objects without value. And although the anxious narcissism, widespread on social media, seeks recognition in displays and performances of radical perfection and independence, this finds its flipside in a 'negative narcissism' (Green, 2002) in which displays of utter abjection close off any chance at social legitimation.

Indeed, while putting together the chapters for this book, we wondered how far the economic logics of demand and supply, so visible in online dating and misogyny, are also present in the political ways of othering online. Not only are they structured around paranoid–schizoid dynamics but, as we discussed via Wendy Hui Kyong Chun (2018, 2021), these dynamics are decisively amplified by the ideas of homophily that are designed into the platform's desired modes of relation. In this respect, the less sure people seem to be about their own social status, the less they seem to be willing to grant any to others. And yet, the fantasies of depriving and destroying the other need this other alive at the same time in order to maintain the status quo. As Jessica Benjamin (1988) writes about Hegel's dialectics of recognition, the master needs the slave in order to constitute themselves as master; once the slave is turned to complete nothingness, no one will be there to recognize the master as master.

The demand for love and care, which we observed in the relationships that digital platforms offer their users, comes to the fore once more in the current design of AI and robots, discussed in Chapter 6, in which mostly men programme their maternal, pre-oedipal longings into smart assistants of all kinds. From our psychoanalytic perspective, the deluge of recorded insults and abuse that has been directed at these female-connoted assistants reflects an intense male ambivalence towards the maternal. This same ambivalence, in turn, is wittily captured in Valerie Walkerdine's (2007) study on videogames, where young boys proved to be extremely dependent on their mothers, especially when it came to propping up their egos when they lost a game, but strongly disavowed this dependence in assertions of their masculinity. Hence, as a precondition for male recognition, women, and particularly mothers, have their recognition denied.

Transitioning objectification

Summing up and overlooking the main themes of our book in the above way, it becomes clear just how omnipresent processes and acts of objectification are in the sphere of digital media. Whether we turn ourselves into ideal objects for the gaze of the big Other, or render others into entirely worthless objects that are best to dispose of, we are confronted with acts of mis/recognition that seem to be ailing and *not good enough* all across the board. Objectification in this respect means a mode of recognizing another that does not do justice to this other, with the reasons for this failure lying in the subject's own needs, limitations and vulnerabilities. Hence, when psychoanalytic theories of racism, presented in Chapter 4, show how the other in racist acts is used and abused so as to stabilize a fragile self, this usage fits to a degree to all of the objectifying modes of recognition we have presented in our book. Consequently, the psychoanalytic question par excellence, in digital media and other sociocultural fields, is what functions a given relational ensemble serves. Translated into our context: what is defended against in acts of objectification? What needs are answered by them and what desires are made possible or impossible?

It is by following and seeking answers to these questions that our notion of 'transitional objectification' becomes relevant. By pointing to the existence not only of a specific structure of desire, but also of a formative need in a given act of objectification, it points to the transitional nature of these needs and desires and thus to the possibility of overcoming them in a mode of sublimation. In contradistinction to a general notion of repression in which unconscious drives, symptoms and desires are defended against, sublimation means to contain and sublate unconscious, regressive tendencies in acts that unfold these tendencies in both socially productive and subjectively creative ways (Whitebook, 1995). Sublimation always remains radically open, unfinished and incomplete – and this makes it a useful concept for thinking about utopian potentials. Thomàs Zicman de Barros (2022) writes that 'it is important to stress that sublimation is never a solitary phenomenon. It implies the construction of social links. It involves social recognition' (p. 12). Sublimation has to be witnessed by others in order to really occur.

In this respect, although it is important to have a positive definition of recognition – for example, to trace in concrete steps where the acts of objectification we have found 'get it wrong' – it will not do to merely counter our critical findings with a set of 'healthy' and 'progressively desirable' formulas of relating with one another. Rather, taking our bearings from Alfred Lorenzer's (2022) psychosocial method of 'cultural analysis', what we want to do here is to uncover the positive, reparative kernel from the conflicted, contradictory and often negative and defensive forms of interaction that we have found in the various contexts of digital media. This orientation also brings the notion of utopia back into play, since, from a psycho*social* perspective, that which cannot be sufficiently understood, but is **acted out**[2] instead, has as much an individually psychic dimension as a social one. Hence, from an ethical, psychosocial point, it is by far not always a given that it is the suffering individual who should change their ways – for example, by entering therapy. Rather, individual suffering often gestures towards a problematic societal arrangement, and it is the scene that this gesture forms together with the social arrangement that holds a utopian potential. It is along these lines that we now want to return to some of the central points of conflict and contradiction in our chapters so as to work out their utopian potential.

1. Transitioning the gaze

Starting with the gaze, in their recent book *Objectification: On the Difference Between Sex and Sexism* (2020), Susanna Paasonen, Feona Attwood, Alan McKee, John Mercer and Clarissa Smith argue that, today, different modes of representation and gazes are possible and are also regularly shown in popular culture which still feature modes of objectification, but in more nuanced and oppositional ways. Referring to Janelle Monáe's (2018) video for the song 'PYNK' as an example, they describe: 'one woman in "sex cells" knickers from which her pubic hair pushes out while another poses in a pair that say "I grab back" in an explicit riposte to the horrors of President Donald Trump's misogyny' (Paasonen *et al.*, 2020, p. 111). The US rapper and singer Lizzo has been similarly described as refusing to conform to hegemonic (white) beauty standards and instead celebrating her body. Whether we think of such forms of representation as nevertheless sexist and (self-)objectifying or not, they demonstrate agency of women who actively frame their 'to-be-looked-at-ness' (Mulvey, 1975, p. 11) in novel terms (Paasonen *et al.* 2020, pp. 114–17) and in distinction to Mulvey's notion of the male gaze. Other examples are contemporary televisual representations of women, such as in *Orange Is the New Black* (Kohan, 2013–19), *Fleabag* (Waller-Bridge, 2016–19), *Killing Eve* (Woodward Gentle, 2018–22) or *I May Destroy You* (Coel, 2020).

These novel gazes can also be used to shed light on the phenomenon of the selfie, which Paasonen *et al.* frame as a socially necessary objectification and 'cultural production' (2020, p. 133). They argue that, 'Selfie exchange and the communication practices connected to it can […] perform a number of functions, from creating, experimenting with and performing identity to receiving validation' (ibid., p. 130). Selfies are uploaded to platforms where others should see, like and comment on them, and this is often meant as a gesture that places the self not in opposition to others, but in line with them. Self-objectification can thus be both communal and solitary, joyful and anxious, all at the same time because there is a necessary disconnect between the selfie that is uploaded and the responses – in the forms of likes, comments, etc. – that it receives. The user who uploads a selfie is caught between subjecthood and (self-)objectification – a state that can be contained and made bearable in the community of, for example, Instagram users who 'like' each other's selfies, but such containment always comes with limits.

Questions of self- and other-objectification touch on a key aspect of psychoanalytic conceptualizations of sexuality in general (see Chapter 5). It is validating and arousing for people to be objectified and to objectify the other, as long as such acts occur consensually. Not being seen and desired as a sexual subject is akin to not existing at all, or as Ann Cahill puts it: 'To have that gaze skip over you, to be rendered sexually invisible by society at large, is to have your full personhood denied' (Cahill, 2011, p. 84, quoted in Paasonen *et al.*, 2020, p. 135). In that sense, sexual desire and to be sexually desired is a key part of subjecthood; what matters is *how* such forms of desire and momentary objectification are realized.

Although the selfie is used in various contexts, for different purposes and by different subjects, its underlying motive remains stable and is important to scrutinize further. From a critical psychoanalytic perspective, however, what we found more interesting about the novel gazes and objectifications is to focus on where they come up short, go wrong and, yes, turn pathological, so as to tell us something about *social* wrongs and injustices, the solution to which cannot be to merely wait for progress to take place. What is implicated in a psychoanalytic conception such as anxious narcissism (introduced in Chapter 2), for example, is an understanding of selfies that, in their most extreme rendering, would pose a *challenge to the sociocultural conception of neoliberal–rational individuality itself*. Putting it bluntly, the ideal representations of a perfect, radically free and totally independent self that are frequently attempted in selfies are indeed shot through with a fundamental, existential anxiety of not fitting in, not being good enough. Hence, the flipside of this anxiety can be seen to reside in a state of total containment and a longing for merging into a community with others where individuality dissolves. In pushing individualism to an extreme, the utopia that shines through is that this might be a point of 'redemption', where individualism ends and 'total community' begins.

Unlikely as it might seem, we have been picking up on a similar scenic constellation in the misogynistic groups of the online manosphere, and especially incels as a subgroup. Paradoxically, incels identify with an impotent and, in their view, feminized masculinity that they perceive as lacking and as disabling them from ever dating women, but at the same time they entrench themselves in this lacking form of masculinity in ritualistic reassertions that this cannot be changed. What becomes perceivable in this paradoxical state is the identification with a soft, non-machismo and female-connoted maleness, even if this identification is a negative one and bemoaned as a curse. Hence, through the harsh hatred of women and rampant forms of self-victimization, the utopian strain that we see as coming to the fore is a mode of sexual relations in which reactionary forms of hypermasculinity and hyperfemininity, which have had a comeback recently, are no longer seen as the ultimate currencies with which to purchase sexual fulfilment. Tragically, this mode of sexual relations is also defended against and always closed down by incels (Krüger, 2021a, 2021b; Johanssen, 2022).

2. Moving beyond exhaustion

In a parallel to the tendency of merging with others in heavily individualistic modes of self-presentation in social media, what seems to announce itself in the harshly self-exploiting forms of working in, with and through the digital we discussed in Chapter 3 is a state of exhaustion at which one breaks down completely. In other words, the promise awaiting people in a burn-out or a breakdown is, paradoxically, to be paralysed in a place of utter immobilization, unproductiveness and quiet – a perverse (in a non-pejorative sense) kind of containment. This place seems to be waiting, somewhere behind the wall against which one bangs one's head again and again, in the repetition-compulsive cycles of counter-phobic acts of labour.

Indeed, this ecstatic place of utter passivity under the spell of overwhelming affective force has been articulated in a beguiling way in advertisements for Alphabet/Google's home automation system, fittingly called 'Nest'. For example, Mark Molloy (2019), in his ad for the brand,[3] shows heart-rendering and disarmingly touching scenes from a broad variety of family lives – family members brushing their teeth together, daddy being smeared with make-up by his little daughter, the cat drinking from the toilet, the baby eating from the dog food bowl – but also scenes of shattering heartbreak, of soaring arguments and fights, desperation and the quiet pain of loss. It speaks to the well-crafted-ness of the clip that the overall feeling the two of us have received from it is one of an exhausted longing for home. When Jeffrey Prager (2011), in his social theory of trauma, explains war trauma as a danger momentarily overwhelming 'any internal capacity to feel invulnerable', adding that dying soldiers in

Iraq were often found 'to call out at the end for his or her mother' (p. 429), there is a distinct sense of this calling out that we also receive from the ad. Hence, when the ad ultimately claims that 'You make a house a home – We make a home a nest', this intensification towards the regressive, from a house to a nest, seems to be intimately tied to the outside of such a nest and to the modern workplace and its constant dangers of being overwhelming and of robbing people of their 'internal capacity to feel invulnerable'. In other words, whereas work, with the help of the digital, has been colonizing much of our social environment, it takes a nest, and not merely a home, to let one's hair down.

By the same token, we must remember, too, that Alphabet is a tech company, and its many sub-companies are hard at work to enable a seamless transition between our professional and private lives, as we discussed through the 'work, work, work' comment on the ad for the smartphone in Chapter 3. In that sense, the Nest brand first and foremost represents an AI-based smart environment designed to enable us to work even more and better, also – or particularly – from home. In this respect, the nest as a metaphor might be understood as the collapsing of the burn-out into the protected sphere of the home itself. After all, the workplaces in the tech companies' headquarters are also full of conveniences – with all kinds of snacks, finger foods, crisps and chocolates, soft drinks and alcoholic beverages, including pizza delivery on speed dial – so that workers can build little nests around their workstations, in case of an all-nighter, for example.

But reflecting even further on the nest metaphor in the context of smart homes, we might just as well believe that there is a genuine desire by the Nest developers to make our homes smarter, cosier, homelier and more practical, so that we can indeed focus on our loved ones. However, since these loved ones might not always be human – the ad, for example, includes a lot of pets – we might understand the metaphor of the nest as breaking a path for an understanding of home that is significantly different from traditional notions of the place where a core family of daddy, mummy and two kids resides. Indeed, this kind of hybrid nest-home might even include the AI of the smart home itself. Hence, adopting a more reparative attitude as regards tech developments allows us to see our relation with the smart home as a 'relation-without-relating' in the sense of Bracha L. Ettinger (see Chapter 6). The Nest devices – smart thermostat, lightbulbs, doorbell, camera and wireless speakers – collect data about their nesting users in order to perform their function; they do so quietly and discreetly and are thus close to us without taking up much space. In this way, the nest need not necessarily be seen as a merely regressive environment; rather it is one in which a transitional space across humans, animals (pets) and AI gradually takes shape.

3. The (re)creativity of negative play and the double layer of trolling

Continuing on our theme of 'transitional objectification' and the tense relations between the two categories comprising the term, we want to shed light on the notions of creativity and the kind of everyday creative acts that have been celebrated in debates on social media and online social networking. David Gauntlett (2018), for example, defines what he calls 'everyday creativity' as 'a process which brings together at least one active human mind, and the material or digital world, in the activity of making something which is novel in that context, and is a process which evokes a feeling of joy' (2018, p. 233). We agree with Gauntlett that human beings have a fundamental desire or, as he says in implicitly psychoanalytic lingo, 'drive', 'to make and share' (ibid.). However, where we fundamentally differ from Gauntlett is that creativity and play include elements of destruction, regression and frustration. Therefore, in this part, and in an attempt at bringing together Balick's (2014) and Turkle's (1995) more positive visions with Žižek's (1998), Dean's (2010) and Flisfeder's (2021) critical ones, we would like to zoom in on the creative potential that can be seen to reside in the negative forms of online interaction, which usually are not taken into consideration when creativity is discussed.

It is especially Dean (2010) and her theory of communicative capitalism that can point us in the direction of negative states of play and creativity. On the basis of Žižek's (1998) dictum of the crisis of the Symbolic in cyberspace, Dean (2010) observes a tendency online for people to articulate all sorts of things – from expressions of absolute beauty to utter abjection – without seemingly being committed to these articulations or their consequentiality at all, making their meaning highly ambiguous. This can be understood as the designation of a realm of free, albeit negative, play and creativity, which comes pre-labelled with the 'whatever' attitude that Dean sees people display online.

Approaching digital everyday creativity from this angle, we argue that the many intricate harassment and trolling campaigns that occur online, from the 'Drachengame' to other forms of abuse (see Chapter 4), need to be understood as acts of such creativity. And this perspective, we argue, helps us shed important light on these social pathologies. Staying with our example of the 'Drachengame', the participants who masterfully execute their elaborate pranks, while continuously emphasizing that everything is just a game and that the Drachenlord himself is merely an actor in a perfectly scripted tragicomedy, *do* have a point when taking this attitude because it has frequently been dubious indeed in how far and in what ways online communication has had actual real-life effects. The aggregated trolling campaigns against the Drachenlord, in any case, appear to us as the cruelly creative attempts at 'turning up the heat' – at increasing the intensity of a game-playing that tests the limits of this lacking consequence in our communications.

In instances of destructive playfulness, such as the Drachengame, recognition is seemingly emphatically rejected in that the victims become entirely flattened out into 'non-playable', disposable characters, and no belief in the big Other, that is, in any kind of binding law, is operative; or, at least any such belief becomes radically questioned. Yet, there is a reflexivity to these forms of play and a mode of awareness of one's actions that is held in a fetishistic spell of denial. The Drachengame, similar to shitstorms and other forms of trolling, is characterized by a mechanistic and repetitive nature that has clear traits of compulsive behaviour, but that must also be seen as a form of play. The haters time and again resort to the same tactics from the trolling playbook. In the case of the Drachenlord: mass pizza orders, provoking or pranking the vlogger online, organizing pilgrimages to his home (until he sold it), trying to spot his car across Germany. Approximating an understanding of the psychology of such 'sadistic merrymaking' in a regressive 'all-against-one', we can draw upon our model for the analysis of videogames again, which we developed via Devereux. Focusing on the methodical and rule-guided behaviour of the game and framing their actions as a game in the first place, we argue, allows the 'players' (the trolls) to distance themselves decisively from feelings of empathy and compassion with their 'plaything' (Rainer Winkler, the Drachenlord). It allows them to manage the game and control any unpredictable or anxiety-provoking elements so as not to get sucked into its sadistic and abusive dimension.

In this respect, saying that the participants in the Drachengame 'know' that what they do is 'just a game' becomes a paradox of sorts which points more to the pathological dimensions of their actions than to any form of containment or transitional potential. The game participants do not play *with* Rainer Winkler (in the sense that he, too, participates in the game willingly), but they play *with* him (in the sense that he is the object of it). At the same time, the emphasis on 'just playing' holds an important element of truth, nevertheless. Emphatically, the trolls' actions are not aimed at having important consequences outside of the internet and their actions are performed in ways that show that they are 'just' trolling. In a sense, although it might seem like they create a new Symbolic Order, this order is only operational when it is forced onto the victim and witnessed by others. The aim of the game is for the poor Drachenlord to work himself into uncontrolled rants and rages; and, unfortunately, this occurs like clockwork and thus reproduces the new Symbolic universe.

These dynamics make trolling on one level 'quasi-psychotic' (Rambatan & Johanssen, 2021, p. 46) as new terms are invented, reality is skewed, meaning is turned upside down or existing Symbolic conventions are completely emptied out of common sense. In that way, the troll creates a new big Other who is there to witness their actions, an imaginary figure or a specific group, such as the participants of the Drachengame. Trolling marks a phallic attack on reality itself and a foreclosure of Symbolic castration. However, the double layer to trolling remains, and that is why we link it to the Lacanian notions of the drive and traversing the fantasy.

After all, there is no new Symbolic Order that is created. Castration has not been undone. Social reality remains intact, and – hilariously, even hysterically – it is the inevitability of the impossibility of actually changing the world and of the insignificance of social media that gives the troll *jouissance*.[4] The very point of trolling is not to persuade others to agree with the troll, but to irritate, enrage, humiliate and abuse them in an endless loop of meaningless nuisance and wretchedness. In a curious twist, then, trolls have *traversed the fantasy* (see Chapter 2) of having any real (Symbolic) power or authority and, in this perversely and nihilistically zen-like state, they also shatter the fantasy of social media platforms being places of true community and care, honest communication and understanding (see Chapter 3), and thus expose a grotesque grimace of the internet. This reflexivity makes them subjects of the drive in the

Lacanian sense.

Returning to the utopian dimension of trolling, then, these forms of negative play almost seem to us to be wilful attempts at testing whether social authority and the law still exist somewhere and whether the absence of the Symbolic and the big Other is finite. In other words, we wonder whether the trolls' schtick of nihilistic play and playing with nihilism should not be seen as the opposite of what their actions claim, namely, as attempts at challenging the social world into an act of recognition by bringing the force of the law down on them. *Show me that I exist by not letting me get away with this!*, their childish, leisurely repetitive and virtual assaults might then say. Hence, although the Drachengame is played as though it should never end, the utopian end point of the game is its validation *in* and *as* reality.

This utopia, however, should not be seen as a benign and happy end point, and we cannot follow the trolls too far in their logic, but need to remember that, despite the emphasis on virtuality and playfulness, real people are being put in harm's way in trolling. The same applies to incels, the manosphere and the Alt-Right, who constantly blame women, the Left and 'Social Justice Warriors' for their predicament, thus delivering justifications for physical attacks against them, while always proclaiming that everything is 'for the lulz' or just a joke and people should have a sense of humour. Yet, the unconscious fantasy that seems to arise here in heavily perverted form is that of *being taken seriously and of the words of small people counting for something again*. As vicious and misguided as the actions in which this fantasy is articulated, with the displacement and projection of guilt and blame on scapegoats, there is nevertheless something ethical in this fantasy in the context of contemporary politics.

4. A new authority

Pushing our speculation about trolling, negative play, recognition and the limits of social consequence a little further still, we started to wonder in our discussions of our book's main themes whether this negative evocation of social–symbolic authority in the trolls' very denial of it might not also speak to the state of the various extremisms – particularly authoritarianism – we have looked at in Chapter 4. Specifically, when supporters of authoritarianism display an eager acceptance of authority from above and a likewise eager willingness to embody such authority when dealing with people lower in the relevant social hierarchies, as Adorno *et al.* (1950) had worked out, is there something about this eagerness for authority that we can empathize with at all? Likewise, when populists blame a 'corrupt elite' for their woes and sufferings, what, if any, positive vision of an elite is entailed in this negative one? And when racists blame othered subjects for having stolen their enjoyment, what authoritative social arrangement might assure them of a more just distribution of *jouissance* (Stavrakakis, 2007)?

Belief structures such as the above cannot by any means be combated at the Imaginary level of reality (i.e. with trying to convince people that their beliefs are misguided), not least since the amount of corruption in contemporary politics – especially on the part of populists promising to end it – is significant indeed, thus offering fresh ammunition to all who want to disbelieve in a just world. Rather, such structures again need to be approached from the perspective of what needs they meet and what desires and fantasies they make possible and impossible. And although we by no means want to suggest that there is anything virtuous about racist sentiments and attitudes, or that our hunch even comes close to satisfactorily capturing the problem of extremism and pathological othering, what can be allowed in certain forms of deliberative and representative systems of democracy as well as in authoritarian discourses to be taken seriously, we argue, are the questions of legitimate authority and social justice in general.

This is something that has been tackled by Žižek in his book *The Year of Dreaming Dangerously* (2012). In a farsighted manner, he discusses here the anti-immigrant backlash in Europe, a few years before the war in Syria would make hundreds of thousands of its citizens flee to European countries, many of them to Germany, and thus add unprecedented intensity to this backlash. Žižek writes:

> The true problem is that the critics of the anti-immigrant backlash, instead of defending the precious core of the European legacy, mostly limit themselves to the endless ritual of confessing Europe's own sins, of humbly accepting the limitations of the European legacy, and of celebrating the wealth of other cultures. (2012, p. 44)

By contrast to the Left's continuous self-critique, what is needed according to him is 'to propose and fight for a positive universalistic project that can be shared by all participants' (ibid., p. 46).

To be sure, Žižek was heavily critiqued, especially from the Left, for his endorsement and creative development of what then-German chancellor Angela Merkel re-introduced as the social need for a *Leitkultur*, a 'leading culture', and its authoritative – or were they authoritarian? – undertones. And yet, when it comes to the question of what a legitimate kind of authority that could bind authoritarians and extremists to itself without giving up a single shred of the principles of democracy, liberalism and human rights might look like, we hold that we need to force ourselves to 'dream dangerously'. In so doing, what we see through and beyond the ressentiments, extreme acts of othering and political violence is a longing for an authority that would guarantee a relatively balanced distribution of wealth, the common ownership of the means of production and the fair contribution to the common wealth by all who profit from it. This authority would facilitate the nation state as a container, as Barry Richards has proposed (2018). Importantly, these utopian fragments can by no means 'explain away' the racist fantasy of stolen enjoyment or the need of the hated other for the stabilizing of one's own existence. However, just as the proliferation of conspiracy theories seems to be correlated with the deregulation of markets and the increasing opening of the income gap (Casara *et al.*, 2022), a longing for a charismatic and violent state authority seems to be at least partly tied to a social reality in which people might still encounter one another, but only as inhabitants of completely different worlds.

5. Changing digital sexual relations

In Chapter 5, we discussed the phallic, arousal-based nature of contemporary digital platforms, as well as instances of digitally mediated sexuality itself, such as hook-up apps and mainstream porn. Contemporary dating culture has been described as an 'apocalypse' (Sales, 2015), a 'tragedy' (Ward, 2020) or driven by 'heteropessimism' (Seresin, 2019). Although the ability to seamlessly hook up may have changed sexuality for many and although porn may reveal erotic desires people did not know they had, people on the whole report having less sex than previous generations, something undoubtedly affected by the levels of stress both at work and in the bedroom that many are faced with today when it comes to questions of performance. However, this omnipresent discourse of a crisis of dating and sex might also offer an opportunity to reinvent and change relevant norms and traditions.

In this respect, Jean Laplanche (1989) points to the relevance of non-phallic, pre-oedipal forms of psychosexuality, reworking the Freudian term of seduction to gesture towards the importance of psychosexuality for subject formation. Along these lines, we want to ask now how inhabitants of a digitized world can be *seduced* (and seduce others) into an enlarged sexuality and more ethical forms of sexual subjectivity. Moving towards such an enlarged sexuality, one formulation of it can be found in Audre Lorde's (1984b) notion of the 'erotic'. For Lorde, the erotic is a non-phallic well of sexuality and in this sense more 'feminine'. In a parallel to Freud's conception of 'Eros' (1920), it stretches over all spheres of life. As Lorde explained:

> the erotic connection functions [as] the open and fearless underlining of my capacity for joy. In the way my body stretches to music and opens into response, hearkening to its deepest rhythms, so every level upon which I sense also opens to the erotically satisfying experience, whether it is dancing, building a bookcase, writing a poem, examining an idea. (Lorde, 1984b, p. 56)

The erotic thus opens up a sensual relationality that includes but goes beyond the sexual and specifically beyond the pornographic. Rather than advocating for a different gaze or different representations, Lorde argues that women, irrespective of their sexual orientation or other markers of identity, should embrace a form of desire and eroticism that is autonomous from patriarchy altogether (ibid., p. 57).

Now, it is easy for us to agree that this is a politically and ethically progressive vision of sexuality and one that for us sounds mostly enticing and desirable. Yet, although sexualities have changed significantly in the last decades, with the internet having been an important catalyst for such change, what we find being reproduced online are still predominantly phallic and patriarchal sexualities. Therefore, the question again is how the transition from these latter sexual realities to more open, fluid and non-phallic sexual possibilities might be achieved. Put another way, what does it take to seduce people into desiring other, more progressive and less domineering forms of sexual desire? Our suggestion is that it is again a process of sublimation – or better, a progress towards sublimation – that leads via 'transitional objectification'.

Arguably, this suggestion returns our argument to Green's (1999) notion of 'negative play' and the question of how such unhealthy play can be turned to progressive means, nevertheless. Breaking with Winnicott's 'refusal to consider play as part of sickness' (Green, 1999, p. 11), Green argues that 'we have witnessed many examples of perverted playing, of dirty playing. Such play is not based on an interchange, but on the will to dominate; it is a way of imposing one's will, and the will to submit' (ibid., p. 12). Furthermore, when Green defines this scene as consisting of an 'interplay of colluding narcissisms', this does not merely capture an unhealthy form of sexual play, but also comes very close to what Jessica Benjamin has called the 'complementarity' of the 'twoness' in the relation between 'doer and done to' (Benjamin, 2004, p. 8). Contrasting the pathological state of complementarity with her concept of thirdness, Benjamin describes the former as a 'coercive dependence that draws each into the orbit of the other's escalating reactivity' – a mutual dependence with an 'underlying symmetry' of a 'takes-one-to-know-one recognition feature' (ibid., pp. 8–9).

It is this conception of complementarity that, despite its denotation of a pathological state, we want to turn productive in our quest for how people's sexual desires might be opened into more fluid relations. Although both Green and Benjamin conceive of these complementarities within the clinical psychoanalytic setting, we wonder how these relations can be assessed and further developed when they become relevant as part of sexual practices. In this respect, a more normative notion of play becomes relevant so as to differentiate forms of sexual complementarity from those of sexual assault and the de facto violent domination of a sexual partner, or victim. In Chapter 3, we quoted Sergio Benvenuto (2016), who writes about the difference between perversion and 'sexual play' that 'we don't consider as perverse those SM games in which, for example, one partner is chained to the bed and maltreated, but derives pleasure from it all. In such cases, we talk about sexual play' (2016, p. 7; see Chapter 3). This is the point we are driving at: as long as people's sexual practices are complementary and as long as all involved derive pleasure from them, they offer an opportunity for opening a realm in which the complementarity of symptomatic acts and expressions might be accessed symbolically. When, in his article on sublimation, Zicman de Barros writes that sublimation also means an 'acceptance of the fact that the subject is affected by others, that one is vulnerable' (2022, p. 12), our psychoanalytic orientation points us towards the question of how these vulnerabilities have evolved over time, how they have crystallized in collusive constellations of twoness and – most importantly here – how they are being expressed in preferences and proclivities of such 'sexual play'. For, once they have become translated into such play – with the normative precondition being that this play is consensual – this playing offers a possibility for remembering, repeating and working through.

Unlike Benjamin, we thus wish to hold onto notions of twoness and complementarity. In this respect, however, we do not present an all-out argument against Benjamin by siding completely with modes of complementarity. Rather, by relating sublimation and the erotic closer to sexuality proper, what we want to argue for is that there lies a transitional potential in such complementarity and the translation of our vulnerabilities into sexual practices – practices that always also articulate the compromised, complementary solutions we have found for them. It is on this 'transitionally objectified' basis of the sexual, then, that, using Benjamin's (2004) words, 'the fact of two-way participation' can become 'a vivid experience' (p. 11) and the desire for erotic union 'a form of the desire for recognition' (Benjamin, 1988, p. 128).

This understanding of desire can then open up different angles along Laplanche's enlarged sexuality and Lorde's vision of the erotic, in which forms of recognition become possible that do 'not privilege the phallus, or masculinity or femininity' (Johanssen, 2022, p. 211). The erotic is thus not an eternal unchanging reservoir that can just be (re)discovered within us; rather, it needs to be reinvented by us, as Bonni Rambatan and Jacob have argued (Rambatan & Johanssen, 2021, p. 146). It is radically open and unpredictable, polymorphous and enlarged. This transitioned erotic then comes to stand for a joy because of the unpredictability of sexuality and life in general. This joy also means embracing the vulnerabilities and doubts of the self and others – embracing 'an enjoyment of an openness to what is impossible, to what is at the margins and limits of the symbolic order that structures our social life' (Zicman de Barros, 2022, p. 12).

6. Non-phallic platforms

Beyond the transitional potential lying in the symbolic and symptomatic aspects of people's sexual preferences – what Green (1986) has called 'private madness' – Laplanche's theories of psychosexuality and seduction can also help us answer the question of what digital platforms might do to create the conditions for people to develop more progressive orientations, sexual and otherwise. Put bluntly: how can digital platforms seduce us into more fluid and open, and less phallic and domineering, sexualities and, ultimately, subjectivities? When in Chapter 5 we move the affordances of digital applications into close proximity to psychosexual configurations, this amounts to pointing to the formative power of such affordances for the process of subjectivation at large.

One simple, yet productive, example of such a difference in seduction – or indeed, a defence against the knee-jerk modes of seduction that users have got so used to – is Twitter's 'read before retweet' prompt, introduced in 2020, by which the platform asks users to take a moment before retweeting an article, from a news outlet, for example: 'when you Retweet an article that you haven't opened on Twitter, we may ask if you'd like to open it first'. Another example is Google Mail's feature, rolled out in 2015, of giving users a few seconds after having pushed the 'Send' button to 'undo' their action, cancel the sending and redraft, or discard the email, without it having reached its recipient(s).

Steffen and Ane Charlotte (Krüger & Spilde, 2019) found similarly reparative options in the paid versions of Tinder, where users are invited to pay fees that patch up and undo to a degree the recklessness and phallic harshness of the basic free version of the dating app. Thus, in the paid version, users can undo a discarding right-swipe and salvage a potential love interest that they did not consider before it was too late. Similarly, the 'super-like' function is designed to counter the inflationary tendencies of liking and right-swiping others that are otherwise built into the service. This latter function basically makes it possible for users to tell others that, *Even if we all know that people match with others here all the time, this time I really mean it!* '[H]ere lies the real cynicism of the platform,' write Steffen and Ane about Tinder and its extra functions in the paid version, 'to "dish out" for free what people *want*, but to let them pay for what they *need*' (ibid., p. 11).

As regards this imbalance between wants and needs, what we

found particularly troubling in forms of online formation are the many dynamics of accumulation – hunting and gathering, pushing and pulling, tugging and nagging, informing, warning and advising, nudging and edging – that are built into the services. A constant excitation and arousal seems to leave little space for the gradual building of relationships, for reflection and slowing down – or what might facilitate the experience of the erotic in Lorde's sense. Hence, forms of online dating and hook-up apps might be developed towards more erotic and non-phallic forms of communication, for instance, by mixing more classical forms of online dating in which images are less central, with the novel affordances of location-based, real-time dating. In this way, people might get to know each other rather on the basis of self-descriptions in writing, or an audio file recorded in their natural voices, as with the app *String*, in which users send each other 'voice notes', than on that of the by-now highly conventionalized visual cues. To be sure, countering the predominance of the visual and emphasizing the auditory are by no means a guarantee for less phallic relations. What they suggest, though, are forms of anticipatory objectification that might be more open to transitoriness.

As a final example, we would like to point out a social media platform that does not feature any metrics: *Minus*, developed by the social media critic and digital artist Ben Grosser, who describes it as:

> a finite social network where users get only 100 posts – *for life*. Rather than the algorithmic feeds, visible 'like' counts, noisy notifications, and infinite scrolls employed by the platforms to induce endless user engagement, Minus limits how much one posts to the feed, and foregrounds – as its only visible and dwindling metric – how few opportunities they have left. Instead of preying on our needs for communication and connection in order to transform them into desires for speed and accumulation, Minus offers an opportunity to reimagine what it means to be connected in the contemporary age. (Grosser, 2021, online)

Of course, moments of doubt, conflict and contradiction will remain present, even in the most non-phallic relations and platforms. They are part of relationships and are sublimated via the erotic and sexual into potential, unpredictable and exciting relations through which human beings connect. As we have shown with Wendy H. K. Chun in Chapter

4, digital networks and platforms are designed so as to suggest relational forms that tend towards the paranoid–schizoid but, as our examples here indicate, with a few changes in design orientations, they can be made to unfold a potential towards more non-phallic modes of experience. Chun writes that recognition 'is an acknowledged reidentification, but, since nothing ever stays the same and no two things are identical, every recognition is also a misidentification' (2021, p. 228). This puts her in proximity to the likes of Aaron Balick and Jessica Benjamin as well as the Lacanian positions we have discussed in this book. Recognition and identification in the psychoanalytic sense never mean complete assimilation but always bear elements of objectifications that are transitional. Moments of recognition and identification, Chun (2021) continues, constitute '"co-relations" that reveal both similarities and differences' (p. 229) between individuals and entities. If conflicts arise, whether mediated through digital platforms or not, whether related to sexuality proper or people's general ways of relating to each other, non-oedipal forms of seduction, nudging or notifying can potentially orient us towards more complementary and relational forms of being together – whether digital or beyond. Such forms might then open up different styles of working through conflicts in which subjects might still 'do' things to each other, but could gradually be made more aware of their complementarities so that Benjamin's 'escalating reactivity' (2004, p. 8) of the 'doer–done to' would instead turn into an escalating, or rather enlarging, creativity of erotic potential and a view towards thirdness.

7. Mourning the self and others

Winnicott (2002) emphasizes that transitional objects are not mourned, but simply lose their significance in the lives of their owners; they pale and recede into the background. And yet, the above scene of recognition and misidentification, as many others we discussed in the book, gestures towards the necessity of a process of letting go of something or someone, whether in fantasy or reality, which is more painful and cumbersome. It implies a distancing from an object of desire, an inspection of one's fantasies and a process of becoming conscious of one's patterns of craving and elation when having, say, 'matched' with someone on Tinder, completed a project at work, received wide attention on social media, managed to capture an important moment on camera, reached a perfect state of flow in a videogame or had a touching encounter with artificial intelligence. Whereas such moments of gratification are always shot through with fantasy, attempts at distancing oneself from them and progressing towards a wider capacity of thinking and reality testing need to go through acts of mourning, in case they prove resistant to a more effortless process of transitioning. In such acts of mourning, the subject struggles with – for and against – the acknowledgement of the gap between them, their fantasies and their objects, as well as their whole psychosocial setting. Although transitional objectification is tied to a certain optimism and the hope that we will gradually arrive at more bearable and less damaging ways of living vis-à-vis the digital and beyond, it is important to face plausible situations in which we become stuck on the way and then need to mourn ourselves and others in order to move on.

For Freud (1917), mourning constitutes a process of letting go of a loved object – for instance, a family relative who has passed away or a partner following separation – in which all kinds of attachments to this object need to be brought to mind and inspected so that they can be reworked into parts of oneself. Gradually, the mourning person uncouples and detaches themselves from the object and acknowledges loss, without, however, completely abandoning what has been lost. Mourning thus entails both a severing of ties to an object and a retaining of these ties in other form. In his later works, Freud describes it as a process of introjecting the lost object into oneself and allowing it to disperse there into an identification. The object is not lost, but lives on in oneself – in mannerisms, gestures, turns of phrases, looks and habits.

In this sense, mourning is a transformational and creative process. 'In mourning the creativity of the psyche straddles the border between the unknown and what is known, between what is lost and what is about to be resumed,' writes the psychoanalyst María Cristina Melgar (2007, p. 112). It may sound paradoxical, but what Freud termed 'the work of mourning' (1917, p. 245) entails traces of joy – an 'enjoyable pain of constructing what we will never know and what we never knew about the mysteries of death and what has been lost' (Melgar, 2007, p. 114). Ever so slowly, and between heavy bouts of grief and despair, moments of sheer disbelief, but also fleeting moments of lightness and forgiveness, loss is turned into a process of growth. This distinguishes mourning from melancholia, in which one does not manage to face loss, cannot allow loss to take place and cannot find a healthy form of parting with and holding dear the object.

We ended Chapter 4 with a discussion of Jamie Steele's (2021) article on whiteness and dismantling white supremacy, and also, in this respect, mourning becomes an important process. Specifically, in order to arrive at a critical sense of their own ethnicity, white people need to mourn their long-standing sense of privilege so as to arrive at modes of relating to themselves and others that acknowledge non-white others as parts of themselves. This would also mean mourning one's fantasies of being only kind, benign, civilized and peaceful, and instead acknowledging the inherent aggression in us all. Just how hard it is to even begin such a process shows in the wildly melancholic instances of racist backlash all over the world.

Turning back to the digital, similar acts of mourning would help us arrive at healthier expectations of ourselves and how we (are made to) occupy both subject and object positions in different contexts and under the spell of different gazes. To what extent can we be recognized and recognize others on social media (Chapter 2)? To what extent and in what ways can we keep working and promote ourselves online (Chapter 3) or transform work into more benign modes of self-realization? How can we live within the limits of complementary romantic and sexual relations with others (Chapter 5), or to what extent do we manage to introduce a measure of thirdness into them? How can we depict others in videogames (Chapter 6), film and television (Chapter 1) so as not to make inevitable who is disposable for whom and who not? And how can we shape future relations with AI (Chapter 6) that do not fall into the trap of regressive phallic fantasies? Finding satisfying answers to these questions requires at least a degree of letting go of idealizations, fantasies and habitual expectations about oneself and others. As with all works of mourning, this letting go must remain an incomplete process. We can never move entirely outside of our fantasies, but, as the proverb has it, the journey is the destination.

The future of psychoanalytic media studies

'If media are increasingly inhabiting all aspects of everyday life, the emerging question is how can we reconceptualise the conscious and unconscious relationalities between people and their evolving media technologies?' (Krüger & Johanssen, 2016, p. 28). This question, as posed by us in 2016, is still relevant now. As we went on to argue, 'what is needed is more hands-on, empirical research from a psychoanalytic and/or psychosocial perspective' (ibid., p. 29). This does not mean that research necessarily needs to be empirical in the sense of conducting interviews or focus groups but that it should connect to examples, case studies and specific phenomena 'out there' in the world. Psychoanalytic media studies, like many other fields, may come with barriers in the form of specific jargon, abstract concepts and taken-for-granted ideas that are not always adequately explained. Indeed, one of the reasons for writing this book was to introduce key ideas and traditions in an accessible manner and to critically develop them further. Scholars in the field could sometimes do more to outline their frameworks, make them more approachable for laypersons and combine them with concrete case studies to broaden their appeal to those outside of the field – academics, students and interested members of the public alike.

Psychoanalysis will continue to be challenged and critiqued by other approaches (such as new materialism, affect studies, Deleuzian or Foucauldian approaches, and many others). Psychoanalytic cultural analysis must face these challenges, but on its own terms. These approaches must be appreciated and recognized for the light they can shed on the limits of psychoanalytic approaches to the digital and, in this way, psychoanalytic scholarship needs to embrace also those positions and ideas that are external to it, as far as this is possible and productive and does not go against the patterns, dynamics and logics of human interaction, the evidence of which our discipline has secured. This is something we have sought to achieve throughout the different chapters.

We further hope that clinicians, who often hold negative views of digital technologies, will appreciate both the beneficial and the damaging aspects of the cases we have discussed in this book. Clinical psychoanalysis itself needs to develop more of a sure-footed cultural orientation and enable more mature understandings of media technology into its conceptual developments. These conceptions thus need to go beyond a simplistic identification of symptoms, such as internet addiction or cyberbullying. Just like Freud and his followers responded to sociocultural change and how it presented or distorted itself in the clinic, contemporary psychoanalytic approaches need to take account of the digital as a psychosocial formation.

Digital media technologies and their use cultures will continue to undergo rapid developments and changes. For instance, the media landscape will continue to diversify, and 'mainstream', traditional media's (symbolic) power will probably decrease, whereas channels and content aimed at particular audiences and demographics will continue to proliferate. Digital platforms, such as those for social networking, will change too, particularly as AI continues to advance and virtual reality and augmented reality technologies are rolled out to consumers. These innovations will present opportunities as much as challenges for the subjects expected to use them and the societies in which these uses take place. Psychoanalytic media studies, in turn, should meet these opportunities and challenges head on.

Notes

1. Arguably, we could also unfold transitional objectification via Lacan's mirror stage but feel that our approach works better in bringing together and further developing the different traditions and examples we have discussed in the book.
2. Freud (1927) conceptualized acting out as a process whereby unconscious fantasies re-emerge in a present moment because something triggered them – for example, an external source or the subject themselves – into action. Acting out is often done repetitively and 'refers to the discharge by means of action, rather than by means of verbalization, of conflicted mental content' (Mijolla-Mellor, 2005, p. 10).
3. https://vimeo.com/337361057 [Accessed 2/5/2022].
4. An exception may be the case of conspiracy thinking, such as the QAnon movement, which has left a lasting impact on American politics. A real danger today is that the crisis of the Symbolic has blurred the lines between the internet and beyond.

Achiampong, L. and Blandy, D. (2015). *Finding Fanon II*. Available at: https://vimeo.com/138951543 [Accessed 10/4/22].
Adorno, T. W., Frenkel-Brunswik, E., Levinson, D. J. and Nevitt Sanford, R. (1950).

Glossary

Acting out
Acting out can be understood as the opposite of what clinical psychoanalysis aims to achieve. Instead of unconscious fantasies and behavioural patterns being remembered, repeated and worked through, acting out means that they are unconsciously re-enacted and reproduced in social situations. Sigmund Freud conceptualized acting out as a process whereby unconscious fantasies re-emerge in a present moment because something triggered them – an external source, say, or the subject themselves. Rather than underlying conflicts becoming verbalized and available to consciousness, acting out means the return of something repressed in the form of it directly acting on the social. These repressed contents tend to be acted out repetitively, either in the consulting room or in other situations. Social media offer spaces in which people do not merely share their rational thoughts and opinions but also act out their undigested, unconscious conflicts.

Alienation
For Karl Marx, workers are alienated in capitalism because they do not own the means of production, that is, the tools, machinery and materials needed for producing goods and services. This absence of ownership creates distance and detachment from one's labour and its end products, which again leads to a detachment from the ways humans are able to realize themselves and recognize themselves as parts of the world. As a result, workers become alienated from themselves and others. Critical theory from the Frankfurt School onwards, not least by drawing on psychoanalysis, has extended the term 'alienation' to refer to the psychological and relational effects of such social–material processes of distancing and detachment, for example in the cases in which people treat others or themselves as if they were a thing that can be disposed of unthinkingly. On corporate social media platforms, scholars argue, one can observe similar effects of alienation, because,

here too, the users do not own the means with which they are invited to express and realize themselves.

Big Other

For Lacan, the Symbolic fulfils the role of a binding structure that subjects enter into. In addition, he claims that what is necessary for our adherence to such a structure is the belief in an authority (a father in patriarchal society) that embodies and stands for the prohibitions, limits and laws erected through and in the symbolic itself. This authority is named the 'big Other'. Crucially, this authority does not really exist but is a more or less shared collective fantasy and social construction. As such, subjects often challenge it.

Castration

Castration literally means the cutting off of sexual organs, first and foremost the penis. However, contemporary psychoanalysis understands castration more at a symbolic level and as a traumatic psychic threat. On the symbolic level, castration refers to phallic, and therefore male-connoted, power – a power that is an imaginary one from the start and that the subject imagines as having been stolen, curtailed or taken away.

Drive

The drive is a major psychoanalytic concept introduced by Freud and revised and discussed by many clinicians and thinkers. We mostly use it in its Lacanian version in this book. For Lacan, the drive is related to his concept of desire. Both relate to jouissance and loss, but in different ways. Drive is an objectless process that knows no goal. Paradoxically speaking, it is through reaching that very non-goal, of getting nowhere, that jouissance is obtained by the subject. It is the repetitive process of the drive itself that is pleasurable. Drive enables only a partial realization of desire. Desire, in contrast, is desire for desire itself, a desire for jouissance, which ultimately remains unfulfilled. We can say that not reaching jouissance via the drive gives the subject pleasure, and not reaching it via desire further amplifies desire and leaves the subject wanting to want more.

Id, ego and super-ego

A tripartite model of the psyche, created by Freud in his later works. Whereas the id comes to represent the unconscious and constantly seeks pleasure and enjoyment, in this way going against and coming into conflict with the laws of the conscience function, represented by the super-ego, it is the ego's job to negotiate between id and super-ego and navigate the arising conflicts so as to keep them in check. Yet, this is no simple task, because the super-ego is seldom benign; rather, as a fantasmatic derivative of parental power and being intimately related to the id and its unconscious desires, it must be seen as the latter's flipside and thus as a hyper-moralistic and exactingly cruel agency which constantly taunts its bearer for their failures and shortcomings.

Homophily
Latin for 'love of sameness'. Wendy Hui Kyong Chun uses the term to describe how digital networks aggregate individuals as datapoints within them into neighbourhoods that display similarities. Commercial social media platforms, in their ongoing analysis and patterning of user data, have proven keenly interested in their users' shared attributes, their main aim being to order this data so as to make it serve the interests of third parties, for example, for advertising purposes.

Identification
Freud saw identification as a form of emotional, loving (indeed, libidinous) tie with an object. Identification essentially means an unconscious process whereby an individual comes to feel a sameness with another person – be this person real or merely a filmic representation – and wants to be like them. The term became particularly useful for early psychoanalytic film theorists such as Jean-Louis Baudry, Christian Metz and Laura Mulvey, who all theorized the often-captivating relationship between audiences and on-screen characters as having to do with identification on the part of audiences.

Ideology
A key term since Marx, ideology refers to a system of beliefs and practices geared to maintaining the existing order and status quo in society. As such guards of the status quo, ideologies often reproduce unequal power relations and protect some social groups while making others more vulnerable. Early Marxists had a straightforward understanding of ideology in which those in power also control the means of mental production and the ruling ideas of a given period. Along these lines, ideology means

a distorted understanding and experience of reality. A key question for psychoanalytic media studies has been how ideology is reproduced or indeed challenged through, for example, film, television or the internet. A more productive and less normatively restrictive understanding has been coined by Antonio Gramsci, who defined ideologies as those beliefs and opinions that seem natural, unchallengeable and common-sensical, and in this way become hegemonic in societies.

Interpassivity
Robert Pfaller and Slavoj Žižek define interpassivity as instances where activities as well as their enjoyment are delegated and performed by someone or something else. An oft-quoted example is the 'canned laughter' in sitcoms that not only signals when to laugh, but de facto laughs for and instead of the viewer. Some psychoanalytic scholars of videogames have used the term to theorize the interactive–passive nature of gaming.

Lacking (or lack)
For Lacan, the subject's sense of existence comes into being through the gap between the Symbolic and the Real, or rather by the gap or lack that exists in the Symbolic Order itself (see Introduction). People can never truly or fully say what they mean. Language is both strangely intimate and alienating all at once. It is a closed system that endlessly runs on, with every word referring to another word, and then another, and another – without us being able to ever properly reach outside of the Symbolic and directly into our lives. The notion of the lack is also related to the Lacanian understanding of desire as always leaving the subject lacking, trying to (unconsciously) rediscover the objet petit a.

Mirror stage
Lacan notes that children from the age of six months start recognizing themselves as themselves in the mirror. However, as at this stage the body is not fully functional, he holds that this act of seeing oneself in the mirror, as whole, coherent and in one piece, results in a misrecognition. Simply put, the baby sees themselves as in much better shape than they really are. This wonderful self-illusion leads to an attitude of the ego to themselves that always struggles to match the ego ideal on the other side of the glass: a vision of oneself that is always somewhat out of reach and that comes to haunt the subject throughout their lives. Film, but also more recent

examples from digital media, such as the selfie, have been discussed by scholars in relation to ideas of the mirror (stage).

Negative transference

Transference is a process in which intimately held desires, feelings, dynamics of interacting with others or modes of relating are unconsciously 'transferred' by one person on to another. This omnipresent process has become available to conscious reflection in clinical psychoanalysis, where analysands transfer their relational patterns on to the analyst, for example by acting in ways that suggest that they unconsciously take the analyst to be their mother. Yet, the analyst is not free of transferential tendencies towards their analysands either; these processes have been captured in the term 'countertransference'. Transference thus means the reproduction of unconscious wishes that the analysand unconsciously projects on to and then inevitably finds to be validated in/by the analyst. These wishes refer back to earlier relationships, often the earliest in a subject's life. Freud further called the phenomenon of transference a 'false connection', where a present experience merges with, or overlays, past ones. There are positive instances of transference, for example, when loving patterns of relating are transferred on to another. Negative transference, in turn, has been vexing clinical psychoanalysis from the start, mostly in instances when analysands defend against interpretations offered by their analyst.

Objects

For object-relations psychoanalysis, objects do not so much refer to things, but rather to other human beings and how they are rendered 'inner objects' or fantasy representations that shape how people relate to themselves and each other both, 'out there' and 'in here'.

Oedipus complex

This key psychoanalytic concept refers to a phase in a child's development, roughly from age four to six, in which the child develops a quasi-sexual attachment to one of the parents, usually that of the opposite sex, and a degree of animosity towards the other parent. As Freud stated, those incestual wishes are given up at some point due to fears of retribution and punishment, which he captured in the image of castration (see 'Castration' and 'Symbolic castration'). By giving up on our first love object, we are prompted to enter into a relationship with the (rest of the) world, and by opening our perspective from a two-person, dyadic relationship (child and mother/primary caregiver) to a triangular one (subject–object–other), the necessity to use symbols to define our place in the world in relation to ourselves and others becomes introduced.

Perversion
A relationship in which the pervert simultaneously loves and abuses, idealizes and dehumanizes the partner. It is a relationship often marked by exploitation, degradation, humiliation and shaming, while also being structured by significant dimensions of care and love. Perverse relationships can be sexual but do not have to be. Rather than being coerced into one, the partner often wilfully enters and stays in a perverse relationship.

Scopophilia
Sexually charged pleasure in looking. This sexual pleasure is not only due to the – preferably attractive – others one looks at, but rather, it means a sexualization of the act of looking per se. Laura Mulvey drew on Freud's use of the term in her Visual Pleasure essay.

Splitting and the paranoid–schizoid position
These terms have been introduced by the object-relations psychoanalyst Melanie Klein, for whom infants, and human beings in general, shift between two main modes for dealing with feelings of anxiety and loss. In the paranoid–schizoid position, the child feels existential, deadly threat and anxiety. In a process of what Klein called 'splitting', 'good' and 'bad' are rigidly kept apart. These terms are useful for analysing contemporary (digital) politics and phenomena such as homophily and filter bubbles. The other main mode for Klein is the 'depressive position' in which the subject becomes able to tolerate ambivalence and loss and exhibits a desire for reparation and healing.

Suture
Lacan understood the term to denote a process through which the gap of the Real is healed and covered over by the Symbolic and, in this way, the subject acquires its status as a sexed and social individual. Films often promise to heal our feelings of lack and castration, enmeshing us in states of abundance and omnipotence. Kaja Silverman applied

Lacan's concept of suture to this function. Film is effective in patching us up in this sense because it responds to a lack that belongs to us in a constitutive, fundamental way and enables us to feel immersed in a film so as to make us momentarily forget our problems and worries. The film's ability to suture us is especially propelled forward through plot twists and unexpected turns, because they make the expected end all the more desirable. Yet, just like in its medical origin, suturing leaves visible a scar and can never fully heal or cover over what is beneath it.

Symbolic castration

The acquisition of and initiation into language of the child represents a major step in terms of both becoming a subject and being part of social life. For Lacan, the entry into language involves a 'marking' of the child by the Symbolic Order. This order determines and fixes subjects in social reality, confronting them with notions of authority, norms and customs that seem to be pre-given and eternal. This 'marking' approximates what he calls 'Symbolic castration' – a castration that is merely symbolic because no actual, physical castration takes place.

The male gaze

Term coined by Laura Mulvey in her 1975 Visual Pleasure and Narrative Cinema essay. Mulvey argues that, in the context of watching Hollywood and other mainstream films, the processes of identification and objectification are achieved primarily through the means of the script, direction, camera and editing that reproduce traditional gender roles and stereotypes, and ultimately the patriarchal order. Hence, many films invite – or create for – their audiences, both male and female, to look at women on screen from a distinctly heterosexual male perspective. Critics have pointed out that Mulvey misinterpreted Lacan's notion of the gaze (see Chapter 1). Yet, this misinterpretation, we argue, has been an immensely productive one.

Transitional object

A term coined by D. W. Winnicott that refers to the objects that small children are highly invested in, such as cuddly toys or soft blankets. Children rely on transitional objects to create a space – between illusion and reality – in which they can negotiate between inner, psychic reality and outer, objective reality. Children animate their transitional objects as objects that can contain anxieties as well as other attachments. The media studies scholar Roger Silverstone, and others in his wake, linked the notion of the transitional object to the comforting nature television can provide.

Traversing the fantasy
A Lacanian concept that refers to letting go of, or working through, the key fantasies that sustain our existence – while being aware that one can never completely move beyond or outside of any fantasy. This letting go may be achieved through psychoanalytic psychotherapy, for instance, or via other means that enable the subject to arrive at a different relationship with themselves, their symptoms and jouissance.

Voyeurism
The term refers to sexual pleasure and gratification that is derived from looking at someone without being seen. Aggressive and violently controlling impulses are involved in that the voyeur appropriates the other as an image, making the other an object of their scopophilic pleasure while remaining detached. Drawing on Freud and Lacan, Laura Mulvey argued that traditional Hollywood cinema facilitates a voyeuristic gaze by turning women into mere objects to be looked at.

Work and labour
For Marxists, work is the universal process whereby humans create things by transforming nature and society as a whole. Work is purposeful, socially needed and not wage dependent. By distinction, we take 'labour' to refer to forms of work that are quantified (e.g. by setting work hours or paying wages) and controlled (either voluntarily by the labourer, if they are self-employed, for example, or by a manager or supervisor). (However, take a look at Hanna Arendt's monograph The Human Condition (1958) for an opposing understanding of the two terms!).

Working through
Working through in the consulting room entails a repetitive process of re-enacting, remembering and bringing unconscious experiences into consciousness so that one may gain a better understanding of one's suffering and, at times, even feel a sense of relief.

Bibliography

Achiampong, L. and Blandy, D. (2015). *Finding Fanon II*. Available at: https://vimeo.com/138951543 [Accessed 10/4/22].

Adorno, T. W., Frenkel-Brunswik, E., Levinson, D. J. and Nevitt Sanford, R. (1950). *The Authoritarian Personality*. New York: Harper.

Ahmed, S. (2012). *On Being Included. Racism and Diversity in Institutional Life.* Durham, NC: Duke University Press.

Ahumada, J. L. (2016). Insight under siege: psychoanalysis in the 'Autistoid Age'. *International Journal of Psychoanalysis*, 97, 839–51.

Almog, R. and Kaplan, D. (2017). The nerd and his discontent: the seduction community and the logic of the game as a geeky solution to the challenges of young masculinity. *Men and Masculinities*, 20(1), 27–48.

Althusser, L. (1971). Ideology and ideological state apparatuses. In: *Lenin and Philosophy* (pp. 170–86). London: Monthly Review Press.

Altman, N. (2009). *The Analyst in the Inner City. Race, Class, and Culture Through a Psychoanalytic Lens.* London: Routledge.

American Psychiatric Association (APA). (2013). *Diagnostic and Statistical Manual of Mental Disorders,* 5th Edition (DSM-V). Washington, DC: American Psychiatric Association.

Andersen, J. (2015). Now you've got the shiveries: affect, intimacy, and the ASMR whisper community. *Television & New Media*, 16(8), 683–700.

Ang, I. (1985). *Watching Dallas. Soap Opera and the Melodramatic Imagination.* London: Methuen.

Anzieu, D. (2016). *The Skin-Ego. A New Translation by Naomi Segal.* London: Karnac Books.

Apprich, C. (2018). Secret agents. A psychoanalytic critique of artificial intelligence and machine learning. *Digital Culture & Society*, 4(1), 29–44.

Ardolino, E. (1987). *Dirty Dancing.* Vestron Pictures.

Arendt, H. (1958) *The Human Condition*, Chicago and London: University of Chicago Press.

Ashtor, G. (2021). *Homo Psyche. On Queer Theory and Erotophobia.* New York: Fordham University Press.

Attwood, F. (2009, Ed.). *Mainstreaming Sex. The Sexualisation of Western Culture.* London: I. B. Tauris.

Bach, S. (1994). *The Language of Perversion and the Language of Love.* Northvale, NJ: Aronson.

Bainbridge, C. (2012). Psychotherapy on the couch: exploring the fantasies of in treatment. *Psychoanalysis, Culture and Society*, 17(2), 153–68.

Bainbridge, C. and Yates, C., eds (2011). Therapy culture/culture as therapy. Special Edition. *Free Associations: Psychoanalysis and Culture, Media, Groups, Politics*, 62, http://freeassociations.org.uk/FA_New/OJS/index.php/fa/issue/view/5.

Bainbridge, C. and Yates, C., eds (2012). Media and the inner world: new perspectives on psychoanalysis and popular culture. Special Issue. *Psychoanalysis, Culture & Society*, 17(2), 113–19.

Bainbridge, C. and Yates, C., eds (2014). *Media and the Inner World: Psychocultural Approaches to Emotion, Media and Popular Culture*. Basingstoke: Palgrave Macmillan.

Baker, R. (1994). Psychoanalysis as a lifeline: a clinical study of a transference perversion. *International Journal of Psycho-Analysis*, 75(4), 743–53.

Balick, A. (2014). *The Psychodynamics of Social Networking: Connected-Up Instantaneous Culture and the Self*. London: Karnac Books.

Bandinelli, C. and Bandinelli, A. (2021). What does the app want? A psychoanalytic interpretation of dating apps' libidinal economy. *Psychoanalysis, Culture & Society*, 26(2), 181–98.

Banet-Weiser, S. (2018). *Empowered: Popular Feminism and Popular Misogyny*. Durham, NC: Duke University Press.

Baraitser, L. (2008). *Maternal Encounters: The Ethics of Interruption*. London: Routledge.

Barker, M. (2005). The Lord of the Rings and 'identification': a critical encounter. *European Journal of Communication*, 20(3), 353–78.

Barker, M. and Pentley, J. (2001). *Ill Effects. The Media Violence Debate, 2nd edn*. London: Routledge.

Baudry, J. L. (2009 [1975]). The apparatus: metapsychological approaches to the impression of reality in cinema. In: L. Braudy and M. Cohen (eds.). *Film Theory and Criticism* (pp. 171–87). New York and Oxford: Oxford University Press.

Bee, S. (2019). Full frontal rewind: the best of big tech at its worst. *TBS*. 27 April. https://youtube.com/watch?v=C8AxA-vh3-ck.

Benjamin, J. (1988). *The Bonds of Love: Psychoanalysis. Feminism, and the Problem of Domination*. New York: Pantheon Books.

Benjamin, J. (2004). Beyond doer and done to: an intersubjective view of thirdness. *The Psychoanalytic Quarterly*, 73(1), 5–46.

Benvenuto, S. (2016). *What Are Perversions? Sexuality, Ethics, Psychoanalysis*. London: Routledge.

Bernstein, J. (2019). How OnlyFans changed sex work forever. *New York Times*. www.nytimes.com/2019/02/09/style/onlyfans-porn-stars.html.

Bersani, L. (2010). *Homos*. Cambridge, MA: Harvard University Press.

Bettelheim, B. (2010 [1976]). *The Uses of Enchantment*. New York: Vintage.

Bhabha, H. K. (1994). *The Location of Culture*. London: Routledge.

Billieux, J., Schimmenti, A., Khazaal, Y., Maurage, P. and Heeren, A. (2015). Are we overpathologizing everyday life? A tenable blueprint for behavioral addiction research. *Journal of Behavioral Addictions*, 4(3), 119–23.

Bion, W. (1962). *Learning from Experience*. London: Karnac.

Black, J. (2020). 'A form of socially acceptable insanity': love, comedy and the digital in *Her. Psychoanalysis, Culture & Society*, 26, 25–45.

Bohle, H. H., Heitmeyer, W., Kühnel, W. and Sander, U. (1997). Anomie in der modernen Gesellschaft: Bestandsaufnahme und Kritik eines klassischen Ansatzes soziologischer Analyse. In: W. Heitmeyer (ed.), *Was Treibt die Gesellschaft Auseinander? Bundesrepublik Deutschland: Auf dem Weg von der Konsens- zur Konfliktgesellschaft* (pp. 29–68). Frankfurt am Main: Suhrkamp.

Böhme, H. (2014). *Fetishism and Culture. A Different Theory of Modernity*. Berlin: De Gruyter.

Bollas, C. (2015). Psychoanalysis in the age of bewilderment: on the return of the oppressed. *International Journal of Psychoanalysis*, 96(3), 535–51.

Boothby, R. (2001). *Freud as Philosopher. Metapsychology After Lacan*. London: Routledge.

Bordwell, D. (1996). Contemporary film studies and the vicissitudes of grand theory. In: N. Carroll and D. Bordwell (eds.), *Post-Theory: Reconstructing Film Studies* (pp. 3–36). Madison, WI: University of Wisconsin Press.

Bott Spillius, E., Milton, J., Garvey, P., Couve, C. and Steiner, D. (2011). *The New Dictionary of Kleinian Thought*. London: Routledge.

Bown, A. (2015). *Enjoying it: Candy Crush and Capitalism*. Winchester: Zer0 Books.

Bown, A. (2017). Video games, capitalism and dreams. An interview with Alfie Bown. *LA Review of Books*. https://lareviewofbooks.org/article/video-games-capitalism-and-dreams-an-interview-with-alfie-bown/ [Accessed 24/2/22].

Bown, A. (2018). *The PlayStation Dreamworld*. Cambridge: Polity.

Boyd, d. (2014). *It's Complicated. The Social Lives of Networked Teens*. New Haven, CT: Yale University Press.

Bratton, B. (2015). *The Stack: On Software and Sovereignty*. Cambridge, MA: The MIT Press.

Brickman, C. (2003). *Aboriginal Populations in the Mind: Race and Primitivity in Psychoanalysis*. New York: Columbia University Press.

Brierley, M. (1937). Affects in theory and practice. *International Journal of Psychoanalysis*, 18, 256–68.

Brinkema, E. (2019). Form for the blind (porn and description without guarantee). *Porn Studies*, 6(1), 10–22.

Bruner, J. (1998). Oedipus Politicus: Freud's paradigm of social relations. In: M. S. Roth (ed.), *Freud – Conflict and Culture. Essays on His Life, Work, and Legacy* (pp. 80–93). New York: Vintage.

Bruns, A. (2019). *Are Filter Bubbles Real?* London: Wiley.

Bucher, T. (2012). The friendship assemblage: investigating programmed sociality on Facebook. *Television & New Media*, 14(6), 479–93.

Bucholtz, M. (2001). The whiteness of nerds: superstandard English and racial markedness. *Journal of Linguistic Anthropology*, 11(1), 84–100.

Bunz, M. (2019). The force of communication. In: P. Bialski, F. Brunton and M.

Bunz (eds.), *Communication* (pp. 51–92). Lüneborg/Minneapolis, MN: Meson Press and University of Minnesota Press.

Cahill, A. (2011). *Overcoming Objectification*. London: Routledge.

Caillois, R. (1958). *Les Jeux et les Hommes*. Paris: Gallimard.

Cartwright, L. (2008). *Moral Spectatorship: Technologies of Voice and Affect in Postwar Representations of the Child*. Durham, NC: Duke University Press.

Casara, B. G. S., Suitner, C. and Jetten, J. (2022). The impact of economic inequality on conspiracy beliefs. *Journal of Experimental Social Psychology*, 98, 1–13.

Celenza, A. (2014). *Erotic Revelations: Clinical Applications and Perverse Scenarios*. London: Routledge.

Chang, W. Y. and Glynos, J. (2011). Ideology and politics in the popular press: the case of the 2009 UK MPs' expenses scandal. In: L. Dahlberg and S. Phelan (eds.), *Discourse Theory and Critical Media Politics* (pp. 106–27). Basingstoke: Palgrave Macmillan.

Chasseguet-Smirgel, J. (1985). The ego ideal and the psychology of groups. *Free Associations*, 1(2), 31-60.

Chaudhuri, S. (2006). *Feminist Film Theorists. Laura Mulvey, Kaja Silverman, Teresa de Lauretis, Barbara Creed*. London: Routledge.

Chow, K. (2018). If we called ourselves yellow. *NPR*. www.npr.org/sections/codeswitch/2018/09/27/647989652/if-we-called-ourselves-yellow.

Chun, W. H. K. (2006). *Control and Freedom. Power and Paranoia in the Age of Fiber Optics*. Cambridge, MA: MIT Press.

Chun, W. H. K. (2016). *Updating to Remain the Same: Habitual New Media*. Minneapolis: University of Minnesota Press.

Chun, W. H. K. (2018). Queerying homophily. In: C. Apprich, W. H. K. Chun, F. Cramer and H. Steyerl (eds.), *Pattern Discrimination* (pp. 59–99). Lüneborg/Minneapolis, MN: Meson Press and University of Minnesota Press.

Chun, W. H. K. (2021). *Discriminating Data: Correlation, Neighborhoods, and the New Politics of Recognition*. Cambridge, MA: MIT Press.

Clarke, S. (2002). Learning from experience. Psycho-social research methods in the social sciences. *Qualitative Research*, 2(2), 173–94

Clarke, S. and Hoggett, P. (2009). *Researching Beneath the Surface. Psycho Social Research Methods in Practice*. London: Karnac Books.

Clough, P. T. (2000). *Autoaffection. Unconscious Thought in the Age of Teletechnology*. Minneapolis, MN: University of Minnesota Press.

Coel, M. (2020). *I May Destroy You*. Various Artists Limited and FALKNA Productions.

Cohen, P. (2002). Psychoanalysis and racism: reading the other scene. In: D. T. Goldberg and J. Solomos (eds.), *A Companion to Racial and Ethnic Studies* (pp. 170–201). Malden: Blackwell.

Cohen, R. (2013). Investments in cinematic constructions of the female serial killer. Re-conceptualising spectatorial 'identification'. *Free Associations*, 64, 37–63.

Coleman, G. (2014). *Hacker, Hoaxer, Whistleblower, Spy. The Many Faces of Anonymous*. London: Verso.

Copjec, J. (1994). *Read My Desire. Lacan Against the Historicists*. Cambridge, MA: MIT Press.

Couldry, N. (2012). *Media Society World. Social Theory and Digital Media Practice*. Cambridge: Polity Press.

Cowie, E. (1992). Pornography and fantasy. In: L. Segal and M. McIntosh (eds.), *Sex Exposed: Sexuality and the Pornography Debate* (pp. 132–52). London: Virago.

Cowie, E. (1997). *Representing the Woman. Cinema and Psychoanalysis*. Basingstoke: Macmillan Press.

Cowie, E. (2017 [1992]). Pornography and fantasy. In: L. Segal and M. McIntosh (eds.), *Sex Exposed: Sexuality and the Pornography Debate* (pp. 132–52). London: Virago, 1992. Availabile at www.academia.edu/31009171/Pornography_and_Fantasy [Accessed 6/5/22].

Coyne, S. M. and Stockdale, L. (2021). Growing up with Grand Theft Auto: a 10-year study of longitudinal growth of violent video game play in adolescents. *Cyberpsychology, Behavior, and Social Networking*, 24(1), 11–16.

Creed, B. (2000). The cyberstar: digital pleasures and the end of the unconscious. *Screen*, 41(1), 79–86.

Crenshaw, K. (1989). Demarginalizing the intersection of race and sex: a black feminist critique of antidiscrimination doctrine, feminist theory and antiracist politics. *University of Chicago Legal Forum*, 8(1), 139–67.

Cubitt, S. (2017). Current screens. In: S. Monteiro (ed.), *The Screen Media Reader. Culture, Theory, Practice* (pp. 39–54). London: Bloomsbury.

Dalal, F. (2001). Insides and outsides: a review of psychoanalytic renderings of difference, racism and prejudice. *Psychoanalytic Studies*, 3, 43–66.

David, G. and Cambre, C. (2016). Screened intimacies: Tinder and the swipe logic. *Social Media + Society*, 2(2), 1–11.

Day Sclater, S., Jones, D. W., Price, H. and Yates, C., eds, (2009). *Emotion. New Psychosocial Perspectives*. Basingstoke: Palgrave Macmillan.

De Beauvoir, S. (1974). *The Second Sex*. New York: Vintage Books.

De Lauretis, T. (1984). *Alice Doesn't: Feminism, Semiotics, Cinema*. Bloomington, IN: Indiana University Press.

Dean, J. (2002). *Publicity's Secret. How Technoculture Capitalizes on Democracy*. Ithaca, NY: Cornell University Press.

Dean, J. (2010). *Blog Theory: Feedback and Capture in the Circuits of Drive*. Cambridge: Polity.

Dean, J. (2018). Still dancing: drive as a category of political economy. *International Journal of Žižek Studies*, 6(1), 1–19.

Devereux, G. (1967). *From Anxiety to Method in the Behavioural Sciences*. The Hague and Paris: Mouton.

Dewey, J. (1981–90). The quest for certainty. In: J. A. Boydston (ed.), *The Later*

Works of John Dewey, 1925–1953, 17 vols. vol. 4. Carbondale, IL: Southern Illinois University Press.

Dimen, M. (1998). Strange hearts: on the paradoxical liaison between psychoanalysis and feminism. In: M. S. Roth (ed.), *Freud – Conflict and Culture. Essays on His Life, Work, and Legacy* (pp. 196–205). New York: Vintage Books.

Doane, M. A. (1982). Film and the masquerade: theorising the female spectator. *Screen*, 23(3–4), 74–88.

Doane, M. A. (1987a). *The Desire to Desire. The Woman's Film of the 1940s.* Bloomington, IN: Indiana University Press.

Doane, M. A. (1987b). The 'woman's film': possession and address. In: C. Gledhill (ed), *Home Is Where the Heart Is: Studies in Melodrama and the Woman's Film* (pp. 283–98). London: BFI.

Doane, M. A. (1991). The moving image: pathos and the maternal. In: M. Landy (ed.), *Imitations of Life: A Reader on Film and Television Melodrama* (pp. 283–306). Detroit, MI: Wayne State University Press.

Drummond, A., Sauer, J. D. and Ferguson, C. J. (2020). Do longitudinal studies support long-term relationships between aggressive game play and youth aggressive behaviour? A meta-analytic examination. *Royal Society Open Science*, 7(7), 1–13.

Duffy, B. E. (2017). *(Not) Getting Paid to Do What you Love. Gender, Social Media, and Aspirational Work.* New Haven, CT: Yale University Press.

Dunagan, C. and Fenton, R. (2014). Dirty Dancing: dance, class, and race in the pursuit of womanhood. In: M. Blanco Borelli (ed.), *The Oxford Handbook of Dance and the Popular Screen.* www.oxfordhandbooks.com/view/10.1093/oxfordhb/9780199897827.001.0001/oxfordhb-9780199897827-e-010?rskey=4lG4H8&result=4 [Accessed 6/5/22].

Durkheim, E. (1997 [1893]). *The Division of Labour in Society* (trans. W. D. Halls, intro. Lewis A. Coser). New York: Free Press.

Eagleman, D. (2021). *Livewired – The Inside Story of the Ever-Changing Brain.* Edinburgh: Cannongate Books.

Ellis, J. (2000). *Seeing Things. Television in the Age of Uncertainty.* London: I. B. Tauris.

Elsaesser, T. and Hagener, M. (2010). *Film Theory: An Introduction Through the Senses.* London: Routledge.

Erikson, E. (1950). *Childhood and Society.* London: Hogarth Press.

Ettinger, B. L. (1996). The red cow effect: the metramorphosis of hallowing the hollow and hollowing the hallow. In: *Art, Criticism and Theory 2: Beautiful Translations* (pp. 82–119). London: Pluto Press.

Ettinger, B. L. (2020). *Matrixial Subjectivity, Aesthetics, Ethics Volume 1 1990–2000.* Edited by Griselda Pollock. Basingstoke: Palgrave Macmillan.

Evans, D. (1996). *An Introductory Dictionary of Lacanian Psychoanalysis.* London: Routledge.

Eyal, N. (2014). *Hooked: How to Build Habit-Forming Products*. New York: Penguin.

Fang, N. (2020). Feeling/being 'out of place': psychic defence against the hostile environment. *Journal of Psychosocial Studies*, 13(2), 151–64.

Fang, N. and Liu, S. J. S. (2021). Critical conversations: being yellow women in the time of COVID-19. *International Feminist Journal of Politics*, 23(2), 333–40.

Fanon, F. (1967). *Black Skin, White Masks*. London: Pluto.

Fanon, F. (2004 [1963]). *Wretched of the Earth*. New York: Grove.

Feldner, H. and Vighi, F. (2018). Finitude of capitalism and the perverse charm of denial. *Berlin Journal of Critical Theory*, 2(2), 99–130.

Fellini, F. (1960). *La Dolce Vita*. Pathé.

Fenichel, O. (1939). The counter-phobic attitude. *International Journal of Psycho-Analysis*, 20, 263–74.

Fidler, D. P. (2015, Ed.). *The Snowden Reader*. Bloomington, IN: Indiana University Press.

Figlio, K. (2006). The absolute state of mind in society and the individual. *Psychoanalysis, Culture & Society*, 11(2), 119–43.

Finn, E. (2017). *What Algorithms Want: Imagination in the Age of Computing*. Cambridge, MA: MIT Press.

Fisher, M. (2013). Exiting the vampire castle. *openDemocracy*. www.opendemocracy.net/en/opendemocracyuk/exiting-vampire-castle/.

Fizek, S. (2018). Interpassivity and the joy of delegated play in idle games. *Transactions of the Digital Games Research Association*, 3(3), 137–63.

Fletcher, J. (2000). Gender, sexuality and the theory of seduction. *Women: A Cultural Review*, 11(1/2), 95–108.

Flieger, A. (2001). Has Oedipus signed off (or struck out)? Žižek, Lacan and the field of cyberspace. *Paragraph*, 24(2), 53–77.

Flieger, A. (2005). *Is Oedipus Online? Siting Feud After Freud*. Cambridge, MA: MIT Press.

Flisfeder, M. (2021). *Algorithmic Desire. Towards a New Structuralist Theory of Social Media*. Evanston, IL: Northwestern University Press.

Florêncio, J. (2020). *Bareback Porn, Porous Masculinities, Queer Futures: The Ethics of Becoming-Pig*. London: Routledge.

Flynn, E. (2017). *What Algorithms Want. Imagination in the Age of Computing*. Cambridge, MA: MIT Press.

Fonagy, P. (2009). Psychosexuality and psychoanalysis: an overview. In: P. Fonagy, R. Krause and M. Leuzinger-Bohleber (eds), *Identity, Gender and Sexuality. 150 Years After Freud* (pp. 1–20). London: Karnac.

Fraser, N. and Honneth, A. (2003). *Redistribution or Recognition? A Political-Philosophical Exchange*. London: Verso.

Fredborg, B. K., Clark, J. M. and Smith, S. D. (2018). Mindfulness and autonomous sensory meridian response (ASMR). *PeerJ*, 6, https://peerj.com/articles/5414/.

Freud, S. (1893–5). *Studies on Hysteria (written with Joseph Breuer)*. *SE II*. London: Hogarth Press and Institute of Psycho-Analysis.

Freud, S. (1900). *The Interpretation of Dreams. SE IV*. London: Hogarth Press and Institute of Psycho-Analysis.

Freud, S. (1905a). *Three Essays on the Theory of Sexuality. SE 7*, 123–246. London: Hogarth Press and Institute of Psycho-Analysis.

Freud, S. (1905b). *Jokes and Their Relation to the Unconscious. SE 8*, 1–247. London: Hogarth Press and Institute of Psycho-Analysis.

Freud. S. (1908). *Creative Writers and Day-Dreaming. SE 9*, 141–54. London: Hogarth Press and Institute of Psycho-Analysis.

Freud. S. (1913a). *On Beginning the Treatment (Further Recommendations on the Technique of Psycho-Analysis I). SE 12*, 121–44. London: Hogarth Press and Institute of Psycho-Analysis.

Freud, S. (1913b). *Totem and Taboo. SE 13*, vii–162. London: Hogarth Press and Institute of Psycho-Analysis.

Freud, S. (1914). *Remembering, Repeating and Working-Through (Further Recommendations on the Technique of Psycho-Analysis II). SE 12*, 145–56. London: Hogarth Press and Institute of Psycho-Analysis.

Freud, S. (1915). *Repression. SE XIV. On the History of the Psycho-Analytic Movement, Papers on Metapsychology and Other Works*. London: Hogarth Press and Institute of Psycho-Analysis.

Freud, S. (1917). *Mourning and Melancholia. SE 14*, 237–58. London: Hogarth Press and Institute of Psycho-Analysis.

Freud, S. (1919). *The Uncanny. SE XVII*, 217–52. London: Hogarth Press and Institute of Psycho-Analysis.

Freud, S. (1920). *Beyond the Pleasure Principle. SE 18*, 1–64. London: Hogarth Press and Institute of Psycho-Analysis.

Freud, S. (1923). *The Ego and the Id. SE 19*, 1–66. London: Hogarth Press and Institute of Psycho-Analysis.

Freud, S. (1926). *The Question of Lay Analysis, SE 20*, 177–258. London: Hogarth Press and Institute of Psycho-Analysis.

Freud, S. (1927). *Fetishism. SE XXI. The Future of an Illusion, Civilization and its Discontents and Other Works*. London: Hogarth Press and Institute of Psycho-Analysis.

Freud, S. (1930). *Civilisation and its Discontents. SE 21*, 64–145. London: Hogarth Press and Institute of Psycho-Analysis.

Freud, S. (1992). *Letters of Sigmund Freud*. New York: Dover.

Friedlander, J. (2008). *Feminine Look: Sexuation, Spectatorship, Subversion*. Albany, NY: State University of New York Press.

Frosh, S. (1999). *The Politics of Psychoanalysis. An Introduction to Freudian and Post-Freudian Theory*. Basingstoke: Macmillan Press.

Frosh, S. (2002). *Key Concepts in Psychoanalysis*. London: The British Library.

Frosh, S. (2005). *Hate and the 'Jewish Science'. Anti-Semitism, Nazism and Psychoanalysis*. Basingstoke: Palgrave Macmillan.

Frosh, S. (2010). *Psychoanalysis Outside the Clinic. Interventions in Psychosocial*

Studies. Basingstoke: Palgrave Macmillan.

Frosh, S. (2011). Psychoanalysis, anti-semitism and the miser. *New Formations*, 72, 94–106.

Frosh, S. (2016). Studies in prejudice: theorizing anti-semitism in the wake of the Nazi Holocaust. In: M. Ffytche (ed.), *Psychoanalysis in the Age of Totalitarianism* (pp. 28–44). London: Routledge.

Frosh, S. and Young, L. S. (2008). Psychoanalytic approaches to qualitative psychology. In: C. Willig (ed.), *The Sage Handbook of Qualitative Research in Psychology* (pp. 109–26). London: Sage.

Fuchs, C. (2008). *Internet and Society. Social Theory in the Information Age*. London: Routledge.

Fuchs, C. (2014). *Digital Labor and Karl Marx*. London: Routledge.

Gadamer, H. G. (2004 [1989]). *Truth and Method. Second,* revised edn. London: Continuum.

Gaines, J. M. (2000). *Fire and Desire. Mixed-Race Movies in the Silent Era*. Chicago, IL: University of Chicago Press.

Gauntlett, D. (2018). *Making is Connecting. The Social Power of Creativity, From Craft and Knitting to Digital Everything. Second Expanded Edition*. Cambridge: Polity.

Gaztambide, D. J. (2019). *A People's History of Psychoanalysis. From Freud to Liberation Psychology*. Washington, DC: Lexington Books.

Gekker, A. (2018). Let's not play: interpassivity as resistance in 'Let's Play' videos. *Journal of Gaming & Virtual Worlds*, 10(3), 219–42.

George, S. (2014). From alienation to cynicism: race and the Lacanian unconscious. *Psychoanalysis, Culture & Society*, 19(4), 360–78.

George, S. (2016). *Trauma and Race: A Lacanian Study of African American Racial Identity*. Waco, TX: Baylor University Press.

George, S. and Hook, D. (2021, Eds.). *Lacan and Race. Racism, Identity, and Psychoanalytic Theory*. London: Routledge.

Gibson, J. J. (1979). *The Ecological Approach to Visual Perception*. Hillsdale, NJ: Lawrence Erlbaum Associates.

Gibson, W. (1984). *Neuromancer*. New York: Ace.

Giffney, N. (2021). *The Culture Breast in Psychoanalysis. Cultural Experiences and the Clinic*. London: Routledge.

Giffney, N. and Watson, E., eds (2017). *Clinical Encounters in Sexuality. Psychoanalytic Practice and Queer Theory*. Goleta: Punctum Books.

Gilbert, J. (2013). What kind of thing is 'neoliberalism'? *New Formations*, 80/81, 7–22.

Gill, R. (2011). 'Life is a pitch': managing the self in new media work. In: M. Deuze (ed.), *Managing Media Work* (pp. 249–62). London: Sage.

Gillespie, T. (2010). The politics of 'platforms'. *New Media & Society*, 12(3), 347–64.

Glynos, J. and Mondon, A. (2016). The political logic of populist hype: the case of right-wing populism's 'meteoric rise' and its relation to the status quo. *POPULISMUS Working Paper Series*, 4.

Gramsci, A. (1971). *Selections from the Prison Notebooks*. New York: International Publishers.

Greedharry, M. (2008). *Postcolonial Theory and Psychoanalysis: From Uneasy Engagements to Effective Critique*. Basingstoke: Palgrave Macmillan.

Green, A. (1986). *On Private Madness*. London: Hogarth Press.

Green, A. (1993). L'analité primaire dans la relation anale. In: B. Brusset (ed.), *La Nevrose Obsessionnelle*. Monographies de Psychanalyse (pp. 61–86). Paris: Presses Universitaires de France.

Green, A. (1999). *The Work of the Negative*. London and New York: Routledge.

Green, A. (2002). A dual conception of narcissism: positive and negative organizations. *The Psychoanalytic Quarterly*, 71(4), 631–49.

Green, A. (2005). *Play and Reflection in D.W. Winnicott's Writings*. London: Karnac Books.

Greenfield, A. (2017). *Radical Technologies: The Design of Everyday Life*. London: Verso Books.

Griffin, C. R. (2012). No more away: techno-attachments and the relational future. *American Journal of Psychoanalysis*, 72(1), 65–75.

Grosser, B. (2021). Minus. https://bengrosser.com/projects/minus/.

Grosz, E. (2006). Naked. In: M. Smith and J. Morra (eds.), *The Prosthetic Impulse: From Posthuman Present to a Biocultural Future* (pp. 187–202). Cambridge, MA: MIT Press.

Grunberger, B. (1989). *New Essays on Narcissism*. London: Free Association Books.

Hall, S. (1993). Cultural identity and diaspora. In: J. Rutherford (ed.), *Identity, Community, Culture, Difference* (pp. 222–37). London: Lawrence and Wishart.

Hall, S., Massey, D. and Rustin, M. (2015). *After Neoliberalism?: The Kilburn Manifesto*. London: Lawrence & Wishart.

Haraway, D. (2003). *The Companion Species Manifesto. Dogs, People, and Significant Otherness*. Chicago, IL: University of Chicago Press.

Harrington, C. L. and Bielby, D. (1995). *Soap Fans: Pursuing Pleasure and Making Meaning in Everyday Life*. Philadelphia, PA: Temple University Press.

Heath, S. (1976). Narrative space. *Screen*, 17(3), 68–112.

Heath, S. (1977). Notes on suture. *Screen*, 18(4), 48–76.

Hein, H. (1968). Play as an aesthetic concept. *Journal of Aesthetics and Art Criticism*, 27(1), 67–71.

Hern, A. (2019). 'The challenge was to play like a human': AI takes on the gamers. *The Guardian*. www.theguardian.com/technology/2019/oct/30/the-challenge-was-to-play-like-a-human-ai-takes-on-the-gamers.

Heywood, A. (2013). *Politics, 4th edn*. Basingstoke: Palgrave Macmillan.

Hiddleston, J. (2014). *Understanding Postcolonialism*. London: Routledge.

Hill, A. (2007). *Restyling Factual TV. Audiences and News, Documentary, and Reality Genres*. London: Routledge.

Hills, M. (2002). *Fan Cultures*. London: Routledge.

Hollway, W. (2006). Paradox in the pursuit of a critical theorization of the development of self in family relationships. *Theory and Psychology*, 16(4), 465–82.

Hollway, W. (2015). *Knowing Mothers: Researching Maternal Identity Change*. Basingstoke: Palgrave Macmillan.

Hollway, W. and Jefferson, T. (2012). *Doing Qualitative Research Differently. Free Association, Narrative and the Interview Method, Second Edition*. London: Sage.

Homer, S. (2005). *Jacques Lacan*. London: Routledge.

Honneth, A. (2010). Verwilderungen. Kampf um Anerkennung im frühen 21. Jahrhundert. *APuZ – Aus Politik und Zeitgeschichte*, 28 December. www.bpb.de/shop/zeitschriften/apuz/33577/verwilderungen-kampf-um-anerkennung-im-fruehen-21-jahrhundert/?p=all.

Hook, D. (2008). Postcolonial psychoanalysis. *Theory & Psychology*, 18(2), 269–83.

Hook, D. (2018). Racism and jouissance: evaluating the 'Racism as (the Theft of) Enjoyment' hypothesis. *Psychoanalysis, Culture & Society*, 23(3), 244–66.

Hook, D. (2020). White anxiety in (post) apartheid South Africa. *Psychoanalysis, Culture & Society*, 25, 612–31.

hooks, b. (1992). The oppositional gaze: black female spectators. In: *Black Looks: Race and Representation* (pp. 115–31). Boston, MA: South End Press.

Hopkins, J. (2018). Darwin, Freud and group conflict. In: S. Krüger, K. Figlio and B. Richards (eds), *Fomenting Political Violence – Fantasy, Language, Media, Action* (pp. 219–52). Basingstoke: Palgrave Macmillan.

Horbury, A. (2019). A psychoanalytic ethics of the pornographic aesthetic. *Porn Studies*, 6(1), 87–99.

Horney, K. (1926). The flight from womanhood: the masculinity-complex in women as viewed by men and by women. *International Journal of Psychoanalysis*, 7, 324–39.

Huang, L. (2018). How to use LinkedIn to find a date. *Medium*, 4 September, https://medium.com/grouvly/how-to-use-linkedin-to-find-a-date-dc529f4adc25 [Accessed 17/6/22].

Huizinga, J. (1955). *Homo Ludens: A Study of the Play-Element in Culture*. Boston, MA: Beacon Press.

Irigaray, L. (1993). *An Ethics of Sexual Difference*. Ithaca: Cornell University Press.

Jagodzinski, J. (2004). *Youth Fantasies. The Perverse Landscape of the Media*. Basingstoke: Palgrave Macmillan.

Johanssen, J. (2018a). Gaming–playing on social media: using the psychoanalytic concept of 'playing' to theorize user labour on Facebook. *Information, Communication & Society*, 21(9), 1204–18.

Johanssen, J. (2018b). Not belonging to one's self: affect on Facebook's site governance page. *International Journal of Cultural Studies*, 21(2), 207–22.

Johanssen, J. (2019). *Psychoanalysis and Digital Culture: Audiences, Social Media, and Big Data*. London: Routledge.

Johanssen, J. (2021). Data perversion. A psychoanalytic perspective on datafication. *Journal of Digital Social Research*, 3(1), 88–105.

Johanssen, J. (2021, Ed). Psychoanalysis, sexualities and networked media. Special Issue. *Psychoanalysis, Culture & Society*, 26(2).

Johanssen, J. (2022). *Fantasy, Online Misogyny and the Manosphere: Male Bodies of Dis/Inhibition*. London: Routledge.

Johanssen, J. (In press). 'For the moment, I am not fucking', I am tweeting: Platforms of / as sexuality. *CLCWeb: Comparative Literature and Culture*.

Johanssen, J. (In press). Incels, MGTOW and heteropessimism. In J. Mercer and M. McGlashan (eds.), *Toxic Masculinity: Men, Meaning and Digital Media*. London: Routledge.

Johanssen, J. and Krüger, S., eds (2016). Digital media, psychoanalysis and the subject. Special Issue. *CM: Communication and Media*, 11(38).

Johanssen, J. and Wang, X. (2021). Artificial intuition in tech journalism on AI: imagining the human subject. *Human-Machine Communication*, 2, 173–90.

Jones, A. (2020). *Feels Good Man*. Ready Fictions.

Jones, D. W. (2008). *Understanding Criminal Behaviour. Psychosocial Approaches to Criminality*. Uffculme: Willan Publishing.

Jones, M. L. (2016). *CTRL + Z – The Right to be Forgotten*. New York and London: New York University Press.

Jonze, S. (2013). *Her*. Sony Pictures.

Juul, J. (2001). Games telling stories? A brief note on games and narratives. *Game Studies*, 1(1). www.gamestudies.org/0101/juul-gts/.

Kale, S. (2018). Erectile dysfunction or performance anxiety? The truth behind a modern malaise. *The Guardian*. www.theguardian.com/lifeandstyle/2018/oct/18/erectile-dysfunction-performance-anxiety-truth-modern-malaise.

Kantor, J. and Streitfeld, D. (2015). Inside Amazon: wrestling big ideas in a bruising workplace. *New York Times*. www.nytimes.com/2015/08/16/technology/inside-amazon-wrestling-big-ideas-in-a-bruising-workplace.html.

Kaplan, L. J. (2006). *Cultures of Fetishism*. Basingstoke: Palgrave Macmillan.

Kavka, M. (2009). *Reality Television, Affect and Intimacy: Reality Matters*. Basingstoke: Palgrave Macmillan.

Kay, A. (1972). *A Personal Computer for Children of All Ages*. Paper presented at the ACM national conference, Boston, MA, August.

Khanna, R. (2003). *Dark Continents: Psychoanalysis and Colonialism*. Durham, NC: Duke University Press.

Kienle, O. (2018–20). *Bad Banks*. Letterbox Filmproduktion and Iris Productions.

King, V. (2021). Autoritarismus als Regression. *WestEnd. Zeitschrift für Kritische Sozialforschung*, 18(1), 87–102.

King, V. and Schmid Noerr, G. (2020). Conceptions of the superego in sociological and socio-psychological analyses. *International Journal of Psychoanalysis*, 101(4), 740–56.

Klein, M. (1935). A contribution to the psychogenesis of manic-depressive states. *International Journal of Psycho-Analysis*, 16, 145–74.

Klein, M. (1946). Notes on some schizoid mechanisms. *International Journal of Psycho-Analysis*, 27, 99–110.

Klein, M. (1975). *The Writings of Melanie Klein. Vol. I, Love, Guilt and Reparation and Other Works. 1921–1945*. London: Hogarth Press and the Institute of Psychoanalysis.

Knafo, D. and Lo Bosco, R. (2017). *The Age of Perversion: Desire and Technology in Psychoanalysis and Culture*. London: Routledge.

Knafo, D. and Lo Bosco, R. (2020). *The New Sexual Landscape and Contemporary Psychoanaylsis*. London: Confer Books.

Knowles, T. (2019). I'm sorry, says the inventor of endless scrolling. *The Times*, 27 April. www.thetimes.co.uk/article/i-m-so-sorry-says-inventor-of-endless-online-scrolling-9lrv59mdk.

Kohan, J. (2013–19). *Orange Is the New Black*. Tilted Productions and Lionsgate Television.

Kovel, J. (1984). *White Racism: A Psychohistory*. New York: Columbia University Press.

Krüger, S. (2011). *Das Unbehagen in der Karikatur – Kunst, Propaganda und persuasive Kommunikation im Theoriewerk Ernst Kris'*. Munich: Fink.

Krüger, S. (2016). Understanding affective labor online – a depth-hermeneutic reading of the My 22nd of July webpage. *Ephemera – Theory and Politics in Organisation, Special Issue: Karppi et al., Affective Capitalism*, 16(4), 185–208.

Krüger, S. (2017a). Barbarous hordes, brutal elites – the traumatic structure of right-wing populism. *e-flux*, 83, summer 2017. www.e-flux.com/journal/83/142185/barbarous-hordes-brutal-elites-the-traumatic-structure-of-right-wing-populism/.

Krüger, S. (2017b). Dropping depth-hermeneutics into psychosocial studies – a Lorenzerian perspective. *The Journal of Psychosocial Studies*, 10(1), 47–66.

Krüger, S. (2018a). Violence and the virtual. Right-wing, anti-asylum Facebook pages and the fomenting of political violence. In: S. Krüger, K. Figlio and B. Richards (Eds.). *Fomenting Political Violence – Fantasy, Language, Media, Action* (pp. 75–102). Basingstoke: Palgrave Macmillan.

Krüger, S. (2018b). Facing Fanon: examining neocolonial aspects in *Grand Theft Auto V* through the prism of the Machinima film Finding Fanon II. *Open Library of Humanities*, 4(1), 12, 1–31. https://olh.openlibhums.org/articles/10.16995/olh.177/.

Krüger, S. (2019a). Goatse & tubgirl – mannlige online-subkulturer og deres hatobjekter. *Arr – Idéhistorisk Tidsskrift*, 3/2019. https://arrvev.no/artikler/goatse-tubgirl.

Krüger, S. (2019b). 'It's over/It never began' – Aggressive Akte der Selbst- und Fremdstigmatisierung in männlichen Internet-Subkulturen. *Psyche – Zeitschrift für Psychoanalyse und ihre Anwendungen*, Special Issue on 'Digitalisierung', Vera King and Benigna Gerisch (eds), 73, Sept/Oct 2019, 771–800.

Krüger, S. (2021a). *Beschmutzungen – anale Sexualität and antisoziale Netzwerke*, texte – psychoanalyse, ästhetik, kulturkritik, 4-2021.

Krüger, S. (2021b). Anal sexuality and male subcultures online: the politics of self-deprecation in the deep vernacular web. *Psychoanalysis, Culture and Society*. https://doi.org/10.1057/s41282-020-00207-z.

Krüger, S. (2022a). Arrested hermeneutics – reassessing Alfred Lorenzer's conceptions of cultural analysis and psychoanalysis. In: K. Rothe, S. Krüger, and D. Rosengart (eds), *Cultural Analysis Now! Alfred Lorenzer and the In-Depth Hermeneutics of Culture and Society* (pp. 205–39). New York: Unconscious in Translation.

Krüger, S. (2022b). Media studies and the psychosocial subject. In: S. Frosh, M. Vyrgioti and J. Walsh (eds), *Palgrave Handbook of Psychosocial Studies*, London: Palgrave Macmillan. www.academia.edu/71042606/Kruger_Medie_Studies_and_Psychosocial_Subject_PREPUB.

Krüger, S. (In press), *Psychoanalysis and Formative Media*, London: Routledge.

Krüger, S. and Johanssen, J. (2014). Alienation and digital labour – a depth hermeneutic inquiry into online commodification and the unconscious. *Triple C: Communication, Capitalism & Critique*, 12(2), 632–47.

Krüger, S. and Johanssen, J. (2016). Thinking (with) the unconscious in media and communication studies. Introduction to the special issue. *CM: Communication and Media*, 38(11), 5–40.

Krüger, S. and Rustad, G. C. (2017). Coping with shame in a media-saturated society: Norwegian web-series Skam as transitional object. *Television & New Media*, 20(1), 72–95.

Krüger, S. and Spilde, A. C. (2019). Judging books by their covers – Tinder interface, usage and sociocultural implications. *Information, Communication & Society*, 23(10), 1395–1410.

Krüger, S., Figlio, K. and Richards, B. (2018, Eds.). *Fomenting Political Violence*. Basingstoke: Palgrave Macmillan.

Krzych, S. (2010). Phatic touch, or the instance of the gadget in the unconscious. *Paragraph*, 33(3), 376–91.

Krzych, S. (2013). Introduction to special section on the digital subject. *Psychoanalysis, Culture & Society*, 18(1), 56–62.

Krzych, S. (2021). *Beyond Bias. Conservative Media, Documentary Form, and the Politics of Hysteria*. Oxford: Oxford University Press.

Kuhn, A. (Ed.). (2013). *Little Madnesses: Winnicott, Transitional Phenomena and Cultural Experience*. London: I. B. Tauris.

Lacan, J. (1966). The insistence of the letter in the unconscious. *Yale French Studies*, 36/37, 112–47.

Lacan, J. (1988). *The Seminar of Jacques Lacan. Book I. Freud's Papers on Technique 1953–54*. New York: W. W. Norton & Company.

Lacan, J. (1993). *The Seminar of Jacques Lacan. Book III. The Psychoses. 1955–56*. New York: W. W. Norton & Company.

Lacan, J. (1999). *The Seminar of Jacques Lacan. Book XX. Encore: On Feminine Sexuality, the Limits of Love and Knowledge. 1972–73*. New York: W.W. Norton & Company.

Lacan, J. (2002). *Ècrits*. New York: W. W. Norton & Company.
Lacan, J. (2004). *The Four Fundamental Concepts of Psychoanalysis*. London: Routledge.
Lacan, J, (2016). *The Seminar of Jacques Lacan. Book XXIII. The Sinthome.1975–76*. Cambridge: Polity Press.
Lacan, J. (2021). *The Object Relation: The Seminar of Jacques Lacan, Book IV*. Cambridge: Polity.
Lang, F. (1927). *Metropolis*. Paramount Pictures Studios.
Laplanche, J. (1970). *Life and Death in Psychoanalysis*. Baltimore, MD: Johns Hopkins University Press.
Laplanche, J. (1989). *New Foundations for Psychoanalysis*. London: Blackwell.
Laplanche, J. (1996). Psychoanalysis as anti-hermeneutics. *Radical Philosophy*, 79, 7–12.
Laplanche, J. (1999). *The Unconscious and the Id*. London: Rebus Press.
Laplanche, J. and Pontalis, J. B. (1973). *The Language of Psycho-Analysis*. New York: Norton.
Laughey, D. (2007). *Key Themes in Media Theory*. Maidenhead: Open University Press.
Leader, D. (2017). *Hands. What We Do With Them – and Why*. New York: Penguin.
Leithäuser, T. and Volmerg, B. (1988). *Psychoanalyse in der Sozialforschung. Eine Einführung am Beispiel einer Sozialpsychologie der Arbeit*. Opladen: Westdeutscher Verlag.
Leonard, D. J. (2004). High tech blackface – race, sports video games and becoming the other. *Intelligent Agent*, 4(4). www.intelligentagent.com/archive/Vol4_No4_gaming_leonard.htm.
Leonard, D. J. (2006). Not a hater, just keepin' it real: the importance of race-and gender-based game studies. *Games and Culture*, 1(1), 83–8.
Leskauskas, D. (2020). Generation Z – everyday (living with an) auxiliary ego. *International Forum of Psychoanalysis*, 29(3), 169–74.
Littler, J. (2017). *Against Meritocracy: Culture, Power and Myths of Mobility*. London: Routledge.
Liu, L. H. (2010). *The Freudian Robot. Digital Media and the Future of the Unconscious*. Chicago, IL: University of Chicago Press.
Löchel, E. (2019). 'Sprache des Abwesenden'. Psychoanalytische Reflexionen zum Subjekt des digitalen Zeitalters. *Psyche: Zeitschrift für Psychoanalyse und ihre Anwendungen*, 9/10, 698–725.
Lorde, A. (1984a). Eye to eye: black women, hatred and anger. In: *Sister Outsider. Essays and Speeches* (pp. 145–75). Berkeley, CA: Crossing Press.
Lorde, A. (1984b). The uses of the erotic. The erotic as power. In: K. Lovaas and M. M. Jenkins (eds), *Everyday Life: A Reader* (pp. 87–91). London: Sage.
Lorenzer, A. (1974). *Die Wahrheit der psychoanalytischen Erkenntnis*. Frankfurt am Main: Suhrkamp.
Lorenzer, A. (2022). In-depth hermeneutic cultural analysis. In: K. Rothe, S. Krüger, and D. Rosengart (eds), *Cultural Analysis Now! Alfred Lorenzer and*

the In-Depth Hermeneutics of Culture and Society (pp. 21–121). New York: Unconscious in Translation.

Lütkehaus, L. (2006). *'Genug von meinen Schweinereien' – Freud zum Vergnügen.* Stuttgart: Reclam.

MacCabe, C. (1974). Realism and the cinema. Notes on some Brechtian theses. *Screen,* 15(2), 7–27.

MacKinnon, C. (2021). OnlyFans is not a safe platform for 'sex work.' It's a pimp. *New York Times.* www.nytimes.com/2021/09/06/opinion/onlyfans-sex-work-safety.html.

MacRury, I. and Yates, C. (2016). Framing the mobile phone: the psychopathologies of an everyday object. *CM: Communication and Media,* 11(38), 41–70.

Makari, G. (2008). *Revolution in Mind – the Creation of Psychoanalysis.* London: Harper Collins.

Malabou, C. (2019). *Morphing Intelligence. From IQ Measurement to Artificial Brains.* New York: Columbia University Press.

Marcuse, H. (1955). *Eros and Civilization. A Philosophical Inquiry into Freud.* Boston, MA: Beacon Press.

Marquez Janse, A., Jarenwattananon, P. and Khalid, A. (2022). Which skin color emoji should you use? The answer can be more complex than you think. *NPR.* www.npr.org/2022/02/09/1078977416/race-chat-emoji-skin-tone-colors.

Marshall, G. (1990). *Pretty Woman.* Buena Vista Pictures Distribution.

Marx, K. (1976). *Capital Volume I . A Critique of Political Economy.* New York: Penguin.

Marx, K. and Engels, F. (1970). *The German Ideology.* New York: International Publishers.

Marzi, A. (2016). Introduction. In: A. Marzi (ed.), *Psychoanalysis, Identity and the Internet. Explorations in Cyberspace* (pp. xxiii–2). London: Karnac.

McGill, A. (2016). Why white people don't use white emoji. *The Atlantic.* www.theatlantic.com/politics/archive/2016/05/white-people-dont-use-white-emoji/481695/.

McGowan, T. (2007). *The Impossible David Lynch.* New York: Columbia University Press.

McGowan, T. (2013). Virtual freedom: the obfuscation and elucidation of the subject in cyberspace. *Psychoanalysis, Culture & Society,* 18(1), 63–70.

McGowan, T. (2015). *Psychoanalytic Film Theory and The Rules of the Game.* London: Bloomsbury.

McLaughlin, N. (2019). The coming triumph of the psychosocial perspective: lessons from the rise, fall and revival of Erich Fromm. *Journal of Psychosocial Studies,* 12(1–2), 9–22.

McNair, B. (2009). From porno-chic to porno-fear: the return of the repressed. In: F. Attwood (Ed.). *Mainstreaming Sex: The Sexualisation of Western Culture* (pp. 55–76). London: I. B. Tauris.

McRobbie, A. (2016). *Be Creative. Making a Living in the New Creative Industries.* Cambridge: Polity.

Melgar, M. C. (2007). Mourning and creativity. In: L. Glocer Fiorini, T. Bokanowski and S. Lewkowicz, S. (Eds.). *On Freud's 'Mourning and Melancholia'* (pp. 110–22). London: Routledge.

Menninger, K. (1942). *Love against Hate.* New York: Harcourt, Brace and Company.

Metz, C. (1975). The imaginary signifier. *Screen,* 16(2), 14–76.

Mijolla-Mellor, S. D. (2005). Acting out/acting in. In: *International Dictionary of Psychoanalysis* (pp. 10–11). Detroit, MI: Thomson Gale.

Millar, I. (2021). *The Psychoanalysis of Artificial Intelligence.* Basingstoke: Palgrave Macmillan.

Miller, J.-A. (1994). Extimité. In: M. Bracher, M. W. Alcorn, R. J. Cortell and F. Massardier-Kenney (eds), *Lacanian Theory of Discourse: Subject, Structure and Society* (pp. 74–87). New York: New York University Press.

Miller, K. (2012). *Playing Along: Digital Games, YouTube, and Virtual Performance.* Oxford: Oxford University Press.

Milmo, D. (2021a). Frances Haugen: 'I never wanted to be a whistleblower. But lives were in danger'. *The Guardian,* 24 October. www.theguardian.com/technology/2021/oct/24/frances-haugen-i-never-wanted-to-be-a-whistleblower-but-lives-were-in-danger [Accessed 17/6/22].

Milmo, D. (2021b). Twitter admits bias in algorithm for rightwing politicians and news outlets. *The Guardian.* www.theguardian.com/technology/2021/oct/22/twitter-admits-bias-in-algorithm-for-rightwing-politicians-and-news-outlets.

Minghella, A. (1999). *The Talented Mr. Ripley.* Paramount Pictures Studios.

Mitchell, J. (1974). *Psychoanalysis and Feminism: A Radical Reassessment of Freudian Psychoanalysis.* London: Allen Lane.

Mitchell, S. (1998). Aggression and the endangered self. *Psychoanalytic Inquiry,* 18(1), 21–30.

Mitscherlich, A. (1966). *Krankheit als Konflikt. Studien zur Psychosomatischen Medizin.* Frankfurt am Main: Suhrkamp.

Moatti, S. C. (2016). *Mobilised – An Insider's Guide to the Business and Future of Connected Technology.* Oakland, CA: Berret-Koehler Publishers.

Modleski, T. (1982). *Loving with a Vengeance. Mass Produced Fantasies for Women.* Hamden, CT: The Shoe String Press.

Mollon, P. (2000). *The Unconscious.* Cambridge: Icon Books.

Molloy, M. (2019). *Google Nest* (ad). 72 and Sunny (agency) for Smuggler (production company).

Morley, D. (1992). *Television, Audiences and Cultural Studies.* London: Routledge.

Mulvey, L. (1975). Visual pleasure and narrative cinema. *Screen,* 16(3), 6–18.

Mulvey, L. (2006). *Death 24x a Second. Stillness and the Moving Image.* London: Reaktion Books.

Mulvey, L. (2019). *Afterimages. On Cinema, Women and Changing Times.* London: Reaktion Books.

Murray, J. (1996). *Hamlet on the Holodeck: The Narrative Future in Cyberspace.* Cambridge, MA: MIT Press.

Musto, M. (2021, Ed.). *Karl Marx's Writings on Alienation: Critiquing Capitalism.* Basingstoke: Palgrave Macmillan.

Nachtwey, O. and Heumann, M. (2019). Regressive Rebellen und autoritäre Innovatoren: Typen des neuen Autoritarismus. In: K. Dörre, H. Rosa, K. Becker, S. Bose and B. Seyd (eds), *Große Transformation? Zur Zukunft moderner Gesellschaften* (pp. 435–53). Wiesbaden: Springer VS.

Nagle, A. (2017). *Kill All Normies: Online Culture Wars from 4chan and Tumblr to Trump and the Alt-Right.* Winchester: Zer0 Books.

Nakamura, L. (2002). *Cybertypes.* New York: Routledge.

Nakamura, L. (2007). *Digitizing Race. Visual Cultures of the Internet.* Minneapolis, MN: University of Minnesota Press.

Neale, S. (1983). Masculinity as spectacle. *Screen*, 24(6), 2–17.

No Author (2021). US supreme court declines to take up bathroom case in win for trans rights. *The Guardian.* www.theguardian.com/law/2021/jun/28/us-supreme-court-transgender-bathroom-case.

Nusselder, A. (2013). Twitter and the personalization of politics. *Psychoanalysis, Culture & Society*, 18(1), 91–100.

OED, *Oxford English Dictionary.* (2022). Selfie. www.oed.com/view/Entry/390063?redirectedFrom=selfie [Accessed 6/5/22].

O'Reilly, T. (2007). What is Web 2.0? Design patterns and business models for the next generation of software. *Communications & Strategies*, 65(1), 17–37.

Overmars, M. (2012). A brief history of computer games. www.stichtingspel.org/sites/default/files/history_of_games.pdf [Accessed 6/5/22].

Paasonen, S. (2011). *Carnal Resonance. Affect and Online Pornography.* Cambridge, MA: MIT Press.

Paasonen, S. (2014). Things to do with the alternative: fragmentation and distinction in online porn. In: G. Maina, E. Biasin and F. Zecca (eds), *Porn After Porn: Contemporary Alternative Pornographies* (pp. 21–36). Milan: Mimesis Books.

Paasonen, S., Attwood, F., McKee, A., Mercer, J. and Smith, C. (2020). *Objectification: On the Difference Between Sex and Sexism.* London: Routledge.

Pariser, E. (2011). *The Filter Bubble: What the Internet is Hiding From You.* New York: Penguin.

Pelletier, C. (2005). Reconfiguring interactivity, agency and pleasure in the education and computer games debate – using Žižek's concept of interpassivity to analyse educational play. *e-Learning*, 2, 317–26.

Peters, J. D. (1999). *Speaking into the Air. A History of the Idea of Communication.* Chicago, IL and London: University of Chicago Press.

Pfaller, R. (2014). *On the Pleasure Principle in Culture. Illusions Without Owners.* London: Verso.

Phillips, W. and Milner, R. M. (2016). *The Ambivalent Internet: Mischief, Oddity, and Antagonism Online.* Cambridge: Polity.

Phillips, W. and Milner, R. M. (2021). *You Are Here. A Field Guide for Navigating Polarized Speech, Conspiracy Theories, and Our Polluted Media Landscape.* Cambridge, MA: MIT Press.

Pinchevski, A. (2019). *Transmitted Wounds: Media and the Mediation of Trauma.* Oxford: Oxford University Press

Pollock, G. (2020). Editor's introduction. In: B. L. Ettinger (2020). *Matrixial Subjectivity, Aesthetics, Ethics Volume 1 1990–2000. Edited by Griselda Pollock* (pp. 1–92). Basingstoke: Palgrave Macmillan.

Possati, L. (2021). *The Algorithmic Unconscious: How Psychoanalysis Helps in Understanding AI.* London: Routledge.

Prager. J. (2011). Social theory of trauma, part 1. *American Imago*, 68/3, 425–48.

Prince, S. (1996). Psychoanalytic film theory and the problem of the missing spectator. In: N. Carroll and D. Bordwell (Eds.). *Post-Theory: Reconstructing Film Studies* (pp. 71–86). Madison, WI: University of Wisconsin Press.

Puwar, N. (2004). *Space Invaders. Race, Gender and Bodies Out of Place.* Oxford: Berg.

Radstone, S. (2007). Clinical and academic psychoanalytic criticism. Differences that matter. In: C. Bainbridge, S. Radstone, M. Rustin and C. Yates (eds), *Culture and the Unconscious* (pp. 242–54). Basingstoke: Palgrave Macmillan.

Radway, J. (1991). *Reading the Romance: Women, Patriarchy, and Popular Literature.* Chapel Hill, NC: University of North Carolina Press. Originally published in 1984.

Rambatan, B. and Johanssen, J. (2021). *Event Horizon. Sexuality, Politics, Online Culture, and the Limits of Capitalism.* Winchester: Zer0 Books.

Rank, O. (1929). *The Trauma of Birth.* London: Kegan Paul, Trench, Trübner and Co.

Redman, P. (2016). Once more with feeling: what is the psychosocial anyway? *Journal of Psychosocial Studies*, 9(1), 73–93.

Reed, T. V. (2014). *Digitized Lives. Culture, Power, and Social Change in the Internet Era.* London: Routledge.

Rehberg, P. (2019). More than vanilla sex: reading gay post-pornography with affect theory and psychoanalysis. *Porn Studies*, 6(1), 114–28.

Ribak, R. (2009). Remote control, umbilical cord and beyond: the mobile phone as a transitional object. *British Journal of Developmental Psychology*, 27(1), 183–96.

Richards, B. (2007). *Emotional Governance: Politics, Media and Terror.* Basingstoke: Palgrave Macmillan.

Richards, B. (2018). *What Holds us Together. Popular Culture and Social Cohesion.* London: Routledge.

Riggs, D. W. (2005). Psychoanalysis as a 'postcolonising' reading practice. In: D. W. Riggs (Ed.). *Taking Up the Challenge: Critical Race and Whiteness Studies in a Post-Colonising Nation* (pp. 33–59). Adelaide: Crawford House.

Riviere, J. (1999). Womanliness as a masquerade. In: R. Grigg, D. Hecq and C. Smith (eds), *Female Sexuality. The Early Psychoanalytic Controversies* (pp. 172–82). London: Routledge.

Rogen, S. and Goldberg, E. (2014). *The Interview*. Columbia Pictures.

Rohrlich, J. B. (1980). *Work and Love: The Crucial Balance*. New York: Summit Books.

Rohrlich, J. B. (1993). Review of: L. Hirschhorn (1990). *The Workplace Within: Psychodynamics of Organizational Life*. Cambridge, MA: MIT Press. *Journal of the American Psychoanalytic Association*, 41, 292–5.

Rose, G. (2001). *Visual Methodologies. An Introduction to the Interpretation of Visual Materials*. London: Sage.

Rosenfeld, D. (2016). 'Lorenzo': psychotic addiction to video games. In: A. Marzi (ed.), *Psychoanalysis, Identity and the Internet. Explorations in Cyberspace* (pp. 135–66). London: Karnac.

Röske, T. (2014). Geschichte und Aktualität der Outsider Art. In: T. Loemke (Ed.). *Annäherungen von Kunstpädagogik und Outsider Art: Ein Projekt des Lehrstuhls für Kunstpädagogik mit dem Kunstraum der Pegnitzwerkstätten/Lebenshilfe Nürnberg* (pp. 22–9). Erlangen: FAU University Press.

Roth, M. S. (1998, Ed.). *Freud – Conflict and Culture. Essays on His Life, Work, and Legacy*. New York: Vintage.

Ruti, M. (2016). *Feminist Film Theory and Pretty Woman*. London: Bloomsbury.

Ruti, M. (2018). *Penis Envy and Other Bad Feelings: The Emotional Costs of Everyday Life*. New York: Columbia University Press.

Said, E. (1978). *Orientalism*. New York: Pantheon.

Saketopoulou, A. (2014). To suffer pleasure: the shattering of the ego as the psychic labor of perverse sexuality. *Studies in Gender and Sexuality*, 15(4), 254–68.

Sales, N. J. (2015). Tinder and the dawn of the 'dating apocalypse'. *Vanity Fair*. www.vanityfair.com/culture/2015/08/tinder-hook-up-culture-end-of-dating.

Sartre, J.-P. (1946). *Réflexions sur la Question Juive*. Paris: Editions Morihien.

Sauvayre, P. (2022). Applied psychoanalysis: cultural and clinical. In: K. Rothe, S. Krüger, and D. Rosengart (eds), *Cultural Analysis Now! Alfred Lorenzer and the In-Depth Hermeneutics of Culture and Society* (pp. 149–77). New York: Unconscious in Translation.

Schimmenti, A. and Caretti, V. (2010). Psychic retreats or psychic pits? Unbearable states of mind and technological addiction. *Psychoanalytic Psychology*, 27(2), 115–32.

Schrader, M. (2021). *I'm Your Man*. Majestic Filmverleih.

Segal, J. (2004). *Melanie Klein*. London: Sage.

Semerene, D. (2016). The female target: digitality, psychoanalysis and the gangbang. *CM: Communication and Media*. Special Issue. Digital Media, Psychoanalysis and the Subject, 38(11), 217–42.

Semerene, D. (2021). Creampied to death: ejaculative kinship in the age of normative data flows. *Psychoanalysis, Culture & Society*, 26(2), 99–216.

Senft, T. (2008). *Camgirls: Celebrity and Community in the Age of Social Networks*. New York: Peter Lang.

Seresin, A. (2019). On heteropessimism. *The New Inquiry*. https://thenewinquiry. com/on-heteropessimism/.

Seymour, R. (2019). *The Twittering Machine: How Capitalism Stole our Social Life*. London: The Indigo Press.

Shields, R. (2006). Virtualities. *Theory, Culture & Society*, 23(2–3), 284–6.

Silverman, K. (1988). *The Acoustic Mirror. The Female. Voice in Psychoanalysis and Cinema*. Bloomington, IN: Indiana University Press

Silverstone, R. (1994). *Television and Everyday Life*. London: Routledge.

Singh, G. (2019). *The Death of Web 2.0: Ethics, Connectivity and Recognition in the Twenty-First Century*. London: Routledge.

Snider, N. (2020). Anti-racism in our institutes: opportunities and challenges. *Contemporary Psychoanalysis*, 56(2), 418–37.

Solms, M. (2018). An introduction to the neuroscientific works of Sigmund Freud. In: D. Barford (ed.), *The Pre-Psychoanalytic Writings of Sigmund Freud* (pp. 17–35). London: Routledge.

Spivak, G. C. (1985). The Rani of Sirmur: an essay in reading the archives. *History and Theory*, 24(3), 247–72.

Srnicek, N. (2017). *Platform Capitalism*. Cambridge: Polity.

Stacey, J. (1994). *Star Gazing: Hollywood Cinema and Female Spectatorship*. London: Routledge.

Stallone, S. (1979). *Rocky II*. United Artists Corporation.

Stanton, R. (2015). *A Brief History of Video Games*. Philadelphia, PA: Running Press.

Starr, R. L., Wang, T. and Go, C. (2020). Sexuality vs. sensuality: the multimodal construction of affective stance in Chinese ASMR performances. *Journal of Sociolinguistics*, 24(4), 492–513.

Statista (2021). Meta's (formerly Facebook Inc.) annual revenue from 2009 to 2021. www.statista.com/statistics/268604/annual-revenue-of-facebook/.

Stavrakakis, Y. (2007). *The Lacanian Left*. Edinburgh: Edinburgh University Press.

Steele, J. (2021). Fear of blackness: understanding white supremacy as an inverted relationship to oppression. *Psychoanalysis, Culture & Society*, 26(3), 388–404.

Stein, R. (2005). Why perversion? 'False love' and the perverse pact. *International Journal of Psychoanalysis*, 86(3), 775–99.

Steiner, J. (1985). Turning a blind eye: the cover-up for Oedipus. *International Review of Psycho-Analysis*, 12, 161–72.

Steiner, J. (1993). *Psychic Retreats. Pathological Organizations in Psychotic, Neurotic and Borderline Patients*. London: Routledge.

Stiller, B. (2016). *Zoolander 2*. Paramount Pictures Studios.

Stone, O. (1987). *Wall Street*. 20th Century Fox.

Stoute, B. (2017). Race and racism in psychoanalytic thought: the ghosts in our nursery. *The American Psychoanalyst*, 51(1), 10–11.

Sunstein, C. R. (2002). *Republic.com*. Princeton: Princeton University Press.

Sutterlüty, F. (2021). Destruktivität des Rechtspopulismus. *West-End – Neue Zeitschrift für Sozialforschung*, 01-2021, 73–86.

Tarantino, Q. (2019). *Once Upon a Time in Hollywood*. Sony Pictures Releasing.

Tate, C. (1996). Freud and his 'negro': psychoanalysis as ally and enemy of African Americans. *Journal for the Psychoanalysis of Culture & Society*, 1(1), 53–62.

Terranova, T. (2000). Free labor: producing culture for the digital economy. *Social Text*, 18(2), 33–58.

Theweleit, K. (1987). *Male Fantasies. Volume 1. Women, Floods, Bodies, History*. Minneapolis, MN: University of Minnesota Press.

Thornham, S. (1999). *Feminist Film Theory: A Reader*. Edinburgh: Edinburgh University Press.

Tugwell, S. (2021). What lurks beneath: the erotic charge of the Laplanchean unconscious and the digital object. *Psychoanalysis, Culture & Society*, 26(2), 165–80.

Turkle, S. (1995). *Life on the Screen. Identity in the Age of the Internet*. New York: Simon & Schuster.

Turkle, S. (2005). *The Second Self. Computers and Human Spirit. Twentieth Anniversary Edition*. Cambridge, MA: MIT Press

Turkle, S. (2011). *Alone Together. Why We Expect More From Technology and Less From Each Other*. New York: Basic Books.

Turkle, S. (2021). *The Empathy Diaries. A Memoir*. New York: Penguin.

Turner, J. (2019). *Robot Rules: Regulating Artificial Intelligence*. Basingstoke: Palgrave Macmillan.

Tutt, P. (2015). Apple's new diverse emoji are even more problematic than before. *The Washington Post*. www.washingtonpost.com/posteverything/wp/2015/04/10 how-apples-new-multicultural-emojis-are-more-racist-than-before/.

Urban Dictionary. (2008). 4chan. 22 July. www.urbandictionary.com/define.php?term=4chan.

Väliaho, P. (2013). Spellbound: early cinema's transformational spaces. *Space and Culture*, 16(2), 161–72.

Van Doorn, N. (2010). Keeping it real: user-generated pornography, gender reification, and visual pleasure. *Convergence*, 16(4), 411–30.

Vanderwees, C. (2019). Paranoid pleasure: surveillance, online pornography, and scopophilia. *Porn Studies*, 6(1), 23–37.

Vertovec, S. (2013). 'Diversity' and the social imaginary. *European Journal of Sociology/Archives Européennes de Sociologie*, 53(3), 287–312.

Vighi, F. (2009). *Sexual Difference in European Cinema. The Curse of Enjoyment*. Basingstoke: Palgrave Macmillan.

The Wachowskis. (1999–2021). *The Matrix films: The Matrix (1999), The Matrix Reloaded (2003), The Matrix Revolutions (2003), The Matrix Resurrections (2021)*. Warner Bros. Pictures.

Walkerdine, V. (1986). Video replay. In: V. Burgin, J. Donald and C. Kaplan (eds), *Formations of Fantasy* (pp. 167–99). London: Verso.

Walkerdine, V. (2007). *Children, Gender, Video Games. Towards a Relational Approach to Multimedia*. Basingstoke: Palgrave Macmillan.

Waller-Bridge, P. (2016–19). *Fleabag*. Two Brothers Pictures.

Walther, B. K. (2003). Playing and gaming. Reflections and classifications. *Game Studies*, 3(2). www.gamestudies.org/0301/walther/.

Ward, J. (2020). *The Tragedy of Heterosexuality*. New York: New York University Press.

Warikoo, N. (2016). *The Diversity Bargain*. Chicago, IL: University of Chicago Press.

Welldon, E. (1988). *Mother, Madonna, Whore: The Idealization and Denigration of Motherhood*. London: Routledge.

Whitebook, J. (1995). *Perversion and Utopia – A Study in Psychoanalysis and Critical Theory*. Cambridge, MA: MIT Press.

Whitehouse-Hart, J. (2014). *Psychosocial Explorations of Film and Television Viewing. Ordinary Audience*. Basingstoke: Palgrave Macmillan.

Whitson, J. R. (2013). Gaming the quantified self. *Surveillance & Society*, 11(1/2), 163–76.

Williams, L. (1989). Hard Core. Berkeley, CA: University of California Press.

Williams, L. (1991). Film bodies. Gender, genre, and excess. *Film Quarterly*, 44(4), 2–13.

Winnicott, D. W. (1960). The theory of the parent–infant relationship. *International Journal of Psychoanalysis*, 41, 585–95.

Winnicott, D. W. (1963). The development of the capacity for concern. *International Psychoanalytic Library*, 64, 73–82.

Winnicott, D. W. (2002). *Playing and Reality*. London: Routledge.

Woodruff, A. (n.d.). What is a neuron? The Queensland Brain Institute. https://qbi.uq.edu.au/brain/brain-anatomy/what-neuron.

Woodward, K. (2015). *Introduction to Psychosocial Studies*. London: Routledge.

Woodward Gentle, S. (2018–22). *Killing Eve*. Sid Gentle Films, BBC America Original Production and Endeavor Content.

Wooldridge, M. (2020). *The Road to Conscious Machines: The Story of AI*. London: Penguin.

World Health Organization. (1993). *The ICD-10 Classification of Mental and Behavioural Disorders: Diagnostic Criteria for Research*. Geneva: World Health Organization.

Yates, C. (2007). *Masculine Jealousy and Contemporary Cinema*. Basingstoke: Palgrave Macmillan.

Yates, C. (2010). Video replay: families, films and fantasy as a transformational text. Commentary on Valerie Walkerdine's video replay. *Psychoanalysis, Culture & Society*, 154, 404–11.

Young-Bruehl, E. (1996). *The Anatomy of Prejudice*. Cambridge, MA: Harvard University Press.

Zaretsky, E. (1976). *Capitalism, the Family and Personal Life.* London: Pluto Press.

Zaretsky, E. (2015a). *From psychoanalysis to cybernetics: the case of Her.* American Imago, 72(2), 197–210.

Zaretsky, E. (2015b). *Secrets of the Soul: A Social and Cultural History of Psychoanalysis.* New York: Three Rivers Press.

Zaretsky, E. (2017). *Political Freud: A History.* New York: Columbia University Press.

Zeavin, H. (2021). *The Distance Cure. A History of Teletherapy.* Cambridge, MA: The MIT Press.

Zicman de Barros, T. (2022). Populism: symptom or sublimation? Reassessing the use of psychoanalytic metaphors. Psychoanalysis, *Culture & Society*, OnlineFirst, 1–17.

Žižek, S. (1994). *The Metastases of Enjoyment.* London: Verso.

Žižek, S. (1996). *The Indivisible Remainder.* London Verso.

Žižek, S. (1997). *The Plague of Fantasies.* London: Verso.

Žižek, S. (1998). Cyberspace, or, how to traverse the fantasy in the age of the retreat of the big Other. *Public Culture,* 10(3), 483–513.

Žižek, S. (2006). *The Parallax View.* Cambridge, MA: The MIT Press.

Žižek, S. (2008). *In Defense of Lost Causes.* London: Verso.

Žižek, S. (2012). *The Year of Dreaming Dangerously.* London: Verso.

Zuboff, S. (2019). *The Age of Surveillance Capitalism. The Fight for a Human Future at the New Frontier of Power.* London: Profile Books.

Index

Karnac Books, founded in 1950 and relaunched in 2020, publishes seminal and contemporary texts on psychotherapy and psychoanalysis. It continues its long tradition of exploring the intricacies of these disciplines, providing space for the best writers on the complexities of the mind.